2

BY DEC 1986

LINGUISTIC STRUCTURES
and
LINGUISTIC LAWS

LINGUISTIC STRUCTURES
AND
LINGUISTIC LAWS

by

FERENC KOVÁCS

B. R. GRÜNER, AMSTERDAM

Translated from the Hungarian into English by
SÁNDOR SIMON

Joint edition by

B. R. GRÜNER, AMSTERDAM
and
AKADÉMIAI KIADÓ, BUDAPEST

Library of Congress Catalog Card Number: 71-170799

ISBN 90 6032 492 7

CONTENTS

INTRODUCTION

This work investigates a given period of the development of "linguistic thought" (the theories of language), analyzing the main motives of certain stages of that development. It is intended to single out the apparent and real contradictions of the development of linguistic thought and on this basis to uncover and, if possible, to solve the contradictions. It is not concerned with the extent and value of the differences doubtless existing in the linguistic theories of the various—rather precisely delimitable—periods, but it focuses attention primarily on the tendencies which help to sum up this course of development as an organic whole, tracing the process in its dynamic rhythm.

In the succession of periods in the linguistic science of the past one hundred and fifty years my study does not seek catastrophic explosions which led to the "dichotomy of the science of language" at the inception of every new school, at the beginning of every period, but it tries to point to the progressive elements of each period and each school, and to draw them up in a line leading to the best possible knowledge of the facts of language.

The standard by which I shall attempt to measure the value of the various theories is their social usefulness in the broadest sense and the role they undertook and played in the evolution of social consciousness, so I shall use this standard to determine the progressive and retrogressive features of those theories, not forgetting, of course, about their "palpable" social utility either.

My purpose is therefore not to invent an "entirely new" linguistic theory, this proposition would even be too bold a venture for me to enter, but I wish to draw the theoretical, ideological lessons for which we can find ample opportunities in a study of the main linguistic schools of the past one hundred and fifty years. We may not even describe as "entirely new" the view which—though it has been somewhat disregarded in the linguistic literature of the past few decades—takes the reflections of every period and every contradiction of the past for a guide leading up to the present, and the "epoch-making" discoveries merely for the "beginnings of an era", not forgetting about its germs appearing in the earlier periods either.

This outlook can be said to be dialectic in the sense that in the substitution of new for older theories it sees a kind of negation which, while eliminating an old theory, claims its progressive elements to be contained in the new one, where it does find them indeed; and it can be said to be materialistic in the sense that it judges every theoretical statement by the facts of language. The same applies to my ideas about the essential features of linguistic laws, too, where the only news is that they recommend, relying on the lessons drawn from the modern concept of natural law, that earlier inflexible formulations be replaced by something more elastic, which might make it easier to solve and explain the seemingly irreconcilable contradictions of the linguistic phenomena.

In accordance with the object of this work I shall therefore investigate the general development of linguistic theory. I shall probe into the results of the joint effort which the linguists of several nations contributed to the general development of the theory. My work is in this sense concerned with the history of science or, more precisely, of theories, inclusive of the fact that it concentrates also on the principal theses of linguistic theory of the so-called modern schools and that it comments also upon the modern concept of linguistic law.

It is a great privilege to me as a Hungarian author to describe how intensively the best Hungarian linguists of the various periods joined the international currents of the general theory of language, and what a fertilizing effect their active participation wrought on the activity of some representatives of linguistic science in Hungary. Nor will it perhaps be taken for national bias if in the appropriate place I refer to the mostly forgotten fact that some Hungarian linguists with their admirable surmises sometimes went ahead of their age. Such reference, however, is by no means intended to be a sort of "chauvinistic parochialism", but it is meant to point to the recognition of the interaction of theories, the principle of *Do ut des* taken in the noblest sense, without which the development of science is hardly conceivable. It is equally true, on the other hand, that the case in point here is a very peculiar kind of interaction. While, towards the end of the eighteenth century and at the beginning of the nineteenth, the results of the Hungarian authors publishing in Latin found very favourable reaction from foreign theoreticians,[1] the works published in Hungarian in the second half of the nineteenth century found almost no response—understandably because of the language barrier between Hungary and the foreign students of language.

Beyond this honouring task I feel also morally bound to introduce to the foreign reader the outstanding representatives of a most colourful period of Hungarian linguistics (the second half of the nineteenth century), to call attention to their scientific results. Obsolete as one or another of their statements might have become, they were excellent representatives of the science of language of their age, and it is not their fault that their activities remained without effect upon the foreign currents of linguistics.

Finally I also consider it my moral duty to inform the foreign reader of the "workshop secrets" of today's linguistic science in Hungary. My reason for doing so is neither a sort of exhibitionism nor an urge to make any "sensational disclosure", but the desire to give an idea of the spirit of scientific polemics which is today one of the characteristic features of the Hungarian science of language. This seems all the more necessary since not much of the Hungarian linguistic production of our days is published in foreign languages, and so the readers abroad cannot get a line on it. Moreover, the few works available to the foreign public might readily be taken as representing the position of the majority of Hungarian linguists,[2] and consequently can provide a source of misinformation.

When, therefore, in my work I deal in more detail with monographic writings of some Hungarian authors, I wish to attain a threefold goal. First, to show the place in the history of science, and the critical character, of the adaptation in Hungary of the new methods. (This, by the nature of my work, is a goal of first importance.) Second, to dispel by my modest means the misbelief which can be inferred from R. M. W. Dixon's remark mentioned before. And lastly, this being a work of comprehensive character

---

[1] See below the opinion of Humboldt and Schwicker on M. Révai's activity (*Antiquitates Litteraturae Hungaricae*, 1803; *Elaboratior Grammatica Hungarica*, 1803), further the appreciation expressed by Benfey, Gabelentz, Thomson, Sanfeld-Jensen with regard to the pioneering merits of J. Sajnovics and S. Gyarmathi (*Demonstratio idioma Ungarorum et Lapporum idem esse*, 1770; *Affinitas linguae Hungaricae cum linguis Fennicae originis grammatice demonstrata*, 1799).

[2] In this respect see R. M. W. Dixon's remark in *Linguistics* 2, p. 96 (1963).

claiming to count as a monograph, detailed discussion of works at the same time enables me to expound also my own opinion on the general theoretical questions raised in those writings.

Hungarian linguistics, like every science of our days, is characterized by ferment, a feverish search for new principles and methods, the demand for a considered improvement of the old ones. The development of our science has reached a stage where the time has come to take stock, to make a critical survey of the theoretical antecedents, to draw the lessons, to find the right way amidst the different trends.

The history of science is to be surveyed and evaluated on the basis of a specific theory. My work is no exception to this rule.

The theses of linguistic theory basically determining the viewpoint of my work can be summed up as follows:

(a) Language as a system of signs, as regards its social "totality", has two functions:

it is a means, and at the same time the result, of the formation of concepts, of thought, the existence form of thought *(gnoseological, reality-reflecting function)*;

it is a means to make intersubjective the subjective body of knowledge, the affective-volitional, etc. elements, accumulated in consequence of the reflection of reality on a social scale *(communicative function)*.

(b) The system of language is thus not merely a complex network of relationships of forms, but an involved system, a social product, which came into being through the simultaneous "co-operation" of social and subjective factors, and which at the same time is a very important means of social intercourse.

(c) The relation between linguistic form and the concepts, thoughts, etc. concerning reality indicates the unity of form and content. This unity is embodied in the process of verbal thinking, which in turn reflects a certain measure of isomorphism of conceptual structures and linguistic structures.

(d) This conception of language at the same time points to the determining features of the linguistic sign and to its place in the semiotic system as well: the linguistic sign is the product of the real sign situation. The real sign situation is a relation of men who want to understand one another and to act upon one another, of men who "create" (linguistic) signs with a view to ensuring their intercourse. But the (linguistic) signs can wholly perform their reality-reflecting and communicative functions only if they reflect faithfully the relation between man and reality, between man and the signs, and between the signs and reality alike;

structurally they can be the tools of complete communication and expression, and form a system whose particular elements are interdependent, hierarchically subordinated to one another (horizontal and vertical networks of relationships between phoneme and phoneme, phoneme and sign, sign and sign, sign and sign combination, sign combination and sign combination, sign combination and sign sequence).

(e) *Linguistic structure is a system of blended interactions of the constitutive elements. The categories reflecting with approximate precision the immanent peculiarities of this complicated structure are the laws of language, the linguistic laws.*

(f) In consequence of the uninterrupted progress of social cognition the conceptual marks of the linguistic laws *are in constant motion, being rearranged and revalued,* for only in this way can they reflect the pattern of motion of linguistic reality with ever greater precision.

(g) The relation of the synchronic and diachronic kinds of motion of language is realized *in the dialectic unity of state and change,* which is at the same time a reference to the interdependence of the two methods of linguistic research.

(h) An entirely worthwhile examination of language has to take into account the extraordinary complexity of the linguistic system. In working out the methodology of special (semantic, phonological, morphological, formal, etc.) investigations, in generalizing the results of such examinations, consideration *of the dynamic relation between the whole and the part* must be the basic standard and starting point.

The historical role of the theories following upon one another, but also the theoretical significance of the modern schools, I seek to value on the basis of the above formulae of linguistic theory.

The main schools of linguistic science *(logicism, the "natural-scientific school", historicism, psychologism, neoempirism: formal description to structuralism)* agree almost unanimously in that each recognized (or at least surmised) one of the features of the extremely involved linguistic structure, unduly exaggerating its importance, and considered the newly discovered feature to be the only characteristic of language. An inevitable consequence of this was that the successive schools failed to build into their respective theories the time-tested partial results of former schools. In determining the worth of the various features of language they did not use as a standard the dialectics of the whole and the part, of state and change. All this, of course, does not negate, or even lessen, the significance of the discovery of part

11

truths; on the contrary, it tries to establish what they are really worth by cutting off their extravagances (the only principle of linguistic explanation).

In conformity with the above theoretical objectives and lessons of the history of science, I shall deal primarily, and in most detail, with those modern schools which absolutized, and elevated to the rank of an exclusive principle of "language description", the importance of one or another part factor of the complex linguistic structure. Even of these I shall investigate the gnoseological motives (empiricism) of what is called formal analysis (formal description), in the light of the international polemic that has started in the past few decades about the interpretation of sign and meaning. Understandably, I will discuss in most detail those monographic works which, based upon the new methods, Hungarian authors have written in the past decade and whose rigid, one-sided views have given rise to lively debates. It may be needless to emphasize specially that the polemic about their theoretical statements and methodological procedures involves also disputes with foreign theoreticians. As regards the foreign theoretical antecedents, I shall deal with them in detail instead of merely referring to them only where there is essential divergence between adaptation in Hungary and the foreign predecessors.

In the second part of the study I shall discuss the genesis and development of the concept of linguistic (phonetic) law. *Phonetic law and linguistic law,* as concerns their most characteristic features, *reflect the correlation of the part and the whole.* Only in this sense do I use them as synonyms.

The most momentous effect upon the formation of the concept law taken in the modern sense was wrought by the concept of natural law of modern times (Newtonian classical physics, Darwinian biology). The modern concept of natural law that sprang out of the ground of the materialist outlook on the world galvanized into life a good number of scientific disciplines, including the science of language. The concept of phonetic law grown out of the soil of physical science comprised all essential traits which we still today take to be the characteristic features of the law (objective character; the laws of science are reflections of the material world; the system of laws, etc.). Of course, the "new" concept of phonetic law was marked also by the white spots of the scientific erudition of the time (absolutization of the objective character, total negation of the role of subjective factors, the principle of the exceptionless working of laws, their operation with blind necessity), a circumstance which has been a source of heated debates up to our days.

Yet the neogrammarian postulate of phonetic law, together with its extravagances and severity, gave an enormous impetus to practical research: a secure grip, a firm basis for the student of language. This much was acknowledged also by those linguists who blamed its severity and rightly so. Consequently the new concept of phonetic law in its time was given a warm reception by progressive representatives of European linguistics. This was highly imputable to the fact that linguistic researches had become scientific, but it was not without effect upon the formation of philosophical thought (Schleicher's physical monism).

It is easy to see why the neogrammarian rigidity gave rise to heated dispute. And, as is usually the case, in the heat of the debate the idea of phonetic law gradually lost its initial spell, so much so that its opponents began to regard it as a brake on scientific progress. The idea of law "infected" by materialistic monism was replaced by "respectable" psychologism.

As phonological research developed, the neogrammarian idea was again attacked by arguments about the gradual or abrupt character of phonetic changes and this in order to obtain recognition for the sound-changing function of the subject.

In the closing chapters of my work I shall investigate the transformation that can be observed in the general concept of law as a consequence of the (natural-scientific) discoveries of the past few decades. By rearranging, revaluing the conceptual marks of the general concept of law I shall attempt to outline the essential traits of the modern concept of linguistic law and to decide the choice between phonetic law and sound-changing tendency.

I. THE AUTONOMY OF LINGUISTICS

"The true life of all science begins with autonomy, when it wants and is even able to solve the questions of its material at home, with its own tools. For the material would practically offer by itself the appropriate arranging principles and fertile evaluative viewpoints, only one must be able to make the material speak", wrote Gyula Laziczius.[1]

The above quotation is suggestive of the well-known struggle which the history of science has recorded as the struggle of linguistics for autonomy. The growing up of linguistic research was characterized by an impatient claim to emancipation, by a rebellion inspired by the "handmaid complex", the exploration of the ways and means by which this branch of science, wishing to rid itself of the yoke of philosophy, logic, psychology, and then of historical science, wanted to get on its own feet and was seeking, and tried to define, its own material, its arranging principles and an appropriate methodology.

The last century, the "collecting century", accumulated a huge pile of linguistic material; this tide of material was even drowning the scholars. It is not by chance, therefore, that they feverishly looked for principles and ways to overmaster that sea of facts, to bring them to talk, to obtain undoubted evidence from initial, medial and final sounds, roots, prefixes, suffixes, and so forth. What in every stage of their search, and at every step forward, the scholars had before their eyes was the aim to grasp the character, the nature of language; this aim helped the representatives of the different schools to get out of the impasse and stimulated them to improve the correct—or supposedly correct—explanatory principles and methods, to give up the unsatisfactory theories for new ones, and to make steady progress.

Commonly known traits of the historical process of human cognition can be seen against the background of particular events of this struggle. The totality of the empirically collected body of

[1] Gy. Laziczius, *Általános nyelvészet* [General Linguistics], Budapest, 1942, p. 9.

material, its varied and manifold questions of detail could no longer be given even roughly satisfactory answers by contemporary philosophy, "the science of sciences", for its explanatory principles and research methods were lagging far behind the professional demands set by the size and quality of the material, its axioms proved insufficient and often improper to answer the accumulated technical questions. The *general* explanatory principles were replaced by *particular,* peculiar interpretations; in other words, *scientific cognition became differentiated.* Various specialized branches of science separated from philosophy and sooner or later set out on the road towards independent existence. The process of separation lasted fairly long; depending on the practical needs and requirements of society and on many other factors, some branches of learning became autonomous already in antiquity (astronomy, physics, geometry, mathematics, logic, etc.), while others had to wait until the nineteenth century. Such a "late-born child" in the family of the specialized branches of learning was also the science of language.

The relatively long period of gestation, of course, did not mean that it was entirely sterile as far as linguistic research was concerned. It is commonly known that the fundamental categories of classical grammar had been established already in antiquity and have survived almost unchanged until the twentieth century as skeleton notions to influence the attempts at a description and classification of various national languages. We must not forget either that already the ancient Greek grammarians made brilliant suggestions to categorize the different elements of language. To mention but one example, in establishing grammatical categories they made allowance for the possibility of association with particular suffixes—an acceptable standpoint even in the present state of our knowledge. There were thus progressive suggestions which, intermediately and by some roundabout way, have come down to the European grammarians of modern times to provide a basis for their experiments in linguistic theories. But this classical heritage—by reason of its genesis—served, expressly or not, as "evidentiary matter" for philosophical axioms; it was called to play the part of a "toy" of logical speculations, it did not—and consequently could not—constitute a unitary whole, a science having an explanatory principle and individual methods of its own.

This special situation may account for the peculiar features and deviations on the way towards autonomy of the science of language taken in the modern sense, for the fact that linguistics "offered itself" to various, more developed branches of learning. The particular lucubrations on the history of science, depending on the theoretical attitude and temperament of the authors concerned, usually censure the principled struggles of the nineteenth century indicating which specialized branch of science, being more developed owing to its positional advantage, should be sought out for closer association, for theoretical and methodological support, or—let us say frankly—to which the science of language should be subordinated. All things considered, these efforts had their own reason of principle. In my view, it was the sudden realization of one aspect of the extremely complicated nature of language that prompted the linguists of the nineteenth century to ask for the help of one or another specialized branch of science. Their choice of this step was dependent on which aspect of language, this complex "physical", mental and social formation, the various researchers were emphasizing and taking as determining.

It is thus no accident that the school hallmarked by K. F. Becker, *linguistic logicism*, turned to logic for help in its attempts at linguistic explanations. The development of this trend was promoted by no lesser factor than the realization *of the indissoluble unity of language and thought*. Or what else could inspire Herbart's disciple, Steinthal, and later Paul and Wundt, when the first two "sought to apply the ready framework" of psychology "to the linguistic material", while the third "wanted to build up his psychology on a linguistic basis" (Laziczius), than the idea that language, speech, is indisputably also a *psychical activity*, consequently linguistics has points of contact, possible explanations in common, with psychology—a fact which is clearly borne out also by our present-day knowledge. It is on the same basis that we have to put in its place what is usually called *linguistic historicism* or *linguistic history*, a tendency that started with Grimm and then expanded rapidly to ascend to hegemony. The emergence of this school was motivated by the discovery of a characteristic feature of language, its *constantly changing and developing nature*. The rapid propagation of the school can be accounted for by the heuristic pleasure of hitting upon the essence of the relations of social and linguistic evolution. This is how we can understand the weak current represented by the subjective idealist Vossler, who turned his attention to the subjective-aesthetic aspect of linguistic expression and outlined his theory on this basis.

This sketchy survey of linguistic exploration would be incomplete if we failed to define what is called physical or *natural-scientific linguistics,* to determine its place and role. I think this school, with regard to its basic motives and effect, is not merely one of the many offers of the science of language. As I wish to prove in detail below, the decisive changes of direction in the history of linguistics occurred when this discipline encountered the natural sciences.

The brilliant achievements of the modern natural sciences had an overwhelming effect on contemporary linguistics, since they woke it up to the unambiguity of the natural-scientific viewpoint and to the exactness of such methods of research. The great successes attained on the basis of the unambiguous viewpoint and exact methods stimulated the linguist of the time to search for similar and identical features of the object of his investigation and other products of nature. The efforts of natural science very soon produced their linguistic results; scholars discovered the most fundamental identical feature of the research material of the two branches of science, *their existence independent of individual men,* which we call *the objective character* today. The highly valuable and significant discovery, a consistent examination of the effect of this discovery—by the logic of things—induced A. Schleicher and his not too numerous followers to draw far-reaching conclusions: they took language for the same kind of natural product, *an organism,* as are the other natural organisms. As the development of all natural organisms is governed by specific regularities, so language cannot be an exception to the rule, and the changes of languages must be governed by the same kind of laws as are the laws of nature. One must not forget either that the neogrammarian postulate of phonetic law resulted from this "linguistic law is a natural law" conception. Nor should one forget that one of Schleicher's conclusions was *his consistently materialistic linguistic outlook,* a direct issue of which is an accurate definition of the concept of linguistic (to him still phonetic) law taken in the modern sense.

The several stages of the linguistic orientation of the nineteenth century (logicism, psychologism, historicism, and last but not least the natural-scientific school) are thus equally characterized by the common feature that representatives of the various schools came to realize the significance of one or another aspect of language and, as is usual in the history of science, exaggerated the significance of the aspect in question, absolutized it, attributed to it an exclusive or at least basically determining character. This posture of the representatives of the various schools settled the essence of their position against other schools: they were categorically opposed to one another, they sternly refused one another. This static, antidialectic way of negation throws light upon the common weakness of all schools: they discovered only one or another feature of the complicated nature of language, and then they swore by it unfalteringly. They clung to their narrow horizon, and could not rise to an elevation from where to determine the place of the common characteristics comprising a synopsis of the partial factors. Briefly, they did not reach the level of the antagonistic unity of the whole and the part, of the dialectical view of language. They failed to recognize language in its complexity, they could not see the coherent nature of its characteristic traits. The implacable mutual criticism of the various schools was therefore antidialectical, metaphysical in character, because they could loosen only one or another thread of the complex linguistic tissue; significant as these threads were, their real value could have been realistically evaluated only in their mutual relation—in their opposition and complementary nature. For true as it is that the categories of language and those of concept-formation overlap, this is still only a half-truth, because language is not only "the living reality of thought" but also a social product—if you like it, a principal means of progress towards society. The logical and historical aspects not only do not categorically exclude each other; on the contrary, they are interdependent and complementary. Also we can accept only as part of the truth the one-sided formulation of the material of language, if it is not complemented with the other half of the truth, the psychical nature of language.

The mutual implacability of the militant representatives of half-truths at the time reflects the same state of "dichotomy" of the science of language as is usually mentioned in the speculations describing the limitations of the clash between exponents of the schools following in Saussure's steps, on the one hand, and representatives of the traditional historical outlook, on the other. As the schools prior to Saussure failed to see the dialectics of the afore-mentioned contradictions of language, so the representatives of historicism and antihistoricism failed to recognize *the unity of state and development*. This is where the underlying motive of the synchronic-diachronic war is to be found.

How significant for the history of science the trend established in the wake of Saussure's teachings is, cannot be too much emphasized, but this may not even be necessary in our days. Representatives of the new schools following in Saussure's footsteps stressed in countless studies and monographs the importance of the teachings concerning the symbolism of the elements of language and the systematism of its signs. Neither do I wish to minimize their role. If I nevertheless take a stand, to the extent of a half-sentence, in favour of the epoch-making influence of Saussure's teachings, I do so because I wish to underscore that, in the explanations for the emergence of the new school, usually no mention is made of the fertilizing effect of the natural-scientific outlook, and that the inaccurate formulation, and even theoretically inappropriate nature, of some details of Saussure's teachings became a source of serious mistakes encountered in the attitude of his followers and in their practical works on linguistics.

In establishing one of the most essential features of the new ideas, the systematic nature of signs, we witness therefore the second meeting of linguistics and natural science in the early years of the twentieth century. The question here is not only that system is a word borrowed from the nomenclature of the natural sciences, first of all from the terminological arsenal of modern discoveries in biology,[2] but mainly that the whole system and the place occupied in it by the constitutive elements were explained by the constitutive elements themselves.

The representatives of the new ideas proclaimed that the long-expected moment had come, the period of the full autonomy of linguistics had begun. For, they thought, if the system of language, the components of the system, the linguistic signs, can be examined in themselves, then there is no need for outside help in the exact description of language. If language is a system of signs, opined Saussure himself, there is nothing to threaten the autonomy of linguistics; namely, at that time there were seen only vague outlines of a science which would deal with the description and systematization of the most varied signs of communication.[3] Laziczius also saw Saussure's scientific significance in the fact "that he secured autonomy not only inwardly, by

[2] Linnaeus, *Systema naturae.*
[3] Semiology (Saussure) or sematology (Bühler): general theory of signs.

specifying the internal tasks of linguistics, but also outwardly, in relation to the other sciences.[4]

How did this "autonomy" really look in the light of Saussure's conception, and chiefly how is it realized in the ideas and activities of his successors? (Here I wish to remark that I use the term "successors" in the broadest sense, in agreement with Benveniste, who sums up the significance of Saussure's teachings, their influence upon modern linguistic trends, in these words: "Il n'y a pas de linguiste aujourd'hui qui ne lui doive quelque chose. Il n'y a pas de théorie générale qui ne mentionne son nom."[5] I have in mind, therefore, not only the camp of Saussureans rallied behind "Cahier Ferdinand de Saussure", but all representatives of modern linguistics, even those who sharply criticize a few details of Saussure's teachings, while at the same time carrying to excess, boldly "developing further", some of his not quite precisely formulated partial statements.)

What should be discussed here for the time being is not the criticism of the opposition of *langue* and *parole*, of synchrony and diachrony, but the Saussurean idea according to which the components of linguistics taken in the broadest sense are by far not homogeneous in character. Saussure himself did not deny their physico-physiological, psychological and social "nature". It is a different matter that he did not regard these factors in their entirety as an object of linguistic research. He did not, and he could not either, because thereby he would have rung the funeral bell over the autonomy that had been a dream and had just "come true". But if we examine the definition of *langue* which, also according to him, belongs to the scope of linguistic research *par exellence*, at once we can see the peculiarity of his conception of *langue:* "le dépôt des images acoustiques",[6] "les associations ratifiées par le consentement collectif et dont l'ensemble constitue la langue".[7] Saussure's *linguistique de la langue* as a whole is interspersed with such and similar expressions.

It is questionable how independent a science can be which, in the definition of its object and its research basis, applies solely

[4] Laziczius, op. cit., p. 28.
[5] E. Benveniste, *Problèmes de linguistique générale*, Paris, 1966, p. 32.
[6] F. de Saussure, *Cours de linguistique générale*, Paris, 1955[3], p. 32 (hereafter referred to as *Cours ...*).
[7] Ibid.

psychological viewpoints and principles, as is amply evidenced by the above quotations. It is equally difficult for the long-awaited and demanded autonomy to uphold the Saussurean conception of the Janus-faced linguistic sign, "la combinaison du concept et de l'image acoustique",[8] which essentially is "une entité psychique".[9] Or if we examine the threefold sign function (image, expression, appeal) based on the above-mentioned definition of the language sign, we can see at once the complexity of the sign, mainly the complex nature of its function, which is impossible to describe "clearly", and especially to explain in an exact manner, without knowledge of the psychical, logical, social factors qualified as "extralinguistic".

Many of Saussure's successors and pupils made several attempts to purify the new doctrines of the Master's "psychological infection", which they imputed to the period. I may not be far from the truth when I see in the sometimes inaccurately worded Saussurean thoughts not the psychological infection of the period (of course, it is difficult to ascertain on the basis of the posthumous texts how much is due to inaccurate notes of the hearers) but a single offshoot of the vibrating train of thought of a ceaselessly cogitating scholar who continually polished and improved his concepts and ideas. I do not insist that these "mongrel" formulations are accidental or downright erroneous, I take it rather that Saussure had at every moment to realize the drawbacks of that autonomy, keeping always in view the extremely complicated nature of language, of linguistic expression, impossible even to approximate by simple description. Hence, his much talked-of inconsistency is not a consequence of superficialness, but rather a reflection of the constant meditation of a very conscientious scholar, who refused to be deceived by his grand discovery. At the most he could not rid himself of the effect of his system compulsion, and this was what drove him into the notorious contradictions. It is common knowledge that he could not solve the contradictions, and today we already can see clearly also that this was a drawback of his grand discovery.

While we have unconditionally to recognize the scientific significance of the discovery of contradictions following from the essence of language, we cannot but make the remark that the Saussurean evaluation of these contradictions was formulated chiefly in the differential opposition of the terms of the system of

[8] Op. cit., p. 99.
[9] Ibid.

language. Having given rise to many disputes and being interpreted in as many ways, Saussure's famous statement, *"dans la langue il n'y a que des différences"*,[10] is in my opinion unequivocal and incapable of misinterpretation. This is what corresponds to the Saussurean conception of the value of the various terms of the system of language, namely that such values are only distinctive values, *"... définis non pas positivement par leur contenu, mais négativement par leurs rapports avec les autres termes du système. Leur plus exacte caractéristique est d'être ce que les autres ne sont pas"*.[11] This is what corresponds to the Saussurean conception of linguistic signifier *(signifiant linguistique)*, which is *"... constitué, non par sa substance matérielle, mais uniquement par les différences qui séparent son image acoustique de toutes les autres"*.[12] This is what corresponds to the Saussurean conception of the essence of the phonemes, according to which *"Les phonèmes sont avant tout des entités oppositives, relatives et négatives."*[13] It was to sum up clearly these partial statements that he drew the general conclusion with regard to language,[14] saying that *"dans la langue il n'y a que des différences"*.

I have to say this even if I pay regard for the Saussurean lines which speak of the relation of identity and difference in the formulation of the characteristic traits of the mechanism of language[15] or mention the paradoxical unity of differing and similar things in another explanation of linguistic value.[16]

Is there a contradiction between the Saussurean passages quoted and referred to above? Undeniably, there is. But a thorough study of Saussure's lifework shows up still more contradictions, as was detailed also by Laziczius,[17] who considered it one of Saussure's principal merits that he had discovered the difference between terms of the system of language, and the opposites mirroring the differences, because "that throws light deep into the very soul of language".[18]

[10] Op. cit., p. 166 (italics in the original).
[11] Op. cit., p. 162.
[12] Op. cit., p. 164.
[13] Ibid.
[14] "Tout ce qui précède revient à dire que ..." Op. cit., p. 166.
[15] Op. cit., p. 151.
[16] Op. cit., p. 159.
[17] Laziczius, op. cit., pp. 15—18.
[18] Saussure, op. cit., p. 36. The oppositive character of the linguistic terms is explained in a different way by N. S. Trubetskoj, *Grundzüge der Phonologie*, Göttingen, 1962³, pp. 60—61.

The successors (taken in the above-mentioned broader sense) educated on the Saussurean heritage also "developed" further Saussure's afore-cited fundamental statement so that they strictly took apart what Saussure still had regarded as an indivisible unity,[19] and in the struggle against much vilified psychologism some of them even went so far—and this is also commonly known—as to refuse to regard meaning as part of grammatical studies. What had thus remained was form, the outward form of the linguistic elements, the examination of this form, of the formal "behaviour" of the different elements of language, as the only exact method of linguistic research, which in the linguistic attitude of some students became at the same time the main pillar of the autonomy of linguistics.

Thereby we have come to some well-known exponents of the schools included (or rather put forcibly) in the generic term "structuralism". The heterogeneity of these tendencies cannot be emphasized often enough. Some of their representatives (Bloomfield and his followers) thought the only task of the science of language was to examine the formal aspect of utterances, while others (Harris, Hjelmslev and disciples), even though they recognized that the examination of the internal content was justified and necessary, regarded the formal aspect as determining, and investigated and explained the content elements as a function of this. Of course, I have referred thereby only to two typical currents of the new trends, and this—I admit—with polarized simplification.[20] In excuse of the simplistic reference I can say only that I have made it on the basis of a certain attitude. And this—if it is not yet clear from the foregoing—is nothing but a criticism of the common trait of the schools in question, of the often mentioned autonomy of linguistics. As a matter of fact, the new trends more or less agree in that they do not consider and describe the function of language in its entirety, but they regard only the communicative function of language as its basic and single determining feature, for if they were to "mix it up" with its role played in human cognition, autonomy would again be in jeopardy.

[19] The Janus face of the linguistic sign—*phonetic form* (true, only in form of an image) + *concept*.

[20] I shall still come back to their detailed analysis; it may then show that I do not fall into the error of considering the new trend in its entirety to be a mass of worthless speculations, as did one or another representative of those schools when they evaluated the linguistic efforts of the times prior to Saussure and even to Bloomfield.

Is it possible to describe the different languages "purely", on the only basis of the formal "behaviour" of its elements? No doubt it is possible to work also with such "formal analysis", even with "description" only. Moreover, there might be, as there have been and may be also in future, cases where the student of language can choose only this method, for he has no other grip to seize (when encountering a totally unknown language, which has no grammar and no written vocabulary either). In such cases the discovery and description of the formal behaviour and possible associations of elements can undeniably lead to incontestable results, which has been a frequent occurrence. While recognizing both the possibilities and the results of the purely descriptive method, I cannot fail to observe at least the disputability of the purely formal character, for even in the case of sound associations of the most different order and level it is indispensable to enlist the help of a "native informant" whose opinion enables the "pure" descriptivist to decide whether a given sound association is an orderly or a "disorderly" set of phonemes, or whether it is genuine "utterance". And this is impossible without questioning the content elements.

From what precedes the reader might gather even that I unequivocally condemn the efforts displayed towards the end of the nineteenth century and at the beginning of the twentieth: the unambiguous establishment of the object of linguistics, the implacable criticism of the former practice which tried to declare linguistics to be a "handmaid" of one or another specialized branch of learning, and mainly the fight waged for the elaboration of specific linguistic methods. No, this was not at all my purpose by putting autonomy between quotation marks.

The history of the development of human cognition explicitly teaches that it was necessary to separate the various specialized branches of science from the "science of sciences". It is also true that the relative homogeneity of the objects of the different branches of science resulted in a relative autonomy of the discipline in question. It depended on the given science, more precisely on its object, how relative its autonomy was. It may not be said with absolute certainty either that the various disciplines of natural science are better off in respect of homogeneity and consequently of relative autonomy. The extent of relative autonomy is not to be approximated on the basis of the undeniably existing peculiarities, identical and different features of the various branches of science, but we have to examine rather the particular periods of their development, the social demand made on them, in order to obtain a nearly accurate answer to this much debated question.

As long as the specialized branches of science were required to provide detailed knowledge and precise description (analysis), such requirements could be met by relatively homogeneous methods. As, however, the requirements increased, so the idea of autonomy lost its original tone and complexion, together with all its progressive elements and stimulating qualities, to become sooner or later an obstacle to progress. As long as the task was to describe the motion of the planets, the astronomer or astrophysicist could perform his task by the aid of relatively uniform methods, physical implements and calculations (the mathematical apparatus served as a "prop" also in this operation). But when the task is to approach the planets or to reach them, no single branch of science can undertake it alone. A close and organic co-operation of a legion of different special sciences is needed to solve the task. It cannot even be said that one or another of the co-operating sciences could play the first violin in this "cosmic orchestra". The only composer and conductor here is the human mind seeking and able to acquire better and better knowledge of the essence of the forms of motion in nature and society, and each branch of science contributes its own part to the composing of this big symphony and to its best possible performance. This does not detract anything from the original worth of the contributing branches of learning; on the contrary, their part played in the ensemble gives them their real worth promoting human cognition and serving man.

Representatives of the natural sciences frankly admit that their discipline has determining features of this character, and it does not even occur to them that they would thereby minimize its worth, its role; on the contrary, they would not dare to undertake otherwise the tasks of "cosmic dimensions" ahead of them. In my judgment, participation of this kind is no hypocritical shyness but a sober realization of the size and dimensions, the ramifications of the tasks, and a courageous approach to the consequences of this realization. This fact is at first sight contradicted by the birth of new branches of natural science (physical chemistry, biochemistry, biophysics, etc., etc.), but this is only an apparent contradiction, because the leading motive for the birth of these new "autonomous" branches of science was the best possible performance of the part to be played in the big "ensemble". The "binomial" branches of science (physical chemistry, etc.) are eloquent products of the development of the natural sciences, pointing to a peculiar "symbiosis" where it is difficult to delimit the various sciences, which "flow" into one another. "Since the science of physics—first of all in the form of what is called quantum chemistry—has increasingly invaded the realm of the chemical sciences, a permanent problem is . . . to delimit the two scientific domains."[21]

It is also very convincing what L. Kalmár said at a working conference devoted to "Problems of Mathematical Linguistics and Computer Translation" (8 to 10 March 1962): "Ours is the age of the evolution of big syntheses, contiguous sciences, complex sciences like cybernetics."[22] During the working conference he once again came back to the idea, elaborating on it in these words: "Characteristic of the scientific development of our age is namely that on the boundary line between two sciences new sciences emerge, such as biochemistry or geobotany, or—mathematical linguistics. Moreover, if I may say after the model of the word *interlingua*, today also 'intersciences' begin to form at the border of several sciences, such as cybernetics."[23]

Linguistics can, of course, take little share in the solution of the tasks of astronautics, but it can assume a part—no small one at that—and has to accept it with a view to acquiring ever more precise knowledge of man who solves the tasks, of *homo sapiens*, and human society. If the linguist not only wants to arrive at trivial generalities in formulating the function of language in man's evolution into *homo sapiens* and thereby in the formation and development of human society, but if he wants to penetrate into the details as well, he shall come to realize still how many white spots there are, and how unsatisfactory is the one-sided conception of the linguistic sign narrowed down to communicative functions, or the fixing of rules of the formal behaviour of signs, if he thinks of the many things the qualifier in the term *homo loquens* means.[24]

[21] P. Rádi, Kísérlet a mozgásformák rendszerének korszerű leírására [Attempt at an Up-to-date Description of the System of Forms of Motion], *Magyar Filozófiai Szemle*, XI/3, p. 389.
[22] Kalmár: ÁnyT II, p. 171.
[23] Loc. cit., p. 297.
[24] While preparing the English edition of my work, I happened to lay hands on the mimeographed manuscript (Linguistics in Relation to Other Sciences. Rapport du Xe Congrès International des Linguistes: *Actes du Xe Congrès International des Linguistes* [Bucarest, 1969], pp. 75—111)

The complexity of the task requires less rigid attitudes and more elaborate methods if we conceive of language as it is and if we want to approach in this way the dynamism of its internal interrelatedness, to uncover the real motive forces of its development, which for plainness' sake we can term linguistic laws.

The starting point is the function of language, of the linguistic sign, both in the formation and in the communication of knowledge; that is, recognition of the synthetic character of the sign, which at the same time determines the method, too.

The stimulus to this kind of investigation has been given by the recent amazing results in the natural sciences and, of course, by the complex methods producing those results. I may not have to stress more specially that this motive, this intention, is not meant to be a repetition "on a higher level" of Schleicher's unsuccessful attempt (linguistics classed as one of the physical sciences). This I want also to lay down in the awareness that I have to face the dangers of the wrong conception which develops an irreconcilable antagonism between the natural and social processes of the phenomenal world and consequently between natural-scientific and sociological cognition. This sort of rigid opposition would disregard such known features of the two processes as their objective character, their immanent networks of relationships, the identical traits of their regularities and the knowability of all these. Today there have already begun to become indistinct the boundaries which have produced only irreconcilable differences of characteristic traits between the natural processes defined by means of classical physics and on the basis of its viewpoint, on the one hand, and the social processes examined through the prism of contemporary social science, on the other. The field investigated by quantum mechan-

---

of a lecture delivered by R. Jakobson at the Tenth International Philological Congress in Bucharest in 1967. I am sincerely pleased to see also Jakobson state his reasons for devising his "interdisciplinary" conception based "on the principal affinities of the objects classified" in these terms: ". . . linguists, whether they like it or not, 'must become increasingly concerned with the many anthropological, sociological, and psychological problems which invade the field of language. It is difficult for a modern linguist to confine himself to his traditional subject matter. Unless he is somewhat unimaginative, he cannot but share in some or all of the mutual interests which tie up linguistics with anthropology and culture history, with sociology, with psychology, with philosophy, and, more remotely, with physics and physiology'." Loc. cit., pp. 1—2. Cf. also E. Sapir, The Status of Linguistics as a Science, *Language* V, 1929.

ics shows a network of such peculiar forms of motion of matter which can no longer be described by the tools of classical physics, cannot be explained from the standpoint which seemed satisfactory at the time. Owing to their complexity, the characteristic features of this pattern of forms of material motion are getting closer and closer to those ideas which modern social science has recently formed of the forms of motion of society. Nonetheless, we must not forget that substantial differences are also to be seen within the fundamental identity, and to disregard them would be just as wrong as to carry to utter excess the significance of the size and worth of the differences.[25] Furthermore, this conception is not intended to squeeze linguistics either into psychology or into logic, even though it recognizes the justification of modern psycholinguistics[26] and the rightness of G. Klaus's opinion regarding the importance of the identical and naturally different features of logical and linguistic systems and last but not least that of the social aspect of language.

The attempt at delimitation, if I have succeeded in demonstrating its elasticity, means at the same time to be a stand on the evaluation of previous attempts, too. By rejecting the demand for exclusivity of logicism, historicism, psychologism and formal linguistic analysis, by removing their excesses and rigidity, it is possible to designate the place of these schools in the history of science, to define the role they play in the struggle for an ever more thorough knowledge of language. The intended differentiation is in fact sustained by the principled consideration which sees both in the results and in the failures of the linguistic efforts of past times individual milestones of the road leading up to the present, hence it declares critical solidarity with the forerunners.

Namely, on the basis of the experience of general human cognition, one can regard as regular that feature of the development of the sciences which necessarily postulates the replacement of old theories by new ones. This "change of place" is lent a dynamic character by the fact that the new, while displacing the old together with its sphere of operation, retains in itself the progressive elements, the promoting tendencies of the old. In the aforesaid manner this theoretical idea is consistent also with

---

[25] The identical and different features of the two processes shall be dealt with later in this study.
[26] Vygotsky and his school.

all experiments which went as far as the empirical apprehension of the facts of language, the description of superficial forms, and was caught in the contradictions appearing between two variants of identical phenomena, and which could not discover the essence of the different courses of development of one and the same linguistic variant, because the means of empiricism alone were insufficient. Here it is entirely irrelevant whether we speak about the descriptive linguists of antiquity or modern formal descriptivists. What determines their role and worth is not the period they lived and worked in but their principles and methods of investigation. The course of researches was usually charted by practical needs from the level of empiricism to that of theoretical generalizations, where the central task was already to grasp the internal interrelations, the regularities of the facts of language.

There is no need to reach for conclusive examples far back in time. Let us think of nothing else than the extremist sort of trend, the "structuralist" school, which did not regard itself as the linguistic embodiment of empiricism but which, by reason of its theoretical unpretentiousness or rather antitheoretical attitude, took account only of the formal behaviour of linguistic utterances. On the basis of sensible considerations it could be expected that the modern schools, overcoming the excrescences of their "Sturm und Drang" period, would embark on the road towards the theoretical pretention enabling them to discover the deeper interrelations, too. Without entering a detailed discussion of this tendency here (which I will not fail to do later), I can state that this process has already started. "Critical solidarity" appreciates this process and blames only those who got stuck within the bounds of the first period "hallmarked" by a lack of theoretical pretention, who confounded the beginning with the end. The blame can be rightly put only on those representatives of the modern trend who take it as the task of linguistics, of all the complicated mesh of linguistic phenomena, only to make a quantitative description of the elements themselves and their external interrelations. The basic gnoseological mistake of this trend is most vividly borne out by the fact that it identifies the methods, possibilities and categories of the first period of linguistic description (formal description) with the methods, possibilities and categories of cognition taken in the general sense, and it holds that the only expedient procedure of linguistic research is to apply its own methods and principles.

If language is a complex physico-physiological, socio-historical and psychical entity, then the true description of its essence and peculiar regularities requires knowledge of all facts which the studies in the above subjects have already uncovered. To what extent this endangers the autonomy of linguistics is clearly demonstrated by the following lines summing up the character of the various part studies in social sciences, of their interrelations, of the essence of their functional interrelations, in these terms: "Every special branch of the socio-historical sciences, in its systematic and historical parts alike, can become an auxiliary science for another branch, or for all the other fields . . . But the utilization, mediatization of the results and methods of the different special fields for another field—those of one for all and those of all for one—expresses a functional interrelation and not the status of an auxiliary science."[27]

I think what I have said so far has quite clearly outlined the motives of principle, the objectives, methods and scope of this work. I have intended it to be an experiment, putting aside a fiction upheld for several decades (concerning the full autonomy of the science of language), to approach the linguistic phenomena in their own complex nature by making use of the results, within the range of my knowledge, of the auxiliary sciences required for this approach. The scope of the opinion to be expressed is determined by the complexity of the system of language, the linguistic sign: their role (1) in the formulation of thoughts and (2) in the communication of thoughts and feelings. This sign conception necessarily calls for consideration of the regularities of language and thought, fixing the relationship between linguistic and other signs (identical but mainly different features), and describing the principal traits of linguistic structures resulting from the systemlike structuralization of the linguistic signs. In this scope I shall explore the relations of semantics (semasiology) and general semantics (semiology, semiotics) and the gnoseological roots of structuralism, and outline their ideological origin. Virtually to sum up all these problems, I shall follow the evolution of the concept of linguistic law, the various interpretations of this concept, and finally I shall try to describe its peculiarities I consider to be most important.

I am aware of the dimensions and weight of this proposition. It is by no means my intention to dwell on all the questions of

[27] J. Szigeti: *Magyar Filozófiai Szemle* VIII, pp. 834—5.

tion→notion→concept-formation), the relation between it and the thing perceived is not natural, but arbitrary and conventional. Between the characteristic traits of the sign and the attributes of the thing denoted by it (part of reality) there is no direct connection, which is simply and palpably proved by the fact that different languages denote one and the same thing by different signs. Aristotle at the same time called attention also to the fact that the arbitrary nature, formulated by him, of the linguistic sign is valid only within certain limits. The usage of individual speakers is determined by definite social norms (objective character). Aristotle's sign conception thus bears all those marks which as a rule are recognized also in the modern definition of the language sign. To the Aristotelian sign conception Dionysius Thrax, author of the first Greek grammar, added a further essential point, *the definition of the representative function of the sign*.

Philosophers and grammarians of the Middle Ages—I have in mind here first of all Thomas Aquinas and the author of *Grammatica speculativa*, Thomas of Erfurt [Duns Scotus]—strove mainly to uncover the relation of the sign, the concept and the objective reality denoted by the sign, and in this way they nilly-willy came up against the problems of the still debated relation between *sign* and *meaning*. The most progressive feature of their theory of meaning was the way they defined the relation between the sign and the thing signified (reality). What is to be noted here first of all is Thomas Aquinas's sensualism, according to which the ultimate source of all knowledge is to be found in sensation. Even though this standpoint disregards the possibility of conceptual operations carried out independently of sensation (and this is just its greatest theoretical defect), it was in any case good for assailing, as it were, the existence of concepts in total independence from objective reality (conceptual realism). From the point of view of the progress of linguistics, on the other hand, an indisputably significant factor was the formulation of the *indirect* character of the relation between sign and denotatum: the sign is connected with the phenomena of the material world only through the interpolation of the concept reflecting the object. The definition of the relation between the concept and the reality reflected by it made less rigorous and less inflexible the idea of arbitrariness that was "developed further" on the basis of Aristotle's conventionalism. We can appreciate as we should the theoretical significance of this conception of the relation between

detail and to venture to bring to a reassuring conclusion the mass of material concerning rather varied opinions. I set out into the immense forest of linguistic structures and linguistic laws with the resolute intention of making a conscious selection of those phenomena of language which promise to provide the most tangible answers necessary for the grasping of the essence of identity and difference between linguistic and other structures, linguistic and other laws.

II. LANGUAGE AS A SYSTEM.
STRUCTURE OF THE LINGUISTIC SIGN

1. THE THEORIES OF THE ESSENCE OF LANGUAGE

Throughout its entire recorded history mankind has always been interested to know the nature, function and characteristic features of language. Among the broadest statements about the world surrounding man, its distinctive features, and man himself (the "dawn" of human thought), we can find views regarding language as a wonderful faculty distinguishing man from all other products of nature (or "creatures"). Among the ideas about the origin of the world, the mysteries of nature puzzling the searching human mind (various mythological explanations), an eminent place is held by a wide range of views on the genesis of language, of the different languages. In almost every one of the tales and legends of the Creation there appears, already at the moment of the creation of man, also speech in some form or other as the most grandiose gift, a distinctive donation from the Creator. The greatest punishment inflicted upon rebel man, who tasted the fruit of the tree of knowledge, was, besides his expulsion from Eden, "the confusion of his language", which again took place, in a peculiar manner, at the time when inquisitive man wanted to pry into the secrets of the higher spheres, to explore them. However smile-provoking and naive this "explanation" may look today, it clearly evidences one thing. In the primitive frame of mind of awakening, thinking man the idea of language and the beginning of growing human knowledge were interconnected from the outset, either so that the only source of knowledge open for man was the incorporeal Creator who gave him language, or so that He would take away the most wonderful gift when man wanted to reveal the "inscrutable secrets" lying beyond the outer limits of his knowledge.

This primitive idea passed through various channels and settled also in the domain of European philosophy. It is no accident that the greatest philosophers of classical antiquity and of later periods almost without exception consciously sought to discover the essence of language, to penetrate the mysteries of the mutual relation of human cognition and language. Heraclitus of Ephesus,

the instinctive materialist and naive dialectical philosopher, w was one of the most outstanding figures of antique philosoph not only added his ingenious idea ("everything flows out") the treasure-house of philosophy, basically influencing the dev opment of all subsequent philosophy, but made his mark al from a gnoseological point of view. The leading motive of h gnoseological doctrine is a general and objective theory hylozoism, according to which *thought must move together wi moving reality*. His jocular etymologies turn around the questic of how far human speech, spoken word, can serve the genera and objective theory of hylozoism, to what extent it can shap and form knowledge. The gnoseological teachings followir Heraclitus already explored the relation of existence (reality) an word (linguistic sign), argued about the necessary (organic) an conventional (arbitrary) character of this relation. In this disput the sophists stressed the polysemantic character of the languag sign, which was to become the basis of sophism (false argumen Aristotle) named after them. In contrast to the sophists, Socrate regarded the unambiguity of the linguistic sign as determinin and endeavoured to catch sight of the "birth of thought" b setting up a clever array of words. It was equally against sophist word-twisting which made the most of the polysemantic chara ter of words that Plato stood up, returning to Heraclitus's fir idea: words are vehicles of all knowledge grasping the essence things, the name mirrors the object in question (reality), mc precisely its mental image.[1] Dealing with the essential traits the relationship of the process of cognition and the linguis sign, he categorically underlined the determining factors of communication of knowledge, the relation of the speaker, hearer, and the material part of reality marked by a linguis term *(somebody tells somebody about something)*. This interpre tion of the language sign traceable to Cratylus has found its v in modern linguistics, too, and has become a source of bit disputes mainly over its part concerning the relation of the s and the thing signified.

Among the historical antecedents of the concept sign take the modern sense special mention should be made of Aristo view. According to him, *word is a mere sign, a sign of the conc crystallized in the process of the acquisition of knowledge (se

[1] As the first categorical formulation of the relation between sig and signified *(word, concept, reality)*, this started a polemic lasting for more than two thousand years.

linguistic sign and reality only if we consider that still today there are many who exaggerate the arbitrary nature of the sign, abuse its incontestably conventional character, and who reduce the complex network of relationships of man, sign and reality, the linguistic meaning, to a system of rules of phonetic form and denotatum.

Great philosophers of modern times (mainly mathematicians, like Descartes and Leibniz) added two new features to the body of knowledge about the linguistic sign, recognizing the *systemlike nature of the signs* and sketching *the outlines of the similarities and differences of linguistic and all other signs*. (The first form of appearance of the contours of semiology, semiotics.) The discovery of the systematism of the language signs, the attempt to build this system into the network of systems of the general theory of signs, inevitably led to a demand, by analogy with universal mathematics, for the creation of a *Lingua universalis* (Descartes) and to an immense work of organization with a view to satisfying that demand (Leibniz). The realization of the new idea was expected to yield no smaller result than the elimination of the contradictions coming up at every step in the system of the linguistic signs, in the signs themselves, the creation of a kind of sign system in which all things and phenomena in the world could be expressed free from contradictions by the aid of unequivocal signs and combinations of signs. The idea could not be carried out because it was meant to "deliver" language of such contradictions (to be discussed in detail later) which belong to its essence, and without which language would cease to exist as a system of signs.

The psychologism hallmarked by Steinthal, Wundt and Paul added nothing worthy of note to the determining features of the linguistic signs, to their systemlike nature, it only embedded its explanation in the conceptual system of psychology, giving a social and then an individual psychological interpretation of the signs.[2]

The nineteenth century, chiefly its second half, was characterized by linguistic historicism, by comparative linguistics. The

---

[2] This is, of course, not a "complete" evaluation of the school of linguistic psychology, it is meant only to hint at the essence of its theory of signs.

contemporary science of language paid attention only to the development of language, to the productive causes of this development. Researches were conducted for the description of only the diachronic features, the examination of synchronic phenomena was neglected. The brilliant successes of the comparative historical method, the efforts to frame linguistic (phonetic) laws and to make them accepted, almost entirely obscured the idea about the symbolism and systematism of signs that belonged to the scope of synchronic investigation. That is why early in the twentieth century Saussure's conception of sign and system came practically as a revelation and laid the foundations of a new school. His ingenious synthesis was determining in mapping out the course of modern linguistic research, and we can safely say that the results and shortcomings of today's linguistic schools are also reducible to the bright and dark sides of the Saussurean teachings.[3]

A historical sketch intended to demonstrate the principal stages of the rise and development of the concept of linguistic sign also shows that one of the characteristic features of language, the systematism of signs, their symbolic nature, was known, in different formulations, already before Saussure's appearance.

[3] H. Steinthal, *Geschichte der Sprachwissenschaft bei den Griechen und Römern mit besonderer Rücksicht auf die Logik*, Berlin, 1890—91², I, pp. 76 ff.; *Platón összes művei* [Collected Works of Plato], Budapest, 1943, I, pp. 501 ff.; U. Willamowitz, *Platon*, Berlin, 1959, I, pp. 614 ff., II, pp. 282 ff.; Arisztotelész, *Organon* [Aristotle, Organon]. Ed.: S. Szalai, Budapest, 1961, I, pp. 13 ff., 111 ff.; Thracis Dionysii *Ars grammatica*. Ed.: G. Uhlig, Lipsiae, 1884; Thomas Aquinas, *Opuscula* 15: "De natura verbi intellectus." Ed.: Grabmann, Toulouse, 1906—13; B. Joannis Duns Scoti Doct. Subtilis O. F. M., *Grammatica spec. nova editio cura et studio P. Fr. Mariani Fernandez Garcia*, Quaracci, 1902, II/2a, II/541b; *Descartes' Letter to Mersenne*, 1629; *Correspondences*. Ed.: P. Tannery, Paris, 1959, I, pp. 80 ff.; Leibniz, *Opuscules et fragments inédits*. Ed.: L. Couturat, Paris, 1903, pp. 27 ff.; G. W. Leibniz, *Lingua Adamica*. Ed.: C. J. Gerhardt, Berlin, 1875, VII, pp. 198, 204; E. Cassirer, *Philosophie der symbolischen Formen: Die Sprache*, Berlin, 1923, pp. 60 ff.; H. Junker, *Sprachphilosophisches Lesebuch*, Heidelberg, 1948, pp. 24, 26—8; G. Ipsen, *Sprachphilosophie der Gegenwart*, Berlin, 1930, pp. 11—15; W. Humboldt, *Gesammelte Schriften*, Berlin, 1905, IV, p. 27, VII/2, p. 53; W. Wundt, *Die Sprache und das Denken*, Leipzig, 1885, pp. 244—85; H. Paul, *Prinzipien der Sprachgeschichte*, Halle, 1898, pp. 12 ff.; F. de Saussure, *Cours...*, Paris, 1955⁵; Gy. Laziczius, *Általános nyelvészet* [General Linguistics], Budapest, 1942, pp. 28 ff.; M. Temesi, A nyelvi jel hagyományos fogalmának kialakulásáról [On the Development of the Traditional Notion of Linguistic Sign], ÁNyT IV, pp. 199—212.

His merit was "only" that, in order to counteract the comparative-historical linguistic theory holding a monopoly position, he renewed the idea of symbolism, of systematism, and by making a selection of earlier partial statements combined them into a unitary theory. From the position of the new theory he fought for the justification of synchronic investigations of language, recognizing the results of the historical comparative method, while pointing up also the ever more evident drawbacks and defects of the latter.

Beyond the known deficiencies[4] of Saussure's teachings, it must still be stated here that he dealt with the network of relationships of linguistic sign and concept, further of sign and reality, only in a sketchy manner and not free from theoretical errors. This then opened the way for the most varied explanations and became the basis of several schools known by the name of linguistic structuralism. The not quite accurate principle (system, structure), the basically oppositive formulation of the interdependence of the signs within the system, the neglect of the most broadly construed social determinedness of the linguistic signs[5]—all served as a basis for the emergence of diverse theories.

Depending on which feature of the linguistic signs, of their system, the particular modern schools regarded as determining and, consequently, on whether they neglected the other components of the sign or even denied their existence, it is possible to get some insight into the rather involved fabric of the new trends.

The debates are today centred *on the functioning of language, of the linguistic sign.* What is the main function (or rather what are the main functions) of linguistic signs, and how (owing to the presence, or rather the interplay, of what factors) can language discharge these functions? This is roughly the way in which we might formulate the substance of these debates. The replies to the question include, of course, the views on the principal peculiarities of the linguistic sign, or rather it is on the basis of these views that the various schools explain the manifestations of

[4] The formulation of the reciprocity of synchrony and diachrony, opposition of language to speech.
[5] Elimination of the factors described as extralinguistic from the scope of linguistic investigation.

language, its function and its functional principle. If we take a look at the various ideological motives behind the particular linguistic explanations, too, we become aware of a very colourful and contradictory panorama, which is characteristic of the theoretical conditions of today's linguistics.

Which are the characteristic features of language conceived in the most general way, and what are their principal functions? Which are the identical and different features of the theoretical answers given to the above question? In my judgment, these questions are at least *essential* to such an extent as they are *general*, and that is why they may serve as qualifying standards to judge the various schools by the answers received.

Opinions generally concur in that human speech composed of articulate sounds is an organic system; but the views regarding the essence of the elements of this system, their place in the system, and the functions they fulfil in it, are still open to dispute.

Also there is agreement in that the principal function of language is to realize social intercourse between men, i.e. social communication taken in the broadest sense. There are, however, different views to explain why the most important elements of the system of language, the linguistic signs, are fit to fulfil this function, what their role is in the "creation", acquisition and "expression" of the body of knowledge about the phenomenal world (the relation of language and thought; the connection between linguistic sign and concept-formation; the essence of verbal thinking; the role of linguistic signs in the mental reflection of objective, material reality; the structures of reality, conceptual structures, linguistic structures, the chances of conceptual, affective-volitional communication, etc.).

Theoretical works generally agree also in that the task of linguistic research, of the science of language, is to discover the immanent peculiarities of language, its internal interrelatedness, its forms of motion, or briefly the linguistic laws. But who understands what by the principal immanent peculiarity of language, how one interprets its interrelatedness, wherein one sees the essence of its forms of motion and chiefly their connection with other forms of motion, is a complex question on which opinions differ widely (the objective character of the laws; the role of subjective factors in the emergence and formation of linguistic laws; the regularities of the relation of form and content; the identical and different traits of phonetic, phonological, morphological, semantic and syntactic laws, of linguistic laws and other social laws, furthermore the laws of nature, law and rule, law and tendency).

An attempt to answer the aforementioned general questions and questions of detail at the same time determines the most characteristic features of the methods of investigation, too. An empirical description of the motion of language, peculiarly enough, does not operate with the usual inductive method, but it tries to deduce, describe and classify the various linguistic manifestations on the basis of axioms, while demanding a rather high-level formalization. This kind of linguistic description endeavours to shed light on the structuralization of the content elements by making inferences from the formal behaviour of the elements, and remains more or less on the plane of the examination of synchronic phenomena. The so-called traditional schools, on the other hand, wish as a rule to come to the necessary generalization inductively, from the manifold evidence of the facts of language. It is by searching after the motives of the development of linguistic elements that they draw general conclusions with a view of a more exact characterization of a given state of language. (Formal description, distribution, transformation, generative grammar; the use of formal-logical, mathematical methods, synchronic and diachronic methods; mediatization of the results of these two methods; application and utilization of the methods and results of the different "related sciences" by making allowance for the complexity of the linguistic sign.)

2. FUNCTION AND IMPORTANCE OF THE LINGUISTIC SIGN

"In the beginning was the Word", says an introductory chapter of the New Testament.[1] Among the conceptual accessories of primitive folklore (superstition, mythology) a very prominent place is held by *incantation* ("the chanting of magical words one after another") in various forms, the idea of belief in the mysterious, supernatural power of magic formulae. The mystical conception of the power of the word[2] can be seen in the view of the neo-Kantian "modern" German philosopher E. Cas-

---

[1] "In principio erat verbum": John I, 1.
[2] Cf. the title of the book by G. Klaus, *Die Macht des Wortes*.

sirer (1874 — 1945) regarding man's — allegedly innate — symbolizing function, which means nothing less than "creation of reality", an attempt to expel objective reality reflected in logical notions from the same categories, and also an intention to reduce reality to mathematical formulae. Or let us think of the "principle of self-reflection" of a recent trend of neopositivism, of the semantic philosophy flourishing in the United States. That principle means that it is not possible, nor is it necessary, in everyday life to confront words with the particular elements of reality. Some representatives of this modern agnosticism go so far, by absolutizing the tool of human intercourse, language, the linguistic signs, as to present the improper use of linguistic signs as the only source of all problems and troubles arising among people, so also of wars and international tensions.

All this enhances the importance of the linguistic signs. Also its exaggeration points out that the sign has come into the focus of interest of modern philosophy, since recent research into the subject matter has prospected heretofore unknown fields, and the latest results could become also sources of new philosophical speculations.[3]

The "philosophical" explanations picked as samples out of the mass of the different sign interpretations are only a drop in the sea, because both in everyday usage and in refined scientific style the *sign* is used in a variety of manner, and its meaning is rather uncertain in the light of manifold usage.

Sign in linguistic literature has a relatively uniform meaning: *signe* in French, *Zeichen* in German, and знак in Russian are all equivalent to 'linguistic sign', while linguistic journals and monographs use also the terms *Kennzeichen, symbol, signal,* and the like, without giving exact definitions of their identical and different features, or stating unmistakably the relation of various signs, their hierarchy, and last but not least their function and meaning. The practice of daily life (in some way or other, nevertheless, men communicate by the aid of signs) and the theoretical significance of the sign equally underscore the importance of the theory of signs, for language as a social product, as a tool of social intercourse, as a system of socially determined signs, is included also in semiology (semiotics), let me add, as its saliently most important part by reason of its significance and function.

---

[3] A. Schaff, *Einführung in die Semantik*, Berlin, 1966, pp. 147—8.

If language as a system of signs is considered the most important element of the general theory of signs, of semiotics, as the pertinent views expressed in international literature usually concur, then it is justifiable, or rather inevitable, to start sketching the characteristic features of the theory of signs by taking stock of the most important peculiarities of the linguistic sign, comparing other signs of general communication to the linguistic signs, in order to discover as accurately as possible, in the light of our present knowledge, the correlations and superposition of the elements of this complicated system.

The significance of the sign as a dominant part of the system of language has inspired leaders of linguistic institutions of universities and academies in the German Democratic Republic, with a view to collating the results of research about the symbolism and systematism of language and reviewing the disputes going on over them, to clear the relevant problems at an international symposium. The only topic of the symposium held at Erfurt in September 1959 was "Zeichen und System der Sprache".[4] One of the papers contained in the publication formulates the significance of the language sign as follows: "The problem of the language sign is of great theoretical and practical significance for the treatment of methodological and gnoseologico-philosophical questions of modern linguistics."[5]

In spite of all, or maybe for this very reason, the symposium could not essentially reconcile the different sign interpretations, especially because the difference of opinion as to the issues of sign and meaning caused insurmountable difficulties. This was a lesson also for the German philologists who, after the symposium, began semantic researches, and although they wished to devote the next international conference to formal analysis, they noted that "the nature (dialectics) of language cannot be overpowered", and the second international symposium[6] dealing with the questions of "Zeichen und System der Sprache" focused its attention on the issues of meaning and structure.[7]

[4] The papers read there and the other contributions were published in 1961 (Akademie Verlag, Berlin).
[5] "Das Problem des sprachlichen Zeichens ist von großer theoretischer und praktischer Bedeutung für die Behandlung methodologischer und erkenntnistheoretisch-philosophischer Fragen der modernen Sprachwissenschaft." E. Albrecht, in *Zeichen und System der Sprache*, Berlin, 1961, p. 358.
[6] September 1964.
[7] *Zeichen und System der Sprache*, Berlin, 1966, pp. 5, 7.

There is no lull yet in the battles around the concept sign taken in the modern sense. Moreover, it cannot possibly be said that the views about the determining marks and basic function of the linguistic sign have come substantially closer together. The disputes are invariably centred on the relation between the sign and the reality it denotes. Even if opinions concur in that the essence of the sign can be apprehended in the role it plays in social communication, this is but a half-truth, because the function of the linguistic sign and that of other tools of general communication, of the other signs, are entirely the same. This agreement does not enhance the deep-rooted difference typical of the two sorts of signs, namely the fact that the language sign is not only a tool of social communication—like the other signs—but it is at the same time its basis. This means that the relation of the sign to the reality imaged is substantially different from that of the other signs. I shall later discuss the two sorts of relationship, here I point them out only because I am going to try my way in the mass of sign conceptions and sign definitions on this basis.

According to their judgment of the relation of sign and signified, representatives of the particular sign theories may be classed in two camps. One is composed of those who regard as determining only the arbitrary nature, the conventional character, of this relation; the other camp includes those who hold that the indirect reference to the significatum—an "organic" reference implemented by means of the concept—is an immanent peculiarity of the linguistic sign, or more precisely, who believe that the functioning of the sign is inconceivable without a faculty to this effect.[8]

[8] If the gnoseological trend launched by H. Poincaré, *conventionalism*, were not reserved for qualifying a specific philosophical school, and if the *conceptualism* represented by P. Abélard were not burdened with reminiscences of the struggle between *nominalism* and *realism*, the adherents of the first camp could be called *conventionalists*, and those of the second *conceptualists*. However much the use of the suggested terms would simplify the task of classing the representatives of different sign theories in the aforementioned two large camps, however much it is fashionable nowadays to differentiate the main theoretical trends by plastic epithets, I refrain from proposing this procedure, because I am aware of the load of new concepts weighing upon the old, "reserved" terms, and consequently of the danger inherent in the various possible interpretations. At the same time I cannot help remarking that, from the point of view of the theory of knowledge, striking similarities can be discovered between certain parts of the said philosophical and sign-theoretical conceptions,

The substance of the principal theses of the aforementioned schools of sign theory can be found in the main features of Saussure's sign conception. As is commonly known, Saussure pointed up the indissoluble unity of sound form and concept. His notorious simile of the sheet of paper—recto: thought *(la pensée)*, verso: sound *(le son)*[9]—unmistakably proves this, as it says nothing else of this unity even when we read in his book the following: "Une suite de sons n'est pas linguistique que si elle est le support d'une idée; prise en elle-même elle n'est plus que la matière d'une étude physiologique."[10] As it is impossible to imagine the metaphorical verso, the sequence of sounds, without the recto, or meaning that makes the sequence of sounds a linguistic sign, so he gives the converse formulation of the same thesis, too: ". . . un sens, une fonction n'existent que par le support de quelque forme matérielle."[11]

Where is the vulnerable spot of this sign conception seeming to be a whole, an unassailably entrenched thesis? For even when Saussure speaks of the definition of linguistic unity placed in the structure of the concatenation of speech, he lays unchanged stress on the function of the sequence of sounds as the signifier of a certain notion, pointing to the unsatisfactory nature of the kind of conception which tries to analyze the sound sequences of an unknown language by taking account only of its phonic (material) aspect, or even questions the possibility of such an analysis.[12] Today we already know that such an analysis is possible, and in given cases one can start analyzing a given language solely in this way, even though one cannot be satisfied with this only kind of linguistic description. The trouble is not here, but in the simple fact that the Saussurean linguistic sign— by its nature—is not a sign at all, because it lacks any feature that basically characterizes all sorts of signs, and this makes the communicative function possible, i.e. the sign is *material* and perceptible by the sense organs (hearing, sight). For Saussure's sequence of sounds is no material reality but its *"empreinte psychique"*. And Saussure unmistakably says so: "Le signe lin-

---

and this I have found it necessary to formulate to the extent of a footnote at least.

[9] Saussure, *Cours* . . ., p. 157.
[10] Op. cit., p. 144.
[11] Op. cit., p. 192.
[12] Op. cit., pp. 145, 146.

guistique unit non une chose et un nom, mais un concept et une image acoustique. Cette dernière n'est pas le son matériel, chose purement physique, mais l'empreinte psychique de ce son . . . Nous appelons signe la combinaison du concept et de l'image acoustique."[13] This definition essentially eliminates the material factor of the language sign. We have to stress this all the more as, already 1,500 years before Saussure, the material nature of the sign was pointed out by Aurelius Augustinus (Saint Augustine), who emphasized that a sign can be only what is perceivable itself and can thereby indicate something to the soul.[14]

If we add to all this that Saussure categorically and rightly combated the views trying to approach the relation of signifier and signified on the grounds of the "resemblance theory", and if we do not have in mind the precisely defined, well-known arbitrary principle, we can see all major vulnerable spots of this sign conception, all its essential features to which the determining marks of the sign theories of the twentieth century can be reduced.

The fate of the Saussurean legacy shows which features are recurring in the history of science. Some representatives of the subsequent generation of linguists developed further one or another feature of the coherent theory of language.

Those who were in favour of the psychological explanations of the linguistic sign reduced everything to notions, to a complex of notions, neglected wholly or in part the gnoseological function of the sign, and eliminated from the linguistic sign even what—though not in a precise definition—still existed with Saussure, the concept as a component part of the linguistic sign. The same happened to Z. Gombocz, the first Hungarian propagator of Saussure's theory of signs, too. According to Gombocz, the linguistic sign or word is composed of two parts: sound form (name) and object image. The name is "a connection of two notion sequences, the acoustic images and the faculties of motion (intentions)".[15] To avoid misunderstandings, he expounded in detail his opinion of the linguistic sign: "The word-sign as the smallest independent unit of intelligible speech is a

---

[13] Op. cit., pp. 98—9.
[14] "Signum est quod et se ipsum sensui et praeter se aliquid animo ostendit." *Patrologiae Cursus Completus* XXXII, p. 1410.
[15] Z. Gombocz, *Jelentéstan* [Semantics], Pécs, 1926, p. 10.

two-faced psychical entity. Seen from one side it is an acoustic image, seen from the other side it is a notion or a complex of notions. I have used the term acoustic image instead of sequence of sounds deliberately to emphasize the psychological character."[16] Stressing the psychical aspects of the linguistic sign would not have mattered in itself, the real mistake was that Gombocz's sign conception lost sight of the entirety of cognition as a psychical process: it stopped at the notions, because it did not know what to do with the relationship of sign and concept. This sudden stop, on the other hand, was a direct consequence of the Saussurean thesis which operates with the notion of sign instead of its material nature (sequence of sounds), since according to this school of thought only notion can be connected with notion.

The neglect of the concept as a factor entailed another danger, namely the failure to recognize the indirect relation between the sign and the reality signified, which in turn became a source of further theoretical mistakes. Namely, it made possible a two-way, wrong interpretation of the arbitrary principle which had a relatively delicate formulation in Saussure's conception. One interpretation took form in the definition of the connection based on similarity between signifier and signified ("resemblance theory"), the other denied even the existing indirect connection by overemphasizing the arbitrary character when it reduced the relation of reality between sign and significatum to the level of a merely arbitrary social convention.

The linguistic sign plays an important part in the mental reflection of objective reality (a commonly known thesis of the materialist theory of knowledge). Though this thesis is known in this general formulation, it is still necessary to define exactly the function, the role of the sign, from the points of view of arbitrary character and motivation alike. What is required here as an explanation for the above statement is a discussion of a relatively new, a Marxist definition to be found in the vast literature dealing with the relation of the sign and the object denoted (thing, process, etc.). The point in case is E. Albrecht's sign definition: "The sign as an image (model) is a reflection of objectively existing things, a reflection that presupposes similarity to what is to be reflected."[17]

---

[16] Op. cit., p. 31.
[17] "Das Zeichen als Abbild (Modell) ist eine Widerspiegelung objektiv existierender Gegenstände, eine Widerspiegelung, die Ähnlichkeit mit dem Widerzuspiegelnden voraussetzt." Albrecht: DZfPh. 1961/3, p. 362.

Doubtless Albrecht is right to speak up against the various idealistic sign theories, which deny—or at best neglect—the connection of the linguistic sign and the reality imaged or determine its essence only from the aspect of the sign (arbitrary nature, convention). It is, however, a serious theoretical mistake that he sees the essence of this connection in the similarity between the sign and the reality to be reflected. To support his sign conception, Albrecht refers to Lenin, who was critical of H. Helmholtz's inconsistent materialism apparent from his lecture entitled "Die Tatsachen in der Wahrnehmung".[18] Namely Helmholtz in his lecture at issue said of the series "reality, sensation, sign" the following: "Our sensations are indeed effects wrought by external causes in our organs, and the manner in which such effects manifest themselves, of course, depends very essentially on the nature of the apparatus on which these effects are wrought. Inasmuch as the quality of our sensation informs us of the properties of the external action by which this sensation is produced, the latter can be regarded as its sign [*Zeichen*] but not as its image. For a certain resemblance to the object imaged is demanded of an image . . . But a sign need not resemble that of which it is a sign."[19] The second half of the quotation rightly incurred Lenin's critical remarks as follows: "If sensations are not images of things, but only signs or symbols, which do 'not resemble' them, then Helmholtz's initial materialist premise is undermined; the existence of external objects becomes subject to doubt; for signs or symbols may quite possibly indicate imaginary objects, and everybody is familiar with instances of *such* signs or symbols."[20]

It is my judgment that by interpreting the quotation from Lenin, Albrecht committed the same mistake for which Lenin criticized Helmholtz. As a matter of fact, Helmholtz, by mingling different psychological, gnoseological concepts, made concessions to idealism. He identified sensation *(Empfindung)* with concept *(Begriff)*, more precisely with its vehicle, the sign *(Zeichen)*. If sensation were identical with the sign, then it would really be difficult to look for resemblance between sensation and the reality imaged. The first, lowermost stage of the process of cognition, however, is not identifiable with the uppermost stage! The result of perception, sensation, visibly bears the "true marks" of the reality perceived; that is why it "resem-

[18] *Vorträge und Reden*, 1896.
[19] V. I. Lenin, *Materialism and Empiriocriticism*, Moscow, 1949, p. 239.
[20] Ibid.

bles" the object which produces the sensation. It is therefore a serious theoretical mistake to identify sensations with signs, with symbols, because what gets lost in this case is just that characteristic feature of theirs which links them to reality, and this must be stated unmistakably: sensations come about as a result of the effect wrought in our sense organs by objective reality, so to speak in an indirect way, and in this process to deny the "true-to-reality" resemblance would really be tantamount to giving a peculiar "green light" to agnosticism, to idealism. There is thus a difference, and not even a small one, between true-to-reality image and linguistic sign, because, as Lenin wrote, "the image inevitably and of necessity implies the objective reality of that which it 'images'".[21]

Thus Helmholtz's idea of the connection of sensation and reality was erroneous, but at least as erroneous is Albrecht's theory built on the resemblance between linguistic sign and reality, which simplifies the exceptionally intricate process of the acquisition of knowledge, and vulgarizes the complex pattern of verbal thinking in need of a subtle analysis. Below we shall still speak of the role which the linguistic sign plays in verbal thought, here I only wish to state, in connection with the unacceptability of Albrecht's sign theory, the simple fact I have already mentioned, that the conceptual reflection of identical parts of reality manifests itself by the aid of the different sound sequences of different languages. The only exceptions to this rule are the onomatopoetic utterances of some languages, but they constitute a negligible part of the vocabulary of most languages.

The "resemblance theory" thus does not help us to know better the essence of the language sign, it even hides it from us by confusing various categories; what is more, it provides fresh fuel for the exaggerators of the arbitrary nature of the sign. If—as the latter think, and they are right on this point—the sign conception based on the resemblance of sign and significatum proves wrong, then there remains no other link to connect the two but social convention. On the other hand, the consequent application of this logic inevitably leads to the identification of linguistic sign with sound sequence, for the concatenation of material sounds is the only concrete grip, the rest (denotatum, concept) are mere unfounded speculations, or, to put it in milder terms, none of them belongs by definition to the concept sign.

[21] Op. cit., p. 240.

Already in 1949 A. Martinet ascribed to the great authority of Saussure the fact that still there were sign theories which viewed the linguistic sign in the unity of *signifiant* and *signifié*, although what was already at that time meant by linguistic sign was in general the *signifiant*, more precisely its "material realization".[22]

This is exactly how the sign was interpreted by a speaker at the Erfurt symposium of 1959, too: "I should like therefore to qualify as the linguistic sign not the word . . . but just this external, phonic side of the word (morpheme)."[23]

At that symposium, as a matter of fact, most of the sign definitions reckoned, in some form or other, with the relation of the sign and the reality imaged, only a few lectures adopted a different view on the matter. Thus, among others, E. Buyssens took as a basis for his sign definition the function of the sign in the sentence: he considered the linguistic sign a kind of smallest unit of the sentence which allows us to compare two sentences whose other parts are dissimilar or similar. Hence, he examined not the mutual relation of signs, but the relation of sentences; and in doing so he did not exclude the meanings from the investigations, but he thought that only sentences have meaning (content), the sign has only function, a function which makes it possible to form various sentences.[24] Others again tried different definitions. N. I. Žinkin, for instance, proposed an algorismic analysis of the elements of texts to apprehend the essence of the sign,[25] again others discussed the problems of the correlation of phoneme and sign. Most speakers eliminated the phonemes from the scope of sign investigations (Vl. Skalička, F. Trojan, J. Kuryłowicz, and many others), though Kuryłowicz found it conceivable to connect with the sign certain speech sounds or some sound quality performing a specific function. M. Bierwisch alone recommended

---

[22] "Il est intéressant de noter que l'autorité de Saussure est parvenue à imposer, dans la terminologie linguistique, au mot 'signe' une signification qui s'écarte nettement de celle qu'on a donnée à ce terme dans l'usage ordinaire où il s'appliquerait plutôt au signifiant saussurien ou, plus exactement, à la réalisation matérielle de ce signifiant." A. Martinet, La double articulation linguistique, *Travaux du cercle linguistique de Copenhague* V, pp. 30—7; loc. cit., p. 32.

[23] "Als sprachliches Zeichen möchte ich daher nicht das Wort . . . sondern eben nur diese äußere, lautliche Seite des Wortes (Morphems) bezeichnen." I. Bauer, in *Zeichen und System der Sprache*, 1961, p. 34.

[24] Loc. cit., p. 45.

[25] Loc. cit., p. 180.

to consider extension of the concept phoneme to the concept sign; in this sense he spoke of "elementary signs".[26]

The other speakers of the conference took up one by one all those criteria which can be found also in international literature dealing with the characteristics of the linguistic sign. Contributions of Marxist inspiration emphasized the historical limitation of the sign, its social character, and pointed to the fact that the emergence and development of the sign truly reflect the genesis and refinement of human thought, and especially that this development and refinement take place in the process of man's productive activity as its cause or its effect.[27] The writings submitted preparatory to the symposium agreed, all without exception, that the essential marks of the sign boil down to its having a perceptible form and that the sign is a means of transmission of the communicative content between the speaker and the hearer.[28] The means of transmission of the communicative content, in the opinion of most participants, can be the language sign only in case it has, in addition to its perceptible form, also internal content marks.

And now we have come to the sign definition proposed by the majority of the symposium. The definition is a formulation of the indissoluble unity of the external (sound complex) and the internal (content, meaning) aspect of the sign: "The linguistic sign is any acoustico-physiological sound complex which has a definite meaning content."[29] The term 'meaning content' became a topic of interest and came into the cross-fire of the disputes. Even G. F. Meier, who read the introductory paper, saw that in deciding the linguistic elements classed in the sign category—in the light of the preliminary written theses of the participants—the meaning has a determining role to play. Since, however, a great number of morphemes, words and syntagms have even several, sometimes entirely contradictory meanings, he held that the definitions built on the "unity of sound complex and meaning" are

---

[26] Ibid.
[27] E. Albrecht, Vl. Skalička, G. F. Meier and others; loc. cit., pp. 139, 178, 365 ff.
[28] "Mittel zur Übertragung eines kommunikativen Inhalts zwischen Sprecher und Hörer." Loc. cit., p. 178.
[29] "Das sprachliche Zeichen ist jeder akustisch-physiologische Lautkomplex, welcher einen bestimmten Bedeutungsinhalt besitzt." Loc. cit., p. 143; cf. also pp. 59, 137, 159.

very problematic. Most of the suggested sign definitions, on the other hand, undeniably were built on this basis, only a few of them were different, more or less with a claim to formal analysis. In trying to reconcile the differences of opinion, instead of solving the problem Meier proposed that the term sign be eliminated from structural analysis: "This problem [the problem arising from the Janus face of the linguistic sign] certainly does not exist if the term 'sign' is given up altogether in works on structural analysis and is applied only as a term of linguistic philosophy."[30]

Of course this proposal did not, and its possible acceptance could not, solve the problem, and this for two reasons. The first reason is the simple fact that if any problem is taken out of the scope of investigations, this is not a solution of the problem but its postponement. The other, and more substantial, reason is that if Meier's proposal had been accepted, it would have been necessary to give up the basic principle of modern linguistics, the symbolism and systematism of the signs, which in the second half of the twentieth century no one could, and no one did, undertake to do.

At the same time we can state that the symposium devoted to the topic of "Zeichen und System der Sprache" could not solve the complex of problems relating to the linguistic signs and the system of signs. The most important result and also a lesson of the discussion was just the fact that it again called attention to the issue, collected the views hitherto expressed, and at the same time demonstrated in the light of the debates that it was indispensable to continue a systematic investigation of the question of sign and meaning.

The problems concerning the formal (external) and the content (internal) aspect of the linguistic sign, and their mutual relation, have remained in the focus of interest also after the Erfurt symposium. The question still is what is to be considered a sign, whether only the materially perceivable sound sequence, sound combination, or also the reference to reality, is an integral part of the most important unit of human communication, the linguistic sign. However we wish to describe the part played by the

[30] "Dieses Problem existiert allerdings nicht, wenn man auf den Terminus 'Zeichen' bei strukturanalytischen Arbeiten überhaupt verzichtet und ihn nur im sprachphilosophischen Sinne verwendet." Loc. cit., p. 180.

language sign in human communication, in some form or other we have to answer the question of how it can fulfil this function, how and why it is apt to serve the communication of emotions produced in man by thoughts about reality and by other effects. Hence, no description of language can evade the problems of *meaning*, because without it no kind of communication is possible. Any material *signal* can be a tool of communication only if it means the same thing to the sign-giver and the receiver, that is if it is "loaded" with meaning, because without this it is only a train of physical (sound, light, etc.) waves. From this point of view it is entirely irrelevant whether they are linguistic signs or other signs of social communication. The "only" question is whether the meaningful load of the signs belonging to the two main groups of the general system of signs, non-linguistic and linguistic signs, is of an identical nature, or whether there is some difference between them, and if so, what does it consist in. More precisely, what are the common features by which we can class every kind of communication unit in a common system, the general system of signs, and what are the distinguishing marks by which we can class them in two main groups. Whether the identical or the distinguishing marks are dominant, and what is the correlation on this basis between signs of the two groups. Whether they can be interpreted by common criteria, or whether one is absolutely necessary in order to interpret the other. These are the fundamental questions which we have to answer accurately to find our way in the complicated fabric of the disputes going on for several decades around the character of the tools of communication, the relations between sign and meaning, and the nature of meaning.

3. SIGN AND MEANING

Theoretical research concerned with the meaning of the word, with meaning in general, is of a relatively recent origin. The general statements on the relation of the language sign and the reality imaged by it (traceable sometimes back to antiquity) have by far not proved sufficient to answer the questions of the general theory of signs, to solve the problems arising in connection with sign and meaning. The importance of the matter was recognized already towards the close of the nineteenth century, in the period of linguistic historicism and comparativism, while the theoretical elaboration of general communication caused the topic of meaning to grow into a cardinal issue of the theory. In a relatively short time a vast body of literature arose in order to grasp the essence of meaning, to define its determining features. This was how the problem of meaning became a key question of the science of language, and at the same time a source of diverse philosophical speculations. "The notion 'word meaning' is one of the most important in linguistics. Without the elucidation of this notion it is impossible to give a sufficient definition of the word", writes A. I. Smirnitsky.[1] E. Albrecht takes the problem of meaning as the "nuclear problem" of communication and comprehension.[2] A. Schaff—stressing the importance of the problem of meaning—views it as an exceptionally significant question determining the sphere of interest of linguistics: "The problem of meaning doubtless belongs to the most important and philosophically most striking questions of our time: it can be subjected to scientific analysis, and it can be used as a springboard for daring metaphysical speculations."[3]

There is no end of the statements underlining the importance of the problems of meaning, but there is today no need to quote them, because—regardless of who means what by meaning—they all recognize its significance in general. Only a few researchers, who had been bogged in the ideology of the stage of the behaviourist formalism of structuralist linguistics, displayed—though not with unbroken consistency—attitudes belittling the role of meaning.

This standpoint came from L. Bloomfield's view on meaning as expressed in his notorious sign definition. Namely, according to Bloomfield, the sign is but a form of language, which in turn is nothing else than "A phonetic form which has a meaning, is a

---

[1] «Понятие 'значение слова' является одним из важнейших в языкознании. Без уяснения этого понятия не может быть достаточно определенным слово.» А. И. Смирницкий, Значение слова, ВЯ 1955/2, pp. 79—89; loc. cit., p. 79.

[2] "... Bedeutungsproblem als Kernproblem der Sprache als Leistungsgröße der Mitteilung des Verstehens." DZfPh 1961/3, p. 360; cf. also K. Ammer, *Einführung in die Sprachwissenschaft*, Halle, 1958, I, p. 54.

[3] "Das Problem der Bedeutung gehört zweifellos zu den wichtigsten und vom philosophischen Standpunkt aus zu den frappantesten Problemen unserer Zeit: Man kann es zum Gegenstand wissenschaftlicher Analyse machen, man kann es auch als Sprungbrett zu gewagten metaphysischen Spekulationen benutzen." A. Schaff, Die Bedeutung der "Bedeutung", DZfPh 1961/5, p. 611.

linguistic form".[4] This not quite reassuring sign conception has one more deficiency: it uses a criterion (namely meaning) of which we know nothing.[5]

A well-known representative of logical semantics, C. W. Morris, recognizes the justification of meaning, and even its utility in practical linguistic work, but does not find it precise enough for "scientific analysis", so he eliminates it as a basic term from the scope of semiotic investigations: "The term 'meaning' is not here included among the basic terms of semiotic."[6]

A much quoted theoretician of the modern schools, Z. S. Harris, in his monograph summarizing the methodological procedures of structuralism, makes a remarkable comment on the role played by meaning in modern methodologies. He is compelled to admit that the function of the native informant so often mentioned in formal analysis, the reliance on the hearer's response, is essentially identical with reliance on meaning used in the ordinary sense. Since, however, meaning is regarded as an obsolete category in the terminology of formalists, so in Harris's view the essence of formal analysis made on the basis of meaning as a criterion boils down to methodological confusion or at least to a mixing of viewpoints. Consequently, he hastens to add that the response of the informant, of the hearer, or if you like, reliance on meaning, is to be ascribed to the actual insufficiency of the formal methods—a deficiency of present-day linguistics which will, with the progressive improvement of the methods, be sooner or later eliminated from linguistic research.[7]

L. Antal, who has been educated on the teachings of Bloomfield, Morris and Harris, pronounces a much more unambiguous judgment in the case of meaning. In an oral contribution he

    [4] L. Bloomfield, *Language*, New York, 1933, p. 138.
    [5] ". . . but it cannot be confirmed or rejected on the basis of our science." Op. cit., p. 162.
    [6] C. W. Morris, *Signs, Language and Behavior*, New York, 1946, p. 19.
    [7] "In accepting this criterion of hearer's response, we approach the reliance on 'meaning' usually required by linguists. Something of this order seems inescapable, at least in the present stage of linguistics: in addition to the data concerning sounds we require data about the hearer's response." Z. S. Harris, *Methods in Structural Linguistics*, Chicago, 1951, p. 20.

made in 1961 he mercilessly took the problem of meaning out of the categories of structural linguistic analysis, of the "really modern grammar": "The task of linguistics is to promote the greatest possible prosperity of structural researches; in Hungary this means that the first object is a structural analysis of the Hungarian language, i.e. the creation of a really modern Hungarian grammar. What should a future Hungarian structural grammar be like? I would raise two fundamental requirements. First, it has to hold consistently to the synchronic plane and should yield not an iota to historicism which is so valuable in its proper place. Second, it has to be based on formal analysis and should yield not an iota to meaning."[8] In my view there is, there can be, no misunderstanding here. For while Antal regards diachrony as valuable "in its proper place", he categorically refuses the justification of meaning in a "structural analysis of the Hungarian language", that is within the scope of "a really modern Hungarian grammar". In the light of the above quotation it is quite clear that in Antal's conception there is no place for meaning in a modern grammar.

Besides, with his inflexible antisemantic position, Antal found himself almost completely isolated at the 1961 conference. Even those researchers who at the conference took a clear stand in favour of the structural analysis of language, with a single exception, dissociated themselves from this rigid categorization. Zs. Telegdi, who delivered the opening lecture and who took a resolute stand in favour of formal analysis,[9] considered it necessary at the same time to express his doubt that the analysis of linguistic structures could absolutely do without testing the content elements: "There is no proof—or at least as far as I know there is no conclusive proof—that in analyzing the structural forms of language we can do without the grips of content."[10] And further on: ". . . the structure of grammar is essential in so far as reference to it is an integral part of meaning."[11] Here is how others responded to Antal's position: "To meaning (content) we think we have to make at least the concession (and this is more than an iota) that we examine the segments also with a view to finding out what is their relation to meaning. This is the

---

[8] Antal: IOK XVIII, p. 54.
[9] "Formal analysis is therefore a fundamental method of grammar." Loc. cit., p. 17.
[10] Loc. cit., pp. 17—18.
[11] Loc. cit., p. 22.

least we have to do."[12] S. Szalai stressed: ". . . formal analysis does not mean at all that we do not bother with the meaning of words. On the contrary: only by means of a profound analysis of the meaning of words can we set apart what in the meaning of the word is contingent and what is essential, pertinent from the point of view of structure."[13] To Antal's rigidity M. Hutterer opposed the more differentiated position of the modern structuralist schools: "The structuralists grown out of the old school are increasingly realizing, and even have realized, the danger and untenableness of one-sidedness (cf. the recent relevant works by Martinet, Foruquet, Weinreich, Hammerich, Grosse and others)."[14]

To point up Antal's anti-meaning attitude I could still continue recalling quotations; a single one must yet be added here, and this from his work where he tried to outline the distinction between word-declension and word-formation, describing the Hungarian case-system in a strictly antisemantic manner. "We once again should like to emphasize that the reason why we consider it impossible to do this [to define the cases of a language from the aspect of meaning] is that we can see no regular connection between case as a peculiar grammatical category and certain types of meaning",[15] because "the case-endings . . . do not rely on the nature of the meaning of stems, they have no forbidden semantic zones."[16]

Although a considerable majority of today's structuralist schools rely upon meaning as a complicated phenomenon and approach it in accordance with its complexity, while trying to establish its regularities, yet this affirmation is only a half-truth. The other half of the truth is the fact that intensive research into the questions of meaning has been only lately reoccupying "its place within linguistic description which has often been denied to it, for lack of theoretical preparedness, in the avant-garde years of structuralism".[17] The full truth is, however, that the vicissitudinous fate of meaning in linguistic descriptions of structuralist pretension is commonly known: the

---

[12] L. Tamás, loc. cit., p. 71.
[13] Loc. cit., p. 67.
[14] Loc. cit., p. 79.
[15] L. Antal, *A magyar esetrendszer* [The Hungarian Case-System], Budapest, 1961, p. 20.
[16] Op. cit., p. 50.
[17] ÁNyT III, p. 278.

problem of meaning has come by great detours and roundabout ways to obtain its present status. Namely those who thought that a modern description of language could be performed on the basis of the examination of the formal behaviour of the elements of a finite set of utterances (behaviourist empiricism) stood up deliberately against reliance on meaning as a criterion of linguistic description. To what extent this could be done in practical work is clearly demonstrated by the above quotations from Z. S. Harris.[18]

Those who have realized that only formal means can lead the analysis of language to satisfactory results, and under the influence of traditional opposition to the conception of meaning have seen it fit to construct some kind of "modern" theory of meaning, have introduced the notion of what they call "grammatical meaning" with its very contradictory nature. Here it will suffice to recall Chomsky's well-known sample sentence ("Colourless green ideas sleep furiously")[19] to get some picture of how this sort of theory of meaning can bring us closer to the essence of meaning.

It is only a recent experience that researchers engaged in formal linguistic description also openly acknowledge the importance of the criterion of meaning and its role in formal analysis. J. H. Greenberg, for example, in his article on the universals of language (based upon data from thirty languages of different types), proposed universals of mostly implicational nature on the basis of the regularities of the order of words. (If a phenomenon x is given in a certain language, then also y is always given there.) In the course of his inquiries he directed his attention first of all to the formal—mainly sequential—behaviour of the elements. Despite all this he did not neglect the function of semantic factors either, as appears from his following statement: ". . . the adequacy of cross-linguistic definition of 'noun' would, in any case, be tested by reference to its results from the viewpoint of the semantic phenomena it was designed to explicate. If, for example, a formal definition of 'noun' resulted in equating a class containing such glosses as 'boy', 'nose', and 'house' in one language with a class containing such items as 'eat', 'drink', and 'give' in second language, such a definition would forthwith be

[18] See footnote 7 above.
[19] N. Chomsky, *Syntactic Structures*, The Hague, 1964, p. 15.

rejected and that on semantic grounds. In fact, there was never any real doubt in the languages treated about such matters. There is every reason to believe that such judgments have a high degree of validity."[20]

At the second symposium on "Zeichen und System der Sprache" M. Bierwisch also spoke clearly about the indefensibility of the earlier often advanced opinion that formal analysis alone could meet the requirements of objective linguistic description.[21]

---

[20] J. H. Greenberg, Some Universals of Grammar with Particular Reference to the Order of Meaningful Elements. *Universals of Language*, Cambridge, 1963, p. 59.

[21] "Auch der . . . häufig auftauchende Gedanke, daß zwar die Form, das meint hier die syntaktische und phonologische Struktur, einer objektiven Beschreibung zugänglich sei, aber nicht oder jedenfalls weniger die Bedeutung, ist offensichtlich unhaltbar." *Zeichen und System der Sprache* III, p. 57.

III. THE NATURE AND STRUCTURE OF MEANING

1. PSYCHOLOGISM AND ANTIPSYCHOLOGISM

The wrangle over the recognition of the linguistic role of meaning is thus to be considered ended. Opinions already concur to the effect that meaning is a complex linguistic problem, to which even a considerable part of the specialists attribute a very important role from a gnoseological, philosophical point of view as well. All this, however, does not mean in the least that there would be agreement as to its determining marks, its functions. As some authors took one or another part factor of the complicated social, logical and psychical unity of the linguistic sign to be determinant—and, as usual, they absolutized that factor by disregarding all or most of the other factors—so this fact left its mark on the meaning conception of the researchers, too.

It is common knowledge, for instance, that the so-called psychologistic school believed the linguistic sign to be only a psychical fact, which necessarily led to the same opinion also about meaning: it is a psychical phenomenon, a relatively independent psychical fact. This meaning theory of Husserlian conception was contested in the early thirties by L. Weisgerber, who regarded this sign conception as the "fundamental evil of semasiology" (Grundübel der Semasiologie).[1] Today we already know that conscious elements, psychical phenomena, are relatively independent; it was Weisgerber's theoretical mistake not to recognize this, yet we have to accept his warning, because numerous authors have made ill use of the substance of the Husserlian idea. H. Kronasser, for example, in interpreting meaning as a rather independent psychical fact (ziemlich selbständige psychische Tatsache), went so far that he could imagine concepts without linguistic expression.[2] I think this calls for no

---

[1] Sprachwissenschaft und Philosophie zum Bedeutungsproblem. Blätter für deutsche Philosophie, Berlin, 1930/31, p. 17.
[2] "... es gibt ... Begriffe ... denen sprachlicher Ausdruck fehlt, dann ist sie vom semasiologischen Standpunkt selbständig und Gegenstand der Psychologie allein." H. Kronasser, Handbuch der Semasiologie, Heidelberg, 1952, pp. 60—1.

further comment; this is just a kind of *contradictio in adjecto* Kronasser takes the opposite idea ("unmeaning words": *sinnlose Worte*) to be.[3]

This sort of meaning theory really is out of place in linguistic science. The meaning interpreted in this way can be neither a part of language, of the linguistic sign, nor—let me add at once—the object of a more exacting psychological study.

The same "result" was arrived at by the opposite camp of linguistic theoreticians. Aware of the insufficiency of the "psychologistic" conception of meaning, one of the founders of American structuralism, L. Bloomfield, carried his meaning conception to the other extreme, to the total neglect of psychical factors. In his view, meaning is identical with the object of the sign, so it cannot be a part of language, it must be an extralinguistic entity and consequently does not call for more intensive linguistic investigation (here begins the controversy of *designatum* vs. *denotatum!*).

Bloomfield's anti-meaning attitude had a lasting influence upon the various schools of American linguistics following the 1930's, in spite of the fact that it proved inapplicable in practical research, but the drawbacks of this simplification became clear from the theoretical point of view, too.

This theory made its impact in Hungary in the period when even the more pretentious structuralist schools contested the rightness of the conception.[4]

The conception of meaning in question is that devised by L. Antal, who in his work *Questions of Meaning* (The Hague, 1963) summed up his views on what he considered the most important problems of the theory of meaning.

I will discuss this work in a little more detail because

(a) to my best knowledge, it is one of the first works in monograph form intended to deal, from the modern angle, with the most comprehensive problems of the theory of meaning;

(b) it reflects, with its clearly antipsychologistic attitude, a very specific viewpoint regarding general theory;

(c) since it has been published in English, it may have become known also to the linguistic public of the world at large;

[3] Op. cit., p. 61.
[4] Cf. the comments by C. C. Fries, *Trends in European and American Linguistics 1930—1960*, Utrecht—Antwerp, 1961, pp. 196 ff.

(d) consequently, it can easily give rise to the belief that the book's findings and conclusions reflect the common standpoint of Hungarian (and Soviet) linguists.[5]

Antal in this book revived Bloomfield's idea of the extralinguistic nature of meaning. It is also true, however, that in a writing of his published a year later he states of Bloomfield, who first formulated the extralinguistic nature of meaning, the following: "There was namely an American philologist, L. Bloomfield, who declared: meaning is no part of language . . . This scholar committed a serious error by confusing meaning with the reality denoted."[6] Any researcher has the right, and even the duty, to rectify theories formerly thought to be correct but proved wrong by the test of practical work ("yield not an iota to meaning"), or even to reject them entirely. On the other hand, it is hardly understandable to the reader that the Bloomfieldian thesis (the extralinguistic nature of meaning) should reappear in a writing of the same author. I have in mind the abridged Hungarian version (1966) of Antal's work published in The Hague.[7] This version came out when the repercussions of the English edition abroad and at home were already known to the author, and he nevertheless published again his former views on the extralinguistic nature of meaning: "The meaning, however, is not a part of the linguistic sign, but a condition of it."[8]

---

[5] Cf. the following passage from R. M. W. Dixon: "*Questions of Meaning* presents a viewpoint which is probably fairly representative of a significant section of Russian and Hungarian linguistics (Antal is a Hungarian); he illustrates it with flowery references to the work of his Russian colleagues; for example: 'S. K. Šaumjan recently pointed out with flawless logic that all linguistic works not conceived on structuralist lines must be metaphysical, because they investigate linguistic signs isolated from their natural interrelations. Structuralism, on the other hand, bears the stamp of instinctive dialections [sic!]'." *Linguistics*, 1963/2, p. 96. Then follows Antal's reference to Zvegintsev: "Zvegincev, in his semantics, is justifiably taken aback by the infantile confusion of meaning and denotation." Loc. cit., p. 97. — I refrain here from analyzing in detail the quotation from Shaumian and the reference to Zvegintsev. Being familiar with Soviet literature on semantics, I can safely say that the said quotation and reference do not yet mean at all that "a significant section of Russian . . . linguistics" professes the same semantic views as Antal. I have already given a foretaste of the views held by "a significant section" of Hungarian linguists regarding Antal's semantic conceptions (cf. Chapter II, Section 3), and I shall continue in this way further.

[6] L. Antal, *A formális nyelvi elemzés* [Formal Linguistic Analysis], Budapest, 1964, pp. 188—9.

[7] NyK LXVIII, pp. 279—325.

[8] *Questions . . .*, p. 26; NyK LXVIII, p. 290.

The quotation cannot be misinterpreted! After Antal's afore-mentioned criticism of Bloomfield (the meaning of the linguistic sign is not identical with the reality denoted) one could at most think that the "rule"—though being an abstraction external to the sign—is yet a part of language, because otherwise the criticism of Bloomfield would be nonsensical. Antal, however, entirely rules out this possibility of interpretation when summing up the "most important aspects of the relationship" between the sign (the object of the sign) and the meaning: "Since meaning is a rule of application of the sign, and is not identical with the concrete sign-object, from this it follows inevitably that meaning can be only abstract, the concrete rule being an absurdity."[9] But, to avoid any possible misinterpretation, Antal openly formulates also the extralinguistic nature of meaning: "What is not a sign cannot be a part of language, since language is a system of signs."[10] The principle of "not an iota" is valid, declaratively by all means, also in the interpretation of language, of the linguistic sign. Or is it?! It being made known that the linguistic sign is a physical reality (material sound sequence) but meaning is an abstract rule, "the concrete rule being an absurdity", it follows that meaning is "no part of the language sign", but "a rule that is external to the sign and cannot be deduced from it", while in another statement, where Antal discusses the meaning correlation of the interpreter and the interpreted word (anticontextual meaning), we can read the following: "Hence [John Smith the interpreter] cannot be a meaning, since meaning is an important component of the linguistic sign."[11] However, in one of his writings Antal forgets not only that at one place of his book published in The Hague he described meaning as extralinguistic. In another place of the same book he describes meaning as a part of language: "If language is an objective phenomenon, then the meaning, being a part of language, has also to be objective."[12]

It is difficult to gather from these quotations what Antal's real opinion is as to whether meaning is an "important component" of the linguistic sign or a "rule external to it".

For the time being let us stop examining the linguistic or extralinguistic nature of meaning. Let us content ourselves to fix

---

[9] *A formális* . . ., p. 189. The linguistic sign, according to Antal, is only a material sound sequence, and the abstract rule can indeed hardly be a part of it.

[10] Op. cit., p. 188.

[11] Op. cit., pp. 195—6.

[12] *Questions* . . ., p. 40.

what Antal says about the essence of meaning. His definition of meaning reads as follows: "The rule which regulates the use of signs and their mode of application is called meaning."[13]

Meaning conceived of as a rule already appeared in Hungarian linguistic literature earlier, too, but it was formulated in a much more differentiated manner. Zs. Telegdi wrote in 1956: "The meaning of a word, as a universal and a constant visible in the particular applications of the word, is nothing else than the regularity of the use of the word."[14] The term 'regularity of the use' is a rather general formulation which can hold very much, and it is by all means more complex than Antal's "rule and mode of application". Another definition given by Telegdi is closer in formulation to Antal's definition of meaning: "The meaning of the sign is usually a rule which determines its application, it is the rule of its application."[15] But if we come to examine this "rule of application", we can see the outlines of a very odd rule: ". . . speakers in possession of this rule are capable of applying uniformly a word to a class of things, the rule has to contain the 'description' of the characteristics of the class as a unit: in other words, the rule which leads us in the application of the word is the mental image, the reflection of a category of things. Of the meaning of the elements of language we can say in general that it is the reflection of some segment of reality."[16] What is here "a class of things", "the mental image, the reflection of the characteristics of the class as a unit", we used to call *concept*. We can state without any further investigation that Telegdi's definition of meaning covers a more complicated rule, or rather a system of rules, than does Antal's.

It is a pity that Telegdi did not expound his conception of meaning in more detail, that he did not strive for a critical development of the source (Morris) he had in common with Antal.

It would have been desirable to make Telegdi's conception more precise also because between his formulations of 1956 and 1963 there is an intermediary one which says the following: "With meaning man possesses something general, which is related to the concept, a [quasi] prefiguration of it; but as long

[13] Op. cit., p. 26.
[14] Zs. Telegdi, *Általános nyelvészet, stilisztika, nyelvjárástörténet* [General Linguistics, Stylistics, History of Dialects], Budapest, 1956, p. 67.
[15] Telegdi, *Bevezetés a nyelvtudományba* [Introduction to Linguistics], I, Budapest, 1963, p. 16.
[16] Op. cit., p. 17.

as it has the form of meaning [manifests itself in it], it is linked to the audible or internal use of language. Meaning develops into a concept when man learns to consider and use it [the meaning] in itself . . ."[17] This thesis is liable to misconstruction, for it does not explain in a satisfactory manner the correlation of concept and its "prefiguration". But if I have understood well the German text which seems to me a little complicated, then we are confronted with such a formulation of "concept-development" about which A. Schaff had this to say: "To Marxists—as also to the great majority of linguists—the concept without word is by all means a figment of the speculative fancy of philosophers."[18]

Returning to Antal's theory of meaning, we seek answers to the following main problems: (a) the relationship between the sign and the reality denoted by it; (b) the relationships between sign and meaning.

Antal takes the right course when he criticizes those conceptions which confuse the meaning with the notions of the objects and processes of the real world (psychologism), but he polemicizes also rightly with the school which takes meaning to be identical with the reality imaged by the sign (Bloomfield and his followers). He is right therefore when—not for the first time in linguistic literature—he states that meaning is identical neither with the reality nor with the notions of reality, but he is wrong when he absolutizes the conventional character in the correlation of sign and reality, reducing this complicated social, psychical, etc. relationship to the level of instructions for use.

What is the basis of meaning which, according to Antal, precedes the use of the linguistic sign? What is the essence of this abstract rule? How can it fulfil the function of connecting two material entities (sound sequence and a segment of the material world) in order to make thereby social communication possible?

[17] "Mit der Bedeutung besitzt der Mensch ein Allgemeines, das dem Begriff verwandt, eine Vorform des Begriffes ist; solange es aber die Form der Bedeutung hat, ist es an die laute oder innere Verwendung der Sprache gebunden. Die Bedeutung entwickelt sich zum Begriff, wenn der Mensch lernt, sie für sich . . . zu betrachten und zu verwenden." *Zeichen und System der Sprache*, 1961, p. 210.

[18] "Jedenfalls ist für die Marxisten — wie übrigens für die überwiegende Mehrheit der Linguisten — der Begriff ohne Worte Hirngespenst der spekulativen Einbildungskraft der Philosophen." Schaff: DZfPh IX, p. 710. Cf. footnote 2 above.

To these questions Antal's description of meaning does not, and cannot even, give an answer.

As a matter of fact, whoever sees only arbitrarily established rules instead of the mutual relation—created as a result of socially determined, complicated operations—between the linguistic sign and the thing denoted, and fails to recognize the sign as an important factor of verbal thinking, of concept-formation, will find it hard to understand the essence of communication and in it the function of the meaning as well as of the sign. For the linguistic sign can have no other function than to form the impressions, sensuous perceptions and notions of a bit of some segment of reality, and finally the "intellectual" product of the abstraction indicating the most characteristic features of that part of reality, to furnish it with a material stamp and facilitate its communication to others. If, also according to Antal, "man is obliged to express his subjective thoughts [which, however, in normal conditions are socially much too determined, consequently their subjective character is relative. — F. K.] through objective signs which are governed by objective meanings",[19] then the essence of this "governing" calls for an explanation. And, briefly, it is nothing else than the common disposition of speaker and hearer to the effect that by the linguistic sign "indicating" a part of reality the hearer understands the same conceptual marks which—under normal conditions, of course—the speaker had in mind. Were it not for common possession of the socially determined distinguishing marks, the sign could not be applied, and consequently no rule of application could exist.

Antal's example of 'salt' is edifying from this point of view. In his above-cited critique Antal rightly condemns Bloomfield for having identified meaning with the reality imaged.[20] This is an obvious mistake the like of which has for a long time not been encountered in serious works. Antal is right by all means when he states in opposition to Bloomfield's thesis that "the meaning of 'salt' does not consist of the expert knowledge of NaCl but the knowledge of the application of the sign 'salt'."[21] The question is only what is to be understood by "knowledge of the application of the sign". If, in conformity with Antal's thesis, there is no need to know even the most important characteristics of NaCl,

[19] *Questions . . .*, p. 41.
[20] ". . . the ordinary meaning of the English word 'salt' is 'sodium chloride (NaCl)' . . ." L. Bloomfield, *Language*, p. 139.
[21] *Questions . . .*, pp. 28—9.

and if we wish to judge an utterance to be grammatical or ungrammatical only by inaccurately defined rules of application of the sign, we feel compelled to accept as regular the appearance of the sign 'salt' also in the following sign environments: *Salt is sweet. Salt serves to decorate fancy cakes. The children do not stop crunching salt. The salt efflorescing on the sodic soil was suddenly melted by the heat of the sun,* etc., etc. These are not absurd sentences (utterances)! I only committed here the grammatically regular method of application of the sign 'salt'. What happened is merely that on the basis of the proposed definition of meaning I dispensed with the "expert knowledge" of NaCl, and I did not require the knowledge of the principal conceptual marks of the thing imaged by the sign 'salt'. If the above utterances are to be considered incorrect also on the basis of Antal's theory of semantics, then we ought to require every speaker (and every hearer, of course) to have the knowledge of a system of rules of application which would govern all possible "regular" associations of every word. In this case few people could claim to possess "knowledge of the application of the sign 'salt'".

In my view it is simpler and more reasonable to take note of the fact that we can use the sign 'salt', place it regularly in the given sign environment, only if we have the necessary knowledge of NaCl. Even if this knowledge is not as exact as that which a researcher of inorganic chemistry must have, it must at least be like the knowledge which a man of average talent can be required to possess. The more profound our knowledge of it is, the more the chances of its regular application. Our minds store the items of knowledge in form of concepts, and the assistance of this conscious element is indispensable for the application of signs. Telegdi writes: "Speech commonly refers to a concrete reality; communication, mutual understanding, comes about if the speakers, who are by turns also hearers, are united by the knowledge of this reality, so that they are capable of filling the general formulae of language with unequivocally definite meaning."[22] Namely we create in vain "empty" sequences of phonemes or combinations of signs where the reference to reality (not reality itself but its abstract image) is missing even in a single element or differing from what is socially given, gnoseologically determined, the sound combination does not become a sign, and the combination of signs, the various sequences of signs, cannot form a socially accepted linguistic utterance.

[22] Telegdi, *Bevezetés* . . ., p. 25.

From the basic thesis of Antal's theory of signs (meaning is the rule of application of signs) it follows necessarily that meanings are homogeneous, uniform and indivisible: namely, every meaning can be covered by only one sign. Such known polysemous signs of natural languages which are fit to image different categories of reality—and which do so indeed with a stubbornness following from the nature of facts—would be excluded by Antal from the scope of the facts of language and could seek refuge at most within the bounds of homonymy.[23] The question is about such known terms as Latin *sacer* which means 'sacred' and 'accursed' alike, and *altus* which means 'high' as well as 'profound', similarly to the French *profondeur* which denotes the 'altitude' of the sky *(profondeur du ciel)* just as well as the 'depth' of the sea *(profondeur de la mer)*. Russian благове-ление means 'good will' as well as its opposite, Hung. *köt* means not only what is equivalent to the English 'to bind', but: *kosarat köt* 'to make a basket', *harisnyát köt* 'to knit stockings', *koszorút köt* 'to make a wreath', *kardot köt* 'to belt on a sword', *sarkantyút köt* 'to put on one's spurs', *kereket köt* 'to drag wheel', even *lovat (el-)köt* 'to lift a horse' and *békét köt* 'to conclude peace'. These linguistic facts, whose numbers are legion, would all lose their polysemous character or, according to Antal, would be treated as homonyms like the Hung. *ár* 1. 'flood', 2. 'awl', 3. 'price', 4. 'are' (a unit of measure in the metric system: 100 square metres), and *vár* 1. 'fortress', 2. 'wait', etc., which, no one would deny, are—from the synchronic point of view—due to accidental formal concordance between different linguistic signs.[24]

When negating polysemy and recognizing homonymy, Antal seems to be consistent with his often mentioned theoretical state-

---

[23] *Questions* . . ., pp. 53 ff.
[24] J. Herman writes convincingly that in some concrete cases—on the basis of synchronic descriptive viewpoints alone—it is rather difficult to decide whether the given expressions are polysemous alternants of the selfsame word or we are faced with a case of homonymity. He is also right in saying that it is problematical whether, in his comparison with French equivalents, the Hung. *tiszt* 'officier' and *tiszt* 'dignité, office' are one sign or two, if we consistently ignore the historical viewpoint. It is imaginable also "that, in the light of the logical structure of meanings and of the syntactic regularities taken in the broadest sense, it would be possible to find a consistent system of criteria facilitating the decision of disputed cases". Cf. ÁNyT III, pp. 254—5. It is also imaginable, of course (if the context does not give us any orientation), that we are confronted with a typical case where we have to recognize the insufficiency of synchronic methodology and to resort to the aid of diachronic considerations for a full explanation.

ment: if meaning is a rule of application of the signs, then any sign can have only one meaning, consequently several meanings presuppose the existence of several signs. Hence the Hung. *ár* is a formal concordance of four different signs. This would not matter yet, because in this case it would really be difficult to speak of polysemy — at least in the sense as it is usual to evoke in the case of the Hung. *toll* ('feather' and 'pen'). The trouble is that, when Antal recognizes the existence of homonymy, he clashes with his own fundamental thesis on semiology and semantics: the sign is the material sound sequence itself, while meaning is the rule of application of the latter. But if the sign is the material sound sequence itself, then a sound sequence identical with itself (*ár* and *ár*) is also a sign identical with itself, so in this case we cannot speak of homonymy. This logical contradiction was pointed up also by J. Herman in his very explicit article critical of Antal's sign theory.[25]

In the formula 'one sign ∼ one meaning' there is, of course, no room for the idea of metaphor, for a metaphorical meaning, either. When contesting Ullmann's position[26] in favour of metaphorical meaning, Antal questions that in the French terms *dents* 'teeth' and *dents du peigne* 'teeth of the comb' we are faced with two meanings of the word *dents*.[27] He argues in the same manner also with Baldinger, who in presenting the meanings of the German word *grün* states that in the case of *ein grüner Apfel* and *ein grüner Junge* the word appears with two meanings: *unreif* 'unripe' and *unerfahren* 'inexperienced'.[28] Antal is categorically against the views which recognize the metaphorical type of meaning, against those who profess the "irregularity of meaning", and states that there is here no kind of irregularity of meaning, that each of the words quoted in those examples *(dents, grün)* always has the same meaning, "since when it develops a different meaning, it ceases to be the same word".[29] Proceeding in this way, his "solution" of the problem arising in connection with the view professing the irregularity of meaning is this: *"Thus the metaphor is irregularity not of meaning, but of denota-*

[25] J. Herman, Antal László, Questions of Meaning, ÁNyT III, pp. 242—58; loc. cit., p. 254.
[26] S. Ullmann, *Précis de sémantique française*, Berne, 1952.
[27] *Questions . . .*, pp. 60—1.
[28] K. Baldinger, Die Semasiologie. Deutsche Akademie der Wissenschaften zu Berlin: *Vorträge und Schriften*, No. 61, p. 22.
[29] *Questions . . .*, p. 52.

tum."[30] That this trend of thought is moving in a vicious circle was pointed out already by Herman, who evaluated this solution not without irony: "However patient the world of denotata may be, it is impossible simply to cast the blame on them for everything that disturbs the idea of the unitary and unchanging nature of meaning."[31]

In agreement with Herman's categorical opinion, it is worth while to take a brief glance at the above italicized quotation from Antal. Before advancing an opinion about the essence of his statement, to avoid any misunderstanding it seems necessary to fix again a few facts of common knowledge. Meaning is, also according to Antal, a product of an act of abstraction. In respect of denotatum he states a number of times the "well-known fact" that it is an extralinguistic reality.[32] Furthermore, we could mention innumerable examples like *dents du peigne* and *ein grüner Junge*, which differ in various languages from the usual forms as linguistic expressions of the part of reality existing outside of consciousness. In the case of *ein grüner Junge* and the like, anyway, we have to do with objective facts of language which serve to reflect in consciousness the extralinguistic objective reality. It is, of course, open to debate whether in the given cases the linguistic expressions used in such sense are fit, as indispensable factors of verbal thought, to present a true-to-life mental reflection of objective reality. The opposite, however, is never debatable, namely not without an exceptionally serious theoretical, ideological concession. But if denotatum is an extralinguistic reality, then it must be taken as it is, its mental reflection and its linguistic expression must be measured against it, and not the other way round. Reality, the world of denotata, must be measured against theoretical constructions formed independently of "regular reality" ("the meaning is constant and fixed but that the denotatum is changeable, in this sense, uncertain"),[33] and if this latter does not square with the theorem, then—and this has to be spelled out—the "adjustment" of an "irregular" reality to the "regular" theory is subjective idealism, which has nothing in common with the materialist theory of knowledge and with all that which we call the materialist theory of language. I am fully aware of the weight of my statement; I

[30] Op. cit., p. 60.
[31] ÁNyT III, pp. 252—3.
[32] *Questions* . . ., p. 25; ÁNyT III, p. 10.
[33] Op. cit., p. 34.

ought to apologize to the author for having made it only if his quoted words ("irregularity of denotatum") should be understood metaphorically.

If the pertinent part of Herman's quoted critique could not convince Antal that it is from the linguistic communication itself and not from the examination of denotata that we know that "identical words in different contexts indicate different types of denotata",[34] then I am also concerned by the "tragic misunderstanding" which, according to Antal, follows from the confusion of meaning with denotation.[35] The charge of misunderstanding, however, would be warranted only if it were necessary to place beside the triplet precisely delimited by Antal (sign, meaning, denotatum) a fourth factor: denotation. Such a construction is theoretically conceivable, only the difference between meaning and denotation ought to be precisely defined.[36] Antal in his work at issue fails to make a precise distinction. For his pronouncement "Denotation is of course not independent of meaning but is not identical with it either"[37] cannot be accepted as such, nor can his statement to the effect that "what is elucidated only in the environment is not the meaning but the denotation".[38]

What then is denotation according to Antal? In another place, though not giving a precise definition of the term, he circumscribes it at least. In his article entitled "Sign, Meaning, Context",[39] while discussing the factors of the sign relationship, he states that this relationship has not two but three factors. Two of them, "the sign and the meaning, are of a permanent nature, while the third, the object of the sign—we might call it the denotatum—is occasional, incidental and variable".[40] Regarding the object of the sign, we can read in the same article the following: ". . . the other is that which we denote by the sign. The latter is called the object of the sign."[41] Accordingly, denotation is identical with the object of the sign (i.e. with the denotatum

---

[34] ÁNyT III, p. 252.

[35] L. Antal, *A magyar esetrendszer* [The Hungarian Case System], Budapest, 1961, p. 24.

[36] It is commonly known that works on semantics use these terms, but it is also true that they give precise definitions of what they mean by what.

[37] Ibid.

[38] Ibid.

[39] *Lingua* X, pp. 211—9.

[40] Loc. cit., p. 212. In the Hungarian version of the article 'denotatum' is rendered as *jelölés* ('denotation'): Nyr LXXXV, p. 204.

[41] Loc. cit., p. 211.

which, in contrast with the stability of sign and meaning, is occasional and variable). Denotation as the object of the sign is therefore nothing else but "the table in question, the concrete table".[42] If this is so, how should we construe the following lines encountered on the same page? "But the process of denotation cannot be realized through these two factors [the sequence of sounds *table* as a sign and the table in question, the concrete table as the object of the sign], nor can the process be fully understood with reference to these two factors alone . . ."[43]

It is rather difficult now to find out what Antal really means by denotation. For if denotation is that something which we name by the sign, that is the object of the sign, then it has objective existence, it had existed before we denoted it by the sign, and there is no need to "realize" it through some linguistic manoeuvre. Antal is perfectly right in saying that "the process of denotation . . . cannot be realized", because it is extremely difficult even to imagine that the concrete table in question should have any kind of process.

Antal is consistent in one thing: the application of his theory of meaning. The meaning of the word *denotation* — in the light of the adduced interpretations — really seems to be "completely and utterly arbitrary", or more precisely: Antal uses it in an arbitrary manner without reserve to denote now a concrete object, now an element of a network of abstract relationships.

It would be pretty difficult to define denotation precisely side by side with "the rule of application of the sign". This would be possible only if we were to regard meaning as a self-contained rule entirely abstracted from everything — even from the denotatum — or as the reality denoted. Antal does not do this, he even resolutely stands up against the proponents of such views (see above).

The metaphorical meaning of the constructions *dents du peigne* and *ein grüner Junge* at the same time fits into the problem of contextual meaning, on which also Antal has a very definite opinion based on his theory of meaning: he denies that meaning is responsive to the context.[44] This cannot even be otherwise, for if he recognized this property of the context, he should give up his thesis of 'one sign, one meaning' as well as his idea that meanings are homogeneous and denotata heterogeneous in character.

[42] Ibid.
[43] Ibid.
[44] *Questions* . . ., pp. 48 ff.

Antal follows a right course when he argues with those who absolutize the contextual aspect of meaning, thus with L. Hjelmslev, who writes this on the determining role of the context: "In absolute isolation no sign has any meaning; any sign-meaning arises in a context . . ."[45] But Antal is dissatisfied also with S. Ullmann's more differentiated formulation opposed to the view of the "absolute contextualists", yet recognizing the existence of the—context-influenced—shades of difference in meaning, and stressing that in the constructions *un homme sain* and *un air sain* the meaning of the word *sain* is not identical.[46] This is how, from the platform of one sign, one meaning, Antal argues against Ullmann's distinction: "The meaning of the adjective *'sain'* is not different in the two sentences quoted by Ullmann, but the word 'sain' refers to two different denotata. The man is 'sain' in a different manner from air."[47] If by the "reference to denotatum" of the adjective *'sain'* as a linguistic sign we understand the rule of application of the sign, the meaning of the sign (what else could we understand on the basis of the above-mentioned principle of meaning vs. denotatum?), the question arises with good reason: How does one sign refer to two different denotata? How can the first part of the sentence be reconciled with the second?

In another of his writings Antal makes a similar criticism of a recent manifestation of the contextual theory, the pertinent part of Y. A. Apresian's structuralistic theory of meaning.[48] In examining the contextual "behaviour" of the verb *идти* 'to go', Apresian analyzes the following examples: *Он идёт в столовую* 'He goes to the dining room'; *Дети идут в школу* 'The children go to school'; *Дорога идёт в Лондон* 'The road goes to London'.[49] The next thing he examines is how the particular sentences can be extended or shortened, and states that the first sentence can

---

[45] L. Hjelmslev, *Prolegomena to a Theory of Language*, Baltimore, 1953, p. 28.
[46] "Le sens des mots n'est pas *homogène*: il offre plusieurs aspects à des contextes différents . . . *Un homme sain* est quelqu'un dont l'organisme n'est pas malade; *un air sain* est un air salutaire pour la santé. Seul le contexte pourra décider lequel des divers aspects est pertinent." Ullmann, op. cit., p. 97.
[47] *Questions* . . ., p. 58.
[48] ÁNyT III, pp. 15—16.
[49] Ю. А. Апресян, К вопросу о структурной лексикологии [On the Question of Structural Lexicology], ВЯ XI/3, pp. 38—46; loc. cit., p. 42. Antal gives the title of the article inaccurately: «К вопросу о структурной типологии», ÁNyT III, p. 15.

be extended in this way: *Он идёт в столовую обедать* 'He goes to the dining room to take dinner'. But it can also be shortened in this way: *Он ибёт* 'He goes'. Similar transformations may be performed on the second sentence: *Дети идут в школу учиться* 'The children go to school to learn' and *Дети идут* 'The children go', respectively. On the other hand, no such transformation is feasible on the third sentence, i.e. there is no such sentence as this: *Дорога идёт в Лондон учиться* 'The road goes to London to learn'; it would equally be a nonsense to say: *Дорога идёт* 'The road goes'. The difference between the first two sentences and the third (the first two are liable to extension or shortening, the third is not) Apresian explains on the ground that the variant of the stem morpheme *(ид-)* of the verb *идти* occurring in the third sentence has a different meaning from the variant *ид-* figuring in the first two sentences.[50]

It is worth noting what Antal views as Apresian's "basic mistake" in applying the methods of transformational analysis so as to recognize that the context has an influence on meaning: "What makes Apresian think", he writes, "that the sentence *Дорога идёт в Лондон* cannot be extended in the said manner [*Дорога идёт в Лондон учиться*] because the *ид-* here is of a different nature? Will not rather the whole of the sentence, or at least a fundamental part of it [*Дорога идёт*], be the reason why the proposed extension is not feasible?"[51] This is a really strange "anticontextualist" reasoning! Namely what cannot tolerate the transformation in question is not the morpheme *ид-* but "the syntagm *Дорога идёт* as a whole".[52] But why not? Antal also asks the question himself, he even answers it by summarizing his lengthy grammatical, lexicological speculations, shifting the responsibility upon the denotatum again: The reason why the syntagm at issue does not stand the said transformation is that "a road cannot go to learn, nor can it go, it can only lead somewhere".[53] I think this does not call for further comment. For, if I were to start discussing in detail that according to the last-quoted view the word *идёт* in the sentence *Дорога идёт в Лондон* does not mean what is meant by *идёт* and *идут* in the first two sentences, but that it means 'lead', the reader could rightly take offence at it.

---

[50] Apresian, ibid.
[51] Antal, loc. cit., p. 17.
[52] Ibid.
[53] Loc. cit., p. 18.

72

By throwing the responsibility upon the denotatum with the same reasoning, Antal "argues" also against Walpole's contextualist semantic conceptions. Namely Walpole writes this: "A symbol has meaning only in its context."[54] In support of his affirmation Antal analyzes the different meanings of the word *case* in the following sentences: (1) *"I thought he was in Mexico, but such was not the case."* (2) *"In this case the detective was completely baffled."* (3) *"If this was the case, why didn't you inform the police?"*[55] According to him, what is different in the three sentences is not the meaning of the word *case* (if it differed in meaning, it would be three different words) but the denotatum of the word in the three sentences.[56] He treats similarly the sentences *Er hat mich nach zehn Uhr geweckt* and *Er hat mich nach dem Tunnel geweckt*. He negates the temporal and locative shades of meaning of the preposition *nach* in those sentences. "The meaning of 'nach' is not temporal in the first sentence but the meaning of 'Uhr' is, and the meaning of 'nach' is not locational in the second sentence but that of 'Tunnel' is. The meaning of 'nach' ist nach." [sic !][57]

H. Walpole, *Semantics: The Nature of Words and Their Meanings*, New York, 1941, p. 105.

Op. cit., p. 35.

His "argumentation" is worth following, since he squeezed in it nearly all important theses of his theory of semantics: "If 'case'$_1$, 'case'$_2$ and 'case'$_3$ do not have the same meaning, then these three forms do not represent the same word but are three different words which happen to coincide in form. If the meaning of 'case'$_1$, 'case'$_2$ and 'case'$_3$ is not identical, then they are only homonyms. If they agree only in form, it is incorrect to put them under one heading. The meaning of the three forms of 'case' is necessarily the same, since the meaning of the word 'case' existed before sentences were constructed with them. But there is, in certain respects, a difference between the three forms of 'case'. *However, this difference is not in their meaning, but in their denotatum.*" Antal, *Questions* ..., p. 53.

Op. cit., p. 55. If we accepted the rule of the expressly temporal application of some signs, then—on the analogy of *Uhr*—we ought to accept as such the word *Jahr*, too. Let us see how this meaning is reflected by the form used without any preposition in the following structures: (a) *Vier Jahre sind noch zurück* 'Four more years are left'; (b) *Vier Jahre hat er dort verbracht* 'He spent four years there'; (c) *Vier Jahre arbeiten wir hier* 'We have been working here for four years'. The syntagm *vier Jahre* occurs invariably in all three sentences, it is *subject* in the first, *object* in the second and an *adverb of time* in the third only. There is thus no question of the general temporal reflection of the word *Jahre* appearing in these sentences, the case is rather the contrary: *the linguistic context not only does the actualization of the possible meanings of the structure but also determines the function of the word within the sentence.*

This is an unambiguous statement, but its positiveness is weakened by what follows there: "Its ['nach'] 'temporality' and 'locality' were not independent of the context."[58] Evidently the question here is about the denotatum of *Tunnel* and *Uhr* again, just as in the case of the Hungarian phraseological unit *csütörtököt mond* 'to fail, to miscarry', where 'to fail, to miscarry' is not the meaning but a "particular denotatum"[59] of the syntagm.

In this conception of meaning it would be pretty difficult to decide the meaning of Hung. *nyelv*[60] in the following sentences: *A nyelv fontos testrész* 'The tongue is an important organ'; *Kérek fél kiló nyelvet* 'May I have a half kilogram of (ox-) tongue?'; *A német nyelv nehezebb, mint az angol* 'The German language is more difficult than the English', because:

(a) If, on the analogy of the interpretation of NaCl, I pass over our knowledge about *nyelv*, if I negate synonymy and the mechanism of the semantic interrelations of the words put together in the context, i.e. if I refuse to recognize any kind of lexical shackles, by virtue of an inexplicable rule I have to accept as regular the following transformational variants of the above utterances: *A boltban kapható nyelv az ember fontos testrésze* 'The tongue to be had in the store is an important organ of the human body' (cannibalism excluded!) | *Kérek fél kiló német nyelvet* 'May I have a half kilogram of German language?' | *A német nyelv súlyra nézve nehezebb, mint az angol* 'The German language weighs heavier than the English'.

(b) If I conceive of the component *nyelv* of the above sentences as a phenomenon of homonymy, I have to speak here of three different words, but in this case I come into conflict with the thesis of 'one material sound sequence, one meaning', etc., etc.

I would be confronted with a still more difficult situation if I accepted Antal's rigid anticontextual stand in determining the meaning of given words where even the sentence as a whole does not disclose which is the rule according to which I use the linguistic sign at issue. The Hungarian phrase *Hordd el magad!* equally means 'Carry it away yourself' and 'Get lost'. In the same way it does not appear clearly from the Hungarian written statement *Apám kifestette a szobáját* alone whether 'My father has

---

[58] Op. cit., p. 56.
[59] Op. cit., p. 78.
[60] Hung. *nyelv* equally means the organ of speech (tongue) and speech itself (language).

painted his room' *(fëstëtte)* or 'My father has made his room painted' *(fëstette)*, for the notorious reason that Hungarian spelling does not distinguish between the sounds of open *e* and close *ë*. (Not to mention that in the spoken language of our days the close *ë* sound is dying out.) We do not make ourselves more intelligible even if we add an explanation to the sentence: *Apám a barátjával kifestette a szobáját*, for in this case there are two possible interpretations: (1) 'My father together with his friend has painted his room', and (2) 'My father has made his friend paint his room'. Further contextual aid is similarly needed to interpret accurately the following Hungarian sentence: *Az ár borzalmas volt*, for in this statement the word *ár* may have any one of its four meanings referred to above.[61]

The above examples as linguistic facts cannot be covered by Antal's theory of meaning, and the facts of language are not responsible for this. If the facts of language—in this case the polysemants—perfectly meet the linguistic requirement that they may refer to different denotata in different contexts, then this "faculty" of theirs is linguistic in character or, if you like, manifests itself in the structure of meaning. This is the reason why it can be "used" in different contexts, or more precisely, this is why the various contexts are apt to actualize the different meanings of the given polysemous signs.

Consistent application of the principle 'one sign, one meaning' in establishing the meaning of sign sequences already makes possible one single interpretation: the meaning of complex signs can be only the sum total of the meanings of the part signs. Antal, after enunciating that "the morpheme is not the smallest but, indeed, *the* sign",[62] states that "The meaning of a polymorphemic word is the sum of the meaning of the morphemic elements".[63] His example to verify the thesis is: the meaning of *Schönheit* = the meaning of *schön* + the meaning of *heit*. In the same place he writes this of German *Kraftwagen:* " 'Kraftwagen' represented three signs, namely 'Kraft' and 'Wagen' and 'Kraftwagen'."[64] Hence, by reason of the above-cited thesis: the meaning of *Kraftwagen* = the meaning of *Kraft* + the meaning of *Wagen*.

---

[61] 1. 'flood', 2. 'awl', 3. 'price', 4. '100 square metres'.
[62] Op. cit., p. 75.
[63] Ibid.
[64] Ibid.

The example speaks for itself! Namely *Kraft* means 'power' and *Wagen* 'vehicle'; through a peculiar arithmetics it becomes 'motor vehicle' or even 'car'. Obviously the equivalent of German *Kraftmaschine* 'power machine' ('engine') is also to be "counted out", for even here there would be trouble with the equality between the addends and the sum ('car'). If we are at arithmetics, a more fortunate example would have been the German *Automobil* 'something propelled by itself, moving without the agency of horses'. Also in this case it would be left out of account that this word is being more and more superseded by *Auto*, which has absorbed not only *mobil* but also *Wagen*, thus there would be no less trouble in arithmetics here either; what is more, by accepting the formula *Auto-mobil-Wagen = Auto*, we ought to accept as an equation the following inequality: $a + b + + c = a$. From the sea of English polymorphemic words we can pick out not only *hairbrush* (='hair' + 'brush'), *haircut* (='hair' + 'cut'), etc. but also *hairdresser, head of hair*, etc., etc. to show that in inferring their meanings we cannot contemplate an addition of the original meanings of the component morphemes. In the same manner the Hungarian syntagm *játszótér* ('playground', literally 'playing ground') ought to signify a 'ground which is playing', and *vasgyúró* ('man with prodigious strength', literally 'one who kneads iron') a 'masseur' employed in the steelmill to work liquid metal by hand; in the segmentation of *istenverte* ('goddamned', literally 'struck by God'), on the other hand, we would be bordering on transcendentality, or at least we would witness a brawl between anthropomorphous gods of Greek mythology, instead of thinking of something 'exasperating, causing unpleasantness, doing harm' or 'wretched, dingy'.

We come to the same result if we place beside the German example for a derivative word *(Schönheit = schön + heit)* the fairly recent Hungarian agricultural term *háztáji* which got very soon established.[65] We have to add here, naturally, that at the moment of its rebirth this term also absorbed its second part *földdarab* or *földterület* ('plot', 'farmland'). But together with any of these it signifies not only the 'plot surrounding the house' but also the farmland situated several kilometres away from the co-operative peasant's house, and it means also the statutory size of that land. It has this meaning even in case the co-opera-

---

[65] *Háztáji* (segmented: *ház + táj + i* 'household farm') would mean a plot of ground, in the vicinity of the settlement, allotted from the land of the co-operative to a farmer for private use and cultivation.

tive peasant has no house of his own. If, on the analogy of *Schön-heit*, we segment the meaning of "modern" *háztáji* in this way: *ház* ('house') + *táj* ('surroundings') + *i*, with symbols: $a + b + c$, then the formula for the household farm of a co-operative peasant owning no house is: $0 + 0 + c = a + b + c$.

In agreement with Antal, this formula could be accepted only at the cost of opposing the unitary, indivisible, homogeneous nature of the rule of application to the heterogeneity of the denotata. "Meanings are homogeneous and denotata are hetero-geneous."[66] This is clear, an unequivocal thesis, which follows inevitably from the axiom one sign, one meaning or may possibly be its starting point. An axiom as long as we wish, against the testimony of the facts of language, to explain the meaning of a complex sign by the sum of the meanings of the component morphemes. If, in turn, Antal wishes to explain some different linguistic fact from a different point of view, he sets up an axiom of quite opposite value without much ado.

When he opposes the more exact nature of formal linguistic analysis to the "shakiness" of an analysis made on the basis of meaning, he examines from both viewpoints the possible segmen-tations of the word *szeretjük* ('we love') in the utterance *Ezt a fiút nem szeretjük* 'We do not love this boy'. He states that going by formal analysis "we indisputably and unequivocally come across two segments, namely *szeret* and *jük*".[67] On the other hand, he continues his train of thought, if we examine the two morphemes on the basis of their meanings, "we have to state that, from the point of view of meaning, *szeret* has a single semantic content, while the meaning of *jük* has different semantic constituents. Namely the semantic value of the morpheme *jük* implies plural-ity, first person, and transitivity".[68] Even if we pass over that Antal does not define precisely the terms 'semantic content' and 'semantic value', we have to agree with his last statement, be-cause it is borne out by facts of language. What is more, we may as well add to the semantic content of *jük* another semantic con-stituent: the segment *jük* of *kertjük* ('their garden') implies, besides plurality, also third person and possessive relation. It is true, however, that this would require us to recognize the role of the context. But this is not the point. The point is that on the basis of Antal's semantic segmentation the word *szeretjük* shows

[66] Op. cit., p. 55.
[67] Antal, *A formális . . .*, p. 95.
[68] Ibid.

four segments: (1) *szeret* 'love', (2) number, (3) person, (4) the morpheme of transitivity.[69] Antal's conclusion is: "While thus on the level of meaning we are facing four segments, on the level of linguistic expression we have to face only two. This is to say that the linguistic correspondence of the levels of sign and meaning is not mechanical, not of a one-to-one character."[70] And to avoid any misunderstanding, he speaks it out in a fleeting remark: "And when we have come so far we may mention that the morphemes whose meaning is not homogeneous, but which consist of several and different semantic constituents ... are called portmanteau morphemes."[71]

We have come so far, indeed! After a year's time the fundamental axiom of a whole theory proclaiming the homogeneity of meaning has become an argument (of formal analysis) built on the heterogeneity of meaning. This is a matter of viewpoint. Our theses can be modified according to when we want to demonstrate what: on the next page of the same book we can read the converse of the thesis "sequence of signs = sum of the meanings of the signs" formulated on the basis of 'one morpheme, one meaning'. In the quoted place Antal proves unable to demonstrate, even by an "exact method", the meaning of the last part of *fabatka* ('farthing' in negative sentences of present usage), although *batka* is a morpheme, he writes, and if it is a morpheme it must have a meaning, too. What is this meaning? "In such cases it is most opportune to define the meaning of *batka* as being the difference between the phonemic sequences *fabatka* and *fa*."[72] The rule of application of *batka* is therefore: the rule of application of *fabatka* minus the rule of application of *fa*!

What does Antal adduce in support of this formula? No less, but no more even, than his principled insistence on his thesis quoted from a number of viewpoints: "Because, if we accepted", he writes, "the view that the meaning of the word is such that it cannot be deduced from the sum of the meanings of the constituent morphemes, this would mean that, in certain cases, we do not use the morphemes according to their meaning. If not, why is this?"[73]

This is just the point. Antal develops axioms or, if you like, adapts them incorrectly, and when the facts of language speak

[69] Op. cit., pp. 95—6.
[70] Op. cit., p. 96.
[71] Ibid.
[72] Op. cit., p. 97.
[73] *Questions* . . ., p. 77.

against his conception, then he clings to his principle, lest harm should come to the axioms. It does not even occur to him that, if the axioms proved incorrect in the light of linguistic facts, he ought to devise another conception, another explanation.

What is the theoretical source of the functionalist, operationalist theory of meaning? Antal himself says that he borrowed his definition from C. W. Morris.[74] Morris, the famous representative of logical semantics, rendered a useful service to semiotics by laying the logical foundations of the theory of signs, by creating a peculiar system.[75]

By systematizing his semiotic views he exerted a very strong influence both on the philosophical school known as logical semantics and on the schools dealing with linguistic semantics. His main theoretical statements therefore are worth discussing in order not only to confront them with Antal's semantic views but also to draw general conclusions.

Morris describes the place held by semiotic in the system of science on the basis of the significance of the sign. This, however, means nothing less than that "Men are the dominant sign-using animals".[76] If man is distinguished from animals by his faculty of using signs, then the most characteristic feature of man, his superior faculty of making abstractions, human thinking, is also inseparable from his faculty of using signs, from the functioning of signs, and consequently the whole of human civilization is a function of signs, of systems of signs.[77]

It is well to emphasize the importance of the linguistic sign, of human speech. But if we examine the genesis and development of the linguistic sign as embedded in the process of evolution into man, in that of the development of human society, Morris's absolutization of the importance of the (linguistic) sign sticks out a mile. Namely man is distinguished from animal by purposive activity (humanistic teleology). A consequence or, if you like, a condition of this purposive activity is human thought, verbal thinking at that, which is aimed at the cognition of reality and intends to place it at the service of human goals. The de-

---

[74] Op. cit., p. 20.
[75] C. W. Morris, Foundations of the Theory of Signs. *International Encyclopedia of Unified Science* I/2, Chicago, 1955, pp. 77—137.
[76] Loc. cit., p. 79.
[77] "Human civilization is dependent upon signs and systems of signs, and the human mind is inseparable from the functioning of signs—if indeed mentality is not to be identified with such functioning." Ibid.

velopment of human society, human civilization, is therefore a permanent function of this process of cognition and conscious transformation. In this process an undeniable part is played by the linguistic sign, which is a means of the material manifestation of the proper mental reflection of objective reality and a means of interaction. It is not the dominant use of signs that makes man of man and distinguishes him from animal, but, on the contrary, the conscious process of cognition and transformation of reality "creates" the linguistic signs, and the latter in the course of development build up an ever improving system. Human civilization, therefore, is not dependent on signs, on the degree of development of systems of signs, on their functioning, but the other way round: the development of human civilization "creates" new and new signs and makes the system of these signs ever more perfect. The working of the system of linguistic signs is not a *"Ding an und für sich"*-functioning which reflects, by the way, also the actual degree of development of human civilization, but an organic function, a causally assumed result, an instrument of the humanistic activity aimed at the cognition and transformation of reality.

The stating of these ideas is not a sort of philosophical primness but a categorical dissociation from all those philosophical views which can be traced back to Morris's above-cited concise formulations (semantic philosophy, pragmatism, etc.). Hence, when recognizing the gnoseological significance of the sign, the role of semiotic in the system of science, we at the same time dissociate ourselves from Morris's opinion that semiotic can perform all functions called "traditionally" philosophical, and that philosophy is identical with the general theory of signs, with descriptive semiotic.[78]

A basic feature of Morris's philosophical nihilism is that he negates the "traditional" conception (which, according to him, is being gradually refused also by its former militant champions) in which a certain measure of isomorphism can be established

---

[78] ". . . semiotic promises to fulfil one of the tasks which traditionally has been called philosophical. Philosophy has often sinned in confusing in its own language the various functions which signs perform. But it is an old tradition that philosophy should aim to give insight into the characteristic forms of human activity and to strive for the most general and the most systematic knowledge possible. This tradition appears in a modern form in the identification of philosophy with the theory of signs and the unification of science, that is, with the more general and systematic aspects of pure and descriptive semiotic." Loc. cit., pp. 136—7.

between linguistic and non-linguistic structures.[79] And this means that he negates the mental reflection of objective reality taking place in the process of verbal thought and manifesting itself in the linguistic sign. As is commonly known, recognition of the mental reflection of material reality (facts, relationships) is the foundation of the materialist theory of knowledge and also one of the axioms of materialist philosophy. If the concepts, the ideas formed of reality fail to reflect objective reality with approximate precision, then the investigation of the most comprehensive questions of reality, the explanation of its most important phenomena (philosophy), is a wild-goose chase or, what is worse, a mass of misleading speculations. A "philosophy" of this kind really has had its day, it has nothing to do with scientific thought.

As is commonly known, there is also a different kind of philosophical system, which, based on the mental reflection of objective reality, not only claims to provide a real knowledge and proper explanation of the world, but, in possession of exact information and scientific conclusions, also tries to transform, to change things and human relationships in the interest of humanistic objectives.

Also I am of the opinion that, viewed from the platform of this philosophy, the philosophy of scientific socialism, Morris's position (philosophy = descriptive semiotic) is unacceptable. Unacceptable because it reduces the complicated relation between linguistic sign and reality to a mere linear relationship when it sees the essence of the semantical dimension of the sign in the assumption that there are semantical rules which govern the application of the sign to certain situations under certain conditions.[80] This is true in itself, only it does not disclose much about the essence of the semantical dimension of the signs. Science, including the science of language, is concerned just by those "certain situations" and "certain conditions" which enable the linguistic sign to be an effective instrument of the process of human cognition and communication. Morris's distinction—as well as descriptive semiotic—confines itself to a mere statement of the fact but fails to uncover the internal interrelations, to explain the "whys".

[79] Loc. cit., pp. 104—5.
[80] "A sign has a semantical dimension in so far as there are semantical rules (whether formulated or not is irrelevant) which determine its applicability to certain situations under certain conditions." Loc. cit., p. 102.

It is precisely in Morris's above formula that Antal sees the essence of modern semantics, which in turn means a simplification of Morris's semiotic.

According to Morris, namely, anything can function as a sign only within the scope of a certain process; this process he calls *semiosis*.[81] Semiosis has three (or four) factors:

(a) the *sign vehicle*: "that which acts as a sign";

(b) the *designatum*: "that which the sign refers to";

(c) the *interpretant*: "that effect on some interpreter in virtue of which the thing in question is a sign to that interpreter", and

(d) the *interpreter*: "the agent of the process".[82]

These factors involve one another, no one of them could be a part of semiosis without the others.

Subsequently Morris elucidates the relation between two factors of semiosis: *sign* and *designatum*, making a distinction between *designatum* and *denotatum*. He states that "A sign must have a designatum; yet obviously every sign does not, in fact, refer to an actual existent object".[83] Just for this reason it is necessary to make a definitive distinction between designatum and denotatum. The definition of designatum as a semiotical term is: "The designatum of a sign is the kind of object which the sign applies to, i.e., the objects, with the properties which the interpreter takes account of through the presence of the sign vehicle . . . A designatum is not a thing, but a kind of object or class of objects—and a class may have many members, or one member, or no members. The denotata are the members of the class."[84] He throws light upon the denotatum from another aspect as well: "Where what is referred to actually exists as referred to the object of reference is a *denotatum*."[85]

---

[81] "The process in which something functions as a sign may be called *semiosis*." Loc. cit., p. 81.

[82] Loc. cit., pp. 81, 82.

[83] Loc. cit., p. 83.

[84] Ibid.

[85] Ibid. It should be noted here that, by reason of the confrontation of the term relating to semiosis (sign situation) in the different sign theories—

Ogden: symbol—thought or reference—referent;

Gardiner: sign—meaning—thing meant;

Morris: sign—designatum—denotatum

—Antal ascribes to Morris the following conception of meaning: *designatum = meaning = semantical rule*. Cf. *Questions* . . ., p. 27, note 14 on p. 30. — The quotations from Morris allow us to state that the distinction between designatum and denotatum does not at all mean that Morris used the terms *designatum, meaning* and *semantical rule* as synonyms.

The differentiation between *designatum* and *denotatum* is extremely important from a theoretical point of view. It is important in respect of the old-established truth—endorsed also by Morris—that there are signs which refer to no actual existent object.[86] But it is important also for Morris to disclaim Bloomfield's thesis according to which the meaning of the sign is identical with a part of objective reality. And, last but not least, a precise distinction would have been important also in order to explain how it is possible for the linguistic sign to refer to something that does not actually exist. Morris still owes us this explanation. His statement that the denotatum is a member of a class of objects (designatum), that a class may have many members, or one member, or no members, is namely unsatisfactory from this point of view. The explanation, the concrete example, of this thesis applied to semiotic is not convincing either, or rather it is wrong. To support his thesis, namely, Morris adduces the argument that somebody may search an icebox for an apple which is not there, or may make preparations for his stay in an island that has never existed or had long ago sunk in the sea.[87]

It is undeniable that there exist innumerable such situations where at the moment of human activity (behaviour) the designatum is not covered by a denotatum. To abide by Morris's example: the concrete apple which somebody is looking for in the icebox, or the concrete island to where somebody is getting ready to go, does not actually exist but is only in the mind of the person concerned. If anybody—like Morris, as we have seen

---

Later I shall discuss the semantical rule. Here I wish to stress only that Morris in another writing, further developing his own terminology, replaces the term *semantical rule* by *significatum*, which is a clear distinction from designatum in his terminology as well. As we have seen, designatum is the class of things (denotata) denotable by signs, while he defines significatum as follows: "Those conditions which are such that whatever fulfills them is a denotatum will be called a significatum of the sign." *Sign, Language, and Behavior*, New York, 1955, p. 17. — Morris's *designatum ~ significatum* weirdly resembles (being almost word for word identical with them) those definitions which modern logic gives of the *concept*, more precisely of the *extent* and *content* of the concept. Cf., e.g.: "That class of objects which the concept refers to is called the extent of the concept." "By the content of a concept we mean the totality of the qualities and conditions supposed by the concept." G. Klaus, *Bevezetés a formális logikába* [Introduction to Formal Logic], Budapest, 1963, p. 140.
[86] ". . . every sign has a designatum, not every sign has a denotatum." Morris, *Foundation . . .*, p. 83.
[87] Ibid.

above—negates the mental reflection of objective reality, it is hard for him to explain why there exists in somebody's mind the concept of the apple which prompts him to look for it where it is not to be found. That somebody nevertheless should search the icebox for a non-existent apple, has the simple explanation that he has found apples there hundreds and hundreds of times in all his life, this fact has been fixed, *reflected*, in his mind, so that is why in the given case an association of the *concepts* of apple and icebox has occurred in his thought, that is why he looks for apples even if none is there. The same applies, *mutatis mutandis*, to the preparations for a voyage to the non-existent island, too. The lack of a covering denotatum of the given situation is therefore strongly relative, it applies only to the concrete case preceded by numberless empirically observed denotata. Negation of the mental reflection is thus fraught with an exceptionally grave theoretical-ideological mistake, it postulates the "reality-producing power" of the mind, which in the parlance of "traditional" philosophy is called *subjective idealism.*

Morris's example and "explanation" are unsatisfactory from other points of view, too, because he tries to elucidate only the pragmatic aspect of the sign, and this by referring to the negative motivation of the behaviour. What then should we do with linguistic signs which have no denotatum at all, either in the given situation or elsewhere? Let us think of facts of language like *centaur, Pegasus*, etc., which have nothing actual to refer to. How have they entered the human mind, what rearrangement of conceptual marks has "created" these concepts manifesting themselves in the aforementioned linguistic signs? It is pretty difficult to answer these questions if one negates the fact of reflection.[88] For Morris's idea of *concept* is entirely different from the "traditional" idea (which, by the way, is being met everywhere in psychological, logical and philosophical writings of our days). Namely Morris says: "A concept may be regarded as a semantical rule determining the use of characteristic signs."[89] This idea of concept could hardly explain the emergence of the concept Pegasus.

After discussing the triadic relationship of semiosis (sign vehicle, designatum, interpretant) Morris, in his analysis of the

---

[88] I will still come back to the relative independence, to the peculiar combinative possibilities of the conceptual marks. See Chapter III, Section 4.

[89] Loc. cit., p. 102. Morris names *icon* a "characteristic sign". Ibid.

dyadic relationship of semiosis, of its various planes and dimensions, states that three dimensions are possible:

(a) *semantical dimension*, which investigates the interrelations of sign and reality; the study of this dimension is *semantics;*

(b) *pragmatical dimension*, which inquires into the interrelations of the sign and the sign-user; the related study is called *pragmatics;*

(c) *syntactical dimension*, which examines the relation of the sign to another sign; the relevant study is called *syntactics*.[90]

Morris holds that, in the semiotical sense, the sign itself can be defined only in the simultaneous relationship of all three dimensions: " 'Sign' itself is a strictly semiotical term,'not being definable either within syntactics, semantics or pragmatics alone."[91]

The factors and dimensions of semiosis are applicable to all signs, systems of signs, including language as a particular sort of sign system.[92]

The analysis of the linguistic sign needs a precise definition of *meaning*. The very term 'meaning', because of its varied interpretation in the past, Morris uses rather with reserve and builds it in his semiotical system provisionally.[93] He holds that the objective examination of meaning is feasible in the rule of application of the sign, more precisely he distinguishes three rules of the use (application) of the sign: (a) syntactical, (b) semantical, and (c) pragmatical rules.[94] His definitions are:

(a) "Syntactical rules determine the sign relations between sign vehicles";

(b) "semantical rules correlate sign vehicles with other objects";

(c) "pragmatical rules state the conditions in the interpreters under which the sign vehicle is a sign."[95]

The full semiotical characterization of language, which at the same time applies also to the "total" characterization of meaning, Morris gives in the complex of the syntactical, semantical and pragmatical rules: "The full characterization of a language may now be given: *A language in the full semiotical sense of the*

[90] Loc. cit., pp. 84—5.
[91] Loc. cit., p. 96; see also p. 126.
[92] Loc. cit., p. 88.
[93] Loc. cit., p. 126.
[94] Loc. cit., p. 113.
[95] Ibid.

term is any intersubjective set of sign vehicles whose usage is determined by syntactical, semantical, and pragmatical rules."[96]

From this conception of meaning Antal gathers the following: "The realization that meaning is essentially a rule, i.e. the regulation of the use of the sign, has been elaborated most clearly by C. H. Morris." [sic!][97] The above quotations are eloquent proof that the semantics of Morris's semiotic does not find the essence of meaning in such one-sided instructions for use.

It is namely a well-known fact that symbolic logic cannot be contented with providing semantical rules for describing exactly what is called the language of logic. Without syntactical rules (the succession of signs, the regularities of their combination, etc.) the definition of meaning in symbolic logic is also incomplete. This applies in a greater degree to the description of natural languages, where beyond what has been mentioned above there exists the possibility of choice between synonymic formal variants, which also must be governed by some rule; furthermore, we should not forget either that the signification of natural languages is overburdened also with stylistic, emotional, etc. factors.

From all this it appears clearly enough that the categories worked out for semiotic—more thoroughly than Antal's theory of meaning—also cannot be applied unchanged and uncompleted in the investigation of the semiotical problems of natural languages. In addition to the concordance between an artificial system of signs and a natural language (both are tools of human communication in the broadest sense) there are considerable differing traits, whose neglect may lead to theoretical mistakes, to incorrect conclusions, as it did in the case of Antal. In fact Antal disregarded the basic differences existing between linguistic and non-linguistic signs, namely that the latter are all without exception signs interpreted by natural languages, i.e. the parties to the act of communication create an artificial and entirely arbitrary connection between the message produced independently of those signs and actually existing material entities which may originally have a different function. Thus the meaning of the various elements of artificial sign systems is really a rule based on common agreement, the semantics of these

---

[96] Ibid. (Italics in the original.)
[97] *Questions* . . ., p. 26. In support of this affirmation Antal repeats in a note Morris's above-cited statement. Cf. footnote 77 above.

systems is neither more nor less than the totality of the rules of application of the signs. To apply "perfectly" the various elements of artificial sign systems one has only to know these rules, and with their knowledge the process of communication will be unhampered and free from every difficulty of interpretation.

On the other hand, the sign systems of natural languages serve not only to communicate some "ready-made" message produced "by different means" but they have an indispensable part to play in the crystallization of the "message" (concept, idea, etc.), in the genesis and uninterrupted development of the process of human cognition. To define precisely the semantical aspect of a system of linguistic signs created under such complicated psychical, social, etc. conditions, it is far from sufficient to reduce it to the level of "a rule of application". One has to agree with Herman's wide-ranging claim: "... the semantics of natural languages has not only, and not in the first place, the task of systematizing the rules of designation of the signs—the primary task of linguistic semantics is to discover these rules of designation, to interpret the signs. Linguistic semantics can for this very reason not refrain from examining the extralinguistic (social, psychological) conditions of the use of signs, because failing this it cannot establish the rules of designation of the signs either."[98]

As appears clearly from what precedes, Antal's conception of meaning has not much in common with the theory of meaning conceived by one of the founders of logical semantics to further the semantical interpretation of artificial signs, let alone that the opinion of the authors referred to above (Morris, Carnap) was entirely different from the view which Antal attributed to them, more precisely which he "adapted" in shaping his own conception of meaning concerning linguistic signs.

The theoretical antecedents are more readily found with the neopositivist, pragmatist writers of whom Antal makes no mention in his book as his ideological precursors, nor does he list

[98] ÁNyT III, p. 251. The same opinion is held also by Carnap, one of the founders of logical semantics, according to whom "Pragmatical observations are the basis of all linguistic research . . . pragmatics is an empirical discipline dealing with a special kind of human behavior and making use of the results of different branches of science (principally social sciences, but also physics, biology and psychology)." R. Carnap, Foundations of Logic and Mathematics. *International Encyclopedia of Unified Science* I/3, Chicago, 1955, pp. 139—214; loc. cit., p. 148.

them in his bibliography. In an article of his he later mentions
Wittgenstein as one of the authors of the definition of meaning,
"a definition called also 'operational' ".[99] I have in mind the
framers of the operationalist, behaviourist conception of meaning, Russel and his pupils, L. Wittgenstein, M. Schlick, and
P. W. Bridgman.

"What is not expressed in the signs", writes Wittgenstein, "is
indicated by their application. What the signs absorb is expressed
by their application."[100] In another place he reduces meaning
expressly to usage: "The meaning of a word is its usage in
language."[101]

A member of what is known as the Vienna Circle advances the
same opinion on the meaning of the sentence, adding to it the
idea of verification: "The establishment of the meaning of a
sentence confines itself to the establishment of the rules of its
use. This, however, is tantamount to establishing how a sentence
can be proved true (or false). *The meaning of a sentence is the
method of its verification.*"[102] Finally, in the operationalist conception, "... the true meaning of a term is to be found by
observing what a man does with it, not by what he says about
it."[103]

The above interpretations of meaning can essentially be traced
back to the behaviourist conception of meaning advanced by
Russel, who explained his relevant views in his work *Logic and
Knowledge* as follows: "A word has a meaning, more or less vague,
but the meaning is only to be discovered by observing its use ...
He (a man) 'understands' a word, because he does the right
thing. Such 'understanding' may be regarded as belonging to the
nerves and brain, being habits which they have acquired while

---

[99] ÁNyT III, p. 115.

[100] "Was in den Zeichen nicht zum Ausdruck kommt, das zeigt ihre
Anwendung. Was die Zeichen verschlucken, das spricht ihre Anwendung
aus." L. Wittgenstein, *Tractatus logico-philosophicus*, London, 1955,
3.262.

[101] "Die Bedeutung eines Wortes ist sein Gebrauch in der Sprache."
Quoted from Philosophische Untersuchungen: *Schriften*, p. 290, by
A. Schaff, *Einführung in die Semantik*, Berlin, 1966, p. 229.

[102] "Die Feststellung der Bedeutung eines Satzes reduziert sich auf die
Feststellung der Regeln für seinen Gebrauch. Das ist aber dasselbe, wie
die Feststellung, auf welche Weise ein Satz als wahr (oder falsch) er-
wiesen werden kann. *Die Bedeutung eines Satzes ist die Methode seiner
Verifikation.*" M. Schlick, *Gesammelte Aufsätze 1926—1936*, Vienna, 1938,
p. 340; Schaff, op. cit., p. 230.

[103] P. W. Bridgman, *The Logic of Modern Physics*, New York, 1927,
p. 5.

the language was being learned. Thus 'understanding' in this sense may be reduced to a mere physiological causal law."[104]

The Russelian conception of meaning had a determining influence on the attitude of pragmatists, behaviourists, which—in a somewhat simplified form—might be summed up as follows: meaning is the relation of the sign to the action, to a peculiar sort of action at that; namely to that which manifests itself in the sign in the processes of speech. This view is but one step away from the behaviourist, pragmatist general conception of meaning which is formulated by Schaff in these words: "Meaning [in this conception] is the very action produced by the sign."[105]

It is with such theories of meaning conceived on a slippery ground that Antal is compelled—unknowingly, it seems—to accept solidarity as a consequence of Morris's misunderstood conception of meaning. For Russel and his school, by practically identifying meaning with the human action produced by the sign, not only mystified it from the linguistic viewpoint as a factor of language, but—as is well known—attributed enormous importance to it: they explained the true cause of human, social conflicts by the wrong use and misconception of the linguistic signs.

The principal theoretical error in Antal's conception of meaning is therefore not his misconstruction of Morris's trend of thought. A peculiarly interpreted part selected at random from Morris's complex conception of meaning is only a theoretical fig-leaf to cover up the wrongness of a theory of signs which equates linguistic with non-linguistic signs. The equivalence is to be found in the conventional character of both sorts of signs, more precisely in the absolutization of the arbitrary nature of the language sign. What to Saussure was still relative *(relativement arbitraire)* becomes absolute for Antal: ". . . the sign is completely and utterly arbitrary."[106] ". . . the sign (for instance, the 'table' sequence of sounds) and the denotatum (the actual table) are not in any way connected or in interdependence with each other",[107] in contrast to the traffic signal x, which with its likeness refers to its meaning: 'road crossing'.[108] Antal is right in saying that the form of the 'table' sequence of sounds cannot

[104] B. Russel, *Logic and Knowledge*, London, 1956, pp. 300—1.
[105] "Die Bedeutung ist das durch das Zeichen hervorgerufene Handeln selbst." Schaff, op. cit., p. 233.
[106] *Questions* . . ., p. 81.
[107] Op. cit., p. 26.
[108] Op. cit., p. 45.

indicate its meaning as does the signal x (or some other road-signs, e.g. ↱ 'sharp curve'). But he makes a mistake when he sees in this the only characteristic of the traffic signals. All drivers know that the reason why most of the road-signs are fit to communicate specific instructions and warnings is not in their likeness but that they have an accepted rule of application. No formal likeness can refer, e.g. in case of circular signboards, to the various kinds of prohibition (no thoroughfare, no standing, no parking, etc.), just as the meaning of triangular signboards (various warnings) is made intelligible not by formal likeness but by virtue of a specific instruction, of a semantic rule of the kind to which also Antal rightly refers when interpreting the lights of the semaphore: *red* 'no crossing', *green* 'open'.[109]

If the 'table' sequence of sounds and its denotatum, or the *red light* and 'no crossing', "are not in any way connected or in interdependence with each other", both must have something in common by which they can become tools of the general process of communication, and this, according to Antal, is the same in both: the often-mentioned rule of application. In respect of their most essential characteristic, therefore, they are equal, they are connected with the denotatum by a single link: the completely and utterly conventional nature. Since in railway traffic, he writes, a lot of confusion and even disaster was caused by the use of *white light* for 'open' signal (engine-drivers mistook the white light signals of the semaphores for the white light of the arc lamps of public lighting), around the turn of the century traffic experts agreed without difficulty, on grounds of expedience, that they would in the future use *green light* for 'open' signal. Everybody took note of the agreement for a change of colour and "learned" it, and since that time there has been no confusion of colour in light signals, which have proved suitable both for vehicles and for pedestrians in railway and road traffic alike all over the world. "It is a matter of social convention", writes Antal, "which colour is used",[110] and in this he is perfectly right. "The case is no different for the linguistic signs either", he continues and points out the well-known examples: ". . . one and the same piece of furniture is denoted by the body of sounds or sign *asztal* in one language,*Tisch* in another, *table* in the third . . . In describing this fact we say that the signs are arbitrary."[111]

[109] Antal, *A formális . . .*, p. 185.
[110] Ibid.
[111] Ibid.

If the linguistic signs also were indeed "completely and utterly arbitrary", by analogy with the successful shift in traffic signals we might rightly hope for success in changing linguistic signs to the effect, for instance, that in English-speaking areas the piece of furniture in question should henceforth be denoted by the sequence of sounds *tiš* and elsewhere by *teibl* because these signs are shorter and may serve communication more economically. It is clear to everybody that a language-sign reform of this kind (that may be approvable from the point of view of language economy) would fail for the simple reason that the case is entirely different with the linguistic signs. Convention, a relative arbitrariness, between the linguistic sign and its denotatum is a sum of much more complex psychical, ethnic, and historical components, and to ignore it would be a serious theoretical mistake and a source of further misconclusions.

Disregard for the basic difference between *red* as the colour of traffic light and the word *red* cannot go unpunished. Red light, as the physical reality of light-waves of a certain length and frequency, has and had an entirely independent existence also when it was not yet associated with the warning notion, which also had arisen entirely independently of it. The subsequent connection of the two notions (red and warning) was indeed "completely and utterly arbitrary". The function of traffic regulation could have been fulfilled by different colour lights with the same effectiveness, only care must have been taken not to allow confusion with other lights (that of the arc lamps of public lighting). For this system of signs to work there was—and still is—need for nothing else than agreement between signal-giver and signal-receiver: *red* 'no passage now in this direction', *green* 'the road is now open for traffic in this direction'.

What is more, this system of signs might unilaterally fulfil its communicative function. If, shall we say, a small boy, who has no idea of the traffic rules, observed only in what order the policeman pushed the buttons setting in motion the traffic lights at an intersection, and could in some way lay hands on the apparatus, by imitating the motions of pushing buttons he could—unwittingly and unwillingly—provide precise instructions for the flow of traffic at the intersection. If, on the other hand, he took a liking for the red button and pushed it all the time, the "disciplined" drivers and pedestrians would obey him until they became aware of the source of confusion. The situation is the same when the traffic signals break down and the red button "gets stuck": no traffic will flow in the direction indicated by the red light until a policeman standing in the middle of the intersection interferes by waving his hand to change the false instructions of the apparatus.

The semantics of this system of signs is really knowledge of the rules of application of colour lights and hand signals.

The meaning of language signs is a far cry from that of this system of signs functioning according to the simplest rules. While traffic signals—as material realities—existed and still exist, even entirely independently of their communicative function, the existence of the linguistic signifier is inseparable from the signified, and conversely, the signified (not the objective reality but its mental image) is inconceivable without the signifier. "L'existence du signifiant présuppose donc l'existence du signifié . . . l'existence du signifié présuppose celle du signifiant", writes A. J. Greimas.[112]

In my judgment, this relationship of interdependence is by no means altered by the fact that certain concepts in the field of algebra, symbolic logic, etc. are expressed not in form of linguistic signs but by algebraic signs and signs of symbolic logic, i.e. the "usual" material sound sequences as expressions *par excellence* of the linguistic sign are missing. It can be stated also without any closer scrutiny that these signs are the results of an abstraction of higher level and can one and all be interpreted only with the aid of linguistic signs. We have thus to do with the same *"ensemble signifiant"*[113] of signifier and signified as those formed by linguistic signifiers and signifieds.[114] More precisely, they cease to exist as algebraic, etc. expressions whenever the background of abstraction, the other aspect of the sign, is missing, and they are "degraded" to the same kind of physical (acoustic, visual) phenomena as are the arranged or unarranged sets of meaningless material sounds or letters.

It appears clearly from Greimas's conception of meaning anyway that in case of references to reality of the linguistic sign we have an entirely different kind of "ensemble" from what we encountered above in the case of references to reality of other

---

[112] A. J. Greimas, *Sémantique structurale: Recherche de méthode*, Paris, 1966, p. 10.

[113] Ibid.

[114] What has to be added as a comment on the use of Greimas's term is that by borrowing it I agree neither with Saussure's conception of *image acoustique* + *content* nor with Antal's "material sound sequence + denotatum". Namely Greimas failed to give in the quoted place a precise definition of the constitutive elements of his *ensemble signifiant*.

signs, and from what Antal thought this complicated relation was like when he reduced the meaning of linguistic signs to the level of the rule of application of other signs.

This matter has to be broached all the more because this rigid "anticonceptualist" idea of meaning is fraught with an ideological error. The idea which, by overemphasizing the arbitrary nature of the linguistic sign, reduces the complex network of relationships of the signs and the reality signified to the level of convention boils down to a denial of the reality-reflecting function of the linguistic sign.[115] Antal's theory of meaning, when combating psychologist subjectivism, describes as merely subjective one of the most essential factors of the reality-reflecting process, the concept, the idea, and by doing so it negates nilly-willy verbal thinking or at least regards it as something outside the range of linguistic research: ". . . the meaning is not identical with the concept."[116] If we come to examine, however, by what kind of argument Antal wants to free the meaning from conceptual "pollution", we find that he fails to understand the essence of the concept. If both meaning and sign are objective, he thinks, then only the concept, the idea, can be subjective,[117] and for this very reason it not only cannot be identical with the meaning, nor can it have anything to do with it. It is thus no accident that the concept—beyond the negative definition—is nowhere to be found in all his conception of meaning.

Nobody contests that the subject plays a specific part in the concept-formation, but whoever infers from this that the concept can be only subjective is grossly mistaken. Mistaken because of his failure to recognize, or to think over, the simple fact that our concepts, our ideas can *also* correctly reflect reality, as is usually the case, and this is why the concepts "conceived" in the subject receive an objective "load". Whoever, either for fear of being charged with conceptual realism or for other reasons, denies the objective aspects of concepts, and on this basis eliminates them from the factors of human communication, can possibly give the "green light" to very dangerous philosophical speculations. That this is not only a potential ideological menace is borne out by the history of science. Let us think only of a subjective-idealist school, started by H. Poincaré, of the theory

---

[115] On this there is agreement with Morris; see above.
[116] *Questions* . . ., p. 38.
[117] Op. cit., p. 40.

of knowledge, conventionalism, according to which "... concepts are established subjectively only by conventions, by agreements between men, and have no objective content. Definitions and axioms are chosen at will, they are therefore arbitrary products of the human mind, but not images of objective reality."[118]

The foregoing makes clear at least that Antal fell victim to the well-known false alternative that is usually worded in these terms: Either there is causal connection between the linguistic sign and the reality it reflects, or they are connected only by convention. Whoever apprehends either one or the other side of this typically metaphysical alternative and makes it a principle of linguistic theory loses sight of the following:

(a) There is really no direct, causal connection between the two categories, but the language sign, as a means or result of the reflection of reality, is in indirect connection with the reality reflected.

(b) Language is a historico-social product, it exists not for its own sake, but came into being to organize social activity, this is why men created it. This activity was directed at nature, and as an organizing force it served the development of society. If there had been (there were) no indirect connection between language and reality, it would have been (would be) unable to fulfil this function.

In this place we must state that the discovery of the reference to reality of the linguistic sign is difficult to imagine without inquiring into the fundamental categories of the reflection of reality. It would be at least as difficult as is to imagine an independent meaning external and anterior to the linguistic sign. About the conceptions of meaning without sign Schaff wrote the following: "... meanings 'an sich' without a sign 'vehicle' are only buzzing through the minds of incorrigible metaphysicists... Meaning without sign is the same kind of product of idealistic speculation as is motion without moving matter."[119]

---

[118] "... die Begriffe nur subjektiv durch Konventionen, durch menschliche Vereinbarungen festgelegt seien und keinen objektiven Inhalt hätten. Definitionen und Axiomen seien beliebig wählbar, also willkürliche Produkte des menschlichen Geistes, nicht aber Abbilder der objektiven Realität." See the entry "Konventionalismus" in *Meyers neue Lexiken*, Leipzig, 1963.
[119] "... schwirren Bedeutungen 'an sich' ohne Zeichen-'Vehikel' nur durch die Köpfe unverbesserlicher Metaphysiker ... Bedeutung ohne Zeichen ist ein ebensolches Erzeugnis idealistischer Spekulation wie die

This context puts the problems concerning the objective character of language, and in general the question of social objectivity, in a quite different perspective. The insufficiency of Antal's approach to these problems was pointed out also by J. A. Fodor.[120] Apart from Fodor's ironical phrases, the reason for us to deal with Antal's relevant statements is that, in his interpretation given of linguistic objectivity, and of social objectivity in general, he refers to K. Marx even in two places.[121] This fact may lead to the conclusion as if Antal's views on this matter had been formulated on the platform of Marxist linguistics, or generally on that of Marxist social science.

When treating the deficiencies of H. Paul's and W. Wundt's psychologism, Antal arrives at the conclusion that the relevant problems can be resolved satisfactorily only if we recognize the objective character of language.[122] The essence of the objectivity of language he sees in that it has nothing in common with the consciousness of the individual but is independent of it.[123] He distinguishes the objectivity of language from the objectivity of the physical world (the objective nature of the stone lying about on the road), he considers the former to be much more complex than the latter and compares it to social objectivity. He sees the essence of social objectivity also in the fact that it has nothing to do with the individuals, with the consciousness of individuals.[124]

It is hardly arguable that the objectivity of things and processes is in the things and processes themselves, not in the consciousness of the individuals. This holds true of the objectivity of the stone lying about on the road as well as of the objectivity of society and even of language. To the best of my knowledge, this fact is no longer contested, except by the philosophers of the subjective-idealist schools. But if we are already at the *basic* definition of objectivity, it is worth laying down the "triviality"

Bewegung ohne die sich bewegende Materie." Schaff: DZfPh 1961, pp. 610—1.
  [120] *Language* XXXIX, p. 468.
  [121] *Questions* . . ., pp. 12, 90.
  [122] Op. cit., p. 11.
  [123] Ibid.
  [124] "This second form is the social objectivity and can also be termed objectivity, because it satisfies the basic definition of objectivity, namely, that it does not exist in the consciousness of the individual but apart from it and independently of it." Op. cit., p. 12. For the first time he refers here to Marx as the one who developed the idea of *social objectivity*.

—which is at the same time the real content of social objectivity—that in defining the connection of *matter* and *consciousness* (mind, etc.) it is usual to stress the objective character of matter, and this to the effect that matter is an objective reality *existing outside and entirely independently of our consciousness*, this being no pleonastic pomposity but a fundamental tenet of materialist philosophy and also of the Marxist theory of knowledge. What this principle means is nothing less than that objective reality exists outside consciousness not only in the given synchronic cross-section of the evolution of human consciousness (this is acknowledged even by the objective idealists), but it means also, and this is not negligible, that it existed also *prior to the consciousness*. This is what gives the materialist stamp of the *basic* definition of objectivity.

Also the classical theoreticians of Marxism pronounced in this sense on the basic definition of objectivity, when they opposed the theses of idealism by the basic tenets of mental reflection, the precedence of matter over consciousness. They emphasized this when they argued with the representatives of conceptual realism, and they wrote about the spirit as being "burdened with matter" when expressing their views on the objective character of language. About the essence of human consciousness, the material genesis of the mental elements, Marx and Engels in their early writings stated that ". . . man also possesses 'consciousness'; but, even so, not inherent, not 'pure' consciousness. From the start the 'spirit' is afflicted with the curse of being 'burdened' with matter, which here makes its appearance in the form . . . of language."[125] It was in this sense that they took language to be "genuine consciousness", the "direct reality of thought".[126] This was how also Lenin evaluated Hegel's dialectics or rather the dialectic features of the Hegelian concept 'notion', this was how he corroborated Hegel's brilliant guess that the

[125] ". . . der Mensch auch 'Bewußtsein' hat. Aber auch dies nicht von vornherein, als 'rein' Bewußtsein. Der 'Geist' hat von vornherein den Fluch an sich, mit der Materie 'behaftet' zu sein, die hier in der Form . . . der Sprache auftritt." K. Marx, F. Engels, *Die deutsche Ideologie*: Kritik der neuesten deutschen Philosophie in ihren Repräsentanten, Feuerbach, B. Bauer und Stirner, und des deutschen Sozialismus in seinen verschiedenen Propheten. Berlin, 1953, p. 27. English text from *The German Ideology*, London, 1942, p. 19.

[126] "Die Sprache *ist* das praktische, auch für andere Menschen existierende, also auch für mich selbst erst existierende wirkliche Bewußtsein." Ibid. "Die unmittelbare Wirklichkeit [Existenzform] des Gedankens ist die Sprache." Op. cit., p. 473.

movement, the change, etc. of notions reflect the movement, the change of the existing world.[127]

Hence, the correlation of "physical reality" and its mental elements throws an entirely different light upon the relation of reality and thought, of reality and language, than what Antal imagined and—to make matters worse—put in the mouth of one of the theoreticians of Marxism.

The classics of Marxism in numerous writings stated the objective character conceived in this sense of the social processes. But it is far from the truth that they should have seen the basic criterion of objective reality in its total independence from the consciousness of individuals (thoughts, emotions, goals, aspirations, etc.). When they emphasized the history-shaping role of the masses, they by no means annulled the role of the conscious element, nor did they belittle it. On the contrary! The recognition of the objective determinedness of social processes and of the role of the conscious elements seems to be an unsurmountable difficulty only to incorrigible metaphysicists.

I shall still discuss in detail the problems of objective and subjective factors, of "determinedness" and "freedom";[128] in this place I content myself with stating that Antal's interpretation of social objectivity is a simplification, vulgarization of one of the very important theses of the Marxist conception of society.

When earlier in this book the talk was about what criteria give also the real content of social objectivity, I wanted by no means to equate the objectivity of material reality with that of social reality, I referred only to the material genesis of the latter, which cannot really be neglected on the basis of the requirements of materialist social science. But to let the basic identity practically obscure the important difference that exists "objectively" between matter and society is at least as serious an error as if someone negated the material origin of society. In the emergence of society we see namely conscious human efforts to

[127] "Hegel brilliantly *divined* the dialectics of things (phenomena, the world, nature) . . . in the alternation, reciprocal dependence of *all* notions, in the *identity of their opposites*, in the *transition* of one notion into another, in the eternal change, movement of notions." V. I. Lenin, *Philosophical Notebooks*, Moscow, 1961, pp. 196—7. Furthermore: "Hegel actually *proved* that logical forms and laws are not empty shell, but the *reflections* of the objective world." Op. cit., p. 180. One of the three members of cognition—besides nature and the human brain—is "the form of reflection in human cognition, and this form consists precisely of concepts, laws, categories, etc.". Op. cit., p. 182.
[128] See Chapter V, Sections 7, 8 and 9.

overcome the hardships of nature, to acquire and later to produce material goods. In the development of society these conscious elements (spontaneously or in "conscious" form) play an important part. In depicting the objective course of the development of society, therefore, we have to reckon with the presence of the subjective element and, let us add, with its influence, too, unless we want to fall into the error of mystifying the social consciousness. The indubitably existing objective character of social consciousness is determined namely not by its being a formation arising entirely independently of the consciousness of the individuals (subjects) constituting the society, but it is the resultant of a mesh of ideas, desires, goals, and aspirations which are basically influenced by the social status of the individuals and are rather variegated and often contradictory. The existence of the individual (subjective) conscious elements which are hidden behind the objectivity of social consciousness, and are palpably perceivable and measurable by objective sociological methods, cannot be ignored or categorically denied without vulgarizing the theses of materialist social science. The socialist character basically determining the consciousness of Hungarian society in our age does not mean at all that it is something objective settled upon the consciousness of the individuals making up today's Hungarian society, neither does it mean that it is a homogeneous mathematical summation of the socialist consciousness of all individuals, nor that it is entirely different from the conscious world of the individuals.

If what precedes applies as a whole to the objective character of (the genesis and the current existence of) social consciousness, it cannot be otherwise in the case of the objectivity of language, a very important social formation, either. Even if it sounds trivial, it nevertheless seems necessary to lay down the well-known fact that man (the individual) is not simply a helpless slave of his language, but that, being aware of the objective regularities of its functioning (objective, that is existing—at the given moment—outside and independently of the consciousness of the individual), he uses them knowingly, and even shapes and moulds that objective formation; often it is found in language that an uncommon individual usage, a formula "alien to the nature" of the given language, becomes prevailing over the language area; one might as well say, it becomes objectified.

Also S. Károly stands up against the one-sided, metaphysical conception of the objectivity of language when, in examining the language-developing function of the subject in the projection of the dialectics of necessity and freedom, determinedness and accident, he states: *"In the process of communication therefore limitation and freedom, determinedness and 'accident', are realized in mutual dependence.* Free movement within the linguistically determinate may again be determined from a different—extra-linguistic—point of view, and conversely: we are free to use the linguistically determinate for the purposes of our communication."[129]

After drawing in his own way the line between the simpler form of objectivity and its more complex form, that of social objectivity as interpreted by him, Antal, starting from the objective character of the forms of motion of language, assigns to the subjects no role in this mechanism; more precisely, in describing the essential features of language, he allows the subject only to have a subjective, that is a necessarily incomplete, mental reflection of the language which came into existence independently of the subject and which exists independently of the subject's consciousness: "What exists in the consciousness of the individual is not the real language, but only its subjective reflection, hence an incomplete image varying from one individual to another.

"Linguistics can only study the language independently of the actual individual. Those feelings about the objective language which live in each individual, for instance, the infamous Sprach-gefühl, etc., are completely neutral from the standpoint of linguistics."[130]

To this definition of the task of linguistics there is not too much to add. At most only that the individual's idea of language is not always, and not necessarily, a naive conception. In the case of given persons and under given circumstances it may coincide with the collective (i.e. socially objectively determined) consciousness of language, or at least may contain a very large number of its elements. One must not forget that the "speakers' consciousness" includes also the consciousness of the linguists professionally concerned with the forms of motion of language, and the conscious elements living therein as "subjective impressions" are still worth studying, not to mention the linguistic views and the works of great writers and prominent representatives of the

---

[129] S. Károly, *Általános és magyar jelentéstan* [General and Hungarian Semantics], Budapest, 1970, p. 179.
[130] *Questions . . .*, p. 11.

conscious language-reform movement who nevertheless had some influence on the development of language as an objective phenomenon. There is also no need to explicate in detail that some proponents of formal analysis, who qualify the "linguistic instinct" as only subjective and thereby doom it to exclusion from the range of linguistic investigations, still use this instinct as a refined "objective" yardstick: it is yet the instinct of the native informant that decides whether a sequence of sounds is an utterance of the given language or a more or less orderly concatenation of morphemes; and also whether a morpheme is a "smallest significant element" of the given language or an arbitrary combination of phonemes, etc.

On the other hand, Antal's statement which describes the view regarding the essence of language, formulated by the last and most advanced stage of the comparative and historical linguistics of the nineteenth century, the so-called neogrammarian school, as a "humanistic-romantic linguistic conception",[131] is a repulsive back-slapping and annoying schematism, which forces the whole of the most developed linguistic conception of the last quarter of the nineteenth century into the bag of subjective or objective idealist psychologism, and therefore does not correspond at all to the historical facts. Whoever knows a little about the results of that period of the science of language is fully aware that not only did posterity inherit from that period the psychologistic explanation of language, but the most progressive linguists of those days, turning categorically against the subjective-idealist linguistic theories, recognized and propagated, among other things, the objective character of language, its nature independent of individual arbitrariness. If there is something to cast up to this linguistic conception it is just the same thing for which Antal's conception is also liable to censure: the blindly working and exceptionless nature of the neogrammarian postulate of phonetic law moulded by a one-sided stress upon the objective character inspired by natural science, as is commonly known, is oblivious of the language-forming, language-generating function of subjective factors.[132]

Stressing of the objective character of language in Antal's interpretation means not only that it is a mechanism functioning

---

[131] Op. cit., p. 16.
[132] I shall discuss this in detail later.

entirely independently of the consciousness of the individual, but also that it is sovereign in other respects as well. Advocating the privileged status of structuralist methodology,[133] Antal formulates first of all the sovereignty of the synchronic condition of language as against the diachronic processes: "We think that synchrony, which deals with the condition of a language at a given phase, will always remain more important than diachrony... Synchrony is more important because language is a system of signs . . . The extent to which a system of signs and, thus, a language functioning in a given phase is independent of its own history, can be proved in the case of Esperanto language."[134]

The sovereignty, formulated with certain limitations, of the synchronic condition of language is a more shaded variant of Antal's notorious conception quoted above in a different context, in which he wanted to resolve "the awfully much debated dilemma of synchrony and diachrony" by a peremptory statement (yield not an iota to diachrony). For the sake of historical truth, however, I have to add that Antal formulated with much greater circumspection the linguistic projection of the dialectics of condition and change two years before the publication of his book in question. Thus his recent position seems to be one step backward. In another of his works he namely professed the interdependence of the methods which observe the correlation of the condition and change of language: "The two basic ways of approaching language, the synchronic and the diachronic method, do not exclude or negate each other but are complementary to each other."[135]

On this point it is possible to agree without reserve, because it wholly meets the requirements of the fullness of linguistic description or explanation, neither of which is in itself fit to satisfy on the basis of either its theoretical objectives or its corresponding methods. It is commonly known that the historical method was successful primarily in describing the history of elements, the changes in the elements of language, in discovering the causes of such changes. These results, however, certainly have their drawbacks, too: that method investigated the changes of elements not as changes of members of a given system. In general it paid no attention to what effects a change of an element of the language system had on the system as a whole, what shifts and

---

[133] Op. cit., p. 14.
[134] Op. cit., p. 15.
[135] Antal, *A magyar esetrendszer*, p. 11.

rearrangements of relations it caused in it. Antal devotes a special section to the limitations of synchrony[136] and displays a really convincing frankness when writing about the limits of this method of investigation; what is more, he keeps the possibilities of synchronic research within so narrow bounds that he includes among his objectives only the answer to "what's what" and "leaves it to historical linguistics to answer the whys and wherefores".[137] From this division of labour he draws the conclusion: "From this, however, it follows clearly that synchronic description cannot be regarded as a complete, full and definitive description of language. Synchrony grasps only one aspect of the language and is consequently always incomplete. Just as historical linguistics is often at a loss how to value one or another phenomenon, although it knows its history well, so synchronic description is also sometimes unable to explain a phenomenon which it can otherwise describe accurately."[138]

What is to be added to this passage is only that today not even the proponents of the synchronic method are content with a mere registration of condition; they see one of the prerequisites for linguistics to become a really theoretical science in the fact that they themselves should be able also to explain synchronic phenomena instead of employing purely descriptive and quantitative methods. Ch. E. Osgood, for example, in the introductory part of his lecture delivered at a conference devoted to the universals of language, said that the conference was an outstanding stage of a "bloodless revolution", just on account of the basic stance that, by breaking the bounds of purely descriptive methods, it focussed attention on the question of why, on the explanation of the phenomena.[139] Also J. Lotz holds a similar view on the tasks of descriptive linguistics: "Not only linguistic history explains, but so does descriptive linguistics."[140]

One can only applaud the latest efforts of modern methodology, with the reserve, of course, that it cannot even so claim to

[136] Ibid.
[137] Ibid.
[138] Ibid.
[139] *Universals of Language:* Report of a Conference held at Dobbs Ferry, New York, April 13—15, 1961 (The M.I.T. Press, Cambridge, Mass., 1963), pp. 234—54.
[140] Expressing his own standpoint, this is a motto which S. Károly uses in his above-cited work to introduce the chapter entitled "Meaning of the Hungarian Sign Combinations". Op. cit., p. 579.

give a complete explanation of language, for it needs completing with explanations based on the diachronic method. The synchronic method alone is really unfit to explain why we have a velar vowel in the suffixes of Hung. *híd* 'bridge', *zsír* 'fat', *hív* 'to call', etc. (*híd-at, zsír-os, hív-ok*, etc.), in contrast to the suffixes of *ív* 'arch', *víz* 'water', *hisz* 'to believe', etc., where we find a "regular" sound harmonizing with the palatal root-vowel (*ív-et, viz-es, hisz-ek*, etc.), just as this method is incapable of explaining why the stem morpheme consisting of the same succession of phonemes is different, as regards suffixation, according as it is a noun or a verb (*szív* 'heart', *szív-et, szív-es, szív-ek*, etc., and *szív* 'to inhale', *szív-ok, szív-ott, szív-ás*, etc.). These "irregularities" can be satisfactorily explained by the diachronic method.

To claim the mutual dependence, the complementary nature, of the two kinds of methods is not tantamount to the affirmation of a mixing of methods, of a kind of methodological eclecticism, but is a direct consequence of the dynamism of language or, if you like, of its dialectics, which shows the unity of condition and change after all. A motive of this kind appears from what was written nearly forty years ago by Laziczius, who contrasted Baudoin de Courtenay's "more elastic" synchronism with Saussure's more rigid alternative of synchrony or diachrony: "The synchronism of the living language is the point from where he [Baudoin de Courtenay] views the genetic yarns of the past. His is a synchronic view, which is made dynamic by the interspersed diachronic aspects, in contrast with Saussure's attitude which always keeps apart the facts of history and thus can be described as rather stationary."[141] Being acquainted with Laziczius's lifework and basic habit, I can safely say that by making this evaluation he did not want to be the standard-bearer of some "mixture of standpoints", for he always spoke up most categorically against "solutions" of this kind. With this opposition he had by no means the intention of minimizing Saussure's significance or contesting the importance of the synchronic research of language, for he was a militant Saussurean and an active applier of the synchronic method of research; but he evaluated the whole of the great predecessor's work, not suppressing its seamy sides either, as he was aware that synchronic description needed completing.

[141] Gy. Laziczius, *Bevezetés a fonológiába* [Introduction to Phonology], Budapest, 1932, pp. 5—6.

In the light of the claim to fullness of linguistic description "the awfully much debated dilemma of synchrony and diachrony" may be treated as a pseudo-problem, since the metaphysical alternative suggested by militant representatives of different schools is being replaced by a dynamism of mutual dependence. It seems therefore that the dispute of several decades is nearing to a close; this is what can be inferred also from L. Benkő's substantial lecture entitled "Linguistic History and Present-day Language" as well as from the ensuing discussion.[142] J. Zsilka's pertinent comments are also convincing: "The synchronic system in its interrelations only imitates, as it were, the process in the course of which the forms have historically developed."[143] Furthermore: "The validity of any form is determined at once by the—mutually contrasting—historical and logical structures of the system."[144] The interdependence of occurrence and the present, of change and condition, is referred to also by J. Szigeti: "The implicit momentum of evaluation is rather that in the last analysis we see in the past the road leading up to the present, consequently an indispensable prerequisite of a fuller understanding of the present."[145]

For this very reason it is impossible to pass over Antal's more shaded conception of sovereignty either, because it again prefers linguistic description relying on the sovereignty of synchrony, for he regards this, in contrast with his former view, as a requirement following from the position of modern linguistics and not as an incomplete description incapable of apprehending one of the aspects of language.

I cannot leave it unmentioned either how Antal erects a solid wall of partition between the results of so-called traditional and structuralist linguistic research: ". . . all linguistic works which are not based on structuralism are out of date . . . Structuralism is not a method relating to one individual field of linguistics, nor is it one of the possible methods, but, if language is really a system, it is the only up-to-date methodology of linguistic study."[146]

[142] Delivered as part of the course in linguistic theory at the Institute of Linguistics on March 3, 1967.
[143] IOK XXIV, p. 309.
[144] Loc. cit., p. 345.
[145] Magyar Filozófiai Szemle VIII, p. 835.
[146] Questions . . ., p. 14.

What lies behind this sharp delineation of the fronts? Nothing less than the negation of the complex nature of language, non-recognition of the interdependent elements [R (M , M); R (M, S)][147] of complex relations, a simplification of the complicated network of relationships, an attitude that sees in the language only a formal system consisting of interrelations of signs. As to the former efforts made as a result of research work done by allowing for the complex nature of language, he dismisses them by a passing remark as useless to modern linguistics.[148] Furthermore, he describes the ideas concerning the dichotomy of linguistic researches, by stressing again the difference between the two methods, as wrong.[149] The fact that language, as a social formation, is not one of the categories of an ideological character does not mean at all that its social, psychical, etc. aspects can be denied, that it can be conceived only as a formal system, and as such can be examined only by formal methods. Hidden behind the negation of the connection of language and mental reflection, consequently of the "organic" connection of language and objective reality, is essentially the view that linguistic structures have nothing to do with the structures of objective reality, with the structure of the mental image of the latter—the concept, because, he writes, "as all languages are systems 'sui generis', all languages divide and classify the outside world in a different way according to their own categories of meaning".[150] Whether, on the basis of Antal's conception of meaning, the proper individual categories of meaning of all languages of the world are sufficient to analyze and classify the outside world can now be left to the reader to decide!

To sum up what precedes, it can be stated that Antal's theory of meaning amounts to a mass of misunderstandings and misconstructions, it is a misapprehension of basic gnoseological, logical and linguistic categories, their arbitrary application, which cannot stand criticism from linguistic facts in practice. It is useless in theoretical synchronic analysis, too, not to mention that there is simply nothing to do with it in the examination of the diachronic projections (formal changes vs. changes of meaning) of the forms of motion of language.

[147] See Chapter III, Section 5.
[148] Cf. footnote 131 above.
[149] *Questions* . . ., p. 14.
[150] Op. cit., p. 85.

The reader may rightly raise the question why, in spite of all this, I have dealt with Antal's theory of meaning in such detail, though without pretending to make an exhaustive criticism of his theses and conclusions. The reason is that his book, despite its small size, is one of the first monographic works of Hungarian linguistic literature prepared with a claim to modern analysis, and that it takes a stand on the most comprehensive questions of the science of language.

Being of a pioneering character, the venture is bound to involve certain risks. That Antal nevertheless undertook this work is a commendable fact in itself. An old truth says also that any kind of theory can in some way or other promote science; either by stimulating progress through creative ideas, or by encouraging debates of varying intensity. I think it is the latter case we are facing in respect to the work at issue: the whole theoretical construction is built on shaky ground, and from this it follows automatically that its partial statements and partial conclusions are also false.

I wish to stress in this place once again that I do not consider myself entitled to give a full evaluation of Antal's work. In accordance with the main objectives of my study I have discussed only those details which are diametrically opposed to the facts of language.

The fact remains: Antal's book was published at The Hague in 1963. It can be stated also in the light of its international reception[151] that it did not add too much to the reputation of Hungarian linguistics abroad. J. Herman's critique in 1965, without aiming at completeness, pointed to a few serious theoretical mistakes in the book. Despite this an abridged version of the book was printed in 1966.[152] True, it was completed with commentaries, but it is also true that it contained an "Epilogue" by the author, who, in that place, used a tone somewhat uncommon to our style of scientific prose when speaking about some "unrelinquishable principles" in the following terms: "To speak frankly, the views expounded in my study are instinctively [?!] too deeply rooted in me to allow me to bow before Herman's often convincing criticism, though rationally it may seem absolutely acceptable. And there are a few basic principles which I shall never be able to relinquish. Apart from insignificant changes,

---

[151] Cf. *Germanistik* IV, pp. 565—6; *Language* XXXIX, pp. 468—73; *Linguistics* II, pp. 96—102.
[152] NyK LXVIII, pp. 279—325.

these principles serve as a basis for my semantical views by and large in the same way as they are explained in my book published in 1963."[153] In view of the criticisms one might eagerly expect to see the time-tested principles. One of these reads that "Language is a system of signs" (to the best of my knowledge this was not contested by any one of the critics of Antal's book), but it may be read also in this way: "Meaning is the rule of application of the sign"[154] (this, however, was all the more challenged).

I am aware that I also shall not succeed in eliminating from Antal's semantic conception this instinctive and deep-rooted principle and the ensuing conclusion; that is why my critical remarks are directed not against Antal but against his still prevailing wrong views.

2. SIGN, MEANING, NOTION, CONCEPT

The negatives of the theory of meaning based on the "completely and utterly arbitrary" nature of the relation of the linguistic sign and its denotatum prompt us to seek to discover the essence, the function of meaning by observing the complexity of this relationship. This realization and intention necessarily make us, for the time being, separate from the linguistic signs all those non-linguistic signs, as "disturbing factors", which become signs only through arbitrary convention. That is why it seems justified and expedient to concentrate all our attention on the linguistic sign, on its function in the process of human cognition and communication, and to try to grasp the nature of meaning on the basis of this function.

The proposed method of investigation is singularly "homocentric", which means that it looks for the characteristics of meaning in the sign situation *(Zeichensituation)* and conceives the sign situation as a relation between men who wish to understand one another and who "produce" signs in order to secure communication. These signs, however, can function to serve the above purpose (undisturbed communication) only if:
(a) they truly reflect the relationship of man and reality;
(b) they express the relationship of man and the signs;

---

[153] Loc. cit., p. 325.
[154] Ibid.

107

(c) they indicate by exact criteria the connection between signs and reality;

(d) they have such a structre that they can perfectly express and communicate the most varied conceptual, emotional, etc. elements;

(e) they form a system whose particular elements are in a relationship of interdependence.

Hence the sign situation conceived in this sense is a complicated network of different relationships which may be objective, subjective, intercrossing and sometimes contradictory; the determining factor in this network is the relation of intercommunicating men, of men who try—and who mostly succeed in doing so— to establish the "balance" of the opposite effects of different factors, and to solve the ensuing contradictions, by relying on the test of practice. The secret of success lies in the simple fact that this is all about thinking and acting people whose "determined" subjective intention (the transmission of thought, emotion and will) is manifested, "objectified" as an outcome of the working of that complex network of relationship. This construction of the sign situation does not underestimate the role of language itself, on the contrary, it stipulates the conditions of its functioning more precisely when it turns against all forms of sign fetishism (Bloomfield's empiricism, the sign fatalism of semantical philosophy, the "signocentrism" of the so-called physicalists, etc.).[1]

The structurally complex conception thus sketched of the sign situation has plenty of extralinguistic (gnoseological, psychological, pragmatical, sociological) elements which were banished from the field of linguistic research by those who advocated the formalistic analysis of language alone, because they wished to protect the autonomy of linguistics against the testimony of these elements. This concern subsists on the known alternative: either an autonomous system of signs or psychologism, logicism, sociologism. If language, the linguistic signs are conceived—from the point of view not only of their genesis but also of their functioning—in the above manner, in their complexity, this alterna-

---

[1] A. Gardiner already stood up against the trends that mystified the linguistic sign when he defined the primary purpose of speech as the establishment of co-operation between men, and strongly emphasized the role of the men taking part in the communication. Cf. *The Theory of Speech and Language*, Oxford, 1951, p. 22; cf. also A. Schaff, *Einführung . . .*, p. 200.

tive will prove just as false as that of the motivated or conventional nature of the linguistic sign. The trouble is not that the descriptive linguist takes notice of all essential components of this complex structure, for his fact-respecting scientific conscience does not let him do otherwise; the trouble begins where somebody accepts as determining only one or another of the interdependent components and treats the rest in a perfunctory way or disregards them altogether. As shown by the history of science, this would occur at the turning point between consecutive schools whenever a new kind of one-sidedness was pushed to counteract the one-sidedness of the preceding school.

I wish to recall here the natural-scientific school[2] which, however respectable in its intentions (the demand for scientific exactness !), adopted a narrow linguistic conception disregarding the social, psychical factors. That conception brought about the psychological linguistic explanation, which in turn recognized only the psychical factors as determining elements of language. The former theory, which took language to be a simple natural organism, was replaced by one which regarded language as a psychical phenomenon only—psychological associationism, which endured for a relatively long time. This is how we can comprehend, and have to evaluate, the formulation given by H. Kronasser who, in his monograph published in 1952, summed up the essence of earlier definitions of meaning as follows: "What was thus understood by meaning *is a more or less complex psychical phenomenon that is linked to a symbol perceivable by the sense organs.*"[3] His own definition of meaning is also imputable to the unbending "anti-organistic" linguistic attitude: "The meaning of a word, psychologically speaking, is a closed, articulated and transformed psychical totality."[4]

This "deeply psychologistic" conception of meaning called forth Bloomfield's antimentalism which was revived by the absolutization of the first part of the false alternative of "mechanism" or "mentalism". The cardinal principles of antimen-

[2] A. Schleicher and his followers.
[3] "Man verstand also unter der Bedeutung *ein mehr oder minder komplexives seelisches Phänomen, das an ein sinnlich wahrnehmbares Symbol gebunden ist.*" Kronasser, *Handbuch der Semasiologie*, p. 56.
[4] "Die Wortbedeutung sei—psychologisch gesprochen—eine geschlossene, gegliederte und durchgeformte psychische Ganzheit." Op. cit., p. 64.

talism are almost word for word repeated in Hall's work published in 1964.[5]

Even in the metaphysical zigzag of the simplistic ideas recorded in the history of science a peculiar place is occupied by a wry grimace of the succession or simultaneity of American linguistic theories: at the same time as Hall's book appeared, J. J. Katz published his article "Mentalism in Linguistics",[6] which, by denying the whole of Bloomfield's heritage, accepts only the mentalistic theory of language as the sole scientific kind of linguistics, because in his view language is a "neurological mechanism" existing in the minds of the speakers, and linguistics is consequently a summation of the ideas about the functioning of this mechanism.[7]

Katz's conception, which is essentially a revival of Paul's individual psychologism, is an unmistakable proof of the feeling of want which was roused also in the readers and linguists of today by the mechanism (physicalism), the rigid antimentalism of Bloomfield's successors.

Stressing of the "mental" aspect of language would not matter in itself, it becomes a mistake when the language-creating part factor grows into an exclusive whole of linguistic explanation, into a psychological phantom. This can be found with Katz as with so many of his psychologist predecessors.[8]

The psychologistic conceptions of meaning have one feature in common—the linguistic application of the theory of associations which happens to appear also in writings of authors who adopt the Marxist outlook.

Followers of this school offer association as an explanation for the correlation of the inside and the outside (content and form)

[5] R. A. Hall, *Introductory Linguistics*, Philadelphia, 1964, p. 404.
[6] *Language* XL, pp. 124—37.
[7] "Now it is clear that the linguist . . . claims that his theory describes a neurological mechanism." Loc. cit., p. 129. A few pages later: "Within the framework of the above model of linguistic communication, every aspect of the mentalistic theory involved psychological reality. The linguistic description and the procedures of sentence production and recognition must correspond to independent mechanisms in the brain." Loc. cit., p. 133.
[8] It is worth mentioning also from the point of view of the history of science that Katz's neurologico-mentalistic theory of language is not too far away from the Pavlovian biologistic conception, according to which meaning is a reflex of the organism produced by the sign (signal).

of the linguistic sign. As is well known, Saussure also saw the unity of the language sign in the associative union of acoustic image and concept: "... dans le signe linguistique sont tous deux psychiques et sont unis dans notre cerveau par le lien de l'association."[9] Saussure's associationism is the product of a very enlightening polemic of principle. Namely Saussure worked out his own association theory in the struggle against the vulgarizing linguistic view, according to which language is a nomenclature, a catalogue which corresponds simply to things and concepts. He strongly criticized the basic flaw of that view, namely that "Elle suppose des idées toutes faites préexistant aux mots".[10] And in another place: "Il n'y a pas d'idées préétablies, et rien n'est distinct avant l'apparition de la langue."[11]

The above ideas of Saussure are clear and unambiguous, we can agree with them even in the light of our present knowledge, because they challenge the idealistic conception of thought without language, they are directed against the mystification of "thought". But, while rightly arguing with the mystifiers of thought, Saussure in the heat of the debate fails to see that he himself in turn arrives at the mystification of language itself, at a mysterious phenomenon in which language combines amorphous masses of sounds and thoughts into meaningful units without the necessity either for the thought to be "materialized" or for the sound to be "spiritualized", which is nothing less than "delivering" thought of its material vehicle. He writes: "Il n'y a donc ni matérialisation des pensées, ni spiritualisation des sons, mais il s'agit de ce fait en quelque sorte mystérieux, que la 'pensée-son' implique des divisions et que la langue élabore ses unités en se constituant entre deux masses amorphes."[12] The "mysterious" thought-sound is actually the linguistic unit which is the result of a complex associative operation. He tries to demonstrate the complex nature of the operation by the following natural analogy: "Qu'on se représente l'air en contact avec une nappe d'eau: si la pression atmosphérique change, la surface de l'eau se décompose en une série de divisions, c'est-à-dire de vagues; ce sont ces ondulations qui donneront une idée de l'union, et pour ainsi dire de l'accouplement de la pensée avec la matière phonique."[13] We are facing a really complex coupling, a myste-

[9] *Cours* . . ., p. 98.
[10] Op. cit., p. 97.
[11] Op. cit., p. 155.
[12] Op. cit., p. 156.
[13] Ibid.

rious phenomenon, in the light of the Saussurean formulation: the pairing of air motion and water surface, both of which perish with this mating, give birth to a third, a dematerialized wave motion: the association of phonetic form (its notion) and of thought, the "thought-sound", in the notorious Saussurean formulation is neither thought nor sound any more, but a logical network of (mysterious) forms.

Other representatives of associationism use a much simpler language: by meaning they understand in general the associative union in which the phonetic form is connected with the notion, with the concept, with the sense. Thus, according to M. Hecht: "Meanings are notions associated with words."[14]

L. Sebag, in his definition of the essence and correlation of the signifier and the signified, has revived Saussure's idea with the difference that he emphasizes the phonic reality of the signifier: "Le signifiant, c'est la réalité phonique de la chaîne parlée organisée en fonction de critères linguistiques; le signifié, ce qu'évoquent les sons utilisés, les concepts qui leur sont associés."[15]

The associationist theory of meaning certainly has the rational kernel that the child's learning of the mother tongue is really based on associations. The reply given to the question *"What's this?"* makes the child associate names with objects and then, after long practice of abstraction, with the concepts reflecting the objects (the word *table* + the object > the word *table* + the concept reflecting the table). Something similar occurs in the course of learning a foreign language, too, with the exception that here we already "translate", i.e. we associate the concepts formed by the aid of the mother tongue with the phonic material of the foreign language. But this is where the range of associationism ends. It is of no help in explaining the meaning of linguistic signs in general, at most it leads us to statements to be made within the bounds of generalities.

The associationist theory of meaning, in spite of its negative aspects discussed above, demonstrates anyway that it sought to

[14] "Bedeutungen sind mit den Worten verbundene Vorstellungen." Quoted from Sprachwissenschaft und Philosophie zum Bedeutungsproblem (*Blätter für deutsche Philosophie*, 1930/31, p. 17) by Kronasser, op. cit., p. 55.
[15] L. Sebag, *Marxisme et structuralisme*, Paris, 1964, p. 95.

discover the complex network of relationships "associating" the sign with the thing signified. This endeavour is disclosed by the hypothesis of psychological associationism, which sees a product of psychical operation in the "concurrence" of language sign and concept, of language and reality, by the mediation of the concept.

3. MEANING AS A KIND OF REFLECTION

The Marxist theories of meaning have from the outset emphasized the unity, the indissoluble connection, of the concept as a product of the linguistic sign, the meaning and the operations of abstraction. Since the inception of the well-known Marxist formula which, though, has not been explained in more detail (language is the living reality of thought), it has been on the basis of this formula that Marxist authors have explained their views on the nature of the linguistic sign, on the relationship of sign and reality. The harbinger of modern psycholinguistics, the young theoretician of prime significance also to today's science of language, L. S. Vygotsky, already in the mid-thirties stated that one of the basic functions of meaning is to reflect reality, and he even used meaning and generalization in the same sense: "Generalization and meaning are synonyms."[1]

The editors of the posthumous publication of Vygotsky's writings, the psycholinguists Leontyev and Luria, also emphatically stressed the generalizing function of meaning, its role in the peculiar reflection of reality. "The meaning of a word", they wrote, "reflects reality. That is why meaning of a word is called reflection in the first place. But we have to do here with a special form of reflection... we understand by it the generalization that was fixed through the meaning."[2] This generalization is always a certain system of connections and correlations revealed just by the meaning; the reflection in it of connections and correlations is settled in a form of ideal, intellectual crystallization[3] of the social experience of mankind, of social practice. This formula

---

[1] "Verallgemeinerung und Wortbedeutung sind Synonyme." L. S. Vygotsky, *Denken und Sprechen*, Berlin, 1964, pp. 256—7.

[2] "In der Bedeutung eines Wortes spiegelt sich die Wirklichkeit wider. Deshalb heißt Bedeutung eines Wortes in erster Linie Widerspiegelung. Doch haben wir es hier mit einer besonderen Form der Widerspiegelung zu tun... versteht man darunter jene Verallgemeinerung, wie sie durch die Bedeutung fixiert wurde." Op. cit., Introd., p. 9.

[3] "... ideelle, geistige Kristallisationsform." Ibid.

meaning ~ generalization' leads us to the most general categories of human cognition which present a really unambiguous reflection of the indissoluble process of thinking and speaking, where it is very difficult, practically impossible, to determine whether word meaning is a phenomenon of language or of thought. It is both, but only together. It is a category of thought from the point of view that as the end-result of a process the concept manifests itself, is realized, "becomes objectified" in the word, and it is a category of language because it is a necessary constitutive element of the word itself, since the word "deprived" of its meaning is an empty voice, is not a word any longer, but merely a physiological, acoustic reality. According to Vygotsky, meaning is "a word viewed from its inside",[4] thus not an external factor that cannot be deduced from the word, but its organic part, which is psychologically a generalization or concept,[5] i.e. a result, a phenomenon, of the closing act of the process of thought.

The conception of meaning advanced by Vygotsky and his school had a determining influence on the position of the authors representative of Marxist literature on semantics. The theses formulated on the basis of the general theory of reflection encompassed really all those basic questions whose exact investigation made it possible to uncover the determining features of the linguistic meaning. Vygotsky's doctrines helped to sketch the conceptions which approached the essence of meaning by examining the social experience of mankind, general human cognition, the ways of successful intercommunication (meaning as concept, meaning as a product of different relationships).

4. MEANING AS CONCEPT

Almost all prominent representatives of Marxist literature on semantics interpreted meaning on the basis of the gnoseological-communicative function of the linguistic sign. Conception of the gnoseological-communicative function in indissoluble unity guarantees the discovery of the fundamental features of the language sign, its role in the sign situation referred to above, where also the essence of meaning can be grasped. The sign situation is a product of conscious human, social activity, which

[4] "... von der Innenseite betrachtetes Wort." Op. cit., p. 256.
[5] Ibid.

114

was "created" for the communication of man's knowledge about the world and of other mental phenomena based on knowledge (emotions, wishes, intentions, aesthetical, religious, etc. "notions"), and is being produced day after day, hundreds and hundreds of times, by human intercourse on the plane of social activities in the broadest sense of the word.

This social intercourse is the result of an "interplay" of peculiar interdependent relations. The peculiar correlation of the elements of the sign situation is composed of relationships, or rather a network of relationships, which are primarily social (between men understanding one another, between men and reality, and between men and signs), further significative as socially determined (between sign and reality), and systematical (between sign and sign). Essentially, this network of relationships is nothing else than a recognition of the simple fact known since antiquity that a real sign situation comes about when somebody thinks something of something (or somebody), or when somebody wants to tell somebody something about something (or somebody) for some purpose.

In the real sign situation conceived in this sense, therefore, meaning as a constitutive element of the process of cognition and communication shows the place and role of the linguistic sign in the same process. Hence, it is not an ideally existing objective entity (mentalism), and not even a subjective feature of the autonomous process of thought (psychologism), but a peculiar social product, whose creation requires the existence of "active co-operation" of all elements of the sign relation.

To understand the essence of meaning it is necessary also from another point of view to stress the real sign situation as a basic criterion. If one or another element of the sign situation thus sketched is missing, or "functions poorly", a false sign situation comes about, which cannot serve human communication in the broadest sense or at least causes disturbances in communication. Let us imagine the following "sign situation": Somebody says to his interlocutor (partner in communication) who knows only English: "*Zeichnen Sie mir einen Pegasus.*" The partner, even if he knows "what *Pegasus* means", looks uncomprehendingly at the sign-giver, since the speaker has a linguistic difficulty in making himself understood to the sign-receiver. Easy communication fails to occur also if, in the case of persons living in one and the same language area (linguistic difficulty excluded), the sign-receiver does not know "what *Pegasus* means" when he is given these signs: "*Please draw a Pegasus*". The com-

115

munication *"Tell me about the genesis of the concept Pegasus"* will also work out only in case the receiver is aware of the relative autonomy of the thinking process, of the nature of human "imagination", of the phenomenon in which imagination arbitrarily combines the mental images ('horse', 'wing') of certain existing elements of reality (horse, wing), thus forming the concept of the winged horse, *Pegasus* (relation between sign and "reality"). No communication takes place either if—although both the giver and the receiver of signs know the "concept" *Pegasus*—the giver transmits to the receiver only the elements *drawing* or *draw* and *Pegasus*. (The total lack of the relation elements enabling and reflecting the syntactical "arrangement" of the elements, the lack of a special requirement of systematism, etc., etc.)

The socially determined sign thus obtains its own true value in the real sign situation; its reference to reality, its meaning, can also be deduced from it. When namely men, as constitutive factors of the real sign situation, communicate with one another, by means of signs, the subjective content of their consciousness becomes intersubjective, socially communicable. The subjective content of consciousness can become socially communicable by means of signs only if the sign is "understood" in the same manner on a social scale, which in turn happens to be the case only if the sign (the linguistic sign, of course) is the same on a social scale or at least is indissolubly connected with similar processes of thought. Identical understanding, identical thinking are the basis of meaning, which requires also language and thought to be conceived in organic unity. In other words: the mental reflection of reality (concept) is conceivable only as the result of verbal thinking. An indispensable element of verbal thinking is the linguistic sign, by means of which amorphous partial products take shape, are crystallized into a concept, and the subjective product of this process of crystallization can be transmitted to others equally "by the agency" of the linguistic sign.

In both the cognitive and the communicative process the linguistic sign figures with its own reference to reality. In the cognitive process the physical impulses of the object of cognition arouse physiological stimuli which then become a subjective concept with the aid of the sign; in the communicative process the subjective concept arouses physiological stimuli with the assistance of the material body of sounds, these stimuli being "processed" into an identical concept in the consciousness of the sign-receivers, and as such they create an identical reference to reality. Here is a very simplified schema of this complex process: *reality→concept* (acquisition of knowledge), or *concept→reference to reality* (communication of knowledge). From the point of view of cognition the mental reflection of reality (reference to reality) can be regarded as the *concept*, from the point of view of communication the reference to reality of the linguistic sign can be considered *the meaning*, both being thus names given to the same cognitive connection from different points of view.

We have now arrived at the much debated problem of concept and meaning, most thoroughly discussed in recent literature on semantics by A. Schaff in his polemic article "Die Bedeutung der Bedeutung".[1] As he writes, "Concept and meaning are the product of an abstraction carried out in the process of cognition by means of word-signs".[2] To this rather general definition of concept ∼ meaning he adds at once that these products of abstraction — created in the process of social cognition — are the results of very complicated and closely interrelated processes, and he proceeds: "According as we approach this intellectual-linguistic product from the angle of the mental or the speech process, i.e. according as we stress one side of it or the other, it comes to light as concept (conceptual content) or as word meaning. There is no other difference between concept and meaning (of the same type)."[3]

Concept and meaning were treated as identical in works of much earlier date as well,[4] and provided a controversial matter already before Schaff's writings.

The question arises rightly, why Schaff "went back" to the "logicist" interpretation of meaning which, in earlier writings, "adapted" meaning to the concept, i.e. advocated the priority of the concept being established independently of the meaning of

---

[1] Schaff: DZfPh 1961, pp. 610—21, 708—23. Cf. also his work *Einführung in die Semantik*, Berlin, 1966.

[2] "Begriff und Bedeutung sind das Erzeugnis der im Erkenntnisvorgang mit Hilfe von Wortzeichen vollzogenen Abstraktion." Loc. cit., p. 722.

[3] "Je nachdem wir an dieses gedanklich-sprachliche Erzeugnis von der Seite des Denk- oder Sprachvorgangs herangehen, d. h. je nachdem wir die eine oder die andere Seite betonen, tritt es als Begriff (Begriffsinhalt) oder auch als Wortbedeutung zutage. Einen anderen Unterschied zwischen Begriff und Bedeutung (desselben Typus) gibt es nicht." Ibid.

[4] V. A. Zvegincev, A jelentéstan helye a nyelvészeti diszciplinák sorában [The Place of Semantics among the Linguistic Disciplines], NyIK VI, pp. 267—75; А. Й. Смирницкий, Значение слова, ВЯ 1955/2, p. 79—89.

the linguistic sign (conceptual realism, which became a theoretical source for a variety of objective-idealistic linguistic theories). With his categorical formulation of the genesis of meaning Schaff pursued the opposite goal. He did not want to reduce meaning to the concept established independently of it; on the contrary, by insisting that meaning is equal to concept he emphasized that there is no concept outside the linguistic meaning, i.e. every concept is the meaning of some linguistic expression. At the same time, while criticizing the adherents of conceptual realism for their objective idealism, Schaff energetically spoke up against the nominalistic theories of language, because these do away with the gnoseological aspect of the subjective reflection of reality, with the objective character of the concept as a generalizing reflection of reality (Wittgenstein and his followers, the modern school of American semantical philosophy).

Schaff had therefore every reason to treat the essence of meaning as a category involved with the process of the socially determined reflection of reality. He combated not ideological phantoms, but much too virulent theories and effective ideologies, when he subjected to thorough and ruthless criticism both conceptual realism and the subjective-idealistic views clad in a *flatus vocis* garb.

His reasoning which is not without irony when he dissects the ideas which oppose meaning and concept to each other (some connect the fullness of experience with the meaning, others with the concept) is convincing to me. Namely Schaff is an advocate of the "full" communication theory: not only "pure", that is emotionless, concepts but also the entire content of consciousness can be communicated by the aid of meanings. Hence the concepts (meanings) comprise not only the totality of the conceptual marks of reality but also the complex of emotional, esthetical, etc. momenta produced by the body of knowledge about reality. I can fully agree with the conception that the communicative process is "full", but I leave it to the gnoseologists, psychologists and philosophers to decide whether Schaff's "concept" used as a synonym of meaning can comprise the various parts of the entire content of consciousness (conceptual reflection of reality + related emotional, religious, etc. notions).

One more question is to be answered with respect to the idea 'meaning = concept'. Many have stated many times that the regularities of the process of thought, of the formation of concepts, are within the province of logic. This is so. To understand the meaning, therefore, it is indispensable to examine its logical

118

aspect. Since, however, the concept, the thought, is not only a logical but also a socially determined psychological, gnoseological category, reducing the linguistic problem of meaning exclusively to its formal-logical aspect would be practically tantamount to the simplification of a complex problem. The logician is namely unconcerned with questions (of basic importance for the materialist definition of the meaning of the linguistic sign) like the role of the objects and processes of the material world in the genesis of concepts, of thoughts, and he does not investigate the relations appearing in the intercourse of men either. These questions, as expressly gnoseological and sociological issues, he either regards as given or he abstracts them from the problem of meaning. If Schaff examined the complex problem of meaning really by the above-mentioned formal-logical methods, the criticism would be justified: the danger of logicism would be looming. But Schaff makes a very refined analysis to find the way towards the understanding of meaning, and he is convinced that a comprehension of the chain of correlations of sign, meaning and concept can be attempted only by relying upon linguistics, gnoseology, psychology, logic and sociology alike.[5]

Schaff's definition of meaning was endorsed by G. Klaus in his article co-authored by W. Segeth,[6] and in their independent works.[7] Both of them sought to grasp the essence of the meaning of the linguistic sign by analyzing the network of relationships of the sign situation. The elements of the network of relationships of the sign situation are the following: (1) the objects of mental reflection *(die Objekte der gedanklichen Widerspiegelung)*, (2) the linguistic signs *(die sprachlichen Zeichen)*, (3) the mental images *(die gedanklichen Abbilder)*, (4) men who create, use and understand the signs.[8] If the linguistic sign can exist as such only according to its place in the network of relationships of the real sign situation, then the meaning of the sign can also be only a reflection of this network of relationships, i.e. a "coexistence" of relationships, which precisely corresponds to the meaning conception of Schaff, who took meaning and concept to be a complex of relationships of different levels: "This product of abstrac-

[5] Schaff, loc. cit., p. 617 .
[6] G. Klaus, W. Segeth, Semiotik und materialistische Abbildtheorie, DZfPh 1962, pp. 1245—60.
[7] W. Segeth, *Semiotik und Erkenntnistheorie*, Berlin, 1963, pp. 39—41; G. Klaus, *Die Macht des Wortes*, Berlin, 1964, p. 13.
[8] DZfPh 1962, p. 1248.

tion [meaning and concept] is, at one or another level, always a complex system of social relationships which are realized by means of the human consciousness."[9]

In plain words: "Meanings are . . . determined relations between men."[10]

5. MEANING AS A RELATIONSHIP OR NETWORK OF RELATIONSHIPS

The conception of meaning as a relationship is not of recent date. Since E. Marti[1] and O. Dittrich[2] we have often encountered in literature certain ideas according to which the essence of meaning lies in the relationship between the name and the sense thereto attached.

L. Weisgerber rejects the views which conceive of meaning as a psychical entity and opposes them by his own "correlative or functional idea" (Beziehungs- oder Funktionsbegriff): ". . . the word is a unit of speech with two substantial components, the phonetic form and the content, which are not, as it were, associatively assigned to each other but constitute rather an inseparable union which is the essential characteristic of the word."[3] From this his own definition of meaning follows of necessity; meaning cannot be a union of phonetic form and content created by psychical association, but "either a function or a relationship which acts upon the content from the phonetic form".[4] He held the discovery of the correlation between phonetic form and

---

[9] "Dieses Erzeugnis der Abstraktion [Bedeutung und Begriff] ist auf dem einen oder dem anderen Niveau immer ein kompliziertes System gesellschaftlicher Verhältnisse, die sich mittels des menschlichen Bewußtseins verwirklichen." Schaff, loc. cit., p. 722.

[10] "Die Wortbedeutungen sind . . . bestimmte Beziehungen zwischen Menschen." Loc. cit., p. 713.

[1] E. Marti, Psychologische Untersuchungen zur Bedeutungslehre, Leipzig, 1901.

[2] O. Dittrich, Die Probleme der Sprachpsychologie, Leipzig, 1913.

[3] ". . . das Wort sei eine Spracheinheit mit zwei wesenhaften Bestandteilen, der Lautform und dem Inhalt, die einander nicht etwa assoziativ zugeordnet seien, sondern vielmehr eine untrennbare Verbindung darstellen, die das wesentliche Merkmal des Wortes ausmache." L. Weisgerber, Die Bedeutungslehre — ein Irrweg der Sprachwissenschaft? Germ. Rom. Monatschrift XV, pp. 161—83; loc. cit., p. 181.

[4] ". . . eine Funktion, oder Beziehung, die von der Lautform zum Inhalt wirksam sei." Ibid.

content (the meaning), the explanation of this special kind of relation *(eine Beziehung eigener Art)*, to be the foundation of semasiology.[5]

Also Gy. Laziczius, following in the footsteps of Weisgerber, defined meaning as a correlative idea: the mutual relation of the signifier *(das Bedeutende: le signifiant)* and the signified *(das Bedeutete: le signifié)*.[6] Under Weisgerber's influence Laziczius saw in the indissoluble unity of the outside and the inside of the word the interrelation of signifier and signified, taking it for the most elementary feature of the facts of language, and stated accordingly: "Strictly speaking, the word has thus no meaning: the meaning is in the word and is a function of the phonetic form."[7] If the word has no meaning, if this "is in the word", then it is pointless to speak of semantics apart from lexicology; this is why he, like Weisgerber, called semantics a "pseudo-science" *(Pseudowissenschaft)*.[8]

The relationship theory advanced by Weisgerber and Laziczius did not, and in this way, on the basis of a simple relation, could not even solve the problem of meaning, nevertheless it meant considerable progress compared to mechanical psychological associationism. Its major theoretical weakness was its just mentioned simplicity, the correlation of phonetic form and content, which was formulated on the basis of linguistic hypostasis and torn out of other interconnections, and which could — and really did — lead to the conception of immutable meaning, since this theory was unfit to explain the phenomena of either homonymy or synonymy, let alone the semantic changes.

What Schaff deserved credit for is just that he regarded meaning as a function of the natural sign situation and as a determined social relation[9] comprising a whole network or system of relationships. In the case of the sign situation this is a network of relationships that was built up as a result of man's socio-historical activity, which serves to reflect objective reality in the

[5] L. Weisgerber, *Muttersprache und Geistesbildung*, Göttingen, 1929, pp. 34, 178 ff.
[6] Gy. Laziczius, *Általános nyelvészet* [General Linguistics], Budapest, 1942, p. 56.
[7] Op. cit., p. 57.
[8] Op. cit., p. 55.
[9] "... eine bestimmte gesellschaftliche Beziehung." Schaff: DZfPh 1961, p. 614.

thinking of men, to communicate for some purpose the body of knowledge about reality.

The elements of this network of historical, psychological, gnoseological and pragmatical relationships are:

(a) the relation between men wishing and able to make themselves understood to one another;

(b) the relation between man and reality;

(c) the relation between man and sign;

(d) the relation between sign and reality;

(e) the interrelation of the elements of the system of signs.[10]

From the network of relationships of the real sign situation Schaff deduces the meaning of the linguistic sign and takes this meaning also to be a network of relationships. Meaning, therefore, is a relation:

(a) between sign and sign;

(b) between sign and object;

(c) between the sign and the notions about the object;

(d) between the sign and human activity;

(e) between men who make themselves understood to one another by means of signs.[11]

The network of relationships may be formalized as follows:

$$
\begin{aligned}
&\text{(a) } R_1 \ (S\,,S); \\
&\text{(b) } R_2 \ (S\,,O); \\
&\text{(c) } R_3 \ (S\,,T); \\
&\text{(d) } R_4 \ (S\,,M); \\
&\text{(e) } R_5 \ (M\,,M).^{12}
\end{aligned}
$$

According to the above schema: *meaning* $= R_1 + R_2 + R_3 + R_4 + R_5$, i.e. *the sum of the elements of the network of relationships*.

The determining element of this network of relationships is the relation between men, the conscious cognitive and full communicative intention, the cognitive-communicative process itself.

If we want to confront the elements of the above network of relationships (structure) with the semantic aspects applied in our days, we obtain the following schema:

[10] Schaff, *Einführung in die Semantik*, Berlin, 1966, p. 237.

[11] Op. cit., pp. 202—3; cf. also DZfPh 1961, p. 614.

[12] R = relation, S = (linguistic) sign, O = objective reality, T = thought (mental reflection of objective reality), M = man (human activity).

(a) R_1 (S, S) = syntactical meaning;
(b) R_2 (S, O) = denotative or lexicological meaning;
(c) R_3 (S, T) = designative meaning;
(d) R_4 (S, M) = pragmatical meaning;

(e) R_5 (M, M) = *the basically determining element of the network of relationships.*

Some theories of meaning take also the relation between man and reality $[R\ (M, O)]$ to be a constitutive element of the semantic structure. In my judgment this is unnecessary or rather wrong for the following reasons:

(a) from the point of view of meaning taken in the narrower sense, from that of the *meaning of the linguistic sign* $(R_1 + R_2 + R_3 + R_4)$, the relevant element is R_2 (S, O), which reflects the relation between *sign* and *reality*; reality as *reflected reality* is namely included also in R_3 (S, T);

(b) the relation between *man* and *reality* is the *foundation*, the *starting point*, of the real sign situation; so it must not be reduced to *one of the elements* of the semantic structure.

Scientific analysis may make it necessary—as is often the case—to remove from this context certain elements of the network of relationships and to examine them "in isolation" with a view to attaining exact partial results. Also this "isolated" examination should not for a moment ignore that it has to do with separate parts of a coherent network, their real value being determined by their place and function in that system, and the results of the partial examinations have always to be co-ordinated with the conception of the whole, because meaning is nothing else than the dynamic sum of the elements of the network of relationships.[13]

Let us remove, say, R_2 from this network of relationships and examine what is the relation of the linguistic sign to the segment of reality which it "indicates". It is not by chance that I use here the word "indicate" instead of "image", for I wish to demonstrate here the result of a removal test which absolutizes R_2 (S, O), i.e. which takes it to be one of the—by definition "lin-

---

[13] I use the attribute "dynamic" in the sense that it expresses, on the one hand, the interdependence of the particular elements of the network of relationships and their ensuing value and, on the other hand, the need that we may interpret the meaning of some sign (sign combination) only by relying simultaneously on all elements of the network of relationships.

guistic"—aspects of the network of relationships.[14] Absolutization means also that we examine R_2 in itself, totally abstracted from the "effect" of the other elements of the network of relationships.

Let us examine the linguistic sign (sign combination) *földjük* (*föld + jük*) 'their land'.[15]

On the strength of the "removed" formula R_2 (S, O) it can be stated that there is no "organic" connection between *földjük* and what it denotes, the actual plot of land + the possessive relation of the third person plural; their connection is entirely arbitrary, which is demonstrated also by the fact that the same part of objective reality in other languages is indicated by totally different sound combinations *(ihr Acker, их земля,* etc.). If the connection between the signifier *(földjük)* and its denotatum (their actual plot of land) is only conventional, it can be imagined forthwith that in the Hungarian language area we should indicate the denotatum at issue by a different sound combination. It is only a matter of convention! Conclusion: language is a conventionally established game (Wittgenstein, Carnap, Hempel), an optional linking of forms to reality. If to this post-Saussurean standpoint, which is practically rooted in Plato's ideology but is formulated a little sharply, we add a random quotation from Marx, who, when interpreting the concept of *value* in opposition to the fetishization of the market relations, stated that "The name of a thing is something distinct from the qualities of that thing",[16] we may as well say that that conclusion is a Marxist formula. It may be needless to stress specially that random quotations, by their nature, either do not verify anything or can be used to verify any kind of view. In the above terms Marx stood up against the nominalist distortion of *commodity* and *value,* and it took no special intellectual acrobatics to make it a theoretical basis for the semantic philosophical school by turning the thought inside out with the excesses of conventionalism, saying:

[14] The other is of course R_1 (S, S), as follows automatically from the systemistic conception of language.

[15] I have chosen deliberately this Hungarian example, mainly because of the suffix *-jük* involved. This latter has a wide range of possible functional loads as well as of semantic possibilities, and these are realized as a function of the context. Also the context determines which of the equivalent (synonymous) alternants (*-uk, -ük, -juk, -jük*) can be added to a given stem morpheme and which not. The suffix *-jük* is therefore a good example to show the contextual sensitivity of the meaning, too [R_1 (S, S)]. See its discussion in more detail later.

[16] K. Marx, *Capital,* New York, 1967, I, p. 100.

the qualities of a thing are external to the name of that thing, and we at once find ourselves spell-bound by *name-magic* and *word-tyranny*. All we need is to "deliver" the linguistic sign of the limitations of the network of relationships, and by the aid of "the conventionally established game which is changeable at will" we can "prove" with the greatest ease that the cause of all evils of human society (class society) is that we do not use the words correctly and that, as a result, incorrect notions and concepts become implanted in the minds of men; that groups of men opposed to one another and their implacable struggle are non-existent in reality; but that such concepts still exist is the result of the fact that nowadays we talk much about *classes, class struggle, imperialism,* etc.

That is how far we get if we disregard the socially determined relations between men, the whole of the complicated network of relationships of the reality-reflecting processes necessitated by men's practical (cognitive and reality-transforming) activity and look for an explanation in a single element of that network. This metaphysics is good to explain anything, i.e. nothing. Weird similarities can be uncovered between the above speculation and the one-sidedness of "meaning = rule of application": if the world of the denotata does not correspond to the imaginary meaning of the sign, so much the worse for the denotata!

The meaning of *földjük* cannot be explained by this method. Namely, the arbitrary nature of R_2 (S, O) is strongly limited and made illusive by a number of other factors, the rest of the elements of the network of relationships. R_5 (M, M) reflects a determined social interrelation of men wishing to make themselves understood and to act upon one another, who since the moment of their birth have always been in contact with their life-giving environment, with objective reality, and who want to know and transform that reality in the interest of their own humanistic objectives. The body of knowledge about reality is stored in the minds of men as a result of the mental reflection of reality, of verbal thinking [R_4 (S, M)]; it constitutes real, useful knowledge if its linguistic expressions truly reflect objective reality [R_2 (S, O)], and if, by means of signs making up a finite system [R_1 (S, S)], the infinite number of objects and processes of reality can be "depicted" for the human mind, and the intellectual, emotional result of this depiction can also be communicated.

Hence the conceptually reflected unity of the correlation 'man—sign—reality' provides the key for the understanding of the meaning of *földjük*. Conceptual reflection is the turning point where the impulses emanating from material reality become "dematerialized" in the consciousness. In communication we are faced with the contrary: the "dematerialized" contents of consciousness can be communicated, transmitted by means of material signs. On the basis of the real sign situation, therefore, we have an objective reality, the actual plot of land, possession of this land (O) by a number of persons, a condition which is reflected (T) correctly in man's (M) consciousness by the aid of the sign (S), and this correctly reflected content of consciousness can in the same way be transferred to the consciousness of another man to produce there the notion 'land + possession' without the sign-receiver's getting into direct touch with this objective fact.

If we view R_1 (S, S) in this correlation, we can define also the meaning of the morpheme -jük of földjük, which indicates at the same time the relative freedom of the elements of the network of relationships. The meaning of the morpheme -jük as a bound morpheme cannot be defined independently of the context. It reflects different relations in the case of ver-jük 'we beat [him]'[17] and in that of föld-jük. In the latter it is an expression of the possessive relation. It expresses ownership in plural and possession in singular. It indicates also that ownership is in the third person plural. The plural character of the morpheme -jük of földjük is the only connection with the element -jük of the word verjük.[18] We can thus establish a certain measure of semantic isomorphism between the two elements. Their distinctive semantic marks are that -jük reflects third person in földjük and first person in verjük. Indicative of the relative freedom of R_1 (S, S) is that we applied just the last one of the alternants -uk, -ük, -juk, -jük having the same meaning, instead of examples like ház-uk 'their house', méz-ük 'their honey', kút-juk 'their well', kert-jük 'their garden'. The selection from equivalent alternants is determined by phonetic laws. It should be frankly admitted, however, that we cannot explain by synchronic methods why the morpheme -jük (-juk) can express relations of both first and third persons plural. This faculty has historical and systemic causes.

By keeping the entire network of relationships in view, let us remove again R_2 (S, O), also now with reference to földjük, and

---

[17] What is more, if we conceive it as a compound morpheme, it also has two meanings: (a) ver + jük (imperative mood: 'let us beat [him]') and (b) ver + jük (indicative mood: 'we beat [him]').
[18] See footnote 17.

let us examine in this context the signification of Schaff's formula "meaning = concept", which in our example can be reformulated this way: the meaning of the word *földjük* is the concept 'their land' (actual land + ownership in the third person plural). If we apply this formula in the light of the network of relationships under discussion, we can state that we have to do here with two aspects of one and the same thing, an approach to two types, essentially with R_2 (S, O) and its converse $[R_2 (O, S)]$. Therefore R_2 (O, S), the relation of mental reflection and sign, expresses that the mental images are the meanings of the linguistic signs; and its converse, R_2 (S, O), expresses that the linguistic signs are "forms of existence of the mental images".[19] Depending on the side from which we approach the question, we arrive at two names of the same thing. If we examine the relation between the mental image and the sign, we obtain the meaning of the sign, and if we approach the mental image from the side of the linguistic sign, the analysis of their relations leads us to the concept.

In this respect a new light is shed upon Schaff's thesis together with the assessment of the debate which was provoked by this formula also among Marxist interpreters of meaning.[20]

This complex conception of meaning protects us against the danger of the objective idealism of conceptual realism, that of the subjective idealism of nominalism, and that of sign fetishism alike; it provides the relation between sign and reality with a theoretical basis on which both synonymy and polysemy as well as the semantic changes can be explained, and it promotes the solution of the seemingly irreconcilable contradictions of autonomous meaning $\sim$ contextual meaning and, last but not least, to the understanding of the dialectics of affective and intellectual communication.

[19] "Existenzform gedanklicher Abbilder". G. Klaus, W. Segeth: DZfPh 1963, p. 1251.

[20] Ю. Д. Апресян, Современные методы изучения значений и некоторые проблемы структурной лингвистики [Modern Methods to Investigate Meanings and Some Problems of Structural Linguistics], *Проблемы структурной лингвистики*, Moscow, 1963, pp. 102—50; K. Ammer, G. F. Meier, Bedeutung und Struktur. *Zeichen und System der Sprache*, Berlin, 1966, p. 5—27.

6. MEANING AS A COMPLICATED STRUCTURE

The realization and recognition of the complex nature of meaning appear in nearly all earlier works dealing with semantics in an exacting manner. Depending on which element of the complicated network of relationships of meaning actualized in the real sign situation they realized and found determining, the various authors conceived someway the meaning as a function of the sign in the form of different triangles. We have to recall only the diagrams produced by K. Bühler, C. K. Ogden and G. A. Richards. They illustrate clearly the interdependence of the correlation of the thing (objective reality), the content (the mental reflection of objective reality) and the form (the linguistic sign), of the expressive, representative and invitational functions of the sign.

In G. Stern's semantic triangle[1], in some of its factors, we can already see, besides the Aristotelian conception, also the emotional factor of meaning:

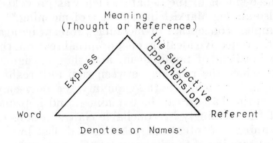

Reliance on the emotional factor is a progressive element in Stern's conception of meaning, but it is a flaw of the theory that it neglects the contextual sensitivity of meaning. Surely Stern refers to the context, but he fails to analyze it, because in his opinion the word standing by itself (lexical unit) has, even outside the context, all shades of meaning it can "assume" in the context; that is why he analyzes only the meaning of semantemes artificially isolated from the concatenation of elements, from the system of elements (e.g., the semantic field).

---

[1] G. Stern, *Meaning and Change of Meaning*, Bloomington, 1931, p. 37.

This method of analyzing can be found also in a number of recent works, some of which use even the word 'structure', that is they realize the interdependence of the semantic elements.[2] New features are encountered mainly in Ullmann's work. The dominant element in his theory is the relation of the name to the meaning, he thus rejects the views interpreting meaning as concept.

A common characteristic of these explanations of sign — meaning is that they miss the determinant factor of the real sign situation, the interrelation of the men who create the sign situation for a definite purpose and take part in the process of communication.

From the viewpoint of this type of more complex interpretation of meaning an important place is held by the definition of meaning given by A. Martinkó in a lecture delivered in 1954, according to which meaning is an "immensely complicated structure in its relation to the thing signified, the form, the speaker, the hearer and to lots of other phenomena".[3] His schema representing his conception of meaning is C. K. Ogden's and J. A. Richards' semantic triangle completed with sign-using man.

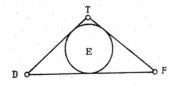

D = dolog 'thing'
F = forma 'form'
T = tartalom 'content'
E = ember 'man (men)'[4]

[2] K. Baldinger, *Die Semasiologie: Versuch eines Überblicks*, Berlin, 1957; H. Kronasser, *Handbuch der Semasiologie*, Heidelberg, 1952; S. Ullmann, *The Principles of Semantics*, New York, 1952; А. И. Смирницкий, Значение слова [Word Meaning], ВЯ 1955/2, pp. 79—89; etc.
[3] Hozzászólás Balázs J.: "A stílus kérdései" c. ref.-hoz [Contribution to a report by J. Balázs on "Questions of Style"]. *Általános nyelvészet, stilisztika, nyelvjárástörténet: A III. Országos Nyelvészkongresszus előadásai* [General Linguistics, Stylistics, History of Dialects: Lectures at the Third National Congress of Hungarian Linguists], Budapest, 1956, pp. 197—219; loc. cit., p. 199.
[4] Loc. cit., p. 198.

His semantic theory is built on the analysis of the sign relations. In the illustration of sign relations he rejects the linear conception of sign—meaning: "The meeting point of sign relations . . . is much more an area than a point, and this is important chiefly for the interpretation of meaning."[5] The meaning of linguistic signs and sign combinations is, in his view, composed not only of lexical, grammatical semantic elements, but an integral part of it is also man's opinion on the denoted object, the concept, etc., the emotional content of consciousness associated with them: "The words and . . . terms, grammatical forms are not only vehicles of definite lexical or grammatical meanings, but they express also the speaker's relation to the particular objects and concepts."[6]

If we "translate" Martinkó's terminology into the technical terms in use today,[7] the network of relationships of the elements of the semantic structure appears as follows:

(a) the relation between the sign and objective reality, reference to things: *denotative meaning*;[8]

(b) the relation between the sign and "content", the content marks of the meaning: *significative meaning*;[9]

(c) the relation of the sign to other signs: *syntactical or structural meaning*.[10]

The significance of Martinkó's theory is only enhanced by the fact that its differentiated and partly still valid formulation preceded the Hungarian attempts at structural linguistic explanation, the antisemantic assaults and the incorrectly adapted foreign interpretations based mainly on logical semantics. A further development of the conception of meaning making critical use of the positive elements of part researches could have spared the Hungarian literature on semantics the notorious detours and theoretical mistakes.

An interesting experiment of the past decade refers to the modernization of traditional semasiology built on Saussurean principles, to the elaboration of a semantic theory sensitive to the linguistic sequence (the system of signs). The reference to contextual sensitivity means recognition of the existence and

---

[5] Ibid.
[6] Loc. cit., p. 206.
[7] See their explication below.
[8] Loc. cit., p. 207.
[9] Loc. cit., p. 211.
[10] Loc. cit., p. 210.

influence of syntactical and lexical factors on which depends the actualization of the (lexical) meaning of the given word.

The possible meanings resulting from the polysemantic nature of the Russian adjective *глухой* are actualized, by its attributive function fulfilled in different structures, in the following manner:

(a) *быть глухим к чему-л* 'to turn a deaf ear to something', 'to be indifferent to something' (cf. *deaf as a post, deaf nut*, etc.);

(b) *глухой звук* 'voiceless sound';

(c) *глухая ночь* 'still night';

(d) *глухая пора* 'quiet period' (cf. *quiet street, quiet market*);

(e) the interaction of *deaf* and *blind* gave rise to *глухое окно* 'blind window';

(f) *глухой голос* 'muffled sound', *глухой шум* 'dull noise';

(g) *глухой лес* 'dense forest'; *глухая тайга* 'overgrown taiga' (cf. *dense darkness, dense ignorance*);

(h) *глухой слух* 'vague rumour';

(i) *глухой овёс* 'wild oats'.

From the polysemous variety it can be inferred at least that the meaning 'dense' is being actualized in structures combined with the elements *forest* and *taiga*, and the meaning 'indifferent' in those with elements signifying man or human activity.

For the word *осёл* ('jackass') to actualize the meaning 'fool' *(дурак)* it is necessary in general that it should have a predicative function: *Ну и осёл же ты!* 'What a fool you are'.[11]

The actualization of the meaning 'to make court' of the verb *бегать* 'to run' requires the preposition *за* going with the instrumental case: *он бегал за ней* 'he made court to her'.[12]

Traditional semantical research in general disregarded the usefulness of these rather well-known facts. A systematic study of the lexical and syntactical sensitivity of meaning was started a relatively short time ago.[13]

---

[11] In Hungarian the connotation 'fool' of the word *szamár* 'jackass' can be actualized as an attribute included in the most different structures and as derivatives and even compounds of the word: *szamár kölyök* 'silly kid', *szamárság* 'foolishness', *szamárfül* 'dog's ear', etc.

[12] The English equivalent is partly identical: 'he ran after her', 'he dangled round her', 'he went with her', etc.

[13] В. В. Виноградов, Основные типы лексических значений слова [The Main Types of Lexical Word Meanings], ВЯ 1953/5, pp. 3—29; J. Firth, The Technique of Semantics. *Papers in Linguistics 1934—1951*, London, 1957; Ю. Д. Апресян, Современные методы изучения значений и некоторые проблемы структурной лингвистики [Modern Methods to Investigate Meanings and Some Problems of Structural Linguistics]. *Проблемы структурной лингвистики*, Moscow, 1963.

On the basis of the principle of contextual sensitivity V. A. Zvegintsev analyzed systematically the semantic complexes of linguistic signs in this sense. The lexical meaning of the word is, in his view, determinable by the objective and the linguistic sequence (language system). Among the factors at issue, contextual sensitivity can be ascertained, or effectively analyzed, according to the so-called "linguistic" factor. In Zvegintsev's conception the lexical meaning can be illustrated by the schema[14] indicating the following network of relationships:

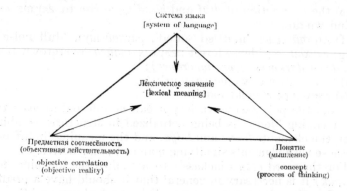

Система языка
[system of language]

Лексическое значение
[lexical meaning]

Предметная соотнесённость
(объективная действительность)

objective correlation
(objective reality)

Понятие
(мышление)

concept
(process of thinking)

Apresian gives a rather negative appraisal of Zvegintsev's conception and methods of research.[15] If, however, we take into consideration the complex character of Zvegintsev's conception of meaning, his views on the network of relationships of the semantic factors, thus also the importance of the contextual factor (its place in the schema is at the apex of the triangle), and consequently its impact upon the lexical meaning, we have to appreciate Zvegintsev's results. His work mentioned above shows the profile of a researcher who "bows" to the partial results of earlier investigations in order to make critical use of all their progressive elements.

Some representatives of modern semiotic, at least in words, treat rather badly the results of what is called traditional semantical research, they do not wish to rely upon their critical application. They accept only those findings of earlier research which

[14] В. А. Звегинцев, *Семасиология*, Moscow, 1957, p. 146.
[15] Apresian, loc. cit., p. 104.

regard meaning as a correlation of various elements, as a special network of relationships. Apresian has this to say: "In modern semiotics the meaning of the linguistic form is identified neither with the concept, nor with the object, nor with any other notion, but is investigated as a correlation."[16]

Apresian's semantic theory, viewed from the aspect of theoretical and methodological considerations, is of a strictly contextual character and examines the meaning of the elements on the basis of their place in the syntagmatic sequence of the elements. At a conference which the Institute of Scientific Information of the Academy of Sciences of the Soviet Union held in 1961 on the subject of information processing, machine translation and automatic text-reading, A. K. Zholkovsky in a lecture, for reasons of principle and translation technique, adopted a position which "requires . . . renunciation of the interpretation of the word as the smallest unit of meaning".[17]

This rigid contextualism is a revival of views encountered also earlier in literature on semantics. According to the view advanced by H. Reichenbach in his work issued in 1947, and by W. Quine in his writing published in 1953, there can be no question of any special meaning of the elements, only the whole utterance has meaning.[18] I think it is not worth wasting time by criticizing the rigid one-sidedness which denies even the relativity of autonomous meaning. The preciseness of scientific terms (which are also elements of utterance) and of a good number of other expressions is eloquent proof to refute the views which recognize the contextual meaning alone. We can of course agree that modern semantic analysis pays special attention to the function of usage, of the semantic unit included in the context, to the meaning of the whole sentence, which basically influences the meanings of the constitutive elements, i.e. promotes the actualization of the various possible meanings.[19]

---

[16] "В современной семиотике значение лингвистической формы не отождествляется ни с понятием, ни с предметом, ни с какой-либо другой сущностью, но рассматривается как отношение." Loc. cit., p. 105.

[17] Quoted from: A szemantikai analízis szabályairól [On the Rules of Semantic Analysis]. Manuscript, p. 2. The article, entitled in Russian "О правилах семантического анализа", was published in the volume of papers *Машинный перевод и прикладная лингвистика* (8th inst.), Moscow, 1964, pp. 17—32.

[18] H. Reichenbach, *Elements of Symbolic Logic*, New York, 1947; W. Quine, *The Problem of Meaning in Linguistics*, Cambridge, 1953.

[19] N. N. Leontyeva, Y. S. Martemianov, E. Benveniste, J. Firth, R. Robins, and others.

We can only approve the endeavour of structuralist research to grasp the meaning of a given speech unit on the basis of the place it occupies in the system of elements. This method of research reckons largely with the determining function of the semantic field, which points at the same time to the degree of semantic affinity of the lexical elements.

Towards the end of the 1950's O. S. Vinogradova, A. R. Luria and N. A. Eisler conducted a series of experiments, on a psychophysiological basis, to discover the structure of the semantic field. The tests, during which the vascular reactions of the experimentees were measured in different situations, proved enlightening.

The first phase of the tests was intended to develop conditioned reflexes upon a stimulating key-word of the semantic field, notably the word *скрипка* 'violin'. An electric current of slight intensity accompanied the appearance of the word. After a brief interval there followed other words *(стена* 'wall', *карандаш* 'pencil', *улица* 'street', etc.), without the accompaniment of electric current. Further on, after a few repetitions of the act, the experimentees developed a conditioned reflex upon the word *скрипка* even if the appearance of the word was not accompanied by electric current. Upon the appearance of the words *стена, карандаш,* etc. which were neutral with regard to the word *скрипка,* of course, no conditioned reflex was developed.

In the second phase the words *смычок* 'violin-bow', *струна* 'string' and *скрипач* 'violinist' appeared but no electric current came with them, and the experimenters found that they produced weaker reaction in the subjects of the experiments. Still weaker reaction was found to come upon the pronouncement of the words *контрабас* 'contrabass', *виолончель* 'violoncello', *музыка* 'music', *оркестр* 'orchestra', etc. Invariably no reaction at all was produced by the appearance of the words *стена, карандаш,* etc. The intensity of vascular reaction thus reflected the semantic affinity of the words.

The third phase of the experiments already drew an outline of the structure of the semantic field: In the centre of the semantic field of *скрипка* were taking place the words *смычок, струна, скрипач,* and the words *виолончель, контрабас, музыка, оркестр* were gradually approaching the peripheral zone of the semantic field The neutral words *(стена, карандаш,* etc.), on the other hand, fell outside the semantic field of the word *скрипка.*[20]

[20] О. С. Виноградова, А. Р. Лурия, Объективное исследование смысловых связей [An Objective Study of Semantic Relations]. *Тезисы кон-*

The strong point and the result of the experiments was the discovery of the semantic field by exact methods. Other semantic fields can be fixed in the same way. The significance of this fact is enhanced by the circumstance that each particular element can usually belong simultaneously to several semantic fields, and the relevant examinations promise to throw light from many sides upon the meaning of the linguistic element.

Modern literature on semantic knows of other field theories as well, which discuss primarily questions of syntactic character, more precisely they examine the possibilities of combining words in syntagms, clarifying at the same time the interdependence, the semantic interaction of the syntagmatic elements. The question is, in plain terms, what words can stand together by what criteria; on what semantic conditions they can form syntagms, syntagmatic series. It is on the basis of this theory that F. Kiefer and L. Dezső in Hungarian literature seek to come closer to a definition of the semantic field.

Kiefer, for example, is investigating which of the Hungarian words *ruha* 'dress', *eszik* 'he eats', *dolgozik* 'he works', etc., further *piros* 'red', *kék* 'blue', etc., *kenyeret* 'bread' (acc.), *húst* 'meat' (acc.), *főzelékét* 'vegetables' (acc.), as well as *gyorsan* 'fast' (adv.), *lassan* 'slowly', *kényelmesen* 'comfortably', etc. can form syntagms and which not, and he states that a syntagmatic unit can be formed by *ruha* with *piros*, etc., by *eszik* with *kenyeret*, etc., by *dolgozik* with *gyorsan*, etc. In other words: *piros*, etc. belong to the semantic field of *ruha; kenyeret*, etc., to that of *eszik; gyorsan*, etc. to that of *dolgozik*. According to him, the semantic field is the sum of all those words which can form (also semantically correct) syntagms with a given word. Formalized: *(X, y)*, where X is the semantic field of (the generator) y.[21]

The semantic correctness of the syntagms is decided by the principle of compatibility; thus the reason why the word combination *kenyeret piros* cannot be considered a (semantically correct) syntagm is that the words *kenyeret* and *piros* are incompatible.

ференции по машинному переводу [Theses of the Conference on Machine Translation], Moscow, 1958; О. С. Виноградова, Н. А. Эислер, Выявление систем словесных связей при регистрации сосудистых реакций [Demonstration of Systems of Word Connections as Registered by Vascular Reactions]. ВПсих № 2; cf. also Apresian, loc. cit., pp. 130—1.

[21] ÁNyT IV, p. 115.

Dezső also defines the concept of the semantic field by the principle of compatibility, but through a different approach. In examining the possible associations of words, the fusion of nouns and adjectives into a syntagmatic unit, he divides all adjectives, by appropriate semantic criteria, into different groups, and he investigates whether or not the particular adjectives classed in one and the same group can associate with a given noun in a given relation. He attaches semantic labels to the words classed in the different groups: [+ Colour] to adjectives like *piros* 'red', *zöld* 'green', *fehér* 'white', etc., [+ Form] to others like *szögletes* 'angular', *kerek* 'round', *ovális* 'oval', etc., [+ Size] to *nagy* 'big', *kicsi* 'small', *apró* 'tiny', etc., and finally [+ Qualification] to *jó* 'good', *rossz* 'bad', *vacak* 'shoddy', etc. He does the same to nouns, which he classes under the semantic labels [+ Concrete] or [+ Abstract], [+ Living] or [+ Non-living], etc., etc. If we take a look at the possible associations between the above adjectives and a noun bearing the semantic labels [+ Concrete] and [+ Object], say, *alma* 'apple', we can establish the following syntagmatic possibilities: *piros alma* 'red apple', *zöld alma* 'green apple', *fehér alma* 'white apple', but two or more of the adjectives of the same group cannot simultaneously associate with the noun *alma* : there is no such thing as *piros, zöld alma* 'red, green apple', or *piros, zöld, fehér alma* 'red, green, white apple'; in the same way there can be *nagy alma* 'big apple', *kicsi alma* 'small apple', *apró alma* 'tiny apple', but there cannot be *nagy, kicsi alma* 'big, small apple', etc., etc. Every member of the group of N_n nouns bearing the semantic label [+ Object] can thus associate with adjectives belonging to the group having the semantic labels [+ Colour], [+ Form], [+ Size], [+ Qualification], but simultaneously only with one of the adjectives classed in the very same group. What Dezső calls the semantic field is these *"adjective groups that are mutually exclusive"* from the point of view of simultaneous association.[22]

The train of thought is clear and unambiguous and easy to follow, but the field theory based on the conclusion drawn from it is inappropriate, or at least we have to do with an inaccurate definition. The above examples show that it is not the "adjective groups" that are mutually exclusive from the point of view of simultaneous association, but the particular elements of the adjective groups bearing the same semantic label. For if the adjective groups with different semantic labels were in general

[22] Loc. cit., p. 45.

mutually exclusive, then—to abide by our example—the noun *alma* could associate only with the adjectives *piros, zöld*, etc. or only with *ovális, kerek*, etc., but it is by no means so.

Dezső views in the same manner also the case when two or more simple sentences are combined to make a cumulative predicate: this can include only one from the groups having the same semantic label. The simple sentences *Az alma piros* 'The apple is red', *Az alma kerek* 'The apple is round', *Az alma nagy* 'The apple is big', *Az alma jó* 'The apple is good' can be reduced, from the point of view of semantic compatibility, to the following sentence with a cumulative predicate: *Az alma piros, kerek, nagy és jó* 'The apple is red, round, big and good'; but the sentence *Az alma nagy és kicsi* 'The apple is big and small' is nonsensical.[23]

Although both field theories are built upon the principle of compatibility, Kiefer's view seems to be more to the point because it demonstrates better the semantic connection of words and expressions, placing greater stress upon the mutual semantic attraction or repulsion of words.

From the point of view of the analysis of the possible syntagmatic constructions the essential is namely not that, from among the group of words (adjectives) distinguished at the level of specific difference within the *genus proximum*, only one can simultaneously associate with a given noun, i.e. that the adjectives distinguished at the level of specific difference from the point of view of simultaneous association are mutually exclusive, but the question is, what word can or cannot form a (semantically correct) syntagm with what other word. That the words *'white'* and *'black'*, or *'big'* and *'small'*, cannot simultaneously be predicates to a given noun is easy to see without any special semantic investigation, merely on the basis of their contradictory character. A much more exciting semantical problem is posed, however, by the examination of why a dress can be yellow *('yellow dress')* and why love cannot *('yellow love')*, etc., etc. It is true that beside *'yellow dress', 'dead man'*, and *'bitter taste'* we have *'yellow trade unions', 'dead line', 'bitter end'*, etc., but these are hard to explain by either Kiefer's or Dezső's semantic field theory, at least neither of them covers the semantic explanation of structures of this kind. The point is not that the compatibility of syntagmatic elements of this sort could not be demonstrated by the addition of diverse—possibly singular—semantic labels,

[23] Ibid.

but this method would make it difficult to have a good grasp of the formal apparatus, and it would say nothing new about the essence of the semantic connection of syntagms of this character, or it would tell only so much that—differently from what is usual—there are also such connections, i.e. the elements of these associations are also compatible on the basis of singular criteria.

If it is true that the strong point of the field theory devised by O. S. Vinogradova, A. R. Luria and N. A. Eisler is that it uses exact methods to point to the semantic affinity of the lexical elements, or more precisely it promises to throw light on their meaning from many sides, then—*mutatis mutandis*—this can rightly be expected also from the theory represented by Kiefer and Dezső. It would seem indisputable, in fact, that the study of the possible syntagmatic constructions of words from the semantic aspect might enrich our knowledge of semantics with numerous results without which our conception of the essence of meaning would be more defective. What is required, however, is a more exact definition of the concepts and criteria to cover a wider scope of elements, the elaboration and consistent application of appropriate methods.

Every semantic field has its own specific semantic property (seme). The meaning of element can accordingly be conceived also as the sum or aggregate, the structure, of the elementary meanings (semes, semantic components, semantic multipliers).[24] The "semantic multipliers" (elementary concept) are the semantical distinctive marks of words.[25] If we want to split a word into its semantic components, i.e. to write it down by semantic multipliers, then we break up the content level of the word—practically by "direct components"—into syntagms. As to meaning, the word *cause* is identical with the syntagm *what produces,* while the word *effect* with the syntagm *what is produced.*[26] The expression *he cannot control himself* is composed of the following semantic multipliers: (a) the concept of *negation (he cannot do something, something cannot happen*; cf. the concept of *affirmation: he can do something,* in our example: *he can master himself)*; (b) the *reflexive* nature of the action compared to its *transitive* alternant *(he controls himself* vs. *he masters another person or the gathering difficulties).*[27]

[24] Apresian, loc. cit., p. 105—6.
[25] Loc. cit., p. 122.
[26] Zholkovsky, loc. cit., p. 3.
[27] Apresian, loc. cit., p. 122—3.

Zholkovsky formalizes the situation arisen when writing down the words *cause* and *effect* with the aid of semantic multipliers by the following symbols: "A→B". In this form the meaning of the word *cause* is represented by the syntagm composed of the first two signs ("A→"), that of the word *effect* by the syntagm composed of the second and third signs ("→B"), and that of the word *produce* by the second sign ("→").[28]

If therefore we break up the meaning of a word into its semantic multipliers, we have to analyze quite a mass of real situations.[29]

Apresian's and Zholkovsky's explanation taken at random from the motley of structuralist theories of meaning unequivocally reveals the conviction that meaning is a complex thing, a complicated structure. In Apresian's view a successful analysis of this complicated object (meaning) needs an adequate breakdown. He himself distinguishes the following sorts of the correlation of sign and meaning:

(a) *structural meaning*: the relation of signs to other signs, syntactical meaning or value, distinctive meaning or simply meaning;[30]

(b) *significative meaning*: the relation of the sign to the signified. This is the same as Saussure's *signifié*, Morris's *significans*, Carnap's *intentionale*, Frege's and Church's *sense*, Quine's *meaning*, and the *designatum* (the content of concept) in the traditional sense;[31]

---

[28] Loc. cit., p. 4.

[29] Apresian, just as well as Zholkovsky, regards the method of semantic multipliers as one of the perspective methods of structural semantic analysis. In use in modern analysis is also the method of the so-called *thesauri*, the groundwork of which was laid by P. M. Roget's dictionary of ideas (named Thesaurus by the author). The dictionary classified the words of the English language into 6 major classes, 24 categories and 1,000 sections. Each section is a typical semantic idea expressible by different words. Cf. L. M. Masternan, Fictitious Sentences in Languages. *Essays on and in Machine Translation by the Cambridge Language Research Unit*, Cambridge, Engl., 1959; R. N. Needham, A. Parker-Rhodes, *The Question of Lattice Theory;* Apresian, loc. cit., p. 124.

I do not intend to give here a detailed analysis of the system of thesauri, because we can regard it as a renewal of an old-established method (thematic dictionaries). Compared to the old attempts, it provides practically nothing new, unless we take its terminological innovations as such. But the literature on semantics of the second half of the twentieth century has made the reader rather familiar with such things.

[30] Apresian, loc. cit., p. 106; cf. Schaff, Klaus: R (S , S); see above.

[31] Ibid.; cf. Klaus: R (S , T).

(c) *denotative meaning*: the relation of the signs to the denotata, which is identical with Frege's *meaning*, Quine's *reference*, Carnap's *extentionale* or the traditional *denotatum* (extent of the concept).[32]

Apresian thus distinguishes the above three sorts of meaning, leaving entirely out of account whether meaning is the linguistic reaction (R) of an external stimulus (S) or the reverse of it, that is a linguistic stimulus, which produces "some extralinguistic" reaction. Hence these three sorts of meaning are not dependent on whether the sign in the succession 'stimulus—reaction' (S→r→s→R; cf. Bloomfield, *Language*) occupies the place of *r* or that of *s*. If we pay regard also to the place occupied by the sign in the above succession, however, we come to see other aspects of meaning:

(a) We can speak of *situative meaning* if we conceive of the language sign as a reaction produced by the denotatum. This practically corresponds to the *denotative meaning* mentioned under paragraph (c) in the former classification. Apresian says that the two can indeed be taken as one;[33]

(b) on the other hand, there is *pragmatical meaning* when the functions are interchanged, i.e. when the "extralinguistic" reaction *(behaviour)* is provoked by the linguistic sign as a stimulus. We can include here also the evaluative (valency: syntactical meaning) and the emotive-expressive constitutive elements of meaning, too.[34]

We can of course imagine different kinds of semantic analysis and semantic types, as such exist indeed.[35] Beside the incontestably existing terminological variety, other systematizations as a rule also agree in that they deal in more or less detail with the above aspects of the correlation of sign and meaning, stressing now one now the other; this, by the nature of things, brings with it a great variety of methods (analysis by components, substitutional and transformational methods, psycho-physiological methods, the methods of mathematical logic and logical semantics, statistical methods, etc.).

[32] Ibid.; cf. Schaff, Klaus: R (S , O).
[33] Ibid.
[34] Ibid.
[35] Ch. Osgood, T. Sebeok, *Psycholinguistics*, Baltimore, 1954; И. А. Мельчук, К вопросу о грамматическом в языке-посреднике [On the Question of the Grammatical in the Intermediary Language], МППЛ 1960/4; U. Weinreich, On the Semantic Structure of Language. *Universals of Language*, Cambridge, Mass., 1963; A. J. Greimas, op. cit.

If in the summary of Apresian's theory we examine a little more closely the concepts of structural semantic analysis and its rather heterogeneous terminology, we can state anyway that we find in them nearly all concepts of so-called traditional semantics, only the terms have changed. No matter by what formulation the representatives of the new school dissociate themselves, the totality of their theory, from traditional semantics, we can see behind their terminology nearly all elements of the more exact results of past researches—of course, in an appropriate re-arrangement (see above).

If we are familiar with the dialectics of scientific cognition, there is here nothing to be surprised at. The way the new in the development of science negates and replaces the old is not that each and every representative of the rising school makes a clean slate and starts from scratch, disregarding the partial results of preceding periods and striving for something "completely new" on the basis of obstinate metaphysics. Modern semiotic has of course a good number of militant metaphysician representatives, who conceive every system of signs, including that of linguistic signs, as a system of only formal relationships, and unbendingly fight against the recognition of any so-called extralinguistic factor alien to the system of hypothetical formal relationships. This, however, puts Marxist linguistic researchers under no obligation, more precisely it stimulates them to point up the defects of that linguistic view, and focus their attention on the complex nature of the socially determined complicated system of signs and on the formulation of appropriate research methods.

The proponents of this outlook on language have to be aware that they are "accused" of dealing with problems which are described by some as "extralinguistic" factors, to destroy phantoms that have been acting for several decades and, last but not least, to rectify a number of theoretical distortions.

7. THE IMPORTANCE OF THE PRAGMATIC ASPECT OF MEANING

If we examine closely how different periods and theoretical schools evaluated the pragmatic aspect of meaning, we can draw enlightening conclusions with regard to the import of the problem pointed out in the above title. It is a commonly known Marxian formula that theory (which, after all, manifests itself in form of linguistic signs, sign combinations, sign sequences), as soon as it has gripped the masses, becomes a material force. As concerns the power of words, already the "enlighteners", the ideological harbingers of the bourgeois society replacing the feudal system, thought that it might become a means of "general popular enlightenment" conducive to fundamental social transformations. This stand of the ideologists of enlightenment sprang from the absolutization of the social function and significance of language, of the linguistic sign, but this does not detract from the true value of the (exaggerated) rational kernel: "... the effect of words is a real power."[1] The rightness of this Marxist doctrine is clearly proved by the historic events and successes of the struggles of the labour movement in the past century.

But the right theoretical principles can be explained in a great number of ways and can be used to support a variety of "truths". This is clearly exemplified by the rather variegated interpretation of the pragmatic aspect of the word, of meaning, with the obvious class interests hidden in the background. It may be needless to explicate that this phrasing is not a revival of the wrong formula according to which language is of class character and belongs in the superstructure. The classification of language as having a class and superstructure character is entirely different from what is recognition of the thesis that the meaning of the linguistic sign reflects specific social conditions, intentions, motives and endeavours which materialize in the "peculiar" polysemy of the particular words and expressions.

Let us think about the real content of the words *equality, fraternity, liberty* in the classical dreams of the era of bourgeois enlightenment, about the "actualized" meaning of these words. The most brilliant "definition" of actualized bourgeois *equality* is given in A. France's formula written with scathing satire (equal right to sleep under the bridge). *Fraternity* in bourgeois society was actualized in the form of *class struggles* provoked by unrestrained *liberty* of exploitation by the bourgeoisie in power.

Does this mean that the respectable slogans of the propagandists of enlightenment came to nothing? No, not at all. The essence of what is actualized of the true meaning of words depends wholly on which is the class from the position of whose interests we look at the materialization of the slogans proclaimed.

[1] "... die Wirkung von Wörtern ist eine reale Macht." G. Klaus, *Die Macht des Wortes*, p. 42.

The real content or "meaning" of formal *equality* is the enormous inequality inherent in the property relations and embodied legally in the Napoleonic Code: what was a *right* for the bourgeois became an *obligation* for the worker. The history of the *class struggles* growing into ever larger dimensions after the victory of classical bourgeois revolution speaks for itself, *liberty* in turn meant a brutal dictatorship of capital. It was a matter of viewpoint only.

After the epoch-making victory of the Great French Revolution even the word *revolution* became a respectable term and was bearing an appropriate historic stamp as long as it helped the bourgeoisie to achieve power, to wield and strengthen it. As soon as it "became a material force" aiming to destroy the power positions of the bourgeois society, it lost its respectability and was degraded to "*Bolshevik revolt*". The "vocabulary" of the progressive forces of the world adopted the "*Bolshevik revolt*" under the term *Great October Socialist Revolution*, which signified the beginning of the real history of mankind and encouraged people either to imitate the Bolshevik example (material force) or to entertain illusions of a "*revolution of quality*", depending entirely on whose consciousness reflected, and how, the possibility of a fundamental transformation of the social conditions [R (M,T)]. The successes of the building-up of socialist society have again lent a "lofty ring" to the meaning of *revolution* as well as of *socialism*. So much so that from the second quarter of the twentieth century onwards no worthwhile political movement could discard them from its "trade dictionary", not even if in the light of the given political aspirations the true meaning of the words was turned inside out. We must not forget that the movement that created the most savage type of fascist dictatorship bore the name of *national socialism*, which had as much to do with socialism as the Hungarian *counter-revolution* of 1956 did with *revolution* (the system of "*revolutionary committees*" was an abuse of the power of the word).

Those who, in the actualization of the semantic potentialities of words and expressions, fail to take account of the reflection of the complicated social conditions put the equality sign between all kinds of manifestation of dictatorship, between the content marks of the *European Common Market* and the *Council for Mutual Economic Aid*, the *Central Treaty Organization* (CENTO) or the *North Atlantic Treaty Organization* (NATO) or the *South East Asia Treaty Organization* (SEATO) and the *Warsaw Treaty*, between *cosmopolitism* and *proletarian inter-*

nationalism (they fall victims to the "fig-leaf words"); they cannot understand the dialectics of *international struggle for peace* and *colonial liberation struggle*, true *patriotism* and workers' *internationalism*.

I am fully aware that by stressing the pragmatic aspect of meaning I come into conflict with the opinion of those who hold that this sort of meaning is no meaning at all because such investigation covers primarily the external effect of the linguistic sign, i.e. it is not of a pre-eminently linguistic nature. In 1966 A. J. Greimas, for example, when analyzing the process of communication, disregarded the intention of the speaker *(l'intentionalité du locuteur)* not only in order to clear himself of the charge of the often mentioned crime of mentalism and pragmatism, but he simply did not take it as being at the level of the analysis of an "exchange of messages", because it "is situated at the level of the emission of messages and not of their reception or transmission".[2]

If, however, we determine one of the basic functions of the linguistic sign, by its role in social communication, as a relation between sign-giver and receiver [R (M,M)], notably so that the sign-giver uses the linguistic sign in order to impart to the receiver identical or at least similar thoughts, emotions, "behaviour", etc., we have to class this kind of meaning among linguistic studies because it is an organic part of the process of communication [sign-giver (communicator)→sign (communication realized by the aid of meaning)→sign-receiver (together with his reaction)]. It is a different matter that the components and aspects of the language sign are studied also by other branches of science (general semantics, psychology, psycholinguistics, ethnolinguistics, pragmatics, etc.); this fact just shows that, in order to uncover and explain the essence of the linguistic sign, close cooperation between the related sciences, a mediatizing synthesis of their results, is an indispensable necessity.

The negation of the pragmatic aspect of meaning results from the non-realization of one of the principal functions of the linguistic sign (complete communication) and is just as serious a theoretical mistake as it is to conceive of this aspect as the only determining factor, which is a characteristic of linguistic and

---

[2] ". . . se situe au niveau de l'émission des messages et non de leur réception ou de leur transmission". A. J. Greimas, *Sémantique structurale: Recherche de méthode*, Paris, 1966, p. 69.

philosophical *pragmatism*. "The fault of pragmatism . . . lies in its having absolutized the social function and significance of language", wrote Klaus.[3] The basis of social coexistence is namely not language but social production. Language is only an instrument, however important an instrument, of social coexistence. If language is not a basis of social coexistence, then the meaning of the linguistic sign also cannot be identified with the effects of action, with definite habits of action, as Ch. S. Peirce opined.[4]

The significance of the pragmatic aspect of meaning follows from the recognition of the real sign-situation, a consequence that is kept distinctly apart from pragmatism, this widespread subjective-idealist current of today's bourgeois philosophy and a virulent type of neopositivism.

The manifold and many-shaded trends of neopositivism (analytical philosophy, linguistic philosophy, logical semantics, logical positivism, logical empiricism, pragmatism, behaviourism, etc., etc.) have one characteristic in common: they deny the possibility of knowing objective reality through theoretical means, they deny the existence of the mental reflection of reality, and representatives of some trends go even so far as to claim that a theoretical verification of the existence of reality is downright impossible (logical empiricism). Their antignoseological position leads directly to the negation of the objective nature of reality. Their notion of truth appears as a function of practical utility, as a category that is most suited to man's various manifestations of life and fits in well with the totality of human experience (pragmatism).

In their view "traditional" philosophy with all its categories has lost its justification and has sunk to the level of "ontological speculations". The only task of "modern" philosophy is to analyze language by a method (analytical philosophy, linguistic philosophy, logical empiricism) free of any ideological "contamination" (Wittgenstein's motive: my language is my world). They regard the problems of traditional philosophy as pseudo-

---

[3] "Der Fehler des Pragmatismus besteht . . . darin, daß er die gesellschaftliche Funktion und Bedeutung der Sprache verabsolutisierte." Klaus, op. cit., p. 25.
[4] "Bedeutung ist nichts mehr als die Wirkungen im Handeln, als bestimmte Handlungsgewohnheiten." Quoted by A. Schaff, *Einführung in die Semantik*, Berlin, 1966, p. 222.

problems arising from the incomprehension of the real nature of language and from its destructive effect upon human thought. From this there follows necessarily the honourable task of "genuine" philosophy: to recognize those difficulties which result from the incorrect use of linguistic terms, for the solution of the problems thus recognized is the only key to the understanding of the essence of social problems and to their solution. Accordingly linguistic philosophy — and also linguistics, of course — has to fulfil primarily a therapeutic function: to cure language of its morbid aberrations and thereby to eliminate the "social diseases". The only task of philosophy and linguistics is therefore to diagnose properly the linguistic diseases and to work out an appropriate linguistic therapy.[5]

Pragmatism, analytical philosophy and also linguistic philosophy — although each has concentrated, instead of artificial language models, on the analysis of natural, everyday language — by their peculiar analysis have blocked the road before the very discovery of the essence of language, since they have given up analyzing the gnoseological problems of language (the relation between language and thought, the connection of language and the cognitive processes in the course of the development of the patterns of thinking, the origin of linguistic forms, the relation between linguistic form and the content elements to be expressed and communicated, etc.) and have confined scientific investigation to the description of different forms of linguistic expressions.

Renunciation of the examination of the relation between linguistic elements and the mental reflection of reality has resulted in a simplification of the characteristic features of language, in the absolutization of the conventional nature of language. Accordingly language is a conventional construction and not a product of the mental projection of objective reality, "a kind of mystical, self-sufficient force",[6] which acts upon man, who then reacts, "behaves", in some way or other (behaviourism).[7]

[5] This latter has nothing in common with the known trends of purism, it is a peculiar sort of therapy which is intended to achieve no less than the solution of all social problems (!).

[6] Cf. the entry "Lingvisztikai filozófia" in M. Rozenthal, P. Yudin, *Filozófiai kislexikon* [Concise Encyclopedia of Philosophy], Budapest, 1964.

[7] "One of the most widely spread doctrines of modern bourgeois psychology. Its philosophical basis is *pragmatism* . . . Behaviourism is the

From the pell-mell of the trends of modern bourgeois philosophy I have picked those which, in one way or another, are concerned with language. Not the last point of view of my selection
was the fact that some of them provided a theoretical motive for
certain — mainly American — schools of modern linguistic analysis. We might consider it natural that the theoretical, ideological
motive should have served as a basis for the most heterogeneous
linguistic schools, because — and this cannot be stressed too
often — neopositivism was the inspirer of the most different and
contradictory philosophical trends from which every researcher
could gather what best suited his educational background and
theoretical conception. By this extremely concise sketch I may
have succeeded in demonstrating what the recognition of the
pragmatic aspect of meaning has to do with these "antiphilo-
sophical" tendencies of philosophy, and in showing also the concreteness of the philosophical background and motive of certain
linguistic trends "free of philosophical speculations".[8]

One thing is certain: The rise of the different descriptivist
schools — whether or not some of them recognizes the pragmatic
component of the meaning of the linguistic sign — was promoted
by the predominance of very definitely formulated "pragmatic"
(political) viewpoints. J. Lotz said in his lecture at the 1966 International Philological Congress in Debrecen that the American
authorities fostered the different descriptive schools neglecting
the basic problems of linguistic theory ("war language program")

---

continuation of the mechanistic line of psychology, in so far as it reduces
the psychical phenomena to organismic reactions, identifies consciousness
with behaviour and regards the correlation of stimulus and reaction as
the basic unit of behaviour. Behaviourism traces cognition back to the
development of the conditioned reactions of organisms (including man)."
See the entry "Behaviourism", op. cit.

[8] I wish to put on record at once that it is not the so-called American
structuralism that my above remarks are intended to value. Such an
intention is far from me, and this for two reasons. First, we cannot speak
about American structuralism in general, just because of the excessive
heterogeneity of the schools covered by the generic term structuralism.
Second, in this place I have not examined these schools on the evidence
of their identical and different features, so I could not venture in good
conscience to evaluate them in general. My purpose in this place has been
to point up what ideological conclusions can be (and have been) drawn
from the gross exaggeration of a very important element of the meaning
of the language sign, the pragmatic aspect of meaning, and conversely,
what general ideological views serve to feed the behaviourist linguistic
outlook.

in order to create, by a formal comparison of languages belonging to different linguistic families, a "theory" for the "cram courses" in foreign languages which would make it possible in the shortest possible time to prepare the leading cadres of the armed forces for administrative and political work among the populations speaking different languages in the areas to be occupied during the Second World War.[9] I know full well that in this place we are faced with a special interpretation of the pragmatic aspect of language, but this interpretation is also an unmistakable proof that the leading circles of the United States realized "the power of the word", which was clear also from the well-known fact that the German fascist propaganda machine already before the war had scored tremendous success among the masses, and this success at the same time served also as a "theoretical background" (pragmatism) for that action of military policy.

8. AN IMPORTANT ASPECT OF SEMANTIC CHANGE

All the foregoing shows clearly that concept has a distinct part to play in the development of a semantic theory free of major errors of principle. Consequently Schaff had every reason to revive this "old view", to examine the genesis of meaning and concept — and also their most typical features — from the angle of Marxist gnoseology, and thus to dissociate himself both from the objective idealism of conceptual realism and from the sign fetishism of semantical philosophy. The starting point of Schaff's analysis and the main prop of his conclusions is the materialist reflection theory in which meaning becomes the central category of social communication because in the generalizing reflection of reality it fulfils the same function as the concept, more precisely both are products of a unitary and indissoluble process (cognition, communication).[1]

[9] J. Lotz, A magyar nyelv története és rendszere [History and System of the Hungarian Language]. *Lectures at the International Philological Congress in Debrecen*, Budapest, 1967, pp. 32—3.
[1] "... unter Begriff verstehen wir dasselbe Erzeugnis der verallgemeinernden Widerspiegelung der Wirklichkeit, das unter dem Aspekt der Verständigung von Mensch zu Mensch den Namen 'Bedeutung' trägt ... wir betrachten sie [Begriff, Bedeutung] als Namen verschiedener Aspekte derselben Erkenntnisbeziehung." A. Schaff, Die Bedeutung der Bedeutung, DZfPh 1961, pp. 610—22, 708—24; loc. cit., p. 717. Furthermore: "Hingegen steht es außerhalb jeglicher Diskussion ... daß der Denkvorgang als Erkenntnisvorgang nicht nur mit Hilfe sprachlicher Mittel — der Wortzeichen —, sondern in organischer Einheit mit den Sprachvor-

It is not by chance that this view was endorsed by Klaus in his paper co-authored by Segeth and in other writings of his.[2]

If we accept the Schaff–Klaus formula, we do so in the same sense that we treat meaning and concept alike as products of abstraction actualized by the help of word-signs in the cognitive process. The concept as a form of social reflection[3] and the linguistic sign—together with its meaning—as a form of existence of the concept can serve human cognition only if they have objective content, which cannot be anything else than the subjective, mental image of objectively given essential features of a part of reality.[4]

The deeper human (social) cognition penetrates the "mysteries" of the immense material world, the more precisely will the concepts (meanings) reflect the essence of this constant motion, this constant change, and the more firmly and effectively will conscious human cognition (action) put reflected reality to use in the interest of its own humanistic objectives. This basic tenet of Marxist gnoseology at the same time refers also to the dynamic character of the conception of notion of Marxist inspiration, providing the key for the discovery of the essential features of semantic developments, semantic changes.

Our acceptance of Schaff's thesis about the genetic identity of concept and meaning does not mean, however, that we can speak

---

gängen erfolgt ... eine außerhalb der Sprache stattfindende Erkenntnis — gehört zur außerwissenschaftlichen Mythologie." Loc. cit., pp. 715—6; cf. also Schaff, *Einführung in die Semantik*, Berlin, 1966.

[2] "Die Frage, warum man für ein und dasselbe zwei verschiedene Bezeichnungen—'Begriff' und 'Bedeutung eines Wortes'—verwendet, wird u. E. hinreichend mit dem Hinweis darauf beantwortet, daß hier zwar ein und dasselbe, aber in verschiedenen Beziehungen betrachtet wird—einerseits in seiner Beziehung zum sprachlichen Zeichen, anderseits in seiner Beziehung zum Objekt der Widerspiegelung. Die Relation R (A,Z) [= mental image and sign] besagt also, daß gedankliche Abbilder die Bedeutung sprachlicher Zeichen sind. Ihre Konverse R (Z,A) besagt, daß sprachliche Zeichen die Existenzform gedanklicher Abbilder sind." G. Klaus, W. Segeth, Semiotik und materialistische Abbildtheorie, DZfPh 1962, pp. 1245—60; loc. cit., p. 1251. Furthermore: "Unter der Bedeutung eines Satzes im engeren Sinne versteht man also die Aussage als Widerspiegelung eines Sachverhaltes." G. Klaus, *Moderne Logik: Abriß der formalen Logik*, Berlin, 1964, p. 40. The sentence is therefore the form of existence of an utterance ("Existenzform einer Aussage"). Ibid.; cf. also G. Klaus, *Semiotik und Erkenntnistheorie*, Berlin, 1963.

[3] Klaus, *Moderne Logik ...*, p. 166.

[4] Cf. footnote 123 in Chapter III, Section 1.

of a total functional identity of the two categories, too. A cardinal point of genetic identity is the identity of the reality-reflecting function which is actualized in the process of social cognition.

The genetic monism of language and thought, however, cannot be interpreted as the identity of language and thought. Schaff also refers to this in one place.[5] In the same way, the organic unity of the cognitive and the communicative process, the causal interdependence of the two processes, cannot blur the functional difference that can be seen between them. Namely language is a means not only of the cognitive process but also of the "work of organization" directed at identical evaluation and even joint action. In this sense it helps to make the total content of consciousness intersubjective, i.e. it is an instrument not only of the communication of subjective statements and judgments but also of the transmission of will, appeal and command. Only in possession of such an instrument can active man not only get to know the reality surrounding him but also to act upon it, transform and "re-create" it to suit his own social interests.[6]

Schaff is certainly right when he contests the existence of "sterile" concepts free of evaluative, emotive, etc. "infections". Such concepts could actually be "born" only in electronic brains, where the "total content of consciousness" would be made only by the interdependence and dynamic interaction of "purely intellectual concepts". All this being recognized, it would seem still indisputable enough that in complete communication based on the meaning of the linguistic sign (and destined to influence man's behaviour and social actions) the factors of conscious influence and transmission of will come more to the fore, and

[5] ". . . it is wrong to interpret the *monism* of language and thought in terms of the *identity* of language and thought." A. Schaff, Nyelv és gondolkodás [Language and Thought], *Magyar Filozófiai Szemle*, 1964, pp. 718—51; loc. cit., p. 739.

[6] "The consciousness of man not only reflects but also creates the objective world." Lenin, *Philosophical Notebooks*, p. 202. — "Speech makes it possible for us to co-ordinate not directly the actions but the psychical phenomena which control and produce them; namely: the co-ordination of actions is realized through the co-ordination of the psychical phenomena controlling the actions . . . This may be the origin of the most fundamental prerequisite of human co-operation—the common goal." L. Kardos, *Általános pszichológia* [General Psychology], Budapest, 1964, p. 156. — "The domain of language is much vaster than that of logic. Namely there is no logical thought that would not appear in linguistic form, but all that appears in linguistic form is not logical." G. Klaus, *Bevezetés a formális logikába* [Introduction to Formal Logic], Budapest, 1963, p. 12.

just this *voluntative* plus is what characterizes the meaning of the linguistic sign, this existence form of the concept burdened with emotive, etc. nuances. Besides the verbal communication of the indicative character of the judgment, it is necessary for the sentence (the existence form of the judgment) to comprise—and it indeed can comprise—the imperative plus which is characteristic of the meaning of the sentence as opposed to the judgment.

Gnoseologically, Schaff's formula does not say more—and this is not an unimportant point—than that no autonomous concept exists outside of meaning, that the process of thought as one of cognition is realized not only by linguistic means but in organic union with the linguistic processes.

The significance of Schaff's formula lies in the fact that it explains the meaning of the linguistic sign as an integral part of man's socio-historical activity which is aimed at the cognition and transformation of reality. In this context meaning is a function of the natural sign situation and as such expresses a determined social relation, comprising a whole network or system of relationships.[7] Also Schaff's formula 'meaning = concept' is valid only in the fullness of the above context.

If we speak of the genetic identity of concept and meaning, then the course of concept-formation, but also the essence of the concept, is outlined on the basis of the natural sign situation. In this sense the concept is the converse $[R_3 \ (T,S)]$ of the designative meaning $[R_3 \ (S,T)]$, a determining element of the semantic structure created in the natural sign situation, it is a relation which says that the mental image of the part of reality, the concept, is identical with the meaning of the linguistic sign. Deduction of the genesis of concept from the real sign situation lends the concept its most essential, its determining feature as well, according to which the component parts of the concept, its distinctive marks, ultimately[8] correspond to the marks of the part of reality, and thus the concept is "a mental summation and reflection of the essential marks of the object".[9]

[7] Cf. the details expounded in Chapter III, Section 5.

[8] The word "ultimately" here means that the products of fantasy (*Pegasus, centaur, heaven,* etc.) are results of a relatively autonomous motion of the conceptual marks or, more precisely, peculiar combinations of the conceptual marks reflecting the marks of the part of reality, thus ultimately distorted reflections of reality.

[9] B. Fogarasi, *Logika* [Logic], Budapest, 1958[4], p. 146.

Deducing the concept from the real sign situation is not undue meticulousness, especially not a linguistic operationalist game, but a clear stand adopted on the central problem of the relation between concept and existence [R (T,O)], which indicates also the role played by this relation in the formation of the semantic structure as well as the value of that relation.

The foregoing helps to bring out and connect the substantial marks of the concept, to give its definition: *"Concept is the highest product of matter, of the human brain, a basic form of thought expressed* [actualized!] *in acoustic language, a form that mentally reflects specified parts and correlations of objective reality by bringing out and connecting (analysis and synthesis), by means of generalization, the common elements of the objective external world, the objects and the interrelations existing between them."*[10]

If the processes of thought are in essence linguistic processes, if the basic unit of thought is judgment, that of judgment is the concept, and the form of existence of the concept is the linguistic sign, then it is not surprising at all that a certain measure of isomorphism can be discovered between the structure of the linguistic sign and that of the concept. Both are products of the mental reflection of objective reality, manifesting themselves in the organic unity of language and thought.[11] The correctness or dialectical interrelatedness of the constitutive elements, the distinctive marks, of the concept is ensured by their inclusion in the network of relationships of the semantic structure.

The constant motion and change of reality, of real relations, and the ever widening and deepening mental reflection of these determining marks of reality bring with them a constant motion of the elements of the semantic structure, the upsetting of the relative equilibrium of relationships, a rearrangement in their order of value, and this underlies also the constant motion, the rearrangement and revaluation of the conceptual marks, the obsolescence of some and the emergence of others, the change and obsolescence of concepts and the emergence of new concepts. This is the organic connection between conceptual change and semantic change, in this sense we can talk of a certain measure

---

[10] Fogarasi, op. cit., p. 140.

[11] "Die dialektische Einheit von Sprache und Denken äußert sich z. B. in dem . . . Zusammenhang darin, daß zwischen den Strukturen von Aussage und Satz eine gewisse Übereinstimmung besteht, wobei die Struktur der Aussage wiederum mehr oder weniger einer Struktur in der objektiven Realität entspricht." G. Klaus, *Moderne Logik . . .*, p. 38.

of isomorphism between conceptual change and semantic change.

Hence the objective content of the parallelism between conceptual change and semantic change is provided by the dynamic pattern of motion of the network of relationships of the semantic structure, on its basis every kind of semantic change can be explained in an exact manner, but also the contrastive unity of the extent and content of the concept[12] is qualified as dialectic in the light of the interdependence and interaction of the conceptual marks.

Let us illustrate the relation between the extent and the content of the concept and the correlations of the corresponding semantic aspect $[R_3\ (S,T)]$ with the following examples:

Simple concepts

In the conceptual system *geometrical figure — plane figure — quadrangle — square* the simple concept which is the smallest as to its extent among all members of the system is the richest as to its content (the totality of the marks interconnected in a certain order). For example, the extent of *square* covers *rectangle, rhombus, rhomboid,* etc. alike on the basis of common conceptual marks (quadrangularity, quadrilaterality). On the other hand, the proper conceptual marks of *square* are the following:

(a) equiangularity;
(b) quadrilaterality;
(c) equilaterality.

The content of the concept *square* is accordingly: $(a) + (b) + (c)$.

If even one of these marks is missing, there can be no *square*. Namely the possible combinations of the set (a) to (c) are:

(1): $(a) + (b) + (c) = $ *square*
(2): $(a) + (b) - (c) = $ *rectangle*
(3): $(b) + (c) - (a) = $ *rhombus*
(4): $(b) - (c) - (a) = $ *rhomboid*
                      trapezium
                      trapezoid

} *quadrilaterals*

(5): $(a) + (c) - (b) = $ *equilateral triangle* } with regard to equilaterality and equiangularity.

[12] See the relevant parts of footnote 81 in Chapter III, Section 1.

The motion of the conceptual marks of simple concepts results therefore in no change of concept, but the differently arranged set of the conceptual marks covers a different concept. Accordingly in such cases there cannot be question of semantic change either.

The case is different with *complex concepts*.

Let us examine, by the Leninist definition of *class* (as a category of political economics),[13] the motion of the conceptual marks of the concept *working class* placed at the third level of this set:

society
class
working class
miner,

i.e. let us investigate the change of concept and meaning of the term *working class*.

The concept *working class* has a narrower extent than *class* and a broader extent than *miner*. With regard to content, the case is the contrary: it comprises a larger number of qualities and relations than *class* and a smaller one than *miner*.

The narrower concepts thus comprise the marks of a broader concept of the conceptual system and some additional mark. From the broader concept we can therefore derive the narrower concept by adding that further conceptual mark which distinguishes it from another concept located at the given derivational level: *class→working class→capitalist class*. Diagrammatically:

class

working class ↔ *capitalist class*

---

[13] "Classes are large groups of people differing from each other by the place they occupy in a historically determined system of social production, by their relation (in most cases fixed and formulated in law) to the means of production, by their role in the social organization of labour, and, consequently, by the dimensions of the share of social wealth of which they dispose and the mode of acquiring it. Classes are groups of people one of which can appropriate the labour of another owing to the different places they occupy in a definite system of social economy." Lenin, *Collected Works*, Moscow, 1961, Vol. 29, p. 421. The second sentence of the definition contains the fundamental characteristic.

In determining the conceptual marks of *working class*, therefore, we have to proceed from the conceptual marks of *class*. On the basis of the aforementioned definition the conceptual marks of *class* are as follows:

(a) a large group of people which

(b) is characteristic of the given stage (the age of class societies) of the development of society (thus it is a historical category);

(c) society in the age of class societies is splitting into basic classes according as it is, or is not, owner of the means of production (economic dependence, possibility of exploitation); this is the basic criterion, a conceptual mark;

(d) each class is a function of a certain historically determined mode of production; an antagonistic mode of production brings about antagonistic classes *(slave-holder↔slave; feudal lord↔serf; capitalist↔proletarian)*; one is a ruling class, the other is a subject class;

(e) in the social organization of labour the *ruling class* controls (directly or indirectly) production, conducts (directly or indirectly) the public affairs, asserts the privilege of most kinds of intellectual labour, while the subject majority is assigned to toilsome, hard manual labour, has no voice in the control of production and the conduct of public affairs, and is mostly barred from intellectual occupations;

(f) the *capitalist* takes away the greater part of the proceeds in form of *profit*, while the *proletarian* as *hired worker* receives a slight portion of the proceeds in form of *wages*, which hardly covers the value of his labour.

Accordingly, the conceptual marks of *working class* in capitalist society are:

(1) a historical category, a product of the capitalist social system in the age of class societies;

(2) for lack of ownership of the means of production (it disposes of its own labour only) it is economically dependent on the bourgeoisie, which thus can exploit it;

(3) its relation to the bourgeoisie is characterized by fundamental antagonisms;

(4) in the social organization of labour it performs toilsome manual labour, has no voice in the control of production and the conduct of public affairs;

(5) as a mass of hired workers, it is compelled to sell its labour to the bourgeoisie and receives in exchange only an approximate value of its labour.

The *concept of working class* (in capitalist society) is: (1) + + (2) + (3) + (4) + (5).

The *concept of working class* is inseparable from that of *bourgeoisie*, and thus the *class structure* of the capitalist system is determined by a union of the bourgeoisie and the proletariat "resting" on fundamental antagonisms.

Included in the *meaning of working class* are, besides the set of the conceptual marks listed above, also all emotive and evaluative elements of positive or negative character (class consciousness, class solidarity, organization of the class struggle, preparations for the revolutionary struggle to eliminate class society, implacable hatred of all forms of oppression, etc.). This is the emotive, evaluative, sociological, pragmatic plus which distinguishes the meaning of the given term from the given concept. All this of course depends on which is the class from whose viewpoint we examine and evaluate the meaning in question. To those excluded from the tenure of power the term *working class* "means" the depositary of the struggle waged for a better future of mankind; to those who are in power and stubbornly defend it, on the other hand, it means an insubordinate mass organizing and advocating the overthrow of "law and order". In this sense (from the viewpoint of the pragmatic aspect of meaning) we cannot even speak of a uniform meaning.

With a change in the *relations of production* [the relations taking shape among people in the course of the production, exchange and distribution of material goods: R (M,M)] which basically determine the essence of classes, with the exclusion of the possibility of exploitation, the *class structure* of the social system also changes, and consequently the conceptual marks of the *working class* are radically transvaluated, but even its meaning is essentially changed.

(1') At the same time as it eliminates the exploiting classes, the *working class* does not suppress itself; what is more, after the victory of the socialist revolution its role will grow temporarily (until the total disappearance of all differences between classes, between urban and rural life, between manual and intellectual labour, etc.). Consequently, the *working class* as a product of the capitalist social system does not cease to exist upon the liquidation of capitalism.

(2') With the socialization of private property the working class ceases to be exploited; what is more, as the leading class of the new social system, it becomes owner of the instruments of production.

(3') With the development of the new social system, with the elimination of the bourgeoisie, the union of the bourgeoisie and the proletariat based on fundamental antagonisms ceases to exist, and the relation of the working class to the other principal class of the new system, the *peasantry*, is characterized by friendship and alliance based on a community of interests.

(4') The working class assumes a leading role in the social organization of labour, in the planning of production, in the conduct of public affairs, and becomes the depositary of the struggle for the success of the cultural revolution.

(5') Individual members of the working class cease to be hired workers, they partake of the goods produced according to the quantity and quality of the work done; the value of their labour input is recovered, indirectly, in full.

(6) As the determinant class of the state of the new social order, of proletarian dictatorship, by realizing socialist democracy at a growing pace, the working class organizes and leads the entire population in the struggle for the consolidation and defence of the new system, for the complete construction of a socialist society. (A new conceptual mark arising from the tenure of power.)

The *concept of working class* (in socialist society) is: (1') + (2') + (3') + (4') + (5') + (6), which means that the essential marks of the concept have changed, their number has increased by one, i.e. in the socialist system of society we have to do with an entirely new concept of *working class*.

Consequently the semantic aspects of the word, according to the new relation between people [R' (M' , M')] and, according to the new relation between people and the changed reality [R' (M' , M')], appears as follows:

$$R_1 \ (S , S')$$
$$R_2 \ (S , O')$$
$$R_3 \ (S , T')$$
$$R_4 \ (S , M').$$

The *new meaning* of the term is then: $R_1 + R_2 + R_3 + R_4$, which means that the old phonetic form of the term is the same, but its meaning has radically changed.

The analysis presented above has been intended to demonstrate the dynamism of the marks of a very complicated political concept, the process and the character of the restructuring of the whole concept, and consequently to discover the productive causes of the semantic change of the existence form (linguistic sign) of the concept. In a similar manner, it is possible to explain, very approximatively, also the dynamism of the conceptual marks of simpler concepts, the semantic change of linguistic signs less complicated from the point of view of the semantic structure. It being considered an important task of semantics to uncover the regularities of semantic changes, I may not be far from the truth if I venture to say that the correlations of concept and meaning have a distinguished role to play in the aggregate of these regular interrelations.

9. CONCLUSIONS

What I have so far expounded in connection with the general problems of sign and meaning permits me to make my conclusions and state the following:

(a) I have no intention to add an "entirely new" sign and meaning theory (or even a definition) to the immense number of existing theories and definitions. By a critical introduction of the most typical representatives (typical from the viewpoint of a certain conception) of the theories and schools engaged in the study of the linguistic sign and its meaning I have wished "only" to examine to what an extent they have based their theories, and consequently their definition, on the complex nature of the network of relationships of sign and meaning, and what theoretical mistakes have resulted from that kind of method which recognized as determining only one or another factor of this complicated structure.

(b) The second purpose of my critical survey has been to follow the way of formation, and mainly the development, of the concepts of both the sign and the meaning, keeping a watchful eye on the dynamic connection of the successive currents, to see how much the new theories and schools relied on earlier results or on what ground they rejected them. This I have held necessary first of all in the sketchy introduction of some of the so-called structuralist trends, because nearly all representatives of the several schools are generally unanimous in flatly denying the rightness of the procedure of the traditional explanations of meaning and thus also the usability of their partial results.[1] Even a general evaluation of these modern trends, mainly of their methods,

[1] See mainly the remarks made in connection with Apresian's theory.

would far surpass the scope of the present study, but it is not even required by the objectives outlined in the introduction to my work. Most convincing to me is the ingenious value judgment given by U. Weinreich: "But even if they [the structuralist linguists] have not found a new passage to India, their navigational experience may yet be useful in unforeseen ways."[2]

I do not wish to swell the number of the existing definitions of sign and meaning, I nevertheless have to say (just for the purpose of further discussion), not by definition but periphrastically, what I mean by linguistic sign and its meaning.

The linguistic sign, as a sensuously perceptible material entity, is a product of man's social-practical activity, appearing in the complex network of relationships of the real sign situation. Consequently it has two functions: First, the part it plays in the cognition of the material world, in the development of knowledge (concept-formation); second, the communication of knowledge about the world, and thus of the feelings, etc. aroused in the subject, in order that the hearer may have the same ideas, feelings, etc. as the speaker. In this sense, therefore, the sign is a means of exercising an intellectual and affective-volitional influence on men. As the most important element of the network of relationships of language, it has a structure in whose forms of motion we can see definite regularities: its constitutive elements are arranged by the phonetic laws, their possible associations are governed by laws of morphology and syntax. Their grammatical functions are realized by the place they occupy in the syntagmatic concatenation of the sign sequences, by interdependence (complement and opposition).

The meaning of the linguistic sign is a constitutive part of the sign, that is not an extraneous rule that cannot be deduced from it, for in this case it would be on the same level as the meaning of other, non-linguistic signs. The meaning of a linguistic sign is distinguished from that of other signs just by the fact that the former is a conscious (social) outcome of the network of relationships of the natural sign situation and not a subsequently determined rule of application which can be interpreted only by the meanings of linguistic signs. The meaning of a linguistic sign, as

    [2] U. Weinreich, Travels Through Semantic Space, *Word* 14/2—3, pp. 346—66; loc. cit., p. 366.

an issue of the mental reflection of material reality, is a connecting link between sign and objective reality, between man and the material world. The reason why men are able to understand one another by means of signs is that the signs are embodiments of the same (or at least a similar) content of consciousness, and this is possible because the phenomena and events of the material world are reflected in the human mind by and large in the same manner. Thus the meaning of the linguistic sign is a complicated structure: reflection of the network of mutual relations between men, of relationships between men and objective reality, between men and linguistic signs, between linguistic signs and objective reality, between signs and signs.

This conception of the sign meaning can provide explanations for the relation of linguistic and non-linguistic signs (for the identities and differences of their features), for the problem of the relatively arbitrary nature and motivation of the linguistic sign, for the manifold questions of the different types of meaning, for the apparent contradiction between autonomous and contextual meaning, for the origin and the process, influenced by many factors, of homonymy, synonymy and also semantic changes, for problems concerning the factors of different contents of consciousness hidden behind one and the same linguistic sign.

The more exact knowledge we have of the particular components of the semantic structure, the more precisely we can define the meaning of each sign, which is a direct consequence of the reflecting function of language, because the structures of objective reality are reflected in linguistic structures, as Klaus put it: "We hold the view that in a certain respect language really performs a function of reflection, and this in so far as structures of objective reality are reflected in linguistic structures. Besides, this is not a perceptibly concrete reflection, but an abstract one, to some extent an isomorphic relation between reality and the sphere of signs, what Leibniz told about . . . when discussing the connection between words and things." The work in question is Leibniz, *Hauptschriften zur Grundlegung der Philosophie* VII: Philosophische Bibliothek Nr. 107.[3]

---

[3] "Wir sind der Ansicht, daß die Sprache in gewisser Hinsicht tatsächlich eine Widerspiegelungsfunktion ausübt, und zwar insofern, als Strukturen der objektiven Realität in sprachlichen Strukturen widerspiegelt werden. Dabei handelt es sich natürlich nicht um eine sinnlich konkrete, sondern um eine abstrakte Widerspiegelung, gewissermaßen um eine

If Klaus's formula based on Leibniz's ingenious guess is correct, if the structures of reality are really reflected in the linguistic structures, then the most promising method of discovering the linguistic laws is by examining, within the scope of this process of reflection, the "behaviour" and forms of motion of the linguistic signs, sign combinations, sign sequences and of their meanings. To discover this complicated system of the forms of motion is possible only on the basis of a complex linguistic view, which is postulated by the simple fact that language is a complicated structure, and its essence can be grasped only by relying on this fact.

This linguistic approach, in the light of the results and failures shown up by the history of science, declares war on all forms and manifestations of the linguistic hypostasis, and is waging an implacable fight against the linguistic conceptions which carry to excess or absolutize the role of one or another constitutive element of this linguistic structure. This opposition is directed not only against sign fetishism, historicism, psychologism, etc., but it is necessarily at loggerheads also with those representatives of the so-called modern schools who try to force language, this complicated social, psychical, etc. product, in the Procrustean bed of the—otherwise highly important—recent results of symbolic logic.

Let me add right away that this "negative standpoint" is far from being tantamount to negating the justification of examinations of this kind and the importance and even practical usability of the partial results attained by such methods, but it means that it negates the "fullness" of these partial examinations and results, the "exact" character of their linguistic explanation. Today no one denies that linguistic investigation conducted by means of formal logic can discover in an exact manner *one* aspect of language, of the meaning of the linguistic sign, but it is certainly denied that this method is fit to achieve the *fullness* of linguistic explanation. Mathematical linguistics, despite its being of recent origin, has remarkable results to its credit, not to speak of the practical utilization of those results (its concrete results in the use of translating machines, its stimulus to the linguist to employ more and more exact methods of research), but that this would

---

Isomorphierelation zwischen Wirklichkeit und Zeichenbereich, um das, was Leibniz ... über die Verknüpfung zwischen Worten und Dingen behandelt hat." G. Klaus, *Semiotik und Erkenntnistheorie*, Berlin, 1962, p. 43.

be the only principle of linguistic theory is hardly conceivable. *Suum cuique!* The most honest thing to do in recognizing the results of partial examinations is to put the whole to the test of critique, but it cannot be safely said either that what cannot be used from the viewpoint of the whole would have no other practical significance at all.

The dialectics of the part and the whole is the exact grip by which the refuse can be separated from the pure stuff. We must not forget, of course, that refuse can be used for *other* purposes, and also that we shall not sow refuse grain if we wish to have a *good* harvest of wheat.

10. THE FORMALIZATION OF SEMANTIC THEORY

In the light of the conception of sign and meaning as outlined above I shall try to analyze the works aimed at a formalization of meaning, among them mainly the voluminous paper by F. Kiefer,[1] who himself said this: "When we speak of a formal theory of meaning, all we wish to do is lay the foundations [!] of the construction of such a theory and sketch its main outlines."[2] Therefore, this is a fundamental work which has few theoretical antecedents to depend on.[3] It was by a critical application of Fodor's and Katz's works that Kiefer built up his own formal semantic theory, which is in essence an elaboration of his research conducted in common with S. Ábrahám. The first results of their joint work was published in English, too.[4] Also their principal views on general and formal semantic theory are accessible to the foreign reader.[5] As the author remarks in his paper, he was the first in literature to give a formal definition of meaning

[1] A jelentéselmélet formalizálásáról [On the Formalization of Semantic Theory], ÁNyT IV, pp. 105—55.

[2] Loc. cit., p. 110.

[3] J. A. Fodor, J. J. Katz, The Structure of a Semantic Theory, *Language* XXXIX, pp. 170—211. The critique of the article is from R. M. W. Dixon *(Linguistics* 1, pp. 30—57), to which the authors replied in No. 3 of the same journal, pp. 19—30. The principles laid down in the joint reply were further developed by J. J. Katz in his work *The Semantic Component of a Linguistic Description,* M.I.T., 1964.

[4] *A Theory of Structural Semantics,* The Hague—Paris, 1966.

[5] Cf. S. Ábrahám, F. Kiefer, Some Problems of Formalization in Linguistics, *Linguistics* 17, pp. 11—20.

relative to natural languages.[6] The bulky study therefore deserves closer attention so that we might draw conclusions also with regard to the correlations of the formal and content elements of language.

Kiefer starts his work by discussing questions of the general theory of language. This is a fairly commendable proposition, for every exact linguistic description can rightly be expected to state its author's position of principle, to define his concepts precisely. This is what Kiefer is seeking to do when he lays down right on the first page that the object of linguistic theory (i.e. not formal linguistic theory, but *the* linguistic theory) is to examine only the problem of *langue*, because "by language we always mean Saussure's *langue*, the *parole* is not a subject of linguistic theory".[7] With this categorical statement we could not agree even if we accepted his distinction between *langue* and *parole,* which he formulates in a more differentiated manner than Saussure: "Departing a little from Saussure's interpretation, we conceive *langue* as an abstract system whose concrete realization is the *parole.*"[8] In the linguistic literature of our days it is no longer usual to interpret the relation of *langue* and *parole* in this way, because it has been proved clearly that *speech*, or the speech act, came before language. A thorough inductive analysis of this act reveals the immanent correlations and their motives that can be called simply linguistic laws governing also the movement (not only the development!) of the "abstract system". To exclude the examination of 'parole' problems from the domain of linguistic theory is at least as serious a theoretical error as is "to examine motion without moving matter". This does not mean, of course, that the "abstract system" cannot be examined separately, as it is possible to follow closely *also* the formal "behaviour" of this system, but it should be said outright that the question is about formalization and not about the theory.

However, even though we agreed with this theoretical stand and examined how it is realized in Kiefer's work, we would come up against a self-contradiction right at the outset. Namely Kiefer, when outlining the scope of the general problems that may be raised in connection with language, gives the following specification:

[6] Kiefer: ÁNyT IV, p. 114.
[7] Loc. cit., p. 105.
[8] Ibid.

(a) How does language come into being?

(b) What are its properties?

(c) How can it be ascertained that a given text is a text of some language?

(d) What laws characterize the development of language?

(e) What is the relation between language and reality?[9]

Let me make the following observations:

(a) If we interpret the problems relating to the first point of Kiefer's specification in the broadest sense, namely so that by the human "faculty" absolutely necessary for the formation of the system we understand the simultaneous existence of all those factors which constitute the network of relationships between man and reality, man and mental reflection, man and linguistic sign, and we recognize all that as belonging in the sphere of investigation of the theory of language,[10] on what ground do we describe the problems under (e) as "not pertaining at all to linguistic theory"?[11] Either both or neither!

It is a remarkable circumstance also that on the following page, as compared to the first formulation, we can observe a considerable transformation of the first item (a) of the "three issues left" (a to c) to the theory. "Instead of man's language-creating faculty we study the generative model", writes Kiefer.[12] It is true, however, that the basic criterion of the rightness of the generative model — if my interpretation of the terse formulation is correct — is that it should agree with man's language-creating faculty: "The model is appropriate if the language L^x generated by the model (the set of generated sentences) agrees with the *langue* L generable in man."[13] Therefore, the linguistic theory postulated by Kiefer has, in the last analysis, to rely on "man's language-creating faculty". This is then the subject of the theory!

(b) After sharply delimiting the subject of linguistic theory and excluding therefrom the examination of parole facts, in the third point Kiefer returns to the question by approaching the problem included in point (c) from two sides: "in what way can an abstract language be realized?", and then he goes on to say, not without any contradictions: "Namely (c) takes *parole* for granted and wishes to decide which *langue* is in fact realized."[14]

[9] Ibid.

[10] Loc. cit., p. 106.

[11] Ibid.

[12] Ibid.

[13] Ibid.

[14] Ibid.

How can the two successive sentences be reconciled? How can the "way of realization" of an abstract language (which, also according to Kiefer, is a parole problem) be conceived so that the parole is given? Hereafter it is really difficult to decide whether or not, in Kiefer's view, the parole questions belong to the sphere of investigation of the theory of language.

(c) Kiefer clearly assigns to the synchronic analysis of language all problems involved in the first three points, namely even that one which inquires into "how language comes into being".[15] However we conceive of that faculty *(faculté du langage)* "which makes it possible to generate a *langue*", it is difficult to imagine how such a question could be answered effectively without thorough diachronic investigations. To investigate the "coming into being" of something is a typically diachronic subject. But, to avoid being accused of arbitrary interpretation, I let Kiefer himself say so: "Therefore our first problem (how language comes into being) is how this abstract system is formed in man; in other words, which are the faculties (faculté du langage) which make it possible to bring about the *langue*."[16] The emphasis is on "how it is formed", because the second part of the sentence, beginning with "in other words", can hardly be regarded as being synonymous with the first.

(d) What I have said so far may possibly show what serious theoretical mistakes can — and did — arise from the neglect of the "relation between linguistic sign and denotatum", from its exclusion from the sphere of linguistic investigations.

(e) Last but not least, according to Kiefer's theoretical introduction, the forces regulating the synchronic forms of motion of language are not laws, they govern only historical development: ". . . our next question concerns the laws of the *historical* development of language, i.e. the diachronic analysis of language."[17] Because the *"langue* characteristics" — which also according to Kiefer belong in the scope of synchronic studies — i.e. such questions as "what are the grammatical and semantical characteristics of the sentences, what is the relation between sentences, and how can this abstract system be realized",[18] are difficult to conceive as linguistic laws. It depends on what we mean by the laws of science. I shall still come back to discuss the

[15] Ibid.
[16] Ibid.
[17] Ibid. (Italics in the original.)
[18] Loc. cit., pp. 105—6.

problems of *rule* ~ *law* ~ *tendency*; all I have to state in this place, for the sake of historical truth, is that Kiefer in that same work of his uses the category of *law* and devotes a whole chapter to its study,[19] but how much this conception of law has in common with the concept that reflects the internal objective interrelatedness of processes and things, their forms of motion, I won't tell, but let Kiefer himself spell it out: "The semantic laws practically give the meaning of a word (morpheme) in a formal manner." In Morris's conception the meaning of a word can be defined only by the rules of its application. This is just what the semantic laws do, because "the rules of application of a word specify the other words in whose environment it can stand".[20] Whether this *rule*, totally separated from the denotative relations and referring only to the superficial arrangement, can be accordingly regarded as a *law* is open to question, to put it mildly; not to mention the issue whether the above categories of logical semantics are "one-to-one" applicable to language, to the meaning of the linguistic sign.

But this is not even the weakest point of Kiefer's conception of law. Its main theoretical flaw is his voluntaristic method of promoting mathematical formulae to laws, as will be clearly seen from the following. Of the possible "definitions" of the semantic laws in matrix form he says: "Of course, we could define the semantic laws in matrix form, too, but in this case we would need as many laws as there are ways of arranging the matrix sets in pairs."[21] It must be a strange semantic law which can be defined also in matrix form, especially if we take into consideration Kiefer's footnote on this question: "As the number of sentences is infinite, the number of matrix pairs would also be infinite. That is, we should have an infinity of laws, for the model is intended to model man's linguistic behaviour, but the capacity of man's brain, though potentially infinite, is practically always finite."[22] Either the semantic law can be defined in matrix form or it cannot. If it really could be, i.e. if the infinite number of matrix pairs truly reflected the semantic forms of motion of language, then—whether you like it or not—there would be an infinite number of semantic laws, no matter what difficulties such a fact of language would raise in the attempt at a formalization of semantic theory.

[19] "Semantic laws". Loc. cit., pp. 140—55.
[20] Loc. cit., p. 150.
[21] Loc. cit., p. 142.
[22] Ibid.

That Kiefer tries to discover the internal interrelatedness of facts not on the basis of a manysided analysis of the facts of language, but that he declares aprioristic schemata to be linguistic laws, is demonstrated by his following conclusion drawn from the definition of matrix values:

"Let further t_i, $t_j \rightarrow t$ be a semantic law [sic !]. The necessary and sufficient prerequisite for this law to be applicable to the matrix pair m_i, m_j [!] is that

$$[t_i]_{r,s} = [m_i]_{r,s}$$

and

$$[t_j]_{r,s} = [m_j]_{r,s}$$

in respect of every natural number r, s for which the left sides of the equations are construed, that is for which the table has a value.

"The type of the table at the right side of the semantic law can be determined as follows. Let t_i be of the type $p \times p$, and t_j of the type $p' \times p'$, then t will be of the type $(p + p') \times v$, where max $(q, q') \leq v \leq q + q'$.

"If the above necessary (and sufficient) requirement is satisfied, the semantic law will be applicable."[23]

I do not wish (I leave it to the mathematician) to comment upon the rightness or wrongness of the mathematical apparatus applied from among the formulae of the theory of sets, but I have to state that the kind of law which is created by the linguist ("let this or that be a semantic law") has nothing in common with the above outlined conception of law.

I know full well that different branches of mathematics successfully apply the several—defined or axiomatic—theorems in the course of deductive procedures, I also know that the formulae introducing the deductions are called "laws", but whether these formulae are applicable to a formalization of the very complicated network of relationships discussed above is open to debate. Everybody is also aware that the *a priori* formulae applied by mathematicians in their deductive procedures are indeed laws reflecting objective reality. These laws have been arrived at by the mathematicians through generalization based on zealous induction, they are therefore not invented premises if they indeed reflect truly the facts of material reality and the objective interrelatedness of these facts. The importance of the

[23] Loc. cit., pp. 142—3.

objective content of "undefined" mathematical axioms cannot thus be overemphasized. But mathematical formulae and axioms are one thing, and the world of semantic laws is another !

To avoid any possible misunderstanding and misinterpretation, I should like to state emphatically that what I have said is not at all directed in general against any possible formalization of semantic problems, because a position of this kind would mean non-recognition of facts. I am also aware that the formalization of some semantic problems is of immense practical significance for machine translation. But let us speak plainly: these are formulae, or rules if you like, however useful they may be, and they are not linguistic laws, not even formalized variations of them. Hence they are not made laws in the above sense by a categorical declaration like this: "These formal operations we shall call laws."[24]

One more commentary to Kiefer's theoretical "foundation": Kiefer takes language to be a system of signs. On this point we can only agree with him, in these days this is no longer denied by anybody. The fact is, however, that he reduces the linguistic system to a set of signs (W) and to a set of relations between signs (R); so he defines the linguistic system as a set $\{W,R\}$,[25] and this is strongly debatable and even unacceptable. There is no misunderstanding about what he has in mind; this is not formal structure, since this he formulates separately: "Formal by definition is what depends only on the outward form and sequence of the signs . . . If we suppose that R is dependent only on the outward form and sequence of the signs, we are speaking of formal structure."[26]

So Kiefer does not speak of formal structure when defining language as a sign system; but it is also true that here he fails to state precisely a set of what relations of signs the symbol R is. Later he mentions surface structure and deep structure, and specifies both: "The deep structure, which is given in the tree diagram, makes semantic interpretation possible; the surface structure, which is expressed by the tree (often called also derivational tree), makes phonological interpretation possible."[27]

One is curious to see what are the characteristics of the said structure which, beyond phonological interpretation, makes also

[24] Loc. cit., p. 109.
[25] Loc. cit., p. 106.
[26] Ibid.
[27] Loc. cit., p. 130.

semantic interpretation possible. Upon the general definitions there follows a definition of morpheme which is a category of the deep structure: "A morpheme is the symbol chains separated by blanks or the sign # in the terminal line of the basic tree diagram providing the deep structure,"[28] and then, a good number of pages later, we can read a peculiar paraphrase of the definition of meaning already quoted and attributed to Morris, saying that the rule of application essentially says in the context of what other words a word can stand.[29] If to all this we add that the relation between linguistic sign and denotatum is barred from the scope of linguistic investigations, and that Kiefer supports its exclusion also with a reference to Antal,[30] we come to see the outlines of a strange structure: the so-called deep structure, in the light of the everyday use of the term, is practically a surface structure, reflecting the interconnections, the formal relations between the particular elements of the sign sequence. In Kiefer's conception, therefore, the linguistic structure is a formal structure $\{W,R\}$, while meaning indicates merely the mutual relation of the various elements of this formal structure.

It is a different question how the linguistic structure conceived in this sense can comprise the problem of "how language has come into being", though language in Kiefer's submission is a structure.[31]

This much about the most important theoretical premises of Kiefer's semantic formalization. Let us now examine what are the hypotheses and methods by means of which he seeks to approach the essence of meaning, how he defines meaning, and how accordingly he interprets the different linguistic signs and sign sequences.

After presuming that language can be conceived as a structure from the point of view of the first three of the general problems that can be raised in connection with language, he sets up — in

[28] Loc. cit., pp. 130—1.
[29] Loc. cit., p. 150. N.B.: The meaning of a word, according to Kiefer, is interpretable also by the deep structure !
[30] "We are therefore fully in agreement with László Antal who excludes the content, as an extralinguistic notion, from the sphere of linguistics." Loc. cit., p. 109.
[31] "Language is not from every point of view a structure. It stands to reason, however, that we can suppose that it is, and this from the point of view of the questions *(a)* to *(c)* discussed under (1.1)" [see the list above]. Loc. cit., p. 106.

accordance with the three topics in question—three models of different types:

(a) generative model;
(b) explicative model;
(c) recognitive model.[32]

Kiefer defines the different models as follows:

(a) "The generative model is an abstract system which produces (generates) sentences, an infinite number of sentences, infinite also according to the nature of *langue*."[33] On the criteria of the rightness or wrongness of the model I have made my comments earlier, in connection with a different problem.

(b) "The explicative model describes the properties of sentences."[34] Kiefer distinguishes three such properties: grammatical, functional, and semantic. The first two of them can be clearly illustrated in tree form, by connecting the explicative and generative models, through the simultaneous generation of sentences. Kiefer calls the tree of a sentence the structural description of the sentence. He considers the explicative model appropriate if the structural description is adequate, i.e. entirely in agreement with the linguistic intuitions, and is simple.[35]

To make the criteria of adequacy and simplicity more explicit, Kiefer in a footnote argues with Chomsky, whose definition of adequacy (elaborated in *Syntactic Structures*) he renders in these terms: "The structural description is adequate if in case of any syntactically homonymous sentence s it produces as many different descriptions as are the values of this homonymity."[36] We can fully agree with Kiefer's criticism, but we can add that this narrow interpretation is at the same time so general that it means nothing for the concrete apprehension of adequacy. There is not much more either in what Kiefer says when he states that the solution of the question is "by formulating first precisely what we require of structural description; the requirements may even be arranged hierarchically. If a single requirement is not satisfied, the structural description is inadequate".[37] Kiefer fails to explicate what he thinks is to be required of structural description, but if we think about his definition of linguistic structure (W,R), i.e. the structure of such simple sets as is, for in-

---

[32] Loc. cit., pp. 106—7.
[33] Loc. cit., p. 106.
[34] Loc. cit., p. 107.
[35] Ibid.
[36] Paraphrased by Kiefer, ibid.
[37] Ibid.

stance, the finite series of natural numbers (1, 2, 3 . . ., n), we cannot expect much from the criteria set up by Kiefer either, because the conception of language as a structure of this kind is contrary to the extremely complicated structure of language. However, a structural description of language has to be adequate to this complicated structure; only if we conceive adequacy in an exact, objective manner shall our system of criteria be free from any danger of voluntarism.

Our opinion regarding Kiefer's *intuition* is not different from that regarding the basic criterion of adequacy. If by intuition we mean that general disposition, "developed" on the basis of the simultaneous existence of an exceptionally great number of factors (see above), in possession of which those taking part in the communicative process can establish that a sign sequence is a sentence of a given language *(langue)* or not, then the question is about such a fundamental criterion which breaks the bounds of merely formal analysis. If that is not the question, however, anybody can formulate at discretion, in accordance with his own theoretical attitude, how far intuition extends or, more precisely, what is to be understood by it. I feel that the latter is the case with Kiefer, as appears also from his description of the instability of the requirement of simplicity: "The requirement of simplicity . . . is a much tougher problem. First of all, it is relative and thus can hardly serve as an objective standard. On the other hand, just by reason of its relative nature it lends itself for comparison within one system only. We consider it an intuitive concept until we have found a better solution."[38] This is plain speech! If simplicity is an intuitive concept by reason of its relative and subjective nature, then we cannot think differently of the general value of intuition either. Besides, as is commonly known, the most often quoted theoreticians of formal analysis[39] are rather unconcerned by informant's and hearer's response *(intuition,* which they call *meaning* in the traditional sense), and they regard reliance on this response as a necessary evil, as a deficiency attributable to the hitherto unsatisfactory state of formal analysis, as a defect which must, therefore, be eliminated from the domain of linguistic researches as soon as possible.[40]

(c) The definition of the third, the recognitive model, reads as follows: "The recognitive model is the reverse of the former

[38] Ibid.
[39] C. W. Morris and Z. S. Harris.
[40] Cf. Harris's remark in footnote 7 in Chapter II, Section 3.

combined model, namely its task is (a) to decide whether a given sentence s is an element of the language L; (b) to recognize its grammatical properties, i.e. to establish the structural description of s."[41] What we have said about the criteria of the explicative model applies, *mutatis mutandis*, also to the "decision" and "recognition" criteria of this model.

The features under discussion of the grammatical properties of language (of sentences) are fundamental to Kiefer's theory because he tries to grasp the semantic properties by proceeding from the same. In his opinion, "grammar has first to uncover the appropriate grammatical relations and only thereafter can we talk about the discovery of semantic relations".[42] In another place, where he writes about answering the questions that may be put to semantic theory, the first such question is the following: "Is a given grammatically correct sentence also semantically correct or not?"[43] Again in another place: ". . . semantic theory presupposes grammatical theory."[44] It is essential therefore to distinguish the grammatical and semantic properties of sentences, in other words to suppose, and to demonstrate by rather diffuse and hard-to-follow methods, that "grammatical correctness does not coincide with semantic correctness".[45] Anyone who knows something about the structure of a simple sentence can recognize at once that the sentences *The dog barks* and *The dog sings* are both grammatically correct (analyzable by the classical method of question and answer), but if we inquire about the meaning of the second sentence ("What does the second sentence mean?"), we meet with an unmistakable smile amounting to recognition of the semantic incorrectness of the sentence.

The case is not so trivially simple with Kiefer! When arguing with the authors who hold that grammatical quality involves semantic correctness, he inquires into Chomsky's already mentioned sample sentence *(Colourless green ideas sleep furiously)* from the point of view of semantic correctness and states that the abnormality found in the sentence is "not in its meaning but in its content; that is, there is nothing in reality that corresponds to the sentence, yet we can 'understand' the sentence itself".[46] If the abnormality of the above-cited sentence is imputable not

[41] Kiefer, loc. cit., p. 107.
[42] Loc. cit., p. 118.
[43] Loc. cit., p. 116.
[44] Loc. cit., p. 120.
[45] Loc. cit., p. 109.
[46] Loc. cit., p. 108.

to the meaning but to the content (what is at issue here is unmistakably the denotatum, which is clearly indicated by the second sentence introduced by "that is"), then there is "no trouble" with the meaning of the sentence, which is also semantically correct. Why then does Kiefer argue with those who hold that the said sample sentence "also would be semantically correct".[47] If the trouble is not in the meaning but in the content, since we "can understand the sentence itself", is *meaning* identical with *understanding?* Or how can exoneration of the above sentence from the blame of semantic anomaly be reconciled with Kiefer's interpretation of the definition (meaning = rule) attributed to Morris: "... the rules of application of the word specify the other words in whose environment it can stand"?[48] In other terms: how does the above sentence comply with the criterion of compatibility of the chain of symbols if the sentence *I eat the hot soup cold* is not a compatible chain of symbols in Kiefer's view either, because while *hot* and *soup* are compatible, and so are *soup* and *cold*, yet *hot* and *cold* are not?[49] If *hot* and *cold* are incompatible, then why are *colourless* and *green* compatible? (The issue of compatibility will be discussed later on.) So many sentences, so many question-marks! A little more exact explanation, or rather formulation, and mainly some coherence of principle would possibly make it easier to understand the above "utterance".

Understanding is not helped by Kiefer's sample sentences divided into two groups, either. Let me mention but one of each group. The first group includes sentences of the following type: *The colourless yellow morals got drowned,*[50] and the second has such types: *The average depth of the Atlantic Ocean is ten centimetres.*[51] What is common and what is different, according to Kiefer, in the two types of sample sentences? Kiefer answers the question—astonishingly enough in view of the foregoing—in the following terms (sorry, I cannot but quote a lengthier passage here, because the reader may with good reason become suspicious that I am using purposely picked parts of Kiefer's text to kill his affirmations explained a few lines before): "In each sentence of

[47] Ibid.
[48] Loc. cit., p. 150.
[49] Loc. cit., p. 112.
[50] For the sake of what follows it is important to note here that this sentence is, from the point of view of grammar and semantics, fully congruent with Chomsky's sample sentence.
[51] Loc. cit., p. 108.

173

both groups the difference from 'the normal' can be explained by the denotatum, hence their difference cannot be explained by the content, only by the meaning. In our opinion the sentences of the first group have no meaning, while those of the second are semantically unobjectionable. If in the case of the sentences of the second group we wished to seek an explanation for the difference from the 'normal', then we ought to rely upon extra-linguistic experience as well."[52]

If Chomsky's sample sentence is abnormal because its content is abnormal, "that is, there is nothing in reality that corresponds to the sentence", then the question arises rightly, what in reality corresponds to Kiefer's sentence *The colourless yellow morals got drowned*. What is the difference between the two sentences, why can we explain Chomsky's by the abnormality of content and Kiefer's by "only the meaning"? Why is the first of the perfectly congruent sentences meaningful and why is not the second one? What is the content of the sentence? Is it identical with reality? If so, how can a factor that is extralinguistic by definition (reality) be a semantically determining component of the sentence? But if content is not identical with reality, then what is? What difference is there between undefined denotatum and reality, between denotatum and content? Is denotatum identical with meaning? (". . . the difference from 'the normal' can be explained by the denotatum, hence their difference cannot be explained by the content, only by the meaning.") Why are sentences like *The average depth of the Atlantic Ocean is ten centimetres* "semantically unobjectionable"? What corresponds to sentences of this type in reality? Why should we "rely upon extralinguistic experience as well" only in the case of such sentences if we want to explain the difference from the normal? Was it not—in sentences like *The colourless yellow morals got drowned*—by the evidence of extralinguistic factors that we could ascertain that there was in reality nothing that corresponded to the "sentence"?

And all these exercises are crammed into one and the same page!

In one place Kiefer has the following to say about the fundamental characteristics of scientific research: "At the present level of research we expect linguistics also to be exact. The concept 'exact', however, does not coincide with the concept 'formal'.

[52] Ibid.

174

An exact theory is required only to use precisely formulated concepts and operations, to distinguish undefined concepts (at least within the theory), so-called basic concepts and defined concepts, and further to distinguish its theses which it proves from those which it uses without proof, that is the so-called axioms."[53] In the deductive method these are fairly long-established requirements, with which we can agree from first to last. Without them the deductive conclusions lose their foothold and may give rise to the wildest speculations. But this must also be accomplished. The criteria are practical work and correct method, requirements that are proved correct or incorrect by the test of practice, which can be substituted for by no kind of declaration.

I do not for a moment wish to affirm that Kiefer uses concepts that are entirely new and unknown to traditional linguistics. *Meaning, denotatum, content, structure*, etc. are old-established terms in the science of language. But I cannot keep silent about the way Kiefer uses these terms. It is no secret from the reader well versed in modern linguistic literature that the different authors interpret these terms very differently, but they tell in general the sense in which they use each term and they stick to the interpretations they give. Just as a reminder: Bloomfield identified *meaning* with *denotatum* (the material reality outside the sign: *salt* = NaCl), and on this basis he regarded it, with good reason, as an extralinguistic factor. (It is a different matter whether his semantic theory is acceptable or not.) Kiefer abides by Morris's theory of meaning. At the same time, by one of his afore-cited formulations, he returns to the Bloomfieldian conception. Or is it only an inaccurate formulation? Who knows? The same applies to the *denotatum*, too. In general, but not unanimously, it is usually meant to be a part of objective reality indicated by the sign, and more pretentious semantic schools keep it strictly distinct from the *designatum*, which is the mental reflection of the former. Many writings use *designatum* and *content* as synonyms; but to confuse the *denotatum* (reality) with the *content* of a linguistic sign or a sign sequence, and to conceive it as a factor of language, is a very strange thing to do. Besides, *content* as a linguistic term also has varied interpretations in modern linguistics.

Also the conception of language as a *structure* is not of recent date, but in our days to return to Saussure's inaccurate formulation—which even among the Saussureans is at least a debated

[53] Loc. cit., p. 110.

point — is anachronism, to put it mildly, but much more a theoretical mistake. Language is a structure, but not a formal structure. To conceive language as a structure consisting of many interacting and inseparable components is one thing, and to formalize this structure is another.

If the above interpretation of the structure of meaning[54] is acceptable, then the attempt to formalize a semantic theory must proceed from this complexity; or rather: one has to tell clearly what of it all can be formalized and what cannot. It is easy to imagine that more and more parts of it can be formalized. But to reduce a multilevelled structure to a linear one for the sake of formalization amounts to contempt of facts. Namely one can fully agree with Kiefer's following distinction: "The object of an exact theory can be much broader than that of a formal theory. Its tasks include also the examination of questions which cannot be discussed in a formal manner."[55]

If Kiefer conceived of meaning really as a set of Morris's (semantic, syntactic, and pragmatical) rules and did not reduce it to the semantic function completed with the criterion of compatibility, to rules "which govern the use of words",[56] then he ought to say clearly in his semantic theory which components of this set of rules can be formalized and which cannot. As a matter of fact, the semantic theory cannot be identified, even according to Morris, with one or another member of this system of (semantic or syntactic) rules, not even with the concept of semantic correctness, let alone that the theory and method worked out for logical semantic analyses, if left unchanged, are unsuited to answer the questions of linguistic semantics.

It is on the basis of the theoretical statements and methodological observations thus sketched that Kiefer approaches the formal definition of meaning, which he requires generally to be in agreement with the intuition related to meaning, or at least not to be contrary to it. Thus he does not require the formal definition to agree in everything with the linguistic intuitions, because in his view "by formal definitions we grasp not meaning itself but the functions of meaning, that is the rules which govern the use of words".[57] What he expects such a definition of meaning to tell

---

[54] See Chapter III, Section 6.
[55] Kiefer, loc. cit., p. 110.
[56] Loc. cit., p. 111.
[57] Ibid.

is not what the meaning of a given sign or sign sequence is, but only whether it is endowed with meaning or not. In this sense meaning is identical with the notion of semantic correctness. Hence, if we want to give a formal definition of meaning, we have to define semantic correctness.[58]

Kiefer thinks the semantic correctness of a sign sequence (symbol chain) can be ascertained by the compatibility relation between the symbols and by the grammatical structure.[59] He gives a description of compatibility as follows: "Let a and b be two consecutive chains of symbols. These two chains of symbols are said to be compatible when and only when there is at least one semantic law on whose left side stand matrices corresponding to the two symbol chains, a and b, and this in the same order in which the symbol chains occur."[60] If to this description we add Kiefer's conception of semantic law discussed before and his view that semantic laws are also laws of transcription, i.e. they appear as $\varphi - \psi$, where the formula signifies that "φ should be replaced by ψ",[61] we have to get used to a very peculiar kind of compatibility: If the semantic laws govern the use of words, the basic criterion of this rule of application is compatibility (what else could it be?), but we can talk about compatibility between two chains of symbols only if they comply with the rule of application of the chains of symbols; consequently we are moving around in a vicious circle where like is defined by like, i.e. we can know neither what is the essence of semantic law nor when we can talk of compatibility between two symbol chains!

Neither can we reach a different conclusion if we take a close look also at the linguistic evidence adduced in support of this theorem of Kiefer's. Of the word associations *liquid* and *shoes*, *colourless* and *green*, *sleep* and *furiously*, *table* and *breathes*, he states that they are not compatible. His explanation: "The words *liquid* and *shoes* are not compatible because there is no law on whose left side stands a matrix corresponding to *liquid* and subsequently to *shoes*."[62] In plain English this means that *liquid* and *shoes* are incompatible because according to the rule of application they cannot stand directly side by side, and that they cannot stand directly side by side because they are incompatible!

[58] Ibid.
[59] Loc. cit., pp. 111—3.
[60] Loc. cit., p. 111.
[61] Ibid.
[62] Loc. cit., p. 112.

To break this vicious circle is not even possible by examining only the formal behaviour of language (the formal combinations of an infinite set of symbol chains), by excluding the "extralinguistic" factors from the province of linguistics. Theoretically, though, it is possible to imagine a "solution" where we would set up in principle all possible combinations of the infinite series of linguistic symbols, then compare them, by an unending "analysis", with the actual combinations occurring in language (in speech), and finally, regardless of the reference to reality of these combinations, we establish which combinations have compatible elements and which do not. But a generalization of the results thus attained would have nothing to do with what we commonly call law, or compatibility. We would thus get an empirically produced set of facts, yet more might be required if we wish to elevate the generalization of the results of our investigations to the rank of theory.

Such a feeling of want appears from the following lines of L. Dezső's study published in the same volume:[63] "The semantic rules reflect the relations of reality; a certain degree of isomorphism obviously exists between the correlations of reality and the rules of semantic compatibility."[64] Old as the truth is which Dezső tells by stating the reference to reality of the linguistic sign (sign sequences), trivial as he may declare these correlations, we still have to agree with him fully that "reliance on them is indispensable",[65] for Kiefer's theory of compatibility demonstrates to what mistakes and to what an impasse one is bound to get by disregarding the reference to reality of the signs.

Between the relations of reality and the rules of semantic compatibility there undeniably exists some isomorphism, even more than "a degree", but we have to explain the cause of isomorphism. The "sentence" *The meadow broke into a grin,* in Dezső's view, is contrary to semantic rules and cannot be covered by the rules of compatibility "because the denotatum *meadow* does no such thing".[66] According to him the denotatum *meadow* "determines compulsorily" that the chain of symbols *The meadow broke into a grin* is semantically incorrect.

---

[63] A szemantika és a lexikológia néhány kérdése [Some Questions of Semantics and Lexicology], ÁNyT IV, pp. 31—67.
[64] Loc. cit., p. 42.
[65] Ibid.
[66] Ibid.

This argument is not convincing. The meadow as denotatum, as part of objective reality, "does nothing", it does not "determine" or "prescribe" anything, it exists irrespective of whether we know of its existence, whether we have notions, concepts, sentences or non-sentences about it. However, as soon as the meadow as denotatum, together with its properties, "gets into" our consciousness and is reflected in our minds, then beside the actual meadow—on the strength of it—there appears the mental image of the meadow, the *concept* 'meadow', which is not identical with the actual meadow, but which is not even independent of it. The more precisely the properties of the actual meadow, the relationships between the meadow and other objects of reality, are reflected in our consciousness, the more precise will be our idea of the meadow, a concept which manifests itself in the form of the linguistic sign *meadow*. The correct mental reflection, the *designatum*, is thus the connecting link which "motivates" the relation between the sign and the part of reality, which creates the isomorphism between the real relations and the rules of compatibility. If this were not so, if the connection between sign and denotatum were "completely and utterly arbitrary", then the sign sequence *The meadow broke into a grin* would not necessarily come into conflict with the rules of compatibility, for in this case the phrase *broke into a grin* might refer, let us say, to the green colour of the meadow, or to its vastness or smallness, etc., etc., depending entirely on arbitrary convention.

Dezső himself feels that the conclusion based on the one-sided conception of the "behaviour" of denotata, on their function radically influencing the rules of semantic compatibility, is unsatisfactory, since he admits that, in case of personification, the sign sequence *The meadow broke into a grin* can constitute a semantically correct sentence. "All" he forgets, or fails to speak about, is that in this case we have no longer to do with the same denotatum; more precisely, the mental reflection of the original denotatum has undergone a radical change. Personification is certainly the product of a conscious operation, the result of the relatively autonomous movement of concepts, where conceptual marks more or less different from the original come to the fore, become determinant from the viewpoint of the semantic marks, and make it possible "for the meadow to break into a grin". Let us recall the formation of the concept *Pegasus*, to which "there is nothing in reality that corresponds", and still we accept as semantically entirely "regular" those sentences which usually qualify a versifier by adding an attribute to his *Pegasus* (lame

Pegasus, broken-winged Pegasus, etc.). Results of similar mental operations are, for example, the expressions *winged altar* and *winged love,* whose denotata are induced by the respective conventional notions, but neither of them has real wings. The mythological figures that have come down to us from the dawns of mankind are not only anthropomorphous figments of man's lively imagination, but some of them are products of the personification of one or another natural object or process. *Jupiter* is the name not only of the supreme god of the ancient Romans but of the largest planet of our solar system; in the same way, *Juno* is the name of Jupiter's wife as well as that of an asteroid, just like *Venus,* which is not only the name of the goddess of love and beauty, but also that of the planet second in distance from the sun, and so forth. When one or the other of their "regular" meaning is actualized depends entirely on the context; one may even say that the meaning refers to the context: the sign sequence *Venus broke into a smile* tells us not only that it is an absurd sentence "from the point of view of the denotatum" in a work on astrophysics, but also that its pair being fully within the rules of semantic compatibility can be found only in writings of mythology.

It is evident that the conception of semantic rule built upon a direct connection between sign and denotatum prevents Dezső from giving an explanation for the correlations "which the denotatum determines compulsorily", and that is why he considers them "specially linguistic".[67] His examples of this type are the Hung. *ül* and Russian *сидеть* referring to the denotatum 'sit', and the Hung. *áll* and Russian *стоять* indicating the denotatum 'stand'. But to express the real situation (condition), as he goes on to say, that an actual suit fits (well, badly), the Hungarian uses the word *áll* 'stand', the Russian the word *сидеть* 'sit'. And then he concludes: "Consequently the rules of application of the words *костюм — öltöny* (referring to the denotatum 'suit') become established so that the word *öltöny* can be associated with *áll* but not with *ül*, while the Russian *костюм* can be associated with *сидеть* but not with *стоять*."[68] But the question why in one language and in the other a word can associate with a second and not with a third word remains unanswered, for Dezső is unable to explain it on the basis of the semantic rule built upon a direct connection between sign and denotatum. Why do the

[67] Loc. cit., p. 42.
[68] Ibid.

sign sequences *Az öltöny (jól) áll* and *Костюм (хорошо) сидит* 'The suit fits (well)' reflect correlations that are linguistic by definition, and why does the sign sequence *The meadow broke into a grin* tell about grotesque linguistic correlations? If the elements of the latter are "regular" linguistic signs, and if only their combination is incorrect, then is it only the testimony of the denotatum that helps to ascertain the "irregular" use of signs? What should be done, on this basis, with a combination of the linguistic signs *God, strike* and *hand* in this form: *God strikes not with both hands...?* Should we accept it as regular only because God (the denotatum!!!) "does no such thing", or is the sequence *God save the Queen* regular because God can be expected to do so? Whether a sign sequence is regular, "semantically correct" or irregular we can know anyway, though not from the analysis of the denotatum at issue, but from the linguistic communication itself. Namely the linguistic signs serve well also for us to dispense with showing up directly the signified things every time, not to mention the "linguistic justification" of signs and sign sequences to which "there is nothing in reality that corresponds", and which thus have no denotatum but only a conceptual background. This, however, we could call denotatum only by subscribing to conceptual realism.

What precedes may possibly have demonstrated that denotata cannot directly determine the value of a given sign or sequence of signs, just as they do not explain why the suit which fits well in English *stands well* in Hungarian and why it *sits well* in Russian, nor do they clear up whether the sign sequence *The meadow broke into a grin* is a sentence or only an arbitrary combination of actual linguistic signs. One is not a bit "more linguistic" than the other; knowledge of the "rules" of designation helps to ascertain right away whether either of them is meaningful or not.

If, from the network of relationships of the real sign situation, we pick one relation, that between sign and reality [R (S,O)], and want to explain the meaning only on this basis, we ought to take the relation between sign and denotatum to be entirely arbitrary. Then we could not understand why the signifier of English *suit* is *костюм* in Russian, nor could we explain why in the same language area one denotatum may have more signifiers (Hung. *eb* ~ *kutya* 'dog', etc.), nor why one and the same denotatum has only one signifier in one language and two or more in another, simply because we would forget the fact that denotata have differently shaded reflections in human consciousness and that mental reflection is most often influenced by evaluative, emotive factors as well. This is not yet (or must at least not necessarily be) a false image, but merely a reflection of different intonations of the particular conceptual marks, hence that of a certain outlook, or maybe a reminiscence or a linguistic fossil of an obsolete idea. Let us consider, for example, the different names of the planet *Venus* in several languages. Hungarian has a compound to denote it: *esthajnalcsillag* (literally 'evening-morning-star'); English, French, German and Russian have separate names for the denotatum according as it is seen in the evening or early in the morning: Eng. *evening star* $\sim$ *morning star*, Fr. *étoile du soir* (also *étoile du berger*) $\sim$ *étoile du matin*, German *Abendstern* $\sim$ *Morgenstern*, Russian *вечерняя звезда* $\sim$ *утренняя звезда*. Why the same denotatum has one name in one language and two or more in another can be explained by a lot of things, except by the function of the denotatum as conceived of by Dezső.

We can therefore agree that the semantic rules reflect relations of reality: in this sense these rules are conceptual images of the real relations.[69] But we cannot accept the idea that the essence of these rules can be explained by the direct evidence of the denotata, by leaving out of account the complicated nature of the process of reflection, the somewhat "autonomous" movement of the conceptual marks. It is a different matter, of course, to know what can and what cannot be formalized in the present state of our knowledge.

After Dezső's commentaries let us return to the question of Kiefer's semantic theory, namely to how meaning can be defined on the basis of compatibility.

Compatibility is marked by ( ). Thus, if a and b are compatible, they can be written in this form: (a, b). The order of the chains of symbols is also important in the establishing of compatibility. Therefore, three consecutive chains of symbols — a, b, c — are compatible only if $[(a, b), c]$ or $[a, (b, c)]$.[70] The generalization of compatibility says: the consecutive chains of symbols $a_1, a_2, \ldots a_n$ are compatible only if either $[(a_1, a_2, \ldots a_{n-1}), a_n]$ or $[a_1, (a_2, a_3, \ldots a_n)]$.[71] On the basis of compatibility, according to Kiefer, the following definition of meaning is possible: "The sentence $a_{x_1}, a_{x_2}, \ldots a_{x_r}$ is said to be semantically correct (or

[69] Cf. Schaff's conception: meaning = concept.
[70] Kiefer, loc. cit., p. 111.
[71] Loc. cit., p. 112.

meaningful) if the chain composed of the words of the sentence is compatible."[72]

Kiefer himself is not satisfied with this definition based on compatibility alone, because it disregards grammatical structure. Namely it is not enough, he says, to ascertain whether the whole of the chain composed of the words of the sentence is compatible, we have to know about each syntagm of the sentence separately whether it is compatible or not.

He defines the syntagm by the tree diagram providing a structural description of the sentence. The sentence *A kis fiú játszik a kertben* 'The little boy plays in the garden' is structurally described by him as follows:

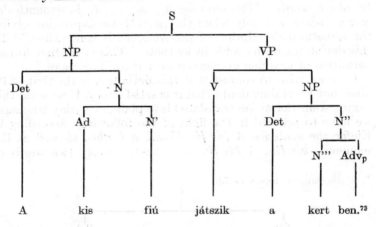

A kis fiú játszik a kert ben.[73]

As appears from the diagram, each nodal point is marked by a grammatical category. On this basis Kiefer defines the syntagm as follows: "A syntagm is the combination of two words or morphemes whose first nodes are the same ... However, a syntagm is formed also by any word-chain which can be traced back to an identical nodal point."[74] According to this conception of the syntagm, each of the sequences *kis fiú, A kis fiú, kert ben, a kert ben, játszik a kertben* is a syntagm in itself, and so is the whole sentence *A kis fiú játszik a kertben.*

[72] Ibid.

[73] As a consequence of the structural difference between Hungarian and English the tree diagram of the English sentence is different from that of the Hungarian sentence. The diagram for the corresponding English sentence is shown on. p. 148.

[74] Kiefer, loc. cit., p. 112.

The tree diagram giving the structural description of the sentence is equivalent to the following parenthetic expression: $((A)$ *kis fiú*$))$ $(játszik$ $(a$ $(kert$ $ben))))$.[75]

On the basis of the parenthetic expression allowing also for semantic correctness (the meaning) of the syntagms Kiefer gives his definition of meaning—to be considered satisfactory now in all respects—based on the criterion of compatibility: "The sentence $a_{x_1}, a_{x_2}, \ldots a_{x_r}$ is semantically correct when and only when there exists at least one such parenthetic form of the above sentence which, proceeding from the innermost parentheses and applying the compatibility operation step by step towards the outer parentheses, gives us a compatible chain of symbols."[76] In other words: "The sentence $a_{x_1}, a_{x_2}, \ldots a_{x_r}$ is semantically correct when and only when the parenthetic expression giving the structural description of the sentence is compatible."[77] To this definition Kiefer adds in footnote: "This is the first formal definition of meaning ever given for natural languages."

I do not wish to contest that this definition is the first of its kind, but I certainly doubt that it is satisfactory. If we want this cumbersome definition translated into plain, everyday language, we have to proceed in the light of the following: According to Kiefer the sentence *A kis fiú játszik a kertben* as well as the sequences *kis fiú, A kis fiú,* etc., that is every two words or

Tree diagram to footnote 73.

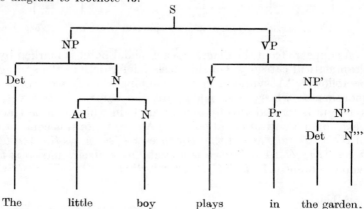

[75] Loc. cit., p. 114.
[76] Ibid.
[77] Ibid.

184

morphemes of the sentence "whose first nodes are the same", are equally syntagms. It is not in Kiefer's formulation that the conception of the sentence as a syntagm is first encountered in literature, but it is really a novelty that he regards both the sentence and the structural formations constituting smaller units of the sentence as syntagms and makes no distinction between them. It is common knowledge that even Saussure, for example, discussed inflected forms and derivations as well as word-combinations and sentences under the heading of syntagmatic relations.[78] It is also true, however, that he regarded the sentence as a "type *par excellence*" of syntagm[79] and clearly distinguished the study of syntagms from syntax.[80] But this is not even the greatest mistake in Kiefer's classification, for in this way – after performing the necessary substitutions – we would arrive at the following tautology: A syntagm is "semantically correct" if its syntagms are compatible. The "parenthetic expression" is namely equivalent to the above tree diagram, which in turn is nothing else but a structural description of the sentence (syntagm).

The greatest problem is caused by the main pillar of the entire theory—the interpretation and application of compatibility. The first possibility of a definition mentioned by Kiefer was held unsatisfactory even by its author because its formulation disregarded the tree diagram indicating the requirements of structural description, i.e. it did not show whether the syntagms constituting the whole sentence are one and all compatible. Yet "the parenthetic expression giving the structural description of the sentence" is compatible only in case the parentheses within parentheses are one and all compatible; in other words, the whole of the chain composed of the words of the sentence is compatible only in case the smaller structural units of the sentence, the words or morphemes with the same nodes (the single elements of the "small" syntagms), are one and all compatible.[81] We have to examine, therefore whether the syntagms *kis fiú, A kis fiú,* etc. are compatible. The method is the same for ascertaining the compatibility of each syntagm, hence all that is needed is to establish the compatibility of a single syntagm of the above sentence in order to come closer to the essence of Kiefer's definition of meaning. Kiefer does not set up criteria for the compatibility

[78] Saussure, *Cours* . . ., pp. 172−3.
[79] Op. cit., p. 172.
[80] Op. cit., p. 188.
[81] Kiefer, loc. cit., p. 113.

of the syntagmatic elements, obviously because he did so earlier when treating the incompatibility of two words (*liquid* and *shoes*). Thus there is no other solution than to apply for the definition of compatibility the converse of the definition of incompatibility. The words occurring in the syntagm *kis fiú* of the sentence under discussion "are compatible because there is a law on whose left side stand matrices corresponding to *kis* and then to *fiú*". More plainly: *kis* and *fiú* are compatible because according to the rule (law) of application they can stand directly side by side (as continuous morphemes they can form a syntagm), and they can stand directly side by side (they can form a syntagm) because they are compatible. The criterion of compatibility is therefore the possibility of a (real) syntagmatic arrangement, and the criterion of this latter is compatibility. The case is the same with the mutual compatibility of the particular syntagms of the "parenthetic expression", so we cannot break the vicious circle in this case either.

But this is not the only weak point of the theory of meaning built on the criterion of compatibility. Kiefer readily betrays his compatibility theory. In some place, where he discusses the semantic status of the inflectional and derivative morphemes,[82] he writes this: "Semantically the inflectional morphemes present no problem, because they do not change the meaning, they only fix the other morpheme by which compatibility is to be verified.[!] The case is different with the derivative endings, for such suffixes can change the meaning (e.g., *ember* ['man']—*emberség* ['humaneness']; but there is no change in this case: *merev* ['rigid']—*merevség* ['rigidity'])."[83] The first sentence of the above quotation is inaccurately worded, since it does not disclose what is to be understood by "verification of compatibility by other morphemes" (stem morphemes or suffixational morphemes?). But, either one or the other, this thesis of Kiefer comes into conflict with his semantic conception discussed earlier. Namely,

---

[82] In Hungarian both the inflectional ending and the derivative ending (formative) are suffixes and thus stand *after* the stem morpheme in morphemic description. As to its function the inflectional ending is equivalent to the *preposition* of the languages of the Indo-European family *(kertben = kert + ben* 'in the garden'). The function of the derivative ending is to change the meaning, and this suffix precedes the inflectional morpheme in the morphemic chain *(kertész = kert + ész* 'garden-er'; *kertésznek = kert + ész + nek* 'to the gardener').

[83] Loc. cit., p. 131.

if we have to examine the compatibility of an inflectional morpheme with another inflectional or derivative morpheme we must reckon with the following contingencies:

(a) An inflectional suffix side by side with another inflectional suffix forms no compatible chain of morphemes. In fact, there are inflectional morphemes like *-ban* 'in' and *-tól* 'from', but the chain of morphemes *(-ban)* + *(-tól)* is incompatible, semantically incorrect, and has no meaning.

(b) The same applies to the chain 'stem morpheme + inflectional morpheme + inflectional morpheme'. The chain of morphemes *ember* + *ben* is compatible, *ember* + *ben* + *tól* is again not.

(c) The sequence 'stem morpheme + inflectional morpheme + + derivative morpheme' generally also forms no compatible chain of morphemes: *ember* + *ben* is a compatible chain of morphemes, but *ember* + *ben* + *ség* is not.

(d) The chain 'stem morpheme + inflectional morpheme + +marker morpheme' is also incompatible. The morpheme sequence *ember* + *ben* + *(e)k* is not compatible, etc. (I have taken up those possible cases where the inflectional morpheme, either standing by itself or following upon the stem morpheme, would precede the other suffixational morphemes, such as derivative suffixes and markers, since other possible associations are irrelevant from our point of view.)

The conclusions to be drawn from this perfunctory enumeration are the following: The chain of morphemes *ember* + *ben* is semantically correct and meaningful, *ember* + *ben* + *tól* is incorrect and has no meaning; in other terms: the meaning of *emberben* was changed by the addition of the inflectional morpheme *-tól*.[84] Literally the same applies to the case of *ember* + *ség* — *ember* + *ben* + *ség* and *ember* + *(e)k* — *ember* + *ben* + *(e)k*. Occurrences like *nagy* + *ban* + *i* 'wholesale' (adj.) are exceptions which can be explained in a different way (not by formal means, at best "we ought to create a singular law" for them, though this would not lead us far), but what is essential is not this exception but the incorrect and even contradictory nature of the thesis that the inflectional morphemes are irrelevant from the semantic point of view.

We must come to the same conclusion if by the compatibility or incompatibility of a possible association with other morphemes we mean the issue whether the single elements of a lengthy chain of morphemes (sentence) remain compatible if we add

---

[84] See above: meaning = semantic correctness. Loc. cit., p. 111.

an inflectional morpheme to one of them. The chain of mor·
phemes *Az ember ír* 'The man writes' is compatible, *Az emberben
ír* is not. Considering what has been expounded, I think, it is
needless to demonstrate at length the wrongness of the statement that the derivative morpheme *-ség* does not change the
meaning in the case of *merev—merevség* 'rigid—rigidity'. Again
on the basis of compatibility: *merev vasgerenda* 'rigid girder' is
compatible, and so is *merev magatartás* 'rigid attitude', but the
same cannot be said of the chain of morphemes *merevség vasgerenda* and *merevség magatartás*.

If Kiefer identifies meaning with the concept of semantic
correctness and, on the other hand, considers the basic criterion
of semantic correctness to be compatibility, which is at the same
time the main pillar of his conception of semantic law ("the rules
of application of a word specify the other words in whose environment it can stand"), how can he write in the same study that the
inflectional morphemes and (in some cases) the derivative morphemes are irrelevant from the semantic point of view?

It is difficult to see what this logic should mean. It is hard to
grow accustomed to the exceptional "elasticity" of Kiefer's
concepts!

From the "first formal definition of [sentence] meaning" thus
we cannot know much about the essence of meaning, because its
starting point (meaning = rule) is false, its concepts are undefined, and consequently its conclusions also are not valid. This
kind of formal semantic theory lets us know nothing more about
the structure of language than we have thus far been able to
state, on the basis of the traditional linguistic theory, about the
correlations or, if you like, the dialectics of the content elements
and formal components of language.

On the basis of the—by no means positive—lessons of the
axioms, definitions and conclusions discussed above, one has to
be rather skeptical also regarding Kiefer's definition of the task
of semantic theory: "One of the most important tasks of semantic theory is to clarify the problems which it can resolve by formal methods,"[85] and we do not find it objectively justified why
formal semantic theory must answer exactly the eight questions
raised by the author.[86] But if this is the fate which semantic

[85] Loc. cit., p. 115.
[86] Loc. cit., pp. 116—9.

theory has to meet, why should the category of semantic interpretation be reduced to sentence semantics? As Kiefer writes, "Having formulated the questions precisely, we can already define also the scope of semantic interpretation: to interpret a sentence semantically is to give precise and satisfactory answers to the questions that may be asked [(1)−(5)] in connection with the sentence."[87] And then he goes on to say: "We have to emphasize that semantic interpretation within formal semantics depends on the questions which relate to the sentence and can be asked, it is a function thereof. As we are able to formulate more questions accurately, also the concept of semantic interpretation will be broadened."[88]

There is no misunderstanding on this point. It is not the possibilities of semantic interpretation that are broadened, and its scope widened, but the concept of semantic interpretation is broadened only depending on what semantic problems we can answer by formal means. Accordingly the range of the problems is not determined by the objectivity of the formal structure of language, but it is left to the discretion of the linguist what questions he recognizes as broadening the concept of semantic interpretation. Either we can or we cannot ascertain that we arrive at the concept of formal semantic interpretation by formulating the questions required to define the formal structure of language, by seeking "precise and satisfactory answers" to those questions which disclose to us the essence of the "formal motion" of this complicated structure. But we can in no way agree with Kiefer's procedure: first he declares that the concept of semantic interpretation is covered by the answers given to the five questions that can be asked in connection with the sentence, and then his idea of broadening this concept is that still more questions need accurate formulation.

Even if we accepted Kiefer's "interpretation" of semantic interpretation (reduced to sentences), what should we do with word semantics, which also according to Kiefer is a subject of formal semantic theory; what is more, the sentence is a *sine qua non* of answering questions of semantics! "However, the sentence is not the only subject of formal semantic theory. Without properly elaborated word semantics there is no way of answering questions of sentence level. The semantic characterization of words has to be at least of such a depth that the questions

[87] Loc. cit., p. 120.
[88] Ibid.

(1) to (6) concerning the sentences might be answered."[89] Is not the semantic characterization of words part of semantic interpretation? Are words only to be characterized and not to be interpreted semantically? What is the difference between the two procedures? These are all questions which are left unanswered by Kiefer's conception of semantic interpretation, not to speak here in more detail about the possibilities taken in the broadest sense, which often provide the sole key to the genuine interpretation not only of a given word but also of a whole sentence. (See the explications above concerning the possibility of interpreting, in the light of the broader context only, the predicate, and even the whole, of the Hungarian sentence *Apám kifestette a szobáját*. Cf. Chapter III, Section 1.) The problem of the interpretative function of the text does not belong in the sphere of semantic interpretation, it only "deserves attention".[90] Or does it? One page later, to demonstrate such a function of the "text", Kiefer probes into the following sentences:

"Er hatte eine rote Feder in der linken Hand.

"Ist sie vom Jägerhut meines Mannes?

"Ja, gewiß".

Kiefer's conclusion: the afore-cited text is an "example to show that in many cases *to make a sentence unambiguous* is possible only in the light of the sentence context".[91]

The italicized phrase in the quotation is not too fortunate a formulation. Objectively, a sentence is either unambiguous or not. If a sentence is ambiguous, i.e. if it admits of more than one meaning, we cannot make it unambiguous by building it in the given sentence context. Is not the point rather that, under the influence of the sentence context, a single one of more possible meanings admitted by the polysemantic nature of the sentence is actualized, i.e. the given sentence context enables the unambiguous interpretation of a polysemantic sentence? What else is this but the semantic interpretative function of the text (sentence context)? Again it is a different question whether this can be formalized or not.

A peculiar train of thought it is! Bold premises, which Kiefer very often raises to the level of axioms; a cardinal system of criteria, upon which he builds his theory, but again very often he operates with criteria of a radically different character to

---

[89] Loc. cit., p. 119.
[90] Ibid.
[91] Ibid. (Italics are mine. — F. K.)

"elucidate" the same theoretical notion from a different point of view; categorically formulated principles and theses, followed by their wilful desertion a few pages later; a series of contradictions; to put it a little more mildly: unusually audacious theoretical selectivity. From this latter Kiefer does not shrink even when he himself comes to see the drawbacks of the theoretical premises of his own thesis.

Let us consider his idea about the basic condition of his theory of meaning, about grammatical theory. After stating that the theory of language consists of three principal parts: (a) grammar (syntactical component), (b) semantics (semantical component), and (c) phonology (phonological component),[92] he writes this about the task of the syntactical component (grammar): "The task of the syntactical component . . . can be discharged by any grammatical system that is equivalent to Chomsky's grammar of type 2 [context-restricted phrase structure grammar]. It seems expedient, however, to choose transformational grammar [?!] whose status is by no means clear from the formal point of view [!], but which, from the point of view of semantic inter- pretation, has advantages hardly to be found in the aforemen- tioned grammars of type 2."[93] One is interested to know what is, from the point of view of formal semantic interpretation, the advantage of transformational grammar, "whose status is by no means clear from the formal point of view", i.e. what can the proponent of formal semantic theory gain by making a not insignificant compromise of principle. Kiefer hints at practical difficulties, maintaining that direct semantic interpretation of diverse sentences would raise practically unsurmountable ob- stacles. For this very reason he has chosen transformational grammar, or rather he endeavours to make use of the advantages offered by it: first he wishes to perform the semantic interpreta- tion of so-called kernel sentences and only thereafter—in the light of the transformational rules—the interpretation of any other sentence, however complicated it may be. Thus what one can suppose is evidently only that the starting point, a *sine qua non*, of transformational grammatical analysis is the kernel sentence and its analysis, and that this is a kind of general "rule" which should underlie the analysis of every language, not to talk about the practical advantages of this method.

[92] Loc. cit., p. 121.
[93] Ibid.

Such is not at all the case. Kiefer himself states: "The recent results in the field of transformational grammar show, however, that the kernel sentences do not in the least play, within transformational grammar, the prominent role attributed to them originally; and in some languages any transformation is feasible without kernel sentences."[94]

Why then does he cling to transformational grammar whose status is by no means clear from the formal point of view, insisting on starting with formal semantic interpretation of kernel sentences which, as has been made clear lately, have no such prominent part to play in analysis as was thought earlier? Kiefer's answer is unequivocal: the reason why he — in opposition to the principles laid down in Chomsky's latest work — votes for "traditional" transformational grammar is primarily that, as he writes, "our semantic theory in its present form is irreconcilable with Chomsky's recent conception".[95]

Of course, Kiefer indisputably has the right to accept any new theory or to oppose it by his own. But if Chomsky's grammatical system can really perform the function of the syntactical component, and if nevertheless Kiefer chooses transformational grammar of uncertain formal status for a starting point of his formal semantic theory, this procedure would call for at least some explanation.

I have presented the cardinal points of Kiefer's semantic theory, but there is no need here to discuss Chomsky's grammatical theory. In spite of all this, I think, the mere affirmation that Kiefer's semantic theory is irreconcilable with Chomsky's recent conception is no satisfactory explanation. Nor is maybe the idea that there are advantages in starting with the analysis of the kernel sentence of equally uncertain status of the theory of transformational grammar. This fact is to be stressed all the more as Kiefer, on the third page following his repudiation of Chomsky's grammatical theory, asserts that the significance of the word-function so important from the viewpoint of the semantic interpretation of words is due to Chomsky's recent works: "Since Chomsky's recent works[96] it is evident that the tree

---

[94] Ibid. J. Zsilka has a more unequivocal opinion on the status of the "elementary sentence", the "linguistic kernel": ". . . Harris's conception of an elementary sentence is a fiction which does not correspond to linguistic reality." IOK XXIV, p. 365.

[95] Kiefer, loc. cit., p. 122.

[96] Including, of course, the incriminated manuscript: "Categories and Relations in Syntactic Theory." Loc. cit., pp. 122, 124.

diagram implicitly shows also the functions of words, i.e. relations which traditional grammar denotes by the terms 'subject of the sentence', 'object of the sentence', 'object of the verb', etc. This functional relation has an important part to play also in semantic interpretation."[97]

Anyway it is obvious that Kiefer's formal semantic theory is built on a shaky basis of grammatical theory open to different evaluations, evidently because this basis can be reconciled with his semantic conception.

One more remark regarding the semantic characterization of words. After stating that the definitions given by the Explanatory Dictionary "are of no use from the formal point of view",[98] Kiefer opines that the semantic characterization of words can be made in the form of a tree diagram. The essence of the semantic tree, however, is nothing else than a combination of Elekfi's idea about a terminal lexical chain and of the definition contained in the Explanatory Dictionary. But it does not matter that Kiefer in one place declares the definitions of the Explanatory Dictionary to be of no use, while a few pages later he writes this: "For the construction of the semantic tree diagram we have made use of the principal definitions given by the Explanatory Dictionary;"[99] what is especially striking is the conclusion he makes for the purpose of defining different concepts, on the basis of the semantic tree diagram, with regard to the semantic properties of the word:

"(a) Two words, w_1 and w_2, are said to be entirely synonymous when and only when their tree diagrams contain exactly the same branches.

"(b) An i-fold synonymy is said to exist between two words, w_1 and w_2, when and only when in their tree diagrams they have i branches in common.

---

[97] Loc. cit., p. 124. I do not wish to discuss here in detail that the semantically also important role of the functional relation of words has been known not only since Chomsky's tree diagrams, I only refer to the converse of the semantic interpretative function of the context, to the old truth that *verbs* in general fulfil the function of the predicate, while *nouns* and *adjectives* would have substantive, objective, attributive, etc. functions. Not only since the diagrams is it known that in the sentence *Egész nap eszem-iszom* 'I eat and drink all day long' the pair of verbs *eszem-iszom* is the predicate, while in the structure *eszem-iszom alak* 'a feasting type' the same chain of morphemes stands as attribute and is an adjective, etc., etc.

[98] Loc. cit., p. 135.

[99] Loc. cit., p. 137.

"(c) Two words, w_1 and w_2, are said to be entirely different [?!] when and only when in their appropriate tree diagrams they have no branch in common.

"(d) A word w is said to be an i-fold homonym when and only when its tree diagram contains i branches.

"(e) A word w is said to be unambiguous when and only when its tree diagram contains only one branch."[100]

Kiefer wishes to defend the above definitions against the charge of tautology by noting that "the semantic characterization to be found in the Explanatory Dictionary [of the Hungarian Language] does not fully agree [sic!] with the characterization given by means of the semantic tree diagram".[101]

What is primarily wrong with these definitions is not even their tautological nature but their system of criteria. For if we come to examine the formation of the tree diagram giving the semantic characterization of the words, we can see that, upon the model of the bifurcations indicating the grammatical categories, the tree diagram divides into as many end branches as the word has meanings. Even though, in his tree diagram of the word *legény*, Kiefer does not enumerate all definitions found in the Explanatory Dictionary: 'bachelor', 'young man', 'tough fellow', 'occupation (journeyman, servant, soldier)', it can be seen at once that the diagram of *legény* has seven branches, since he accepted seven principal meanings of the word.[102] If for the above definition we rely on the genesis of the tree diagram, we come to the following conclusions:

(a) Two words are entirely synonymous when their tree diagrams contain exactly the same branches (they have as many and exactly identical meanings), and they contain exactly the same branches because they are entirely synonymous (they have exactly as many and identical meanings).

The same applies, *mutatis mutandis*, also to the criteria of:

(b) i-fold synonymy,

(c) the total difference of two words,

(d) i-fold homonymy, and

(e) unambiguity.

This set of definitions has led us again to the notorious vicious circle: defining a thing by itself. So this method lets us know nothing more about the "non-redundant" semantic characteriza-

<hr>

[100] Loc. cit., p. 138.
[101] Ibid.
[102] Loc. cit., p. 137.

tion of a word or morpheme than we have so far known from either the definitions of the Explanatory Dictionary or even from earlier works on semantics.

A summary of what precedes necessarily leads to the conclusion that Kiefer's theory of meaning starting from false premises is unacceptable, and his formal definition of meaning based on the principle of compatibility—by its *idem per idem* nature—does not mean anything. The logic of his trend of thought is difficult to follow because of its inconsistency and voluntaristic eclecticism. The most striking indication of this is given where, in discussing the semantic function of suffixational morphemes, Kiefer builds his conception on the traditional semantic criteria he himself criticized before, and leaves entirely out of account the corner-stone of his whole semantic theory, the principle of semantic compatibility.

11. CONCLUSIONS

I should like to emphasize that this summary is not intended to be an evaluation of the formalization of semantic theory, but it is meant to be a critique of Kiefer's fundamental theoretical statements. Although it is impossible to agree with Kiefer's definition of the tasks of semantic theory wishing to confine the whole theory to the clarification of those questions which can be solved by formal methods, there is no need to demonstrate specially that a semantic theory, like any other theory, can be formalized and that formal analysis can even disclose such aspects of meaning as could not so far be discovered by other methods. But this calls for irrefutable axioms, precisely defined concepts and clearly described categories, which—as is evidenced by the foregoing—can hardly be found in Kiefer's work destined "to lay the foundations of the construction of a formal theory of meaning".

One cannot help asking the question why, besides the false theoretical premises, the basic tenets of Kiefer's semantic theory, his definition of compatibility, his semantic characterization of compatibility, his semantic characterization of words, his distinctions in respect of synonymy, homonymy, etc. are stuck within the limits described above. In other words: is it an inevitable consequence of formal analysis that his findings, theses, definitions remain inside the magic circle of "freedom from redundancy" bordering on tautologism? It certainly is not. One of the strong points of the formalization theory taken and applied in the right sense is just the requirement of exactness, the possible grasping of the pattern of motion of phenomena and processes by discovering cardinal points that can be defined with the aid of symbols and schemata, and elevated to a very high level of abstraction on the basis of properly applied mathematical formulae.

The high level of abstraction, however, is not to be confused with schematic representation. The mathematical formulae picked without proper circumspection entail the danger of schematism by themselves. The characteristic feature of mathematics is just that it is the result of a very high degree of abstraction: the diverse phenomena and processes of the world can find room in a simple mathematical symbol, say a, furthermore the most complicated structure—and such is language—can be expressed by a symbol enclosed in braces ($\{W,R\}$), where W is the set of the signs and R is the set of all relations between signs.

Is mathematics right when it works with such a large measure of generalization? Absolutely, because without that it would cease to be mathematics. But until mathematics arrives at the symbols reflecting an extremely large measure of generalization, the result presupposes an unpredictable number of sets of operations of generalization, because without these its system of symbols would be a lifeless schema, or worse, an invented fiction. Therefore, when we apply a sort of mathematical formula to represent some phenomenon of reality, when we "substitute a formula" that serves to represent other relations, we have to traverse the road in the opposite direction (in thought at least) and to subject the main phases of our deduction (the final conclusion by all means) to the test of practice, unless we want to be left stranded at the level of hypotheses and schematic operations.

A trivial but unforgettable truth was told by F. Papp in one of his lectures: "Mathematics gives so general schemata that they can hold everything, indeed."[1] That is why all that he said of the mathematical models and of the three main phases of the related method, modelling, is worth considering: "The model is ... a consciously simplified pattern of reality which, by reason of its relative simplicity, enables us to study through it the phenomenon under examination. And consequently modelling means that mathematical linguistics, like other exact sciences, tries to

[1] Papp: ÁNyT II, p. 76.

express more or less accurately, in the language of mathematics, the relations between elements of the discovered body of facts (i.e. to build a model); in the next phase of the task it can make some alterations on this model, and finally it re-applies the model thus obtained to reality and examines which facts meet the requirements raised by the new model and which do not. The construction of models, the operations performed on the model and the re-application of the models to reality are the three main phases of the work of modelling."[2]

And still something that must be kept in mind. In preparation and in support of its varied operations, mathematics—just like formal logic—very often makes statements which sound like very trivial truths to the ears of a non-mathematician. Among the many relevant cases let us recall only the qualification of the equivalency relation applied also by Kiefer:

(1) a is equivalent to a: $a \Rightarrow a$;

(2) if a is equivalent to b, then b is equivalent to a: if $a \Rightarrow b$, then $b \Rightarrow a$;

(3) if a is equivalent to b and b is equivalent to c, then a is equivalent to c: if $a \Rightarrow b$ and $b \Rightarrow c$, then $a \Rightarrow c$.[3]

Are these statements true? They certainly are, and however evident they may seem, they should be fixed as premises of other operations. It is doubtless that these formulae can be applied in the formalization and characterization of language. If we make the appropriate "substitutions", we come to the following truth of irrefutable validity:

Let the meanings of Hung. *ár*[4] be formalized as a, "the four-branched tree diagram" as b, and "a fourfold polysemant" as c. From the reflexive, symmetrical and transitive character of the equivalency relation we can infer the following:

(1) The formalization of the meanings of the word *ár* (a) is equivalent to the formalization of the meanings of the word *ár* (a).

(2) If the formalization of the meanings of the word *ár* (a) is equivalent to the four-branched tree diagram (b), then the four-branched tree diagram (b) is equivalent to the formalization of the meanings of the word *ár* (a).

(3) If the formalization of the meanings of the word *ár* (a) is equivalent to the four-branched tree diagram (b), and the four-branched tree diagram (b) is equivalent to the formalization of a

---

[2] Ibid.
[3] Kiefer, loc. cit., p. 115.
[4] See the discussion about the Hungarian word *ár* in Chapter III, Section 1.

fourfold polysemant (c), then the formalization of the meanings of the word ár (a) is equivalent to the formalization of the four-fold polysemant (c).

These statements of irrefutable validity, however, tell us not too much about the essence of the fourfold polysemantic charac-ter of the word ár, or about the essence of the meaning of poly-semants in general, even if we describe one of the above state-ments, e.g. that under (2), in a more general form:

If the formalization of the meanings of an i-fold homonym (a) is equivalent to a tree diagram having i branches (b), then the tree diagram having i branches (b) is equivalent to the formaliza-tion of the meanings of an i-fold homonym (a).

Let us add as a reminder the already discussed variant of Kiefer's definition of homonymity:

A word w is said to be an i-fold homonym when and only when its tree diagram contains i branches, and the tree diagram of the word w contains i branches because it is an i-fold homonym.

Weirdly similar trains of thought! I may not be far from the truth if I say that the symmetrical character of the equivalency relation so important for mathematical analysis might be re-sponsible for the genesis of Kiefer's definition of homonymity and of his definition of compatibility as well.

Homonymity, the polysemantic character of words, etc. con-stitute a complicated semantical problem. The grasping of their essence is inconceivable without dissecting the complex body of the semantic structure, and their formalization promises satis-factory results only if it is made with due respect for what has been said above.

If we compare the above train of thought, the mathematical apparatus, of the paper written in an attempt to formalize semantic theory with the conception of meaning as a compli-cated structure, we cannot help thinking of the mathematician L. Kalmár's convincing opinion: "... what is called abstract algebra ... obtained its name from a further abstraction: namely that the mathematician disregarded even whether he performed operations on quantities or on other objects, and what objects at all he operated on. All he considered was what kind of opera-tion can be made among the objects which are operated on, and what is the nature of these operations ... Abstract algebra engaged first in the examination of such special systems for which the technical term used in mathematics is structures."[5]

[5] Kalmár: ÁNyT II, pp. 29—30.

A few pages later he describes the elements of the said structures as follows: "In case of such types of structures the elements of the system are not necessarily numbers any longer, but they may be elements of any nature whatever; the definition of the operations performed on them and of the relations existing among them also may be optional, we only require them to satisfy some axioms. The axioms still show, however, that the mathematician originally started out from the structural examination of systems consisting of numbers."[6]

And it is an old truth that what is relevant from the point of view of the structural examination of systems consisting of numbers is not necessarily relevant, and may even be unsatisfactory, for the description of other systems.

Everything depends on what kind of system we take language to be, whether we hold meaning a constitutive element of members of that system, or whether we interpret it as an extraneous rule that cannot be deduced from them. For if we conceive of language as a system which is a network of relationships that can be described by categories of formal logic, where it is possible and even necessary to disregard the essential features of the constitutive elements (vehicles) of the relations, the factors of the sign which is actualized in the real sign situation (reference to reality, etc.), then the results and axioms of abstract mathematical investigations which grow out of the structural analysis of systems consisting of numbers are also applicable directly to the examination of the network of relationships of the linguistic structure; what is more, some aspects of language "can be examined successfully only by means of the categories and methods of certain mathematical disciplines", as Zs. Telegdi said when summing up the lessons of the working conference on "Questions of Mathematical Linguistics and Machine Translation".[7] Telegdi's opinion quoted below is already a more shaded formulation of the way he at the time described—in the wake of Saussure—the linguistic structure: "According to Saussure, language is a system whose elements are determined merely by the place they occupy in the system as a whole; in other words, it is a network of relationships which we have to examine aside from the nature of the vehicles of those relationships."[8]

[6] Loc. cit., p. 33.
[7] Telegdi, loc. cit., p. 315.
[8] Loc. cit., p. 314.

I do not wish to deal here with this simplification of the complicated linguistic structure, but I deem it necessary to compare Telegdi's above view with the linguistic conception of Kalmár, who delivered the principal lecture at the conference: ". . . language is a much more complicated system than those systems whose structures have ever been analyzed by algebra."[9] With this statement Kalmár surely did not want to propagate the opinion that language, just because of its complicated nature, is not liable to formal description, to interpretation by mathematical apparatus. On the contrary! A wide application of mathematical methods is made feasible by the very fact that their formulae are the products of a great degree of generalization, by which it is possible to describe, to formalize the structure of language like any other complicated structure. Since, however, every formal system has a large variety of possible interpretations, we cannot stop at the formal definition of language either, we cannot rest satisfied with indicating which of the formulae are axioms and which of the transformations into other formulae are rules of deduction, but we have also to make a semantic interpretation of the formal system. Kalmár writes: "With a view to making the interpretation we have to define the meaning of each expression, of each formula (to state at least when its meaning is considered true and when false). Only on the basis of such semantic definitions can we ask what are all the adequate interpretations of the formal system, interpretations in which each of the demonstrable formulae is a true judgment, whether the formal system is complete with respect to some interpretation, or whether every formula signifying a true judgment is demonstrable."[10]

The significance of Kalmár's above statement can duly be appreciated only if we take into account the following:

(a) At that conference again L. Antal, this militant representative of "consistently formal" linguistic analysis, made this categorical statement: "Examination of the content [which, in the light of Antal's terminology and of his opinion advanced at the conference held one year before, is identical with semantic investigation] is from the outset certainly outside the province of linguistics . . . The *true* and the *false* are no categories of linguistics."[11]

(b) At the same working conference F. Papp doubted that the linguist might be able to do anything with any material "even

[9] Kalmár, loc. cit., p. 36.
[10] Loc. cit., pp. 170—1.
[11] Antal: ÁNyT II, p. 139.

slightly contaminated by intellective momenta",[12] and therefore he held that "maximal formalization" was, besides exactness, "an essential requirement of modernity".[13] Namely, in his judgment, "we must not the least bit confound the two sets of phenomena—those of form and meaning—, we have to separate them as consistently as possible".[14]

(c) It is true that Gy. Szépe was in favour of semantic investigations: ". . . the comprehensive theory of the whole of language would be incomplete without a semantic theory."[15] His espousal of semantics, however, was not a recognition of the importance of any kind of semantics, but it was an espousal of the semantic theory of Antal, whose work was in the press at the time of the working conference. Szépe thought that the strongest point of Antal's theory was its consistent criticism of semantics encumbered with psychological or ontological categories, and—in unison with Antal—he demanded the "development of linguistic semantics" as opposed to those categories.

(d) In his theses summarizing the lessons of the working conference Telegdi responded neither to the conception of meaning represented by Antal, Papp and Szépe, nor to Kalmár's related opinion.

Thus it is not surprising that Kalmár has recently been joined by another mathematician, A. Rényi, in trying to defend the linguistic justification of the examination of "content" elements against the total negligence of linguists abiding by "maximal formalization". In his lecture at the conference Rényi[16] distinguished information theory taken in the narrower and the broader sense. The first is engaged in theoretical questions of all kinds of message transmission (applied in telecommunication, in the operation of electronic computers, in automation, etc.), and it can in itself be of great help to the science of language. According to Rényi, however, "in fact, the linguist needs more: he needs a theory which is able to grasp the deeper interrelations of language, too. A theory which examines information not only from the quantitative point of view, but also with regard to content, we can call *information theory in the broader sense*".[17] He defined the scope of reference of the theory of information

[12] Papp, loc. cit., p. 293.
[13] Ibid.
[14] Ibid.
[15] Szépe: ÁNyT II, p. 291.
[16] "Information Theory and Linguistics."
[17] Rényi, loc. cit., p. 245.

in the broader sense as follows: "The subject of information theory in the broader sense can be language not only as a series of symbols (for, as such, it is already a subject of information theory in the narrower sense as well), but also as a series of signs having content or meaning. The statistical properties and laws of language are in themselves important and interesting, and deserving of more attention than they received so far. But mathematical linguistics today is striving for more, namely to discuss also the content of language somehow mathematically."[18] He saw the essence of the difference between the two kinds of theory in the study of questions of content: "As to the difference between the two kinds of information theory I consider the issue of the content of information to be decisive."[19]

The content of information is a complicated, complex thing, composed of both objective and subjective elements which the linguist has to deal with. As Rényi said, "Thus, for example, the quantity of information is an entirely objective notion, while in the issue of content and meaning it is much more difficult to separate subjective from objective elements."[20]

This is how the problem of "pure linguistics"[21] free from semantics was viewed by the mathematicians taking an active part in the working conference on the questions of mathematical linguistics and being "sensitive to the semantic problems of language", and let me add, also by the only sociologist who took the floor at the conference, S. Szalai, who is of the opinion that the mechanical summarizing of scientific publications can be automated only "by selecting the content characteristics—descriptors—of specified discursive types of texts" and "by selecting passages relevant from the point of view of content".[22]

With all these questions, however, we have come already to the problem of the dialectics of content and form, described in the linguistic literature of the past few years as the relation of meaning and linguistic form.

[18] Loc. cit., p. 246.
[19] Ibid.
[20] Loc. cit., p. 247.
[21] Kalmár's expression, loc. cit., p. 171.
[22] Szalai: ÁNyT II, p. 243. For details cf. S. Szalai, Gépi kivonatolás. Elméleti és kísérleti adalékok a magyar nyelvű tudományos közlemények kivonatolásának kérdéséhez [Mechanical Summarizing. Theoretical and Experimental Contributions to the Question of Mechanical Summarizing of Scientific Publications in Hungarian], Budapest, 1963. Published as No. 5 of Időszerű Műszaki Dokumentációs Kérdések [Timely Questions of Technical Documentation].

IV. THE RELATION BETWEEN CONTENT
(MEANING) AND (LINGUISTIC) FORM

1. PRE-SAUSSUREAN THEORIES

Authors of theories concerning the most characteristic features
of language (beginning from the great philosophers of antiquity),
as far as we can look back, have all, in one form or another,
stated their views regarding the relations between the content
elements and formal components of language. Ever since thinkers
of different periods have been studying the nature of the basic
function of language, the communication of ideas, emotions,
etc., they have inevitably had to face the problem of the relations
between language and the reality denoted by it. Those who
observed the difference indisputably existing between the characteristics of language, of the linguistic sign, and the segment of
reality denoted by it, emphasized mainly the lack of direct connection, the arbitrary character of the relation of language and
reality, adding that this arbitrary nature prevailed only with
some reservations, within the scope of socially determined norms
(Artistotle and his school). On the basis of the conventional
character the polysemous nature of the linguistic sign became
overemphasized, which only made it difficult to understand the
real connection of language and objective reality (sophists,
sophism). Against sophistry fed by such excesses, Plato with his
idealistic definition of the relation between ideas and reality,
with his view on the priority of ideas, perforce became acquainted with the relation of words and ideas, of language and
knowledge about reality, and, returning to Heraclitus's original
thought, stressed that language is the "vehicle" of knowledge
grasping the essence of things, a representative of the mental
image of reality. If to this we add the discovery of the imaging
function of the linguistic sign (Dionysius Thrax), we come to see
the essence of all those questions which constitute the problem
of the linguistic aspect of content and form, a problem that was
handed down, through various channels,[1] to Saussure, one of the
greatest linguistic theoreticians of the twentieth century.

---

[1] Thomas Aquinas, Duns Scotus, Descartes, Leibniz, Wundt, Paul.

2. SAUSSUREAN "UNITY"

As is commonly known, Saussure with his sign theory (not entirely free from contradictions) was in his own way very categorical on one point: in the linguistic sign he saw the indivisible unity of the signified *(signifié)* and the signifier *(signifiant)* or, in other words, the concept and the phonic form *(son)*,[1] so much so that he regarded the sequence of sounds as being of linguistic nature only in case the "vehicle of the concept" *(le support d'une idée)* eliminated from linguistic research the examination of phonetic form abstracted from the concept.[2] Momentous as Saussure's thesis regarding the inseparability of the external and internal aspects of language is, the formula is devalued greatly by the well-known fact that, based on the unity of concept and phonic form, the Saussurean sign in the above formulation is, as to its essential traits, not a sign at all, because it is not the unity of the concept and the sensuously perceptible material sound sequence, but the unity of concept and phonic notion, of a psychical impression of the material sound sequence.[3] Accordingly, the combination of content and the phonic elements taken in the above sense produces form, not substance.[4]

In the light of Saussure's definition, therefore, the unity of content and form is not a substantial unity but a network, a combination, of formal relationships.

3. CRITIQUE OF THE SAUSSUREAN CONCEPTION

It is no accident that this conception of the unity of content and form gave rise to extensive debates. The Marxists rightly criticized Saussure for his surrender of the material character of the linguistic sign, for his "dematerialized" interpretation of content and form, for his deformation of the reality-reflecting function of language, of the linguistic sign. Representatives of other schools also could not see what to do with this "unity" and were increasingly disposed, just like many Marxist students of language, to understand by linguistic sign only Saussure's

---

[1] Saussure, *Cours* . . ., pp. 157, 158.
[2] Op. cit., p. 144.
[3] ". . . l'empreinte psychique de ce son." Op. cit., p. 98.
[4] ". . . cette combinaison produit *une forme, non une substance*." Op. cit., p. 157. (Italics in the original.)

signifiant, or rather its "material realization".[1] This kind of sign conception, of course, threw a different light upon the relation of content (identical with meaning in most linguistic works) and form (linguistic form, material sound sequence). In other words, they viewed this relationship not as an immanent peculiarity of the linguistic sign (the above sign conception prevented them from doing so), but they lowered the relation of meaning and phonic form to the level of association. More simply, this denies the dual character of one of the most essential elements of language, the linguistic sign, and gives up the idea about the unity of content and formal elements being actualized in the linguistic sign, namely it negates all that which was and is still regarded, by both the traditional and the Marxist sign theory, as one of the most essential features of the linguistic sign.[2]

4. THE VARIOUS FORMAL METHODS

The insufficiency of Saussure's sign theory based on the inseparability of content from the phonic form deprived of its material garb, besides other ideological considerations, was also responsible for the fact that some theoreticians[1] in describing the structure of language (descriptive analysis) sought to neglect entirely (but whether they accomplished it consistently is a different question) the content elements, the meaning. Thinking that such questions did not belong to the realm of language, they eliminated their investigation from the scope of linguistic research. I only wish to remind the reader of Bloomfield's concep-

---

[1] Cf. A. Martinet's view in footnote 21 in Chapter II, Section 2.

[2] Cf. L. Weisgerber's opinion in footnote 3 in Chapter III, Section 5; Laziczius's standpoint in his *Általános nyelvészet* [General Linguistics], Budapest, 1942, p. 56; the position taken up by Leontyev and Luria in the introductory part of the German edition of Vygotsky's work, *Denken und Sprechen*, Berlin, 1964, p. 15; Schaff's statement: "... das Wort — nicht der Laut, sondern das Wort, das die Einheit von Laut und Bedeutung ist — ...", in DZfPh IX, p. 712; O. S. Akhmanova's categorical definition: "Ясно, что основной задачей современного языкознания является выяснение вопроса о содержании (значении) языковых единиц в его соотношении с их выражением (в частности, звучанием)." [It is clear that the basic task of modern linguistics is to examine the question of the content (meaning) of linguistic units in correlation with their expression (in particular, with their phonation).] О. С. Ахманова, *О точных методах исследования языка* [On Precise Methods of Linguistic Research], Moscow, 1961, p. 9.

[1] L. Bloomfield, Z. S. Harris, B. Bloch and their followers.

tion of meaning, according to which meaning is the very object denoted by the sign and for this very reason cannot claim the attention of linguistic research.

According to the *distributional analysis* of language, for example, the sign itself is the material sound sequence, and if language is a system of signs, the only task linguistics can have is to examine these signs according to their places in the system; this is called the distributional analysis of language, which includes also the investigation of the possible reciprocal combinations, the formal "behaviour", of the various phonemes. Harris holds that distribution is "the freedom of occurrence of portions of an utterance relatively to each other".[2] Accordingly, "The distribution of an element will be understood as the sum of all its environments".[3] The only exact criterion of recognizing the linguistic elements and classifying them is, therefore, the ascertainment of the narrower or broader environment in which a given element can occur and in which it cannot.

The other method of linguistic research seeking to eliminate consideration of the content elements is the so-called *transformational analysis*, whose essential traits are the following: structures, sentences occurring in different linguistic utterances are considered to be the results of the single- or multi-stage transformation of a few simple sentence types, called *nuclear* or kernel *sentences*. As to its basic structural features, every complicated sentence can be reduced to a few kernel sentences, and with this procedure transformational analysis arrives at a grammatical schema which seems fit to generate an infinite number of linguistic utterances of the most varied construction.

This latter trait of transformational grammars is a connecting link to what is called *generative grammar*, which can be regarded also as the converse of transformational grammar. Namely, while transformational grammar makes analyses by means of a certain number of rules of transformation on different levels, i.e. while it reduces complex constructions to simpler ones until this "method of reduction" leads to the kernel sentence, generative grammar is intended to provide a set of "generating rules" which can help to build up sentences of the most complicated construction meeting also the criteria of good grammar.

Beyond mentioning the essential features of the methods in

---

[2] Harris, *Methods in Structural Linguistics*, Chicago, 1951, p. 5.
[3] *Word* X, p. 146.

question, I do not wish to discuss every one of them; there are vast volumes discussing their advantages and drawbacks. I should like only to refer to the fact—which I have mentioned already when speaking of Kiefer's semantic theory—that the status of what is called transformational grammar is, from the formal point of view, not so clear in the light of recent research; the supporting pillar of theory and methods, the kernel sentence, plays no such distinctive role as was thought earlier.

The discussion of *generative transformational grammar* would go beyond the scope and the purposes of this study,[4] therefore I am going to discuss (to the extent of a few remarks) only one of the said methods, distributional analysis, against the background of practical usefulness.[5]

Thus I shall examine how it is possible, by completely excluding the content elements marked as extralinguistic, to describe language in an exact manner, to carry out the analysis of language by the sole criteria of its formal behaviour.

The reason for my choice is that the formal methods, in spite of some differences, agree by and large in their essential traits, their fundamental theoretical motives and their approach, thus the testimony of one allows us from a certain point of view to make general inferences with regard to the others, too.

5. DISTRIBUTIONAL ANALYSIS

To begin with, I should like to stress my agreement with those views which welcome a "new revolution of linguistics" when pointing to the importance of linguistics satisfying the production-technological requirements of human society (information theory, daily tasks of telecommunication and automation, machine translation, etc.). These pressing needs really call for research methods different from the so-called traditional methods of linguistics; more precisely, they necessarily require that the old methods be combined with the new ones, to ensure that the new achievements of linguistic research are, strictly speaking, "socially useful" results.

---

[4] For its elaborate critique based on a careful analysis of some types of motion of linguistic reality, see J. Zsilka, Nyelvi rendszer és valóság [Linguistic System and Reality]. A doctoral dissertation in manuscript (1968).

[5] I use the term "practical usefulness" in a double sense: (a) what is its "concrete" social advantage; (b) as a theory and method, how it can stand the test of practice taken in the philosophical sense.

In addition to direct practical usefulness, the new features of linguistic structure discoverable by formal means can be expected to bring results likely to serve as the starting point of new theoretical generalizations and to encourage further research work.

Lots of examples could be cited from the history of science to demonstrate the stimulating nature of the interaction of theory and practice. One or another branch of science underwent sudden, "revolutionary" changes when its representatives "heeded the call of the times", when they realized the significance of meeting social requirements, and placed their work of research at the service of this objective. Let me quote, from among the many relevant instances, what the Hungarian F. Kempelen, who lived in the second half of the eighteenth century, told about the real value and the significance of the invention of his talking machine, which was viewed as a mere exotic wonder at the time: "All the benefits, all the merits of all my discoveries may well consist only in that some deaf-mutes can thereby learn to speak more easily, and part of the persons of defective speech can be cured through my instructions."[1] He pointed to the incontestable correlation of theory and practice in the following categorical terms, which are in harmony even with the modern views: "Hence my speech machine and my theory of language have continually progressed side by side, leading the way for each other."[2]

Let us see what E. Brücke had to say about the influence of Kempelen's "mechanical" discovery upon the sudden development of phonetics: "Towards the end of the eighteenth century, on the other hand, phonetics made still another considerable move forward . . . in Vienna, through Wolfgang von Kempelen who, in his efforts to construct a talking machine, was led not only to

[1] "Aller Nutzen — alles Verdienst, das meine gesammelte Entdeckungen haben dürften, mag wohl nur darin bestehen, daß dadurch bey einigen Taubstummen der Unterricht im Sprechen erleichtert, und ein Teil derjenigen Menschen, die eine fehlerhafte Aussprache haben, durch meine Anleitungen davon geheilt werden kann." Wolfgang von Kempelen, *Mechanismus der menschlichen Sprache nebst der Beschreibung einer sprechenden Maschine*, "Vorerinnerung", Vienna, 1791, first unnumbered page.

[2] "Daher ist meine Sprachmaschine, und meine Theorie von der Sprache beständig neben einander fortgeschritten, und hat eine der anderen Wegweiserin gedient." Op. cit., pp. 396—7.

examine how man produces the speech-sounds, but to explore the conditions of their production in general."[3]

To state these facts today seems, so to speak, trivial. Yet I have found it necessary to cast my vote for the justification of formal analysis, because still in our days there are opinions questioning the practical significance of formal methods, of formalization. The total negation of the correlation of content and form is one thing (this can and even must be contested), and the formalization of the results attained by exact research methods is another.

I think the above preliminaries have been necessary also because I am of the view myself that the formal analysis related to the problems of the correlation of form and meaning (content) has not only a polemic aspect. "If we proceed", writes J. Herman, "from the almost generally accepted and correct objective that we should describe language as a system of signs that serves the purposes of communication, and if we examine from this angle its various elements, its structure, the mechanism of its working and the regularities of its development, we have perforce to take into account what influence is exerted on the structure of the system by the content aspect of the elements of the system and of the particular acts of communication; this question can be answered only on the basis of an examination of the relation between the formal and the content aspect."[4]

If we conceive the correlation of form and content in this manner, the role of the content elements comes inevitably to the foreground—a fact that does not matter by itself, because it is an application to linguistic research of the old-established thesis which says that every content looks for an appropriate form, i.e. the content is expressed in an appropriate form. But this formula grasps only one aspect of the correlation of content and

[3] "Dagegen sollte die Lautlehre gegen das Ende des achtzehnten Jahrhunderts . . . in Wien, noch einen wesentlichen Fortschritt machen durch Wolfgang von Kempelen, der bei seinen Bemühungen, eine sprechende Maschine zu construiren, darauf geführt wurde, nicht allein zu untersuchen, wie der Mensch die Sprachlaute bildet, sondern die Bedingungen ihrer Hervorbringung überhaupt zu erforschen." E. Brücke, *Grundzüge der Physiologie und Systematik der Sprachlaute für Linguisten und Taubstummenlehrer*, Vienna, 1896², p. 6.
[4] Herman: ÁNyT I, pp. 125—6.

form, and for the sake of completeness let me add the other aspect as well: form also acts upon the content and shapes it. The determining role of the linguistic form was stressed also by Zs. Telegdi, who wrote this: "It can be said, therefore, that the sentences of a language are made valid by their form; to describe these forms which in their totality determine the sentences possible in the given language—that is in fact the task of grammar, of grammatical description."[5] Even though we cannot agree with Telegdi's one-sided formulation, which utterly exaggerates the role of one of the elements of the relation of content and form, the form ("the sentences of a language are made valid by their form"), this view bears witness anyhow that the significance of the formal aspect must not be ignored.

Formal descriptivists, however, established the linguistic validity of utterances by the formal behaviour of the elements of the utterances, and closed the debates over the priority of content and form so that they refused to recognize content as a constitutive element of language, turned dialectic unity into a sovereign form, distorted the indivisible unity of the constitutive elements by their one-sided interpretation, we may as well say that they annulled it.

This procedure was followed among others by Z. S. Harris, the well-known theoretician of distributional analysis, who relied only on formal distinctions and omitted to take note of the content elements, of meaning.[6] If the problem of meaning, within the scope of linguistic analysis, cannot play a role, what is left is only distribution as a criterion of relevance.[7] On this basis the only task of descriptive analysis is to investigate the linguistic utterances.[8] And even if we have to accept the expert opinion of the native informant, which can be called "meaning" in the terminology of "traditional" linguistics, it refers only to the

---

[5] Loc. cit., p. 7.

[6] "The procedures given below, however, are merely ways of arranging the original data; and since they go only by formal distinctions there is no opportunity for uncontrolled interpreting of the data or for forcing of the meaning." Z. S. Harris, Methods in Structural Linguistics, Chicago, 1951, p. 3.

[7] "The main research of descriptive linguistics, and the only relation which will be accepted as relevant in the present survey, is the distribution or arrangement, within the flow of speech, of some parts or features relatively to others." Op. cit., p. 5.

[8] "An UTTERANCE is any stretch of talk, by one person, before and after which there is silence on the part of the person." Op. cit., p. 14.

insufficient nature of formal descriptive analysis, which can sooner or later be eliminated by improving the methods.[9]

All this does not mean, of course, that within unity there is no way of examining separately the forms of motion, the "behaviour" of the formal aspect, only we cannot expect this kind of investigation to lead to complete linguistic explanation, to a linguistic theory, and not even its method can be regarded as the only exact, or even the most important, method.

If language, as to its essence, were really a rule, i.e. a set of formal distinctions governing the narrower and broader environments of the constitutive elements of utterances, then the grasping of this essence could be expected only by way of formal analysis, because formal analysis makes only formal comparisons, establishes identities and differences, and thereby qualifies, classifies, categorizes, defines, etc. If, however, language is more than a system composed of formal relationships, the insufficiency of the essence-grasping nature of formal analysis would become conspicuous at once, since it is really unfit to discover the "intrinsic qualities" of the utterances. This method of approach leaves the internal, and let us add, determining interrelations of language hidden from the researcher. Well, then, it is a primary task of every science to uncover the essence hidden behind the regularities of superficial forms, the internal interrelatedness of things and phenomena, to find out the motives that basically determine the manifestations of phenomena which do not become apparent in the initial phase of cognition, at the time of empiric inquiries.

But let us stop conducting a declarative polemic with Harris's principal theoretical statements at issue, and let us oppose his only example by the evidence of the facts of language. With two forms taken from the paradigm of the Arabic equivalent of the verb 'write' Harris wishes to support his thesis on "Non-contiguous Phonemic Sequences".[10] What is of interest to us, in this place, is not the problems of contiguous and non-contiguous phonemic sequences, but the question whether or not the proposed theory and method are acceptable. Namely, whether the end-results of the acts of segmentation performed on the basis of formal distinctions can stand the test of linguistic facts.

[9] See Harris's remark in footnote 7 in Chapter II, Section 3.
[10] Subtitle, op. cit., p. 165.

Harris operates with the opposition of two forms of the Arabic verb and states the following: "In Arabic, for example, we have such utterances as *kataba* 'he wrote', . . . *katabtu* 'I wrote' . . . from which we extract the following as independent morphemic segments: *k-t-b* 'write', . . . *-a* 'he', *-tu* 'I' . . ."[11] In the light of American typographical usage the formulae "*-a* 'he' " and "*-tu* 'I' " can be interpreted in one way only: *-a* means 'he', and *-tu* means 'I', that is they ought to denote pronouns of the third and the first person singular!

The paradigm of the masculine singular of the above verb of class I and the corresponding personal pronouns are as follows:

3rd person:	*kataba*	'he wrote'	— *huwa*	'he',
2nd person:	*katabta*	'you wrote'	— *anta*	'you',
1st person:	*katabtu*	'I wrote'	— *anā*	'I'.[12]

This table shows many things but just not that *-a* is 'he' and *-tu* is 'I', that they are personal pronouns. The pronouns at issue are *huwa* and *ana*. The morphemes *-a* and *-tu* occurring in the paradigm are personal suffixes of the verb, and all they have in common with the personal pronouns of the third and the first person singular *huwa* and *anā* is that in the singular of the perfect form the morpheme *-a* is compatible with *huwa* and *-tu* with *anā*. But it has to be fixed categorically that compatibility is something entirely different from identity.[13]

The wrongness of Harris's conclusion can be demonstrated by formal comparison, too, regardless of the real personal pronoun. One has only to look about the other paradigmatic forms of the

---

[11] Ibid. At the places marked (. . .) other Arabic examples are introduced, but the conclusions drawn from the formal opposition of *kataba* and *katabtu* are to us sufficient.

[12] I have compiled this torso of paradigm on the basis of the verb type *qatala* found in C. Brockelmann, *Arabische Grammatik*, Leipzig, 1953[13], Part II, pp. 4—5. Its conjugation is identical with that of *kataba*. The personal pronouns are to be found on p. 27 of Part I of the same work. The transliteration is by Miklós Maróth, to whom I express my thanks in this place.

[13] If we are looking in any case for morphological similarity or genetical identity between the above paradigmatic forms and the corresponding personal pronouns, we may presume, in respect of the second person singular, that the morpheme *-ta* in *anta* and *katabta* is of the same origin (verbal communication from Károly Czeglédi), but thereby we have already departed from synchronic description and have fallen victim to a confusion of viewpoints. From the point of view of synchrony, *anta* is not identical with the morpheme *-ta*.

212

Arabic verb in question. The three forms of the imperfect singular are:

3rd person: *(huwa) jaktubu* 'he writes',
2nd person: *(anta) taktubu* 'you write',
1st person: *(anā) aktubu* 'I write'.[14]

Let us separate the morphemes which appear as preformatives: *ja-*, *ta-*, *a-* (they have *-ktubu* in common). If *aktubu* means 'I write', then it follows necessarily from Harris's formal comparison that *a* means 'I'. Accordingly the morpheme *a* means either 'he' or 'I', depending on whether it occurs in the paradigm of the perfect or in that of the imperfect. If the facts of language directly contradict this logic, this is for the facts of language to worry about! But it may be proposed anyhow that, as to the rightness of the conclusions drawn from formal comparison, one should consult the native informant, or Brockelmann's Arabic grammar, or at least one should examine the inflectional system of the language concerned.

In his conclusion drawn from the formal comparison of *kataba* and *katabtu* Harris was deceived by the same method by which, on the basis of Harris's distinctions, Antal, in his book on the Hungarian case-system, "established" the meaning and function of the morpheme *-os* of Latin *hortos*. Also Antal tries to approach the meaning and function of the given morpheme from the aspect of expression, and he separates from the whole paradigmatic system those forms which are liable to formal comparison with the elements of the segment *-os*. His train of thought is worth following to the end.

He begins with stating that part of the Latin nouns take the ending *-os* in the accusative plural: *hortos*. What is the function or meaning of the morpheme *-os*, can it fulfil the function of signifying plurality and direct object? He answers in the negative, because the two supposed functions of the morpheme *-os* cannot be found out from the segments *o* and *s* of *-os*.[15] For this very reason he would accept the double meaning or double function of the morpheme *-os* only if *horto* were to mean 'gardens' and the ending *-s* would change the form to an accusative, or *vice*

---

[14] Brockelmann, ibid.
[15] This perfectly agrees with the already discussed conception of one morpheme, one meaning.

213

versa. Since, however, *horto* signifies neither direct object nor plurality, he states that "the *o* of *horto* has nothing to do with the *o* of *hortos*". On the same basis "the *-s* of *hortos* also cannot be related to the *s* of *hortus*".[16] The conclusion he arrives at through the above speculation and "argumentation" is the following: "All this points to the complete indivisibility of the segment *-os*, which has a semantically unanalyzable, unitary meaning, function, etc."[17] We could thus speak about two functions only on the basis of a forced adaptation, e.g. from the angle of the Hungarian language, which has separate means to express plurality (*-k*) and the accusative (*-t*). The only concession Antal makes is that "*-os* contains logically [? !] what is contained in the Hungarian *-eket*",[18] and he states categorically again that "linguistically the Latin *-os*, from the aspects of expression and meaning alike, is the same kind of unit as is the *-t* of the accusative in Hungarian".[19]

Let us take these statements one by one.

We shall first examine what endings are taken in general by Latin nouns in the accusative plural: *aulas, hortos, oppida, homines, montes, exercitus, cornua, res.* On the basis of Antal's segmentation of *hortos*, let us separate the morphemes of the accusative plural: *aul-as, oppid-a, homin-es, mont-es, exercit-us, corn-ua, re-s.* What is left after the separation of the morpheme of the accusative plural can obviously be only the stem morpheme, because according to Antal the plural is not suggested by any separate instrument of linguistic expression.[20]

This method of segmentation leads to the following astonishing result: with the exception of the stem morpheme of the ut-

[16] Antal, *A magyar esetrendszer,* p. 73.
[17] Ibid.
[18] Ibid.
[19] Ibid.
[20] Regarding the above segmentation of *aulas, exercitus, cornua* it should be noted that I have made it strictly in accordance with Antal's segmentation principle; namely I took as a stem morpheme only what is common to all paradigmatic forms. The segment *-ae* of *aulae* (gen. and dat. sing. + nom. plur.) I have treated as a morpheme, which in fact appears in pronunciation as a single sound (ē); in other words, the form *aulis* (dat. and abl. plur.) does not involve "the stem morpheme that may possibly be taken for *aula*". I observed the same principle in dealing with *cornua;* the form *cornibus* (dat. and abl. plur.) again does not involve "the stem morpheme that may possibly be taken for *cornu*"; the case is the same also with *exercitibus.* I have segmented *-ibus* as a unitary inflectional morpheme, because also according to the "law of lower limit" it may occur in utterances other than *cornibus* and *exercitibus,* for instance: *homin + ibus, mont + ibus,* etc.

terance *res*, the stem morphemes of Latin nouns of all declensions end in a consonant! This discovery really revolutionizes the views stated in so-called traditional grammar regarding the stem and the thematic morpheme of the noun, and it throws a different light upon the Latin declension system, simplifies its description, for in this way there can be only two instead of the conventional five declensions: (a) stems ending in a consonant and (b) in a vowel. To classify the nouns with a stem ending in a consonant in further subclasses is needless, not only because this would complicate description, but also because then we would have almost as many subclasses as there are consonants in Latin.

The other hypothesis: We should segment *hortos* not the way Antal does, saying that "a group of Latin nouns in the accusative plural take not the ending *-os*" but, let us suppose, the ending *-s*, just like nouns of other groups: *aula-s, exercitu-s, re-s*, etc. Thus, on the basis of synchronic description, the segments *aula-, exercitu-, re-* left after the separation of the case-morphemes can be taken for stem morphemes, while leaving it to diachrony to explain why the stem morphemes in some cases have different forms, and what were the phonological, morphological, analogical, etc. influences and the shifts in systems and functions which caused their "transformation".

What can we lose by accepting this hypothesis? No doubt we have to renounce the stem morpheme *hort-* and the case-morpheme *-os*, just like the formal-arithmetical segmentation of *-os*, as well as a possible comparison between the segment *-us* of *hortus* and the segment *-o* of *horto*, the fiction of the unitary and indivisible meaning and function of the morpheme *-os*. On the profit side we shall have the real stem of the word, together with the alternant to be found in the paradigmatic system, and we shall be compelled to determine the real value of the formal expressions of the case-morphemes (function, meaning) by their places in the inflectional system, by their horizontal and vertical opposition.

Let us put side by side (horizontal opposition) the forms of the accusative plural of the nouns of all declensions:[21]

    (a) *aula-s,*
    (b) *horto-s,*

---

[21] With the exception of neuters; we do not deal here with the origin of their uniform morpheme *-a*, which is in fact a subject for diachronic research.

(c) *mont(i > e)-s*, by analogy with *homin(e)-s*,
(d) *exercitu-s*,
(e) *re-s*.

The separated inflectional morphemes present a uniform opposition to the other inflectional morphemes of the plural: *-rum, -um, -bus*, etc. (vertical opposition).[22] If this vertical opposition shows that (what else can it show?) the morpheme *-s* distinguishes the accusative also formally from the genitive, dative, etc. in the plural, then the function and meaning of the morpheme *-s* can be only plurality and the accusative case.

We arrive at the same result if we compare the singular equivalents of the accusative:

(a) *aula-m*,
(b) *hort(o > u)-m*,
(c) *mont(i > e)-m*, by analogy with *homin(e)-m*,
(d) *exercitu-m*,
(e) *re-m*.

The *-m* as the inflectional morpheme of the accusative singular stands in vertical opposition to the inflectional morphemes *-is, -i, -o*, etc. of the genitive, dative, etc. in the singular.

Both the *-m* of *hortum* and the *-s* of *hortos* are inflectional morphemes of the accusative but, on the basis of their places in the paradigms of the singular and the plural respectively, they express—without a special morpheme or, if you like, with a morpheme Ø—both the singular and the plural, i.e. either of them has more functions and meanings than does *-t* in Hungarian, where a special morpheme serves to indicate the plural. It is true at the same time that the singular is indicated here also by a morpheme Ø.

Being at the subject of the function and meaning of case-suffixes, let us state that we can know more from their places in the paradigmatic system than from their negative value established by formal comparison. If we conceive language really as a system, we can establish the value and function of the elements of this system only on the basis of the place they occupy in it. The suffixes and markers in this system are opposed to one

---

[22] Of course, we leave out of account here the occurrence of morphemes which have different functions, but have one single form; at most we shall call them homonymous morphemes.

another as suffixes and markers, whether they are composed of one or more phonemes or whether they are simply morphemes Ø. (A segmentation of these latter is hardly imaginable.)

Regarding the Hungarian utterance *vár* ('1. fortress, 2. wait') we could hardly tell whether it is a noun or a verb, but if we place it in the paradigm

$$vár\text{-}ok \quad \text{'I wait'}$$
$$vár\text{-}sz \quad \text{'you wait'}$$
$$vár\text{-}\emptyset \quad \text{'he waits'}$$

we can state at once that it is the indicative present third person singular of the verb *vár* in "subjective" conjugation, where the mood, the tense, the number, the person, and the type of conjugation are all "represented" by the morpheme Ø: $vár + \emptyset + \emptyset + \emptyset + \emptyset + \emptyset =$ stem morpheme $+ \emptyset$ (mood) $+ \emptyset$ (tense) $+ \emptyset$ (number) $+ \emptyset$ (person) $+ \emptyset$ (intransitive conjugation). If to this we compare the paradigmatic forms

$$vár \quad \text{'fortress'}$$
$$várak \quad \text{'fortresses'}$$
$$vártól \quad \text{'from the fortress', etc.}$$

we can see at once that the morphemes Ø added to the utterance *vár* have an enormous potential functional load, and these potentialities are realized only within the given paradigmatic system. However, the morpheme Ø being a product of the paradigmatic system-compulsion, its functions in the given system can be precisely "described".

The examples I have presented clearly point to the main theoretical weakness of distributional analysis, the shortcoming of its method: the linear conception of the linguistic structure, the absolutization of the significance of the linguistic form, the establishment of the value, meaning and function of the linguistic elements on the basis of distribution alone. This theory and method conflict with the fact of the extreme complexity of the linguistic structure, because they are confined to the examination of the correlations of the surface structure and are incapable of discovering the deeper and more complex interrelations. This method is stranded on the level of the object of cognition, of the empirical apprehension of human speech, and what is more, it considers this level the only exact form of linguistic knowledge, the result—or origin—of which is the negation of the correlation of linguistic form and content.

It follows necessarily from the theoretical and methodological limits of "modern" gnoseological empiricism that, when examining the norms of superficial forms, the researcher comes up against contradictions which cannot even be solved on this level of cognition. To mention only one of them: empirical knowledge is unable to solve the contradiction between two different forms of identical configurations, which is adequately exemplified by Harris's morphemic segmentation of the Arabic *katab-a* and *katab-tu*: the separated morphemes are the linguistic forms to express that one of the verbal forms at issue is in the third person singular, and the other in the first person singular, but this does not imply at all that *-a* should mean 'he' and *-tu* should mean 'I'. The function to express the person is not identical with the personal pronoun.

The well-known antitheoretical attitude of modern empiricism is not of recent origin. Already the representatives of pre-Marxian empiricism regarded experience based on sensation as the only source of knowledge and belittled the role of theory and scientific abstraction. The modern type of empiricism is a real or potential danger just because—its gnoseological basis being indubitably composed of materialist elements—it can easily deceive the uninformed reader. Let us think only of the linguistic projection of this school: the only apprehensible element of language is the utterance, the material sequence of sounds as we hear it, that is, what we have to segment with eager studiousness, only we have to discern the interrelations of the surface structures.

The matter at issue is not that it would be possible to deny the importance of the first phase of cognition, the empirical description of the thing or process involved. On the contrary, an indispensable momentum and the starting point of all knowledge is the empirical apprehension of the object of cognition, the most precise description possible and systematization of its elements and the external interrelations thereof. But we must not for a moment forget that this is not an ultimate aim but the starting point or, if you like, a means towards a superior level of cognition, towards theoretical elaboration.

It is also a long-established truth that the first phase of cognition—the case at issue being social cognition—cannot be merely empirical, free from any theoretical consideration. In a more exact investigation of the surface structure of the thing involved we cannot operate without the earlier, relevant or less relevant, theoretical results of the efforts of earlier times. Cognizing man, when viewing and examining a thing that is new to him, cannot put aside his earlier knowledge, the categories which refer, or can be made to refer, to the thing in question, etc. Let us recall the above-mentioned enlightening segmentation of *kataba* and *katabtu*. If Harris had kept in view the general peculiarity of languages that personal pronouns are autonomous linguistic categories or free morphemes from times of old, he would not have seen in the Arabic suffixes at issue the Arabic equivalent of 'he' and 'I'. I do not for a moment intend to suppose that Harris did not know this. But the use of his knowledge in his analysis would have shaken the supporting pillars of the basic habit which always treats every utterance as a sum of particles or elements separable by formal criteria on all levels of analysis. This standpoint is unmistakable: this is an unadulterated kind of empiricism, according to which the object of linguistics is to make a possibly precise quantitative description of the external interrelations of language.

The examples we have introduced show conspicuous deficiencies of the empirical outlook on language. Over and above this we have to bear in mind, even in a general way, the following statement on the limitations of empiricism: "The capital mistake of empiricism as a school of research and a gnoseological standpoint was just that it transformed the methods, potentialities and categories of the first phase of cognition, both gnoseologically and in the process of scientific investigation, into methods and categories of cognition taken in the general sense, and identified them with scientific cognition itself."[23]

However improbable it may sound after what I have said so far, I did all this in defence of the real values of formal analysis, of its socially usable results conceived in the most general way. I still have the firm conviction—which I have already expressed before—that a reliable examination (which is exact and based on a critical use of the time-tested results of linguistics) of the pattern of formal behaviour of language may lead to the discovery of such interrelations which have thus far been unknown and which can serve as a basis for further investigations, setting the correlation of linguistic form and content in a new perspective.

[23] *Magyar Filozófiai Szemle* VIII, p. 829.

V. ESSENTIAL FEATURES OF THE LINGUISTIC LAWS

1. GENESIS AND EVOLUTION OF THE CONCEPT OF LINGUISTIC LAW

"Nur das Gesetzmäßige und innerlich Zusammen-
hängende läßt sich wissenschaftlich erforschen."

Curtius

The history of science has registered the linguistic endeavours of the past century as efforts made to provide sufficient answers to the comprehensive questions raised with regard to the principle and methodology of linguistics. What was time and again in the centre of interest was the grasping of the essence, of the "nature" of language. The "modern" needs of the contemporary linguist were by far not satisfied by the linguistic conceptions of the philosophers of classical antiquity, by the repetition of their opinions and interpretations based on a great variety of ideas and ideologies. The linguist of that time was looking, with respectable eagerness, for an explanatory principle and a pertinent method by which to uncover the nature of language, to explain its phenomena. This purposeful eagerness has the indisputable merit that it discovered one of the essential features of language, its constant motion, its constant change. The magic spell of heuristics then developed an essential trait of language into its universal and unique determinative feature: The nature of language resides in its historicity, so the task of the linguist is to keep track of its historical motion, of its constant change, as far back as the first beginnings — the genesis of a primitive language or languages. If the nature of language is in its historicity, the explanatory principle can only be a historical one, and the method should consist in the comparison of the change and evolution of the several languages, in the determination of the identical and different features of this process of growth. The historical approach and the comparative method are the most typical aspects of the new theory which unfolded in the early decades of the nineteenth century and which we would call comparative historical linguistics.

This new science, comparative historical linguistics, had to grapple with a burdensome theoretical heritage. It espoused the progressive results and positive elements of earlier researches, the rational kernel of the linguistic "theories" burdened with extravagant contradictions. It is true, however, that it could not even do otherwise on the basis of the objective logic of human cognition. At the same time the new theory and method, resting on the ground of linguistic historicism, necessarily became opposed to any theoretical conclusion and methodological procedure that failed to stand the test of historicism, of comparatism.

It was a multilevelled opposition. In the first place, for reasons of principle and methodology, it necessarily negated the cogency of descriptive grammar and questioned even its scientific character. It subjected to the same merciless criticism the previous statements of "linguistic theory"—the mystical ideas about the origin of language, the evolution of the various languages, the simplified logicism of Leibniz's "Lingua Adamica" or Rousseau's linguistic conception based on the musicality of language just as well as the diverse naive etymological experiments of which Voltaire depicted—in his own manner—the image of a science where "les voyelles ne font rien et les consonnes fort peu de chose".[1] The founders of the new school evolved their theory as well as the pertinent method in the light of the inexorable criticism of the aforementioned motley heritage fraught with gross theoretical and methodological mistakes. The significance, the essence, of the new theory and method was summed up by K. Brugman as follows: "Linguistic research at the beginning of our century made tremendous progress compared to former times inasmuch as it saw the essence of language in its historical development and introduced the historical method . . ."[2] This conception became more and more established during the nineteenth century, it grew supreme in the course of time, and could boast really impressive results after the lapse of a century: ". . . it explored and gave a general outline of the evolution of languages and of a whole series of linguistic families; it has shown how it is possible at all to conduct scientific investigation into the motion, change and transformation of languages".[3]

The new school undertook no smaller task than to explore the historical interrelations of the given linguistic facts and elements, to attempt to draw a precise sketch of their growth over many centuries, to grasp the objective order, "sensible liberty" (ver-

[1] Brunot, *Histoire de la langue française* I, quoted by L. Kukenheim, *Esquisse historique de la linguistiq ue française*, Leiden, 1962, p. 38.
[2] "Die Sprachforschung machte im Anfang unseres Jahrhunderts insofern einen gewaltigen Fortschritt über die frühere Zeit hinaus, als sie als das Gr undwesen der Sprache ihre geschichtliche Entwicklung erkannte und die historische Methode einführte . . ." K. Brugman, *Zum heutigen Stand der Sprachwissenschaft*, Strassburg, 1885, p. 31.
[3] Telegdi: ÁNyT I (1963), p. 295.

nünfte Freiheit: Grimm), discernible from the course of development, and to work out a method satisfying this theoretical requirement—the comparative and historical method. This mode of outlook, a theoretical requirement, seeks to conceive language as it is, considers its changes and their interrelations to be immanent peculiarities of language, and defines the task of the linguist as consisting in the exploration of these historical interrelations, regular correspondences, regularities. It looks for order in the superficial disorder, necessity in the sea of accidental manifestations; briefly, it explores the "physical" interrelatedness of linguistic facts, i.e. the laws of language. It is true that in the given period the concept of linguistic law was primarily and basically confined to the category of *phonetic law*, but it is also true that this category reflected, together with all its shortcomings and extravagances, everything that is called law in the modern sense. It is in this and only in this sense that I put the equality sign between linguistic law and phonetic law.

The formation of the concept of phonetic law opened a new chapter in the history of linguistic research. This process, the intensity and the extent of the disputes about it are interesting and valuable not only from the point of view of the history of science (with no knowledge of all this, in fact, it would be difficult to see the real significance of the formation of the comparative historical method) but they present an opportunity to draw from it general lessons of principle.

The modern conception of law, as a philosophical category, was induced by the needs of modern scholarship. Namely a simple, commonplace description of the superficial manifestations of phenomena could no longer satisfy these needs, because it failed to give an idea of the real, more profound interrelations of things, phenomena and processes. It is a striving after the essence hidden deep below the surface, after generalizations on an empirical basis, that impels the scholars of modern times to give expression to the intrinsic, substantial, necessary, continuous and recurrent interrelations of phenomena and processes. The concept of law taken in this sense "emerged from the soil of the materialist ideology as an integral part of determinism, of the doctrine professing the objective causality, the objective necessity of nature".[4]

---

[4] Gy. Nádor, *A természettörvény fogalmának kialakulása* [Genesis and Evolution of the Concept of Natural Law], Budapest, 1957, p. 533.

It was not by chance that the most significant effect on the development of this conception of law was exerted by the formation of the modern concept of natural law, which is now, in modern times, a central category of the natural sciences. Newton's classical physics and then Darwinian biology formulated those essential features of natural law which are still today characteristic of the concept of natural law: the objective character, the laws as reflections of the material world, the interrelation of law and substance, the system of laws, etc.

The new concept of natural law had a fertilizing effect on several branches of science, because they "increasingly rise above the primitive level of registering the particular phenomena and strive after a generalization on the basis of empiric knowledge of the phenomena".[5]

Not even linguistics could escape this influence. The spread of the natural-scientific outlook and methods can be clearly seen in the progress of language studies in the first half of the nineteenth century.

The birth of the new school, of the comparative historical method, is usually put in the year 1816, when 25-year-old F. Bopp published his work *Über das Conjugationssystem der Sanskrita-Sprache in Vergleichung mit jenem der griechischen, lateinischen, persischen und germanischen Sprache* (Frankfurt a. M.). All that should be added here is that already eight years earlier A. W. Schlegel, in his work *Über die Sprache und Weisheit der Inder* (1808), raised the idea about an Indo-European linguistic family and comparative grammar.[6] This, however, does not eclipse the merits of Bopp, who was the first to outline the theoretical and methodological questions of comparative philology by showing an array of data about members of that family of languages.

In Bopp's first book we still look in vain for the concept *law* or *regularity*, all the more often we come across terms like *Willkür, Zufall, Verwechslung, zufällige Verwandlung*.[7] The terms *Regel, Regelung* in that work are to be taken literally ('rule').

The evolution of Bopp's linguistic view was considerably influenced by his sojourn in Paris, where he became familiar with the ideas of the Encyclopaedists. An equally remarkable factor

[5] Op. cit., p. 252.
[6] Kukenheim, op. cit., p. 44.
[7] Op. cit., pp. 57, 118, 119, 128, 144.

in the rapid advance of the claim for exact methods was his relationship established with Schlegel, Grimm, and especially with Humboldt.[8]

For, as is commonly held, it was Humboldt who first formulated the concept of phonetic law *(phonetisches Gesetz)* in a letter written to Bopp in 1826.[9] According to Kukenheim the idea of a phonetic law had already come up eight years before, in 1818, in a work by the Dane R. Rask. Since, however, the Danish researcher published his work in his native tongue, his conception of phonetic law remained for a long time inaccessible and consequently unknown to European linguists.[10]

According to a conclusive reasoning of E. Wechssler the evolution of Humboldt's conception of phonetic law was a necessary consequence of his entire theoretical attitude: "For after he [Humboldt] had recognized that the phonetic phenomena and their changes are conditioned by the natural constitution of the language communities, it stood to reason that they are reducible to laws."[11]

In evolving his conception of phonetic law Humboldt started out of comparisons with natural organisms, with the natural laws, by comparing the characteristics of the latter with those of the former, from the basic position which determined his entire scientific habit of mind: "If you want here to pry into the formations of creative nature, then you should not interpolate ideas but take it as it shows itself."[12]

Let me remark here that the generally known technical term *(Lautgesetz)* is a creation of Bopp. He first adopted the former

---

[8] E. Wechssler, *Gibt es Lautgesetze?* Festgabe Suchier, Halle a. S., 1900, p. 395; Kukenheim, op. cit., p. 44.

[9] Wechssler, op. cit., p. 392.

[10] Kukenheim, op. cit., p. 44; B. Delbrück, *Einleitung in das Sprachstudium*, Leipzig, 1880, pp. 32—3.

[11] "Denn nachdem er [Humboldt] erkannt hatte, daß die phonetischen Phänomene und ihre Veränderungen durch die natürliche Konstitution der Sprachgemeinschaften bedingt sind, war die Zurückführung derselben auf Gesetze eine selbstverständliche Folgerung." Wechssler, op. cit., p. 392.

[12] "Will man hier die Bildungen der schaffenden Natur nachspähen, so muß man ihr nicht Ideen unterschieben, sondern sie nehmen, wie sie sich zeigt." Quoted by H. Steinthal, *Die sprachphilosophischen Werke von Humboldt*, Berlin, 1884, p. 191; Wechssler, op. cit., pp. 392—3.

expression *Wohllautsregel*[13] and used it until 1827.[14] Then he changed over to the use of *Wohllautgesetz*, in the coining of which a fundamental role was played obviously by the previous *Wohllautsregel* and Humboldt's *Gesetz*.[15] Finally the union of the two and the curtailment of the first term gave birth to the form *Laut-Gesetz*.[16] For a short time Bopp still used also the former *Wohllautgesetz*,[17] and later he abided by the sole use of *Lautgesetz*.[18]

As a result of the strengthening of his relationship and cooperation with Humboldt, Bopp's linguistic conception was increasingly prevailed upon by the natural-scientific view; this, however, did not obscure his earlier philological attitude, it even added new elements to it. The new aspects of his mode of expression showed most definitely when he opposed the new features of his linguistic conception to the older ideas, when he emphasized, e.g., that language is not an arbitrary creation, that its emergence was necessary and its evolution takes place on the strength of specific laws. As he put it: "Languages are to be regarded as *organic physical bodies* which are shaped according to *specific laws* and develop upon an internal life-principle . . ."[19] He defined the task of scholarly grammar as follows: "Grammar in the higher, scientific sense has to be *a history and natural description* of language; as far as possible, but especially in terms of *natural history*, it has to comply . . . with the *laws* according to which its development took place . . ."[20] His natural-scientific terminology is most conspicuous when he opposes it to the pre-existing terms: '*Zergliederung der Sprachen*; *Sprachanatomie*; *anatomische Zerlegung* oder *chemische Zersetzung des Sprachkörpers*; *Physik* oder *Physiologie der Sprache*, etc.[21] In the first

---

13 *Vergl. Zerglied. der Sanskrita* . . .: Abh. d. Berl. Akad. Phil.-hist. Kl. 1824, p. 118.
14 *Ausführliches Lehrgebäude der Sanskrita-Sprache*, Berlin, 1827.
15 *Berl. Jahrb. 1827*, pp. 733, 735, 736, 749.
16 *Vergl. Zerglied.* II, 1825, p. 195.
17 Op. cit. III, 1826, p. 69.
18 Op. cit. IV, 1829, pp. 28, 30.
19 "Die Sprachen sind als *organische Naturkörper* anzusehen, die nach *bestimmten Gesetzen* sich bilden, ein inneres Lebensprinzip sich tragend sich entwickeln . . ." *Berl. Jahrb. 1827*, p. 251.
20 "Eine Grammatik in höherem, wissenschaftlichem Sinne soll eine *Geschichte und Naturbeschreibung* der Sprache sein; sie soll, so weit es möglich ist . . . besonders aber *naturhistorische* die Gesetze verfolgen, nach welchen ihre Entwicklung . . . vor sich gegangen." Ibid.
21 *Vergl. Gr.*, pp. I, VI, VIII, IX; quoted by Delbrück, op. cit., p. 17.

sentence of the preface to his comparative grammar we encounter the terms Beschreibung des *Organismus der Sprachen, physische und mechanische Gesetze.*[22]

With the details thus sketched I may have succeeded in demonstrating the quick propagation of the natural-scientific outlook in the activity of the first prominent representative of the new linguistic school. This effect appeared primarily and basically in the adaptation of the concept of natural law at the time of the birth of the concept of linguistic (phonetic) law.

G. Curtius, an active representative of the natural-scientific view and method, still used some nuances in his style: ". . . it is possible just in the life of sounds most positively to recognize firm laws which assert themselves almost with the consistency of natural forces."[23]

The *phonetic law* here is not a *law of nature* as yet. Linguistics is not yet classed among the natural sciences, but the latter have an indisputably fertilizing effect upon the development of the new linguistic view. The frequent use of various adjectives with the term 'law' (physical, mechanical, etc.) reflects, in my judgment, primarily a metaphorical character just as does the *chemical dissolution of the body of language* ('linguistic analysis') or language conceived of as an *organism.* The newly created linguistic terms — even if one or another of them provokes a smile today — unanimously testify of a vigorous tendency towards natural-scientific exactness in the linguistics of the first half of the nineteenth century. But it may not be needless to point out that some of the linguistic terms devised at the time have been so widely accepted by usage that they are still in use today *(family of languages, root, stem, assimilation, dissimilation,* etc.).

The first militant "naturalist-linguist", August Schleicher, was a personal friend of the great natural scientist E. Häckel and an active propagator of the Darwinian doctrines.

In the first stage of his activity Schleicher was still a follower of what was called the school of "moral science"; he was particularly influenced by the periodization theory of Hegel's natural philosophy. According to him: "The life of language is divided

---

[22] *Vergl. Gr.*, pp. I, III.

[23] ". . . lassen sich gerade in dem Leben der Laute am sichersten feste Gesetze erkennen, die sich beinahe mit der Consequenz von Naturkräften geltend machen." G. Curtius, *Einleitung zu: Grundzüge der griechischen Etymologie*, Leipzig, 1858, p. 81; Delbrück, op. cit., p. 102.

into two entirely distinct periods—the history of the evolution of language, the *prehistoric* period, and the history of the decadence of the linguistic form: the historical period."[24] The Hegelian "theory of language evolution" left so deep an impression in the young scholar that he organically built in his later theoretical system the Hegelian tenets on the two periods of the "life" of language.

From 1850 on he moved further and further away from the school of "moral science" and, under the influence of Schleiden, then of Vogt, Häckel and especially Darwin, and prompted by the need for scholarly exactness, he became more and more an advocate and active promoter of the natural-scientific view and method: "Natural philosophers let us understand that only the fact deduced from secure, strictly objective observation and the right conclusions built upon it are of value to science; this is a realization that would be useful to many of my colleagues. Subjective interpretation, unsteady etymologizing . . . in short, all that spoils linguistic studies of their scientific strictness and degrades and even ridicules them in the eyes of sensible people, is thoroughly disgusting to anyone who has learnt to adopt the position of calm observation I have referred to above. Only accurate observation of the organisms and their laws of existence, only total devotion to the scientific object should be the basis also of our discipline."[25]

He explained his theoretical theses and methodological ideas about language in two brief treatises. The first of them—the one

---

[24] "Das Leben der Sprache zerfällt in zwei völlig gesonderte Perioden: in die Entwicklungsgeschichte der Sprache: *vorhistorische* Periode, und in die Geschichte des Verfalles der sprachlichen Form: historische Periode." A. Schleicher, "Zur vergleichenden Sprachgeschichte (Zetazismus)." *Sprachvergleichende Untersuchungen* I, Bonn, 1848, p. 16.

[25] "Bei den Naturforschern kann man einsehen lernen, daß für die Wissenschaft nur die durch sichere, streng objektive Beobachtung festgestellte Thatsache und der auf diese gebaute richtige Schluß Geltung hat; eine Erkenntniss, die manchem meiner Collegen von Nutzen wäre. Subjektives Deuteln, haltloses Etymologisieren . . . kurz alles, wodurch die sprachlichen Studien ihrer wissenschaftlichen Strenge beraubt und in den Augen einsichtiger Leute herabgesetzt, ja sogar lächerlich gemacht werden, wird demjenigen gründlich verleidet, der sich auf den oben angedeuteten Standpunkt nüchterner Beobachtung zu stellen gelernt hat. Nur die genaue Beobachtung der Organismen und ihrer Lebensgesetze, nur die völlige Hingabe an das wissenschaftliche Objekt soll die Grundlage auch unserer Disciplin bilden." A. Schleicher, *Die Darwinsche Theorie und die Sprachwissenschaft*: Offenes Sendschreiben an Herrn Dr. Ernst Häckel, a. o. Professor der Zoologie und Direktor des zoologischen Museums an der Universität Jena, Weimar, 1863, p. 6.

cited above—was written three years after the first German translation (1860) of Darwin's work.[26] The other is entitled *Über die Bedeutung der Sprache für die Naturgeschichte des Menschen* (Weimar, 1865).

Schleicher's first polemical essay *(Darwin)* stirred up a very big storm, just as Häckel's consistent Darwinism incurred "the hatred of bigoted dailies".[27] A most eloquent proof of Schleicher's unfailing courage is that he knew about the attack against Häckel and was aware that a similar future was in store for his own consistent materialism, and he nevertheless made his above essay public in form of an open letter to this friend and comrade-in-arms Häckel. Consciously evolved on the basis of militant philosophical monism, Schleicher's "naturalist conception of language" also invited furious attacks from the idealist camp; the large scale and vigour of these attacks can be inferred from the preface to the second edition devoted to a "detailed motivation" of the principles laid down in that open letter: "I have been denied namely the right to treat languages as material existences, as natural realities."[28]

What is language, what characteristic features does it have, what methods of research can help us to penetrate its nature? These are undoubtedly the primarily fundamental questions of linguistics. Schleicher's two polemical writings give unequivocal replies to these problems.

His definition of language is unequivocally materialistic: "Language is an aurally perceptible symptom of the activity of a complex of material relationships produced by the brain and the speech organs with their nerves, bones, muscles, etc."[29] If this definition formulated with German ponderousness and sounding a little unusual to foreign ears is analyzed with the aid of our present-day terminology, we can find out no less than

[26] Five years later the treatise appeared also in French translation by M. de Pomayrol under the title *La théorie de Darwin et la science du langage*, Paris, 1868.

[27] "... den Zorn glaubenseifriger Tagesblätter". *Darwin*, p. 29.

[28] "Man bestritt mir nämlich das Recht, die Sprachen als materielle Existenzen, als reale Naturwesen zu behandeln." Schleicher, *Über die Bedeutung der Sprache für die Naturgeschichte des Menschen*, Weimar, 1865, p. 2.

[29] "Die Sprache ist das durch das Ohr wahrnehmbare Symptom der Thätigkeit eines Complexes materieller Verhältnisse in der Bildung des Gehirns und der Sprachorgane mit ihren Nerven, Knochen, Muskeln u.s.f." Op. cit., p. 8. With regard to the definition Schleicher himself states that the main outlines of the idea can be found also in L. Diefenbach, *Vorschule der Völkerkunde*, Frankfurt a. M., p. 40.

that (a) language is an acoustic phenomenon—but, anyway, this was not much contested earlier either; (b) language is the expression of concepts by means of the "speech organs"; (c) if I understand correctly the phrase "Complex materieller Verhältnisse in der Bildung des Gehirns", this is a case where the essence of concept is grasped in its modern, materialistic sense: concept as the reflection, in the consciousness (in the brain), of part of the material world, of objective reality. This is already genuine materialism. It has nothing to do with the earlier mythical, idealistic theories of language.

Schleicher was not concerned to refute the earlier idealistic linguistic theories, he ruled them out with a single categorical sentence: "I think it is convenient that I can save myself the trouble to refute the view that language might be the invention of the individual or that it might have been imparted to man from outside."[30]

From this basic position, the most essential feature of language is describable in one way only: Language is a product of nature. an organism, essentially identical with other organisms, a natural phenomenon that arises and evolves independently of God and man (!): "Languages are physical organisms which came into being independently of the will of man, grew and developed according to specific laws and which, on the other hand, would become old and die off: the many phenomena by which the term 'life' is usually meant are peculiar also to them."[31] Here we have to take notice of two things. The first emphasizes, and indeed overemphasizes, a very essential trait of language, its independence of individual men, its objective character; this overemphasis was due to the failure to recognize the dialectics of the objective and at the same time subjective character of language, and became the source of irreconcilable contradictions later, when it came to defining the features characteristic of language. The second important thing is that language was conceived to be a natural organism (no longer in its metaphorical acceptation).

---

[30] "Eine Widerlegung der Ansicht, die Sprache sei die Erfindung eines Einzelnen, oder sie sei dem Menschen von Außen her mitgetheilt worden, glaube ich mir füglich ersparen zu können." Schleicher, *Über die Bedeutung . . .*, p. 20.
[31] "Die Sprachen sind Naturorganismen, die, ohne vom Willen des Menschen bestimmbar zu sein, entstunden, nach bestimmten Gesetzen wuchsen und sich entwickelten und wiederum altern und absterben; auch ihnen ist jene Reihe von Erscheinungen eigen, die man unter dem Namen 'Leben' zu verstehen pflegt." *Darwin*, p. 6.

This was the first appearance of social Darwinism in philology, with overemphasis on the physical and physiological aspects of linguistic facts—based on unawareness of the psychical nature of language, absolutizing one of its aspects, which perforce led to new contradictions.

The conception of language as an organism could readily be adapted to Hegelian historical philosophy. What Hegel says of the progressive and retrogressive stages of society is essentially in agreement with the main peculiarities of organisms and is in reality nothing but an adaptation of the most typical peculiarities of organisms to social history: "Within history we see languages grow old in sound and form only according to specific laws of existence. The languages we now speak, like all . . . languages of historically advanced peoples, so far as they are on the whole sufficiently known to us . . ., have for a long time been more or less in a state of retrograde metamorphosis. Language formation and historical life succeed in turn in the course of the life of mankind."[32] It is not difficult to discover here also the influence of Darwinian doctrines, but Schleicher himself is unmistakable about this: "Darwin's explanations and views influenced me in fact increasingly as I brought them into relation with linguistics.

"Namely the views applicable to speech organisms are similar to those which Darwin holds about the living being on the whole, and which in part almost generally, in part incidentally in 1860, i.e. in the year of publication of the German translation of Darwin's work, I expressed in a way that was, apart from the terminology, strikingly in agreement with Darwin's ideas about the 'struggle for existence', the extinction of old forms, the wide dissemination and differentiation of particular classes in the field of language."[33]

If language is a product of nature, a natural organism, then "Glottology, the science of language, is . . . a natural science; its

[32] "Innerhalb der Geschichte sehen wir die Sprachen nur nach bestimmten Lebensgesetzen in Laut und Form altern. Die Sprachen, welche wir jetzt sprechen, sind, wie alle . . . Sprachen geschichtlich entwickelter Völker, soweit sie überhaupt uns in hinreichendem Maaße bekannt sind . . ., längst mehr oder minder in rückbildender Metamorphose begriffen. Sprachbildung und geschichtliches Leben lösen einander im Lebensverlaufe der Menschheit ab." *Über die Bedeutung* . . ., p. 27.

[33] "In noch höherem Grade wirkten nämlich Darwins Darlegungen und Ansichten auf mich, in so ferne sie in Verbindung brachte mit der Sprachwissenschaft.

method is by and large the same as that of the other natural sciences."[34]

This is how he explains the evolution of language on the basis of the theory and method outlined above: "The comparative anatomy of languages shows that the more highly organized languages have evolved step by step, from lower speech organisms, probably in the course of very long periods; at the least glottology does not find anything to contradict the assumption that the simplest thought expressions came about by means of sounds, that the structurally simplest languages arose gradually from sound-gestures and vocal imitations common also to animals."[35] There is no need to talk much about the metaphysical character of the above process of evolution, though we might have expected Schleicher—considering his knowledge about Hegel—to present a more elastic description of evolution.

Schleicher held that these theoretical and methodological conclusions were very important, and he thought the greatest merit of his entire scientific activity was that he had introduced the natural-scientific methods in linguistic researches.[36]

Schleicher's theses came into the limelight of interest in the second half of the nineteenth century. If language was a natural

"Von den sprachlichen Organismen gelten nämlich ähnliche Ansichten wie sie Darwin von den lebenden Wesen überhaupt ausspricht, theils fast allgemein, theils habe ich zufällig im Jahre 1860, also in demselben Jahre, in welchem die deutsche Uebersetzung von Darwins Werk erschien, über den 'Kampf ums Dasein', über das Erlöschen alter Formen, über die große Ausbreitung und Differenzierung einzelner Arten auf sprachlichem Gebiete mich in einer Weise ausgesprochen, welche, den Ausdruck abgerechnet, mit Darwins Ansichten in auffälliger Weise zusammen stimmt." *Darwin*, p. 4. Cf. *Die deutsche Sprache*, Stuttgart, 1860, pp. 43, 44.

[34] "Die Glottik, die Wissenschaft der Sprache, ist . . . eine Naturwissenschaft; ihre Methode ist im Ganzen und Allgemeinen dieselbe, wie die der übrigen Naturwissenschaften." *Darwin*, p. 7. A footnote added to this statement reads as follows: "Von der Philologie, einer historischen Disciplin, ist hier natürlich nicht die Rede."

[35] "Die vergleichende Anatomie der Sprachen weist nach, daß die höher organisierten Sprachen aus einfacheren Sprachorganismen ganz allmählich, wahrscheinlich im Verlaufe sehr langer Zeiträume sich entwickelt haben; die Glottik findet zum Mindesten nichts, was der Annahme widerspräche, daß die einfachsten Gedankenäußerungen mittels des Lautes, daß die Sprachen einfachsten Baues allmählich aus Lautgebärden und Schallnachahmungen, wie sie auch die Tiere besitzen, hervorgegangen sind." *Über die Bedeutung . . .*, pp. 19—20.

[36] Delbrück, op. cit., pp. 42—3.

organism and linguistics belonged to the natural sciences, then the *linguistic laws* disclosing the essential, intrinsic properties of language—chiefly the phonetic laws—had to be identical with the *natural laws*; according to the view based on the natural-scientific achievements of the time, they admitted of no exceptions and operated with iron consistency.

The first linguistic researcher who explained clearly, and formulated in relatively flexible terms, the circumstances determining the operation of phonetic laws was A. Leskien. He stated: "In my investigation I proceeded from the principle that the case-form we have inherited is never founded on an exception to the phonetic laws otherwise observed. To avoid any misunderstanding I wish still to add this: if by exception are meant cases in which the expectable phonetic change has failed to set in for certain recognizable reasons, ... where thus a rule conflicts with another to a certain extent, there is of course nothing to object to the thesis that the phonetic laws are not exceptionless. The law is just not nullified thereby and is operative as expected where this or other disturbances and the effects of other laws are not present."[37]

H. Osthoff, together with K. Brugman, held that one of the most important principles of the neogrammarian school consisted in stipulating the exceptionless regularity of phonetic changes: "Every phonetic change, so far as it occurs mechanically, takes place according to exceptionless laws, i.e. the direction of the sound-shift is the same in all members of a language community, except in case a dialect split sets in, and all words in which the sound exposed to the shift appears under the same conditions are affected by the change without exception."[38]

[37] "Bei der Untersuchung bin ich von dem Grundsatz ausgegangen, daß die uns überlieferte Gestalt eines Casus niemals auf einer Ausnahme von den sonst befolgten Lautgesetzen beruhe. Um nicht mißverstanden zu werden, möchte ich noch hinzufügen: versteht man unter Ausnahmen solche Fälle, in denen der zu erwartende Lautwandel aus bestimmten erkennbaren Ursachen nicht eingetreten ist ... wo also gewissermaßen eine Regel die andere durchkreuzt, so ist gegen den Satz, die Lautgesetze seien nicht ausnahmslos, natürlich nichts einzuwenden. Das Gesetz wird eben dadurch nicht aufgehoben, und wirkt, wo diese oder andere Störungen, die Wirkungen anderer Gesetze nicht vorhanden sind, in der zu erwartenden Weise." A. Leskien, *Die Declination im Slavisch-Litauischen und Germanischen*, Leipzig, 1876, p. XXVIII.

[38] "Aller lautwandel, so weit er mechanisch vor sich geht, vollzieht sich nach ausnahmslosen gesetzen, d. h. die richtung der lautbewegung ist bei allen angehörigen einer sprachgenossenschaft, außer dem fall, daß

The cogency of phonetic laws was regarded as the main pillar of all linguistics. Whoever refused to recognize it was charged with subjectivism: "Only he who strictly holds to the phonetic laws, this main pillar of our entire science, has generally a firm ground under his feet during research. On the other hand, he who ... permits of exceptions ... slips of necessity into subjectivism and caprice."[39] The two philologists several times referred to phonetic law as a main pillar.[40]

The thesis about phonetic law's being a principal instrument of comparative historical linguistics, the only secure basis, was upheld also by scholars who otherwise criticized the Brugman–Osthoff postulate of "exceptionlessness". Th. Benfey, for example, mentioned, when treating the significance of the phonetic laws, "... the investigation of the phonetic laws as a principal means of comparison after all, the only secure basis for the demonstration of related, particularly primary, forms".[41]

And finally about the necessity of exceptionlessness: "Phonetic laws work with blind necessity."[42]

The "semblance" of exception—which is practically a real exception—comes about, also according to Brugman, when two different laws operate simultaneously: "The semblance of exception comes about when two laws act side by side."[43]

In his lectures as well as in other works Max Müller regarded

---

dialektspaltung eintritt, stets dieselbe, und alle wörter, in denen der der lautbewegung unterworfene laut unter gleichen verhältnissen erscheint, werden ohne ausnahme von der änderung ergriffen." H. Osthoff—K. Brugman, *Morphologische Untersuchungen auf dem Gebiete der indogermanischen Sprache* I, Leipzig, 1878, p. XIII.

[39] "Nur wer sich an die lautgesetze, diesen grundfeiler unserer ganzen wissenschaft, sträng hält, hat bei seiner forschung überhaupt einen festen boden unter den füßen. Wer dagegen ... ausnahmen ... zuläßt ... der verfällt ganz notwendigerweise dem subjektivismus und der willkür." Op. cit., pp. XIV—XV.

[40] Op. cit., p. 134; cf. also pp. 137—8, where phonetic law appears, besides being exceptionless, as a "mechanisch wirkender factor".

[41] "... die Erforschung der Lautgesetze endlich als Hauptmittel der Vergleichung, als die einzig sichere Grundlage für den Erweis des Verwandten, speziell der Grundformen." Th. Benfey, *Geschichte der Sprachwissenschaft und orientalischen Philologie in Deutschland seit dem Anfange des 19. Jahrhunderts mit einem Rückblick auf die früheren Zeiten*, München, 1869, p. 476; Delbrück, op. cit., p. 3.

[42] "Die Lautgesetze wirken met [misprint for *mit*] blinder Notwendigkeit." Brugman quoted by Kukenheim, op. cit., p. 68.

[43] "Der Schein der Ausnahme entsteht dadurch, daß zwei Gesetze nebeneinander wirken." Brugman, op. cit., p. 55.

the cogency of phonetic laws as a scientific criterion of linguistics: "The new school asserts, as I did many years ago, that phonetic laws admit of no exceptions at all; if they did, language would not be a matter for really scientific treatment."[44]

H. Paul, on the other hand, wrote in a more moderate and differentiated manner: "The phonetic law does not lay down what must always happen under certain general circumstances, but it states only the uniformity within a group of specific historical phenomena ... If we therefore speak of consistent operation of the phonetic laws, it means only that a phonetic change within one dialect equally affects all particular cases where the same phonetic conditions exist."[45]

For the sake of truth we have to point out that even advocates of "iron consistency", of "exceptionlessness" acknowledged that the operation of phonetic laws was limited in time: "It is namely a frequent phenomenon that every phonetic law in the language has its time limits within which it alone works. Sounds and sound combinations that fall safely outside the scope of operation of this phonetic law remain unchanged."[46] The same view was held by Delbrück regarding the limitation of phonetic laws in place and time: "Phonetic laws ... which occur within a given language and time and are valid only for these."[47]

[44] "Die neue Schule behauptet, wie ich selber vor vielen Jahren, daß die Lautgesetze durchaus keine Ausnahmen zulassen, wenn sie dies thäten, die Sprache kein Gegenstand für eine wirklich wissenschaftliche Behandlung sein würde." M. Müller, *Die Wissenschaft der Sprache*, Leipzig, 1892, pp. X—XI.

[45] "Das Lautgesetz sagt nicht aus, was unter gewissen allgemeinen Bedingungen immer wieder eintreten muß, sondern es konstatiert nur die Gleichmäßigkeit innerhalb einer Gruppe bestimmter historischen Erscheinungen ... Wenn wir daher von konsequenter Wirkung der Lautgesetze reden, so kann das nur heißen, daß bei dem Lautwandel innerhalb desselben Dialektes alle einzelnen Fälle, in denen die gleichen lautlichen Bedingungen vorliegen, gleichmäßig behandelt werden." H. Paul, *Prinzipien der Sprachgeschichte*, Halle, 1898, pp. 61—2.

[46] "Es ist nämlich eine vielfach zu beobachtende erscheinung, daß jedes lautgesetz in der sprache seine begrenzte zeit hat, innerhalb deren allein es wirkt. Laute und lautverbindungen, welche im wärend [!] der zeit seiner wirksamkeit unfelbar [!] verfallen sein würden, bleiben unverändert." Quoted from J. Schmidt by Osthoff, *Morph. Unters.* IV, 1881, p. 389.

[47] "Die Lautgesetze ... welche in einer gewissen Sprache und Zeit auftreten und nur für diese Gültigkeit haben." Delbrück, op. cit., p. 128.

Schleicher and his followers (Osthoff and especially Brugman) fought doggedly to make the principle of "iron consistency" and "exceptionlessness" accepted. Schleicher's doctrine on "speech organism", just like the theory of the two-period evolution of language, found a great many adherents, and still much more opponents. A similar fate was in store also for the (natural-scientific) research methods applicable to language and for the neogrammarian views concerning the classification of the science of linguistics.

The polemic was started by G. Curtius with his article "Bemerkungen über die Tragweite der Lautgesetze, besonders im Lateinischen und Griechischen",[48] was continued by Th. Benfey with his study entitled "Die Spaltung einer Sprache in mehrere lautverschiedene Sprachen",[49] and was joined in by H. Collitz with his "Besprechung von Osthoff–Brugman: Morphologische Untersuchungen I."[50] Again the Osthoff–Brugman conception was criticized by A. Bezzenberger in his "Besprechung von Osthoff und Brugman: Morphologische Untersuchungen I",[51] as well as by O. Brenner in his *Einleitung zur "Deutschen Phonetik".*[52] Foreign authors also took a hand in the debate, among them: N. Kruszevsky, "Die Laute und ihre Gesetze";[53] P. Regnaud, *Eléments de grammaire comparée du grec et du latin, I: Phonétique* (Paris, 1895, pp. XVII—XXV); W. D. Whitney, "Further Words as to Surds and Sonants, and the Law of Economy as a Phonetic Force";[54] M. W. Easton, "Analogy and Uniformity";[55] M. Bloomfield, "On the Probability of the Existence of Phonetic Law".[56]

The sharpest criticism and the most categorical objections to the theory of "exceptionlessness" were formulated by H. Schuchardt in his work *Ueber die Lautgesetze: Gegen die Junggrammatiker* (Berlin, 1885).

[48] Berichte der kgl. sächs. Gesellschaft der Wissenschaften. Phil.-hist. Kl. 1870, pp. 1—39.
[49] *Göttinger Nachrichten 1877*, pp. 533—8.
[50] *Anz. f. deutsches Altertum* V, 1879, pp. 318—23.
[51] *Gött. Gel. Anz. 1879*, pp. 641—69.
[52] Grammatiken deutscher Mundarten (Leipzig, 1893).
[53] "Prinzipien der Sprachentwicklung", *Techmers Zeitschrift f. intern. Sprachwissenschaft* I, 1884, pp. 301—4; II, 1885, pp. 260—8; III, 1887, pp. 145—70; the article is an abridged version of a paper published at Kazan in 1883.
[54] *Proceedings of the American Philological Association*, July 1889, pp. XII—XVIII.
[55] *The American Journal of Philology* V, 1884, No. 6, pp. 164—77.
[56] Loc. cit., pp. 178—85.

Schuchardt recognized the existence of phonetic laws but denied that they were exceptionless. This still would not matter, since he was right here. But he failed to uphold the existence of exceptions to the phonetic laws; on the contrary, bypassing the gist of the problem (laws with exceptions), he declared that there existed sporadic sound-shifts.[57] In this there was nothing special or anyway nothing new, since he could not thus grasp the nature of *law* or *regularity*; or, as a matter of fact, by "really" *regular* he also understood the realization of the natural-scientific conception of law in the mechanical sense (law admitting of no exceptions): ". . . so we can speak of absolute and of relative regularity."[58] Schuchardt spoke rather disparagingly of the significance of the neogrammarian discovery of phonetic law: "In short, the establishment of the neogrammarian principle means to me no turn in the history of linguistics, no turn which would have started it on the road of more definite and rapid progress."[59]

The same view was voiced later by Vossler, the founder of the "idealist school", and that position was adopted also by representatives of neolinguistics who stated that the neogrammarian conception was definitely harmful to the development of the science of language.[60]

Nor does it correspond to the historical truth that Schuchardt arbitrarily confined the results of the neogrammarians to the Achilles' heel of their conception of phonetic law, which is that this law is exceptionless: "The only thesis that the so-called neogrammarian school can regard as its exclusive property is that concerning the exceptionless operation of the phonetic laws."[61] Nevertheless, linguistics owes quite a bit more to the neogrammarian school. This is why I feel it is unjust to pass an extremely severe, "dogmatic" judgment on the neogrammarian concept of phonetic law as Schuchardt did: "The teaching of the exception-

[57] ". . . es gibt sporadischen Lautwandel". H. Schuchardt, *Ueber die Lautgesetze: Gegen die Junggrammatiker*, Berlin, 1885, p. 31.
[58] ". . . so mag man von absoluter und von relativer Gesetzmäßigkeit reden". Op. cit., p. 32.
[59] "Kurz, die Aufstellung des junggrammatischen Prinzips bedeutet für mich keinen Umschwung in der Geschichte der Sprachwissenschaft, mit dem sie sicherer und rascher fortzuschreiten begonnen hätte . . ." Op. cit., p. 33.
[60] Al. Graur, *Studii de lingvistică generală: Varianța nouă* [Studies in General Linguistics: New Variant], 1960, p. 235.
[61] "Der einzige Satz, den die sog. junggrammatische Schule als ihr ausschließliches Eigentum betrachten darf, ist der von der ausnahmslosen Wirkung der Lautgesetze." Schuchardt, op. cit., p. 1.

less working of phonetic laws can be demonstrated neither deductively nor inductively; anyone who clings to it must espouse it as a dogma . . ."[62]

The new theory of phonetic law was equally branded as a dogma by Meyer in an obituary devoted to Curtius and by Bloomfield in his pertinent discussions.[63]

When Schuchardt, starting from the position of subjective idealism, made a fierce attack on the principle of the cogency of the neogrammarian law, he stood up practically against the conception of law. He must be blamed for his conduct all the more because, when he wrote down his thoughts without bias against the neogrammarian conception of law and with sober moderation, he nilly-willy got quite close to the idea of linguistic law taken in the modern sense: "The exceptions which should be left out of account in the cogency of the phonetic laws consist in the cross-breeding with other phonetic laws, in the dialectical mixture and in the influence of conceptual associations."[64]

The exposition of the neogrammarian tenet about speech organism also was followed by heated debates. While the criticism of the exceptionless operation of phonetic laws concentrated the fire against the mechanical materialist conception of law, the opponents of the organism theory, understandably, combated successfully the simplified adaptation to language of the characteristic features of natural organisms. The organism dispute lasted, with varying intensity, more than three decades, in spite of the fact that this natural-scientific simplification, or working hypothesis, with its drawbacks quite soon proved to be untenable. Indicative of the persistence of the polemic is that, towards the turn of the century, V. Henry was still engaged in a very vehement dispute with the proponents of the organism theory: "Douer de vie cette entité [langue], c'est déjà énorme; mais, sous prétexte qu'on l'a douée de vie, vouloir y retrouver les caractères essentiels et distinctifs de la vie, la naissance, la croissance, l'assimilation, la mort, ce qui enfin constitue un organisme vivant,

[62] "Die Lehre von der Ausnahmslosigkeit der Lautgesetze läßt sich . . . ebensowenig auf deductivem wie auf inductivem Wege beweisen; wer ihr anhängt, muß sich zu ihr als einem Dogma bekennen . . ." Op. cit., p. 29.
[63] Ibid.
[64] "Die Ausnahmen, von welchen bei der Ausnahmslosigkeit der Lautgesetze abgesehen werden soll, bestehen in der Kreuzung mit anderen Lautgesetzen, in der dialektischen Mischung und in der Einwirkung begrifflicher Associationen." Op. cit., pp. 3—4.

c'est simplement parer des grâces du style la sécheresse de la constatation scientifique; sinon, c'est ne rien comprendre à cette constatation même."[65]
The storm that arose around the organism theory, as a matter of course, was a hard blow also to the Hegelian idea of the two periods. It would have been really difficult to defend this Hegelian thesis contradicting all practical experience. The evolution of language is not induced by factors typical of natural organisms, neither is the "draining of natural life fluids" that causes it to "become old and die off".

Farthest in the polemic against phonetic law went Delbrück, who, as a reaction to the extravagances and simplified adaptations, negated everything that the neogrammarians believed in. Based on the criteria he knew of the natural laws in his time, he negated even the existence of phonetic law: "The phonetic laws ...are... nothing but uniformities... Whether the term law is applicable to them in general is doubtful ... I cannot approve that phonetic laws are labelled as natural laws. These historical uniformities have obviously no similarity to chemical or physical laws."[66]
It is also a part of the historical truth that Delbrück valued highly the activity of Schleicher and Curtius (regarding them as principal representatives of a new school) and admitted that their views exercised an enormous influence on linguistic researches.[67]
As a consequence of the furious attacks, one of the most militant neogrammarians, Brugman, felt also compelled to stand up against some extravagances in the teachings of the new school. He dissociated himself from those who classed linguistics among

[65] V. Henry, *Antinomies linguistiques*, Paris, 1896, p. 10; Wechssler, op. cit., p. 416.
[66] "Die Lautgesetze ... sind ... nichts anders als Gleichmäßigkeiten... Ob für dieselben der Ausdruck Gesetz überhaupt anwendbar sei, ist zweifelhaft ... Nicht billigen kann ich die Bezeichnung der Lautgesetze als Naturgesetze. Mit chemischen oder physikalischen Gesetzen haben offenbar diese geschichtlichen Gleichmäßigkeiten keine Ähnlichkeit." Delbrück, op. cit., p. 128.
[67] "... dagegen darf man mit Recht Schleicher und Curtius als Haupt-Repräsentanten einer Richtung ansehen, die nicht nur auf den Betrieb der einzelnen Sprachen, sondern auch auf die Ansichten über Ziel und Methode der Sprachforschung überhaupt einen mächtigen Einfluß ausgeübt hat und ausübt." Op. cit., p. 55. "... sein [Curtius'] Streben vorzüglich darauf gerichtet war, in der Lautwelt eine strengere Ordnung nachzuweisen, als seinem Vorgänger gelungen war, und somit für die Etymologie eine festere Methode zu begründen." Op. cit., p. 101.

the natural sciences, and rejected also the Hegelian tenet about periodization, branding both views as erroneous: "Some of these erroneous views were even formally systematized by adherents of Bopp. Such are, e.g., the opinion that linguistics should be classed in the natural sciences, and the conception that languages were organized and perfected in prehistoric times in order to degenerate and decline in historical times . . ."[68]

In the seventies the "anatomical" theory was also abandoned. As a matter of fact, the anti-neogrammarians rightly criticized the procedure which reconstructed a "primitive language" just in order to decompose (dissect) it again into its elements by deftly operating with its sounds (letters). The result of these operations was a formation broken up into its constitutive elements, a conglomerate of *"roots"*, *"stems"* and suffixes, without the haziest outlines of their interrelations. The reconstructed elements of the reconstructed primitive language became a mass of unrelated parts, where comprehension was provided by the regular behaviour of the elements, determined by their phonetic position. This isolating method did of course not help to describe the real process of evolution of the history of language, and it was no accident that it incurred strong opposition and sharp criticism from the contemporaries.

Owing to this criticism, the study of spoken language, of the different dialects came gradually to the forefront of linguistic research and eclipsed the endeavours aimed at reconstructing primitive elements of a primitive language. The new material of investigation called for new methods. The new methods required new devices of investigation. This situation led to the rise and rapid development of an entirely new branch of learning, called linguistic physiology or phonetics.

If we add that, as a result of the stormy clash between flatly contradictory views, the attitude of linguistic psychology was slowly but surely gaining ground (Osthoff, Brückner, Paul, Delbrück, Brugman, Wundt), then we can see clearly the alter-

---

[68] "Einige von diesen irrigen Ansichten wurden von einem Theil der Nachfolger Bopp's sogar förmlich systematisiert. Dahin gehören z. B. die Meinung, die Sprachwissenschaft sei zu den Naturwissenschaften zu rechnen, und die Vorstellung, die Sprachen organisierten und vervollkommneten sich in vorhistorischer Zeit, um in historischer Zeit zu entarten und zu verfallen . . ." Brugman, op. cit., p. 32.

native of "either *phonetic law* or *analogy*" for an explanation of sound changes.

To the above alternative set up by the younger generation was added another fundamental innovation of principle and methodology: the application of the principle of causality to linguistic (phonetic) changes: every phonetic change must have its own necessary cause. The introduction of causality in linguistic research was viewed as the scientific foundation of phonetics. Afterwards, as is usually the case, the followers of the new conception and methods of investigation absolutized the necessary aspect of causality and entirely eliminated the accidental as a "factor inadmissible" in science. As early as 1827 Bopp resolutely declared war on every kind of explanation for linguistic changes which recognized the accidental as a language-changing factor: "*It cannot be viewed as an accident* that the genius of language makes it a condition for the change of *a* to *ê* that the root must not end in two consonants, because accident and mysterious caprice should be kept out of the explanations of everything that operates according to natural laws."[69]

On the basis of the law of causality Wundt accepted the views regarding the phonetic laws, stating that the phonetic laws "are certainly based on causal relations".[70]

The causal explanation of the exceptionless working of law was categorically challenged by Schuchardt: "On the other hand, the teaching of the exceptionless phonetic laws seems to me an obstacle for science to develop further in accordance with the law of causality."[71]

An account of the polemic, an evaluation of its various episodes could go on endlessly. It may be needless to recall that the second

[69] "*Es kann nicht als Zufall angesehen werden*, daß der Genius der Sprache der Verwandlung des *a* in *ê* die Bedingung setzt, daß die Wurzel nicht mit zwei Konsonanten schließen dürfe, da bei der Erklärung von allem, was nach natürlichen Gesetzen wirkt, Zufall und rätselhafte Willkür ausgeschlossen bleiben müssen." *Berl. Jahrb. 1827*, p. 270; cf. also Wundt, *Phil. Stud.* III, p. 212.

[70] ". . . sie [die Lautgesetze] beruhen zweifellos auf kausalen Verhältnissen . . ." W. Wundt, "Der Begriff des Gesetzes in den Geisteswissenschaften." *Logik*, Stuttgart, 1906, II/2, p. 138.

[71] "Mir hingegen erscheint die Lehre von der Ausnahmslosigkeit der Lautgesetze als ein Hinderniss für die Wissenschaft sich im Sinne des Causalitätsgesetzes fortzuentwickeln." Schuchardt, op. cit., p. 33.

half of the nineteenth century knew no worthwhile philologist who did not take stand either for or against the neogrammarians. Even the intensity of the dispute was determined not by the temperament of the members of one or the other camp, but by the topic of the debate: the nature of language, the classification of linguistic science and the search for the most expedient methods of investigation. If we add to all this the strong ideological motives which had a part in the polarization of the views, then we can really understand the significance of the first "big litigation". The firm objections raised by the mind in quest of order and rationality dethroned authorities overnight, trampled peremptory principles under foot, and tore down axioms and altars reputed to last for ever. Many things were exposed as *a priori* speculations alien to the nature of language, as ideas smuggled into the state of language and its forms of motion just to serve a certain ideology or institutional system.

The first half of the nineteenth century was in the history of linguistics the period of great experiments, brilliant achievements and tragic blunders, a period of exploration and orientation with all the essential symptoms of a general crisis of the social sciences of the time. The "great example" was given. The imposing results of the natural sciences made a fascinating impression of which the linguist searching for immanent relations could not, or perhaps did not even want to, rid himself. The mechanism of the Newtonian world outlook is an attractive one, for it tries to view the "universe" as it "appears by itself"; you have nothing to detract and nothing to add!

Thus the neogrammarians were on the right track when, in the interest of making a science of their own science, in their efforts to sketch the essential features of linguistic laws, they appealed to the natural sciences for help. The natural-law idea glittering through the alembic of the naturalist then enthralled the philologist of the age. Instead of the explanations for the mythical origin of language, the primitive attempts at a classification of languages (idiomatic reflections of the refined Greek, the practical Latin and the philosophical German mentality, etc.), it promised something palpable or "visual" to go by. The linguist was unable to resist the temptation and he let the "spirit" of natural science "loose" on linguistics. This "spirit" thereafter, breaking the bounds set by the natural philosophers, overpowered the neogrammarians. With its approach and research methods, with its conception of law, it undoubtedly turned the methods of linguistic investigation (exactness) in the right direction and stimulated the merciless criticism of formerly established "theories".

It is beyond doubt that it was both theoretically and methodologically a mistake to adopt without any change the natural-scientific outlook and research methods, not to mention the limited range of the results of the natural sciences of the time; and the drawbacks came to appear rather soon.

The deficiencies of the natural-law concept are positively recognizable also in the synopsis describing the essential features of *linguistic law* (phonetic law).

The neogrammarians were right when they conceived language as a product of the objective evolution of nature and society, when they recognized no outside interference in its inception (Schleicher and his adherents), but they were wrong in equating language with other products of nature, in failing to recognize the rise and development of society, together with the emergence and evolution of language, as a special "process of natural history" (Lenin).

We can only commend the efforts made to place the physical, physiological aspect of language in the foreground of investigation, for it is these efforts that we have to thank for the birth of physiological phonetics, but we have to criticize the one-sidedness of that method of investigation, the neglect of the psychical, the social factor .

We have to agree with the neogrammarians in that they condemned the rule of the arbitrary, of the accidental, and that finally they overthrew it to replace it by the necessary, the regular, but we have to censure them for having eliminated the accidental entirely from the factors promoting the evolution of language. So they practically lessened the significance of the necessary, for they elevated the accidental to the rank of the necessary.

We can only applaud their endeavour exerted in seeking, among the stimuli of the evolution of language, for objective or objective-looking factors instead of the linguistic theories proposed by the followers of subjective idealism, but they made the mistake of failing to recognize the role of the subject as a language-creating factor. We must not, however, forget that in formulating their conception of phonetic law they were inspired by their staunchness in opposition to subjective factors and in favour of objective grips. As it was therefore erroneous to formulate in a one-sided manner the objective character of the neogrammarian postulate of phonetic law, it was at least as much —

if not more—of a theoretical mistake for the opposite camp to think that the laws of language have "no similarities" to the laws of nature. This view meant nothing less than a negation of one of the fundamental traits of the linguistic (and in general the social) laws—their objective character. There was a great deal at stake. What was involved was the main pillar of the possibility for linguistic research to become a science. This accounts for the fact that in the heat of the debate the neogrammarians slipped to the other extreme; one-sided rigidity generated another kind of one-sided rigidity.

An undeniable proof of the tendency towards scientific exactness was the adaptation of the causal principle to the explanation of the various forms of motion of linguistic elements, while at the same time a source of theoretical confusion resulted from the simple application of causality, from the failure to recognize that the multiform and complicated evolution of linguistic elements cannot be found out by the sole means of either cause or effect, but that it is a complex association of both; what is effect in one stage may become a cause producing effect on another level, and so forth.

It is not difficult to see in the deficiencies of the early view on the characteristics of linguistic (phonetic) laws the limitations of the mechanical natural law, of mechanical materialism. An inevitable consequence was also that the opposite camp at once vehemently criticized these deficiencies, thus giving rise to that polemic lasting for several decades which I have tried to sketch above by selecting at will from the multitude of polemists those opposing parties whom I consider to have been the most typical personages in the litigation, and by picking those points of the controversy which reflected the substance of the debate clearly and unambiguously. And this was nothing else but the enforcement of the concept of phonetic law. The fight against the neogrammarian extravagances was essentially an obstruction to the spreading of the conception of law in the modern sense. Those who criticized the extravagances and deficiencies really existing in the neogrammarian concept of phonetic law were unable—but, by reason of their ideological commitment, could not even have been able, or may not even have wanted—to recommend something better instead. The reason for the "anti-law" attitude was clear: either objective law or "something else". The neogrammarians solved this dilemma for themselves unambiguously when they voted unmistakably for *phonetic law*. That this conception of phonetic law is fraught with the above deficiencies follows of necessity from the white spots of the scholarism of its age, and even if I have criticized these mistakes on the basis of our present-day knowledge, I have been trying to do so with all due respect to principled courage and determined militancy. It is also part of the truth that the opponents of the neogrammarian school did a good service to science also by pointing to minor and major flaws in the new theory of linguistic law, thereby impelling the members of the "pro-law" camp, with their knowledge of the contrary opinions, to render their theory more exact, to unburden it of its defects and distortions.

History has practically concluded the first "big litigation" on the strength of the brilliant results of comparative historical linguistics. This does not mean, of course, that today everybody has a uniform opinion of the merits of that age of militancy, not to mention the questions of detail. But it is hardly debatable today that this militant period of the history of linguistics — with all its defects and extravagances — was of great help in making linguistic research a really scientific pursuit.

2. RECEPTION OF THE IDEA OF LINGUISTIC LAW IN HUNGARY

As is generally known, it is with a visible "phase lag" that Hungarian linguists take notice of the new trends in the world of linguistics: the "worm's-eye-view" of Hungarocentrism hampers the introduction of activities relying on recent theoretical and methodological results; our philologists keep clear of the great, comprehensive problems of principle; Hungarian linguistics is too unpretentious to reach the required theoretical level, etc. It would take a separate study to analyze all this in detail, and such a study would certainly yield useful lessons, too, but the scope of the present book forbids me this venture. Yet it seems unavoidable to investigate and sketch briefly what features were characteristic of Hungarian scientific public opinion when the rippling "new wave" starting out from German soil reached Hungary, with what delay, and especially how, contemporary Hungarian linguistics and its various representatives responded to the principal theoretical theses and methods of the new school, how they developed them further and, consequently, what contribution they made to the universal development of linguistics.

The nineteenth century, especially its second half, was undeniably one of the most colourful and perhaps most conflicting periods of the history of Hungarian linguistics. A burdensome theoretical heritage was weighing upon the linguistic mentality of the time. Parallel with the idealistic tenets of "linguistic theory" confined to the realm of naive myths there were devised, on the soil of overheated nationalism, jingoish explanations of the origin of language; those entertaining illusions based on the will-o'-the-wisp of wild etymologies traced the origin of the Hungarian language back to Paradise (affinity between Hebrew and Hungarian), while at the same time the overpowering influence of Greco-Latin grammar so alien to our tongue only retarded the formation of a proper linguistic outlook.

On the other hand, it is also part of the general picture that before the inception of the German comparative-historical school Hungarian scholars suggested ingenious ideas which preceded J. Grimm's work in evolving the principle of linguistic history and also F. Bopp's activity in applying the method of comparative linguistics. It is a fact of history that it was sixteen years prior to Volume I of *Deutsche Grammatik* (1819) that M. Révai published his works *Antiquitates* and *Elaboratior*[1] (1803), furthermore the first representative of the principles of comparative philology taken in the modern sense, J. Sajnovics, had come out with his *Demonstratio*[2] (1770) almost half a century before Bopp's *Conjugationssystem* was published (1816), and S. Gyarmathi's *Affinitas*[3] was issued before the end of the eighteenth century (1799).

The way the Hungarian precursors of the new doctrines were received both at home and abroad is fairly well known. The requirement and practice of genuine historicity, of scientific comparison met with resistance from the illusion-inspired domestic public mind. In addition, Révai's view of *"veneranda antiquitas"* forced him into opposition in the litigation between neology and orthology, and his anti-reformist stand gave rise to a heated dispute among progressive Hungarian linguists, which then effaced even Révai's indisputable merits in the eyes of the scientific public of the time. The fact remains, however, that Révai preceded Grimm. W. Humboldt, the great European scholar

---

[1] *Antiquitates Litteraturae Hungaricae*, 1803, and *Elaboratior Grammatica Hungarica*, 1803.

[2] *Demonstratio idioma Ungarorum et Lapporum idem esse*, 1770.

[3] *Affinitas linguae Hungaricae cum linguis Fennicae originis grammatice demonstrata*, 1799.

who responded sensitively to every scientific accomplishment, said, to underline the significance of the fact: "I am glad to be able to name the man whose works, methinks, are far from being known so much as they would deserve to be by virtue of the efficient investigative mind which appears from them and which was led by right ideas relating to the origin and growth of language."[4] J. H. Schwicker in his history of Hungarian literature called Révai the "originator of historical philology" and the "precursor of Bopp and Grimm".[5]

In Hungary Révai had his own camp of enthusiastic followers, who were often extremely biassed in favour of orthology, and his reception abroad was hallmarked by appreciation from none other than Humboldt himself. The pioneering activity of Sajnovics and Gyarmathi was equally recognized by the profession abroad (Benfey, Gabelentz, Thomsen, Sanfeld-Jensen).[6] Conservative domestic opinion, however, "honoured" the work of the Hungarian precursors of comparative linguistics with the notorious anathema based on protestation against the "kinsfolk smelling of fish oil".

Naive "theories" for tracing the origin of language and thick-headed conservatism, on the one hand, and ingenious discoveries ahead of the age and preceding the elaboration of the new principles and methods of European linguistics, on the other: these were the cardinal features of the conflicting nature of scientific life in Hungary! It was in this scientific environment that the impact of the new school reached the science of language in Hungary. Consequently, the new thoughts were not entirely unknown or alien; depending on their learning and knowledge, the Hungarian linguists responded to the new doctrines in some way or other.

Thus the most outstanding Hungarian philologists of the age — in spite of the far from friendly or encouraging reception at home — unfalteringly plodded the rugged way designated by their scientific conscience, making critical use of the results of domestic precursors and keeping a watchful eye on everything achieved by the aid of the new methods on the native soil of new linguistic researches, in the German universities.

They consciously strove to acquire the knowledge and mastery

[4] Quoted by D. Trócsányi, *Humboldt Vilmos nyelvbölcselete* [Wilhelm von Humboldt's Linguistic Philosophy], Budapest, 1914, p. 55.
[5] Quoted by M. Rubinyi: Nyr XXXII, p. 59.
[6] IOK IV, p. 313.

of the new methods and results. Sz. Riedl, for example, wrote in 1859: "If we wish to make progress in linguistic science or to take a share in its promoting, we must needs know what has so far been made clear and established in this field not only by Hungarians but by mankind in general. If we do not know this we must inevitably fall behind."[7] They persistently studied the results of the historical comparative school that had started with Bopp and Humboldt, they were not averse from a critical analysis of the results of so-called natural-scientific linguistics either and became active popularizers and appliers of the phonetic-law conception of the neogrammarian school.

In 1863 P. Hunfalvy also took a positive stand in favour of the new doctrines and formulated the task of Hungarian linguistics in the light of those teachings.[8]

The lion's share in the propagation of the new doctrines in Hungary was assumed by P. Hunfalvy, Sz. Riedl and Zs. Simonyi. Hunfalvy became an active propagator of the new ideas under the influence of his readings, while Riedl and Simonyi were linked by personal ties also to eminent representatives of the neogrammarian school.

The scientific public does not usually keep in evidence the effect which the so-called natural-scientific outlook on language initiated by Schleicher wrought upon some excellent representatives of Hungarian linguistic science. What is commonly known is mainly and only a memory of the simplification resulting from the direct adaptation of the natural-scientific viewpoint and method (language is a living organism, a product of nature, like other organisms; the laws of language are identical with the laws of nature, and therefore linguistics is a natural science). It is generally forgotten what stimulating effect the positive kernel of the natural-scientific attitude had upon progressive philologists of the second half of the nineteenth century (exact requirements and methods, emphasis on the objective character of language, efforts to have the laws of language accepted), and, let me add, also upon the development of Hungarian philosophical thinking (materialistic monism).

Riedl, one of the most talented, versatile and open-minded scientists of the nineteenth century, was very much influenced by

---

[7] Sz. Riedl, *Magyar hangtan* [Hungarian Phonetics], Prague—Leipzig, 1859, Intr. p. XII.
[8] NyK II, p. 70.

A. Schleicher, a professor and colleague of his at Prague University, his spiritual guide and great friend in every respect. Thus it was not by chance that on November 15, 1871, his first academic paper was devoted to the memory of Schleicher, an "external member", whom he exalted as one of the most outstanding scholars of Europe.[9] We know from the same source also that in the fifties Schleicher, as a professor of Prague University, proposed the establishment of a Hungarian chair in Prague "for purely scientific purposes", that is because he had become aware of the importance of the Hungarian language in comparative Altaic researches.

That Riedl used also his academic lecture for the propagation of Schleicher's doctrines was an inevitable consequence of the profound respect he consciously developed in himself for the Schleicherian teachings. He pointed to the fundamental characteristic feature of Schleicher's scientific "attitude" which takes language as it is (objective character). From this there follows unequivocally the Schleicherian formulation of the task of the linguistic researcher: ". . . to investigate empirically the interacting laws of sounds."[10] The stress laid upon the empiric character in linguistic researches was directed here against the speculative, *a priori* principles and methods alien to the nature of languages, and did not lead Schleicher to the examination of the "physiological nature of sounds" by accident.[11] A necessary consequence of this scientific posture was the Schleicherian conception of phonetic law, "recognition of the natural laws of language".[12]

The investigation of the "natural laws of language" and their recognition, by the logic of things, called forth the entry of natural-scientific terms in the terminology of linguistics, as can be seen in Schleicher's works just as well as in Riedl's. In the introduction to his book on this subject Riedl describes *phonetics* as the *"chemism of linguistics"*, *word-stem* as *"root"* and *linguistic family* as *"stock of language"*, furthermore we encounter in his book terms such as *"dialectic ramification"*, *"stock language"*, *"linguistic species"*, etc.[13]

Schleicher's striving after scientific exactness, however, inspired Riedl not only, and not even in the first place, to obtain

[9] AkNyÉrt III/7, p. 3.
[10] Loc. cit., p. 4.
[11] Loc. cit., pp. 7—8.
[12] Loc. cit., pp. 8, 12.
[13] Riedl, op. cit., Intr. p. XIII and pp. 19, 30, 32, 40.

recognition for the natural-scientific terminology introduced by the German scholar, since this was only a much contested, and often rightly questioned, by-product of the natural-scientific school of linguistics. The essence of the school's teaching consisted in the stressing of the objective character of language, in respect for linguistic facts; this is what we call today recognition of the motion of language, recognition of the laws of relations between the elements of language.

In addition to his personal friendship with Schleicher, conscious determination also stimulated Riedl to acquire the new linguistic knowledge accumulated abroad, to propagate extensively the new doctrines. Besides, the foreign masters (Pott, Bopp, Humboldt, Steinthal and, of course, Schleicher) he did not forget the accomplishments of his Hungarian precursors either, he spoke in terms of praise about the merits of the "Hungarian Bopp", P. Hunfalvy: "And as regards the Hungarian and other Altaic languages, I have been relying, understandably, on the inquiries of the Hungarian Bopp, namely Pál Hunfalvy, whose activity led to so important results in so short a time."[14] He seems not to have known, or not to have valued, the work done by Sajnovics and Gyarmathi, for in another place he called Hunfalvy the founder of comparative linguistics: "The man who at the time [in the early fifties of the nineteenth century] not only introduced comparative linguistics but, we may as well say, created it was Pál Hunfalvy."[15]

The Schleicherian natural-scientific outlook was observable, judging by contemporary domestic reactions, not only in the field of linguistic research and teaching activity in the strict sense (Riedl), its theoretical and methodological aspects were also made known to the scientific public of the country. In the decade of the publication of Schleicher's two programme-giving polemical treatises[16] the Society of Natural Science arranged two debates to discuss Schleicher's doctrines. The lecturer of both meetings was the founder of the modern school of classical philology in Hungary, E. Ponori Thewrewk. The first lecture under the title "Linguistics as Natural Science" was read on May 5, 1869, and the other, entitled "The Optics of Language",

[14] Op. cit., pp. XIII—XIV.
[15] Op. cit., p. 64.
[16] A. Schleicher, *Die Darwinsche Theorie und die Sprachwissenschaft*, Weimar, 1863; *Über die Bedeutung der Sprache für die Naturgeschichte des Menschen*, Weimar, 1865.

on December 15, 1869. Both were published also in print, the first in the same year, the second a year later.

The scene of the debates and the titles of the lectures speak for themselves as indications of the interest for a theoretical summary of the contemporary results of modern natural-scientific research. At the same time it is worth having a look at some cardinal points of the lectures, because in their time they represented a clear philosophical stand which must have taken rather great courage to represent.

Let us come to the point. Under the influence of Schleicher's polemic treatises and on the basis of modern scientific results, Ponori Thewrewk plainly professed materialistic philosophical monism and described idealistic dualism as a "wholly obsolete standpoint": "The thinking of modern times, as Schleicher explains in his open letter on the Darwinian theory, unmistakably claims monism, the principle of unity. For our contemporary natural science dualism ... is a wholly obsolete standpoint."[17] I think this calls for no special comment. If we add only that in the framework of this lecture he investigated in the first place the role of vision in the evolution of thought, of language, and definitely underlined the role of sensation in the process of human cognition, this view inspired by materialistic monism is a telltale indication of his quite modern knowledge of gnoseology. What is important here is not even to know to what extent vision had an effect on the evolution of language, but to demonstrate the unmistakable and unequivocal theoretical foundation from the other side: the only direct or indirect source of every notion and thought is perceivable matter. What is needed for the world to be known is man who has senses, notions and thoughts, and who speaks, and perceptible matter which has its various outward forms. For thinking, an intellectual activity of high order, to come about, there is thus no need for any kind of external interference, the psychical activity is of material origin. As he wrote: "The linguist learns from physiology furthermore that the seat of the soul is in the brain alone, which is thus the only organ of thought and of all intellectual activity of higher order."[18]

How does the psychical activity of the highest order, thinking, take place, and what role does language have in this activity?

[17] E. Ponori Thewrewk, *A nyelv optikája* [The Optics of Language], Pest, 1870, p. 1.
[18] E. Ponori Thewrewk, *A nyelvészet mint természettudomány* [Linguistics as Natural Science], Pest, 1869, p. 15.

Does one of them precede the other, does language exist before or without thought, and *vice versa?* To these important ontological questions of language the already explained philosophical view can provide a single answer: "...there is no thought without language ... thinking takes place only through language. Independent (absolute) thought is non-existent, but thought exists in certain of its various forms and effects, which not even the most pretentious, most ambitious talent of thinking can surpass."[19] As to its function, therefore, language is not a simple thing—as is held by many still today—it not only serves to pass on "ready-made" thoughts (communicative function), but plays an irreplaceable part also in the "preparation", formation of thoughts. Relying on the teaching of Humboldt, Ponori Thewrewk formulated this function of language in these terms: "... language is the formative organ of thoughts, it occurs only with thought, on the one hand; and on the other, thought expands only through the union of intellectual activity with sound. It does not exist before thinking, nor does thinking exist before it, but both are one and the same as regards their origin and essence. Ultimately language is, properly speaking, not a means to communicate the truths already known, but much rather one to discover the still unknown ones ..."[20] From the foregoing there follows of necessity the acceptance of Schleicher's definition of language: "... thus language can be only what it is said to be by Schleicher, namely the audible symptom of the aggregate activity of the brain and the speech organs."[21]

On the basis of all this the most general definition of the function of language—as distinguishing man from the "other animals" by means of speech—came only to top the concept of language formed in the light of Schleicher's ideas: "... man is distinguished by language from the other animals, and, according to Huxley's notorious investigations, only by language from the nearest anthropoids."[22] It was on the basis of the view on the transition from ape to man—a view propounded by Huxley, this far from entirely consistent propagator of Darwin's doctrines— that Ponori Thewrewk explained also the origin of language, which he formulated tersely, built "in cosmic proportions": "The beginning of the universe includes also the origin of lan-

[19] Op. cit., p. 4.
[20] Op. cit., p. 8.
[21] Op. cit., p. 15.
[22] Op. cit., p. 4.

guage."[23] One cannot read without awe the beautiful lines where he depicted the highest product of the universe, man in his "social totality", rising from the animal world: "Nothing moves us so much as the being who, rising from his animal state, produced in our earth this great effervescence which has brought with it intellectual development, culture, morals, religion, science—in one word, humanity."[24]

From all this it follows logically that "spiritual man" is also an object of natural-scientific investigation, together with the factor that makes him human—language. Thus linguistics belongs to the disciplines of natural science, and the laws of language are laws of nature: "If therefore natural science claims not only animal man but also spiritual man, so also language belongs to its domain."[25] And in plainer terms: ". . . we shall never hesitate a moment to regard linguistics as a genuine *historical natural science*."[26] "One [the linguistic worker] provides the *material obtained by historical means*, the other [natural science] supplies the *laws of nature* required for an explanation."[27] To oppose the earlier phonetic conceptions "built on guesswork" he demanded a physiological phonetics based upon really scientific results: ". . . phonetics is worth something only if it is not built on mere guesswork, but if it is in agreement with the laws of nature, that is, if it rests upon physiology."[28]

The above conception of language necessarily gave rise to a whole series of linguistic terms borrowed from the terminological arsenal of the natural sciences. Let us give a sample of it: *"the chemism of the particular sound elements of language"* ('phonetics'), *"the protoplasm of language"* ('root'), *"the natural growing age of language"*, *"the artificial growth of language"*, *"the optics of language"*.[29]

This much may be enough to demonstrate the influence of the "ingenious Schleicher",[30] the first representative of the natural-scientific school of linguistics. Even if we have to consider somewhat exaggerated what A. Edelspacher, the Hungarian translator of the "naturalist-linguist", said of the monopolistic

[23] Op. cit., p. 5.
[24] Op. cit., p. 3.
[25] Op. cit., p. 4.
[26] Op. cit., p. 12.
[27] Op. cit., p. 13.
[28] Op. cit., p. 15.
[29] Op. cit., pp. 15, 18, 19.
[30] Op. cit., p. 9.

position of Schleicher's doctrines in Hungary,[31] Ponori Thewrewk's two lectures clearly evidence the keen interest which the Hungarian scientific public of the late nineteenth century took in the teaching of the most consistent German representative of social Darwinism.

Another typical imprint of the teaching of the "natural-scientific" school can be observed in the light of its reception in Hungary. The point in case is the organism doctrine "enriched" with the Hegelian theory of two-period social evolution. The theory conceived in Darwinian terms was explained by Schleicher in one of his aforementioned polemical treatises[32] in 1863. Schleicher's relevant ideas were known to Riedl — obviously owing to their friendship and scientific co-operation — already before the publication of the treatise in question. Proof of this is the fact that in his book published in 1859 Riedl spoke of two periods of the "evolution" of language: (a) prehistoric period, in which language came into being, or towards the end of which "its process of growth was completed"; (b) historical period, during which "the historical evolution of finished and essentially grown-up language, i.e. the changes to which it was to be subjected in its future life, consisted not so much in evolution as rather in deterioration and decay".[33] Still more clearly and plainly: ". . . in general we can see the languages through the entire process of their historical life in the state of slow decay and deterioration . . ."[34]

How could Riedl reconcile this characteristic feature of evolution which manifested itself in constant and "slow decay and deterioration" with the idea of the genuine development, of the progress of human society? It was not easy and not without any

[31] "Hardly was anybody more qualified than him [Schleicher] for arguing linguistically in favour of Darwin's doctrines, or for introducing and implementing them in linguistics. Schleicher has thereby created a new era in the genealogical system of languages, which became soon so widely accepted that today it is alone dominating linguistics." A. Edelspacher, *Darwin és a nyelvtudomány* [Darwin and Linguistics], Budapest, 1878, p. 7.

[32] *Die Darwinsche Theorie* . . .

[33] Riedl, op. cit., p. 28.

[34] Op. cit., p. 29. The same thought was formulated — almost word for word — on page 15 of his Hungarian grammar five years later. For comparison it is worth recalling the pertinent passage of Schleicher's treatise published four years later (cf. footnote 31 in Chapter V, Section 1). The concordance of content is striking!

logical somersaults ! "But if we regard language from the view-point of its essential purpose, according to which it is a means and form of the free manifestation of thinking spirit, we must of necessity know only progress towards higher perfection."[35] This is plain talk, too. But it is in flat contradiction to the above exposition. How did Riedl attempt to solve the irreconcilable contradiction between the two ideas? He introduced (or took over from Hegel?) the dualistic thought of "the spiritualization of matter" [of the "sensuous" factor of language], which again involved him in fresh contradictions. "The relationship between the sensuous and the spiritual factor of language is namely decaying slowly, which results in the spirit's getting rid of vocal matter, in the spiritualization of language."[36]

This here is the overpowering effect of Schleicher's authority, of the Schleicherian doctrines. Obviously Riedl was overawed by the discoveries of natural science about the laws of motion of natural organisms just as much as was Schleicher by the organismal conception of the Darwinian doctrines. We must not forget either that Riedl devised his formulation in the moment of the birth of the idea of "language as a living organism", not to mention that the organism debate lasted, with various intensity, for over three decades, in spite of the fact that one of the most militant neogrammarians, K. Brugman, the very man who formulated the phonetic law in physical terms (as a law working with blind, absolute necessity), also dissociated himself from this Schleicherian natural-scientific simplification as an untenable working hypothesis.[37]

The idea of "language change being equal to decay and deterioration" occurred, though sporadically, still around the turn of the century in the linguistic literature of Hungary, in spite of the fact that in 1874 G. Szarvas and later also others resolutely opposed this "anti-evolutionistic" thought. Szarvas already mentioned the confrontation of the old and the new as a polemical question: "We have affirmed, and we still maintain, that victory in the struggle between the old and the naturally [objectively] evolved new always goes to the latter."[38] Even if Szarvas's formulation conceived in the heat of the debate is not wholly true, his stand is unequivocal to the effect that a later

---

[35] Riedl, *Magyar hangtan*, pp. 31—2.
[36] Op. cit., p. 28. This idea occurs again on page 19 of his grammar.
[37] See the remark in footnote 68 in Chapter V, Section 1.
[38] Nyr III, p. 538.

formation of language is equal to "degeneration". Zs. Simonyi pronouncedly stated his "anti-deterioration" view: ". . . the older language cannot govern the language of today . . . modification of language is not all deterioration, but evolution at the same time, replacing old regularity by new regularity."[39] This notwithstanding, mainly in phonetic treatises, the thought of "degeneration" came up until 1907. S. Szabó wrote this in connection with palato-velar disharmony:[40] "Part of the Finns know only the first kind of harmony, but that is no longer perfect, either in Hungarian or in Cheremiss or in Finnish, because, the sounds *ë*, *é*, *i*, *í* are common to all three, getting on well together with front and back vowels alike. This is already degeneration, since the sounds in question are in reality front vowels."[41] Also he entitled a chapter "Degeneration of the Order of Sounds".[42] J. Szinnyei held the view that the disappearance of terminal vowels was due to a "gradual process towards imperfection".[43] The Indo-Europeanist J. Schmidt declared that "The general course of linguistic evolution, as undeniably appears from the reductions of vowels, is atrophy."[44]

It is indisputable that the change of language is not always and not everywhere tending uninterruptedly upwards, but it is hard to accept that the "general course of linguistic evolution" would be continuous degeneration, a process towards imperfection and atrophy. If we keep in view the changes dealt with

---

[39] Zs. Simonyi, *A magyar nyelv* [The Hungarian Language], 1889, p. 30*

[40] Originally, Hungarian words (stem morphemes) could have either only palatal or only velar vowels: *ember* ('man'), *háló* ('net'), etc. (this is what is called the "order of sounds"). The quality of the vowels of the stem morpheme determines the quality of the vowel of suffixes ("vocalic harmony"). Accordingly, words (morphemes) containing palatal vowels can take only suffixes with palatal vowels, and words containing velar vowels only suffixes with velar vowels: *ember-nek* ('to man'), *háló-nak* ('to a net'). Since, however, in the course of evolution, some velar vowels disappeared from the Hungarian stock of sounds, the original harmony broke down: *fiú* ('boy'), *leány* ('girl'), etc. Today stem morphemes having palatal vowels happen to take not only palatal suffixes *(szív-nek* 'to heart', *víz-ből* 'from water'), but also suffixes with velar vowels when the vowels of the stem morphemes originally were velar: *híd-nak* ('to the bridge'), *nyíl-lal* ('with arrow'), *szív-ok* ('I inhale'), etc. Diachronically, therefore, this type of suffixation is "regular", but synchronically this is palatal disharmony.

[41] S. Szabó, *A magyar magánhangzóilleszkedés* [Vocalic Harmony in Hungarian], Budapest, 1902, p. 4.

[42] Op. cit., p. 7.

[43] NyK XXXIV, p. 8.

[44] Nytud I, p. 48.

by phonetics, we must see at once that the sound changes do not merely consist of reductions, let alone the grammatical changes which are undeniable factors of the improvement of language.

I still should like to point out that the idea of "change of language being equal to degeneration of language" was raised, long before the organism debate, also by Révai who during his research into language history became enthralled by old linguistic records *(veneranda antiquitas)* and thus inevitably came into conflict with the neologists. This conflict culminated in what was called the "war of *-ik*", which I will not discuss in detail here. What should be added is only that the fiction of language degeneration came in very handy for Révai's followers who, relying on the authority of their master, stood rigidly by the "lex perpetua sanctitate donata", the "dogma of grammars", "what is in sharp contrast to public usage", the "gentlemanly conjugation" of the "adulterated language".[45]

I do not wish to analyze here the significance of the "natural-scientific school", its positive and negative aspects. As concerns the merits of its representatives, especially in the struggles waged to establish and make acceptable the conception of phonetic law in the modern sense, I have tried to outline them above. What I have written there could only be repeated here *mutatis mutandis*.

The range of the interest taken in general questions of linguistics was still more widened by the appearance of M. Müller, one of the most active popularizers of the neogrammarian doctrines. This professor of Oxford, who was set on formulating the principal laws of linguistics, checking the results of comparative philology with the big problems of philosophy, was really an interesting personage of European linguistics in the second half of the nineteenth century. His activity aroused a very spirited and rather varied reaction throughout Europe: some extolled him to the skies, others attacked him relentlessly. M. Bréal described him as a "luminous point"[46] of science in the focus of interest of the philosophers of the time. Hunfalvy wrote of him: "He is one of the scholars who have won European fame

[45] Nyr III, p. 538; XXII, p. 515; III, p. 538; XLVII, pp. 196, 193.
[46] "... un point lumineux, vers lequel dans le monde entier, les hommes de pensée aimaient à tourner leur regard." Quoted by I. Goldziher: NyK XXX, p. 459.

for their knowledge of Sanskrit and other linguistic studies."[47] Towards the end of his life Müller himself revealed that professional philosophers resented a "new Saul's intrusion" upon the anointed prophets of philosophical disciplines.[48] Goldziher, on the other hand, saw the essence of Müller's writings in the striving after a philosophical synthesis of linguistic problems and the results attained in this field. "The questions of linguistics in his mind and under his pen came into touch with the highest problems of the philosophical and moral sciences."[49] Without dwelling here upon an evaluation of Müller's lifework, I can state that his activity—especially his lectures at the London Royal Institution[50]—excited very great interest all over Europe and even in the New World. The lectures passed through seven editions around the middle of the second half of the nineteenth century, and the London edition of 1861 obtained a prize from the French Academy.[51] They were translated into German, French, Italian and Russian, and were published also in America.[52]

It was no accident that the activity of the "new Saul" pretty shortly arrested the attention of Hungarian philologists and then of the "official circles".

The propagation of the lectures in Hungary was started by a sharp-witted polyhistor, endowed with considerable critical sense, a nineteenth-century scholar of Hungarian linguistics, the "Hungarian Bopp", P. Hunfalvy, with his lecture "On the Science of Language", at the Academy on March 2, 1863.

The lecture, drafted in a definitely critical tone, went far beyond the scope usual at that time, for it took up many important questions of principle of Hungarian and European linguistics. The introductory part acknowledged the results which "the scholarly professor of Oxford University" had attained by

[47] NyK II, p. 69.
[48] "... Während die berufsmäßigen Philosophen das Eindringen eines neuen Saulus unter den alten Propheten der Logik, Psychologie und Metaphysik sehr übel aufnahmen." M. Müller, *Die Wissenschaft der Sprache* I, Leipzig, 1892, Vorwort p. V.
[49] NyK XXX, p. 458.
[50] *Lectures on the Science of Language*, Vols. I and II. — The quotations printed in this book I have taken from the sixth edition (London, 1871); hereinafter referred to as *Lectures* I and *Lectures* II, respectively.
[51] NyK II, p. 69.
[52] Hungarian translation by Zs. Simonyi, *Müller Miksa újabb fölolvasásai a nyelvtudományról* [Max Müller's Recent Lectures on the Science of Language], Budapest, 1876, p. 3; hereinafter referred to as *Fölolvasások* II.

applying mainly the methods of natural science (the claim to exactness !).[53] Müller's activity and accomplishments were given a symbolic construction in the lecture and encompassed the new linguistic school as a whole, all of its outstanding representatives, those "who lead the way and are sweating in the efforts of a European spirit".[54] It was in the light of the multicoloured results of this manifold activity that Hunfalvy defined the task of Hungarian linguistics as consisting in "reading interpretatively the geological script of languages", because "there can no longer be a nation whose science would not be interested herein".[55] As construed by Hunfalvy, the "geological script of languages" does not mean that he uncritically took over from German "natural-scientific linguistics" the simplified conception in which language is the same sort of "natural product" as other natural organisms. By no means. The use of the natural-scientific term here was called to underscore that essential feature of language according to which "man's will has no sway over the languages",[56] and this is nothing else than laying stress on the objective character of language. In his opinion this thesis, which is often encountered in Müller's lectures and which has several times been discussed from different angles, was very important, and Hunfalvy referred to the notorious slip of the tongue committed by the Emperors Tiberius and Sigismund, more precisely to the related arrogant remarks of those "highly distinguished gentlemen", in order to prove that the "happenings" of language (the process of linguistic evolution) "are not subject to man's will".[57] If the evolution of language is not directed by the will of individual men, linguistics can be classed, just because of its "happenings", neither as a historical science nor as a natural science.[58] Hunfalvy underlined especially Müller's genealogical

[53] NyK II, p. 70.
[54] Ibid.
[55] Ibid.
[56] Loc. cit., p. 73.
[57] Ibid.
[58] Even if, relying on our present knowledge of linguistics, we cannot agree with this kind of opposition of the two branches of science (stressing the objective character of one against the obviously non-objective character of the other), we have to commend anyway this "non-classification", for what is at stake here is no less than that the scientific investigation of language is a task of a special science, the science of language. I well know that this statement today sounds as a banal truth, but we must not forget that Hunfalvy took this position at a time when the first waves of the new linguistic theories were reaching Hungary, with the

classification of languages and his views of the criteria of the affinity of languages. He did not censure Müller's idea about the monogenesis of language. He blamed the Romans for not having seen their linguistic kinship with so many peoples. In his view they were made blind to the fact by the bias that "for them all peoples who spoke other than Latin or Greek were barbarian".[59] He did not fail to remark either that there were some who still in the second half of the nineteenth century declared Hungarian to have been the language of Paradise (Hebrew-Hungarian kinship!). To this "primitive-language theory" which could be met also in Germany, and which had sprung from the soil of "religious prejudice", Hunfalvy responded with Leibniz's ironical comparison: "To take Hebrew for the primitive language is tantamount to thinking that the branches and twigs are the beginnings of the tree."[60] To the procedure of the differently motivated daydreaming probers into the origin of language he replied by stressing the importance of the study of living languages. He spoke in appreciative terms about the Spanish Jesuit Hervas, who during his missionary journey in America had been busy studying languages, and who after his return to Rome, with the help of fellow members of his order, obtained further information on various languages. As a result of his systematic work "he collected samples and records of more than 300 tongues, writing grammars of 40 languages by himself . . . He was the first to claim [in his Spanish-language catalogue of languages published in 1800] that the affinity between languages should mostly be based on grammatical evidence . . . he recognized the kinship of the Hungarian with the Lapp and Finnish languages . . ."[61]

When referring to the small number of *root-words* in the different languages, Hunfalvy mentioned also language economy: "Language economizes, makes much out of little."[62] He stressed particularly the importance of *sound reduction* (Hegelian reminiscences in Müller's linguistic theory), because this explained the origin of the various suffixes in Hungarian.[63]

---

result that linguistics was regarded as belonging rather definitely to the exact sciences. (See the views of Riedl and Ponori Thewrewk, Simonyi's translations of Müller, Edelspacher's translations of Schleicher, etc.)

[59] Loc. cit., pp. 75—6.
[60] Loc. cit., p. 76.
[61] Loc. cit., p. 77.
[62] Loc. cit., p. 81.
[63] Loc. cit., p. 73.

The picture Müller's linguistic theory presented in Hungary would not be complete if we failed to make mention of Hunfalvy's positive view in which sounds "change according to a specific law".[64]

In addition, Hunfalvy dealt with Müller's lifework on two occasions. First, still in the year of his lecture at the Academy (1863), in his review of Ch. J. Bunsen's book *Outlines of the Philosophy of Universal History, Applied to Language and Religion* (London, 1854),[65] and secondly, in his "Remarks"[66] published at the end of the first translation of Müller by Zs. Steiner (Simonyi).[67]

The greater part of Bunsen's book (pp. 263—520) consists of the letter Müller wrote to Bunsen in August 1853.[68] The letter sketches the main features of Müller's morphological classification of languages, which he discussed later in his lectures. (I shall still come back to Hunfalvy's review later on.)

Hunfalvy expressed his opinion, very smartly and pregnantly, on Bunsen's general description of evolution as well, giving evidence of his extensive interest and even of his distinct philosophical attitude. It is really worth reading! As he came to the subject, he quoted from Bunsen: "Evolution is possible only through the play of opposites . . . historical evolution and natural manifestation follow the same course. History brings forth in time what creation puts forth in space—to wit, the triumph of spirit, advance from the inorganic to the organic, from unconscious to conscious life."[69] Hunfalvy with his sharp eyes caught out Bunsen at once: the question is essentially about Hegel's theory of evolution, about the views expounded in the "phenomenology of spirit". "Who does not know Hegel's speculation", he writes after his quotation from Bunsen and goes on, "but who can think he unravels thereby the secret of creation,

---

[64] Loc. cit., p. 86.
[65] NyK II, 1863, pp. 381—460.
[66] "Észrevételek Müller Miksa nyelvtudományi felolvasásaira, különösen a nyolczadikra" [Remarks on Max Müller's Lectures on the Science of Language, with Special Regard to the Eighth Lecture]; published on pp. 395—413 of the volume referred to in footnote 67 below. (The eighth lecture is entitled "Morphological Classification".)
[67] *Müller Miksa fölolvasásai a nyelvtudományról* [Max Müller's Lectures on the Science of Language], Budapest, 1874; hereinafter referred to as *Fölolvasások* I.
[68] A turáni nyelvek osztályozásáról [On the Classification of the Turanian Languages], NyK II, pp. 384, 403.
[69] Loc. cit., pp. 384—5.

the origin and the final goal of all that exists? The triumph of spirit, advance from the inorganic to the organic, from unconscious to conscious life. How good it sounds, and how little or how much it means! Spirit! But whose spirit? The spirit of man or the spirit of God? For if the two are identical, then the individuum cannot be responsible."[70] It is indisputable that the formulation to the point is indicative of Hunfalvy's thorough knowledge of the Hegelian theory of evolution and bears eloquent evidence that he put his finger on the cardinal weakness of that idea of evolution, on its inconsistency, more exactly on the wrongness of its starting point, the idealistic conception of "spirit". Hunfalvy's criticism touches upon the most important problem of philosophy, and by posing the problem of "either-or" speaks out straight what Hegel tried to bypass with his sophisticated theory: the divine origin of spirit, namely the untenableness of that theory ("For if the two are identical, then . . ." !).

Müller also embraced this Hegelian-Bunsenian theory of evolution. In the explanation of the evolution and especially of the origin of language it was not by chance that he came into conflict with the consistent materialists. Already Ponori Thewrewk blamed him for his inconsistency: ". . . When speaking of the nature of language he is beating about the bush, but elsewhere he defends Schleicher's theory [the claim to scientific exactness, appropriate methods]."[71]

It may be of interest not only for the history of science that Müller knew and highly valued the results of S. Gyarmathi. In the first series of his lectures he told this about Gyarmathi's work: "The affinity of the Hungarian and the Finno-Ugric dialects was first proved philologically by Gyarmathi in 1799."[72] Already in his letter to Bunsen he recognized the difficulties of Gyarmathi's pioneering work and achievements: ". . . if we consider that Gyarmathi had written his work before the foundations of comparative philology were laid, he deserves a high place among the founders of this science."[73] Speaking in support of this appreciation, Hunfalvy stated: "Gyarmathi did much in a short time; if he was mistaken on many points, it was because he had not broken the crust; he had no inkling of the laws of the change

[70] Ibid.
[71] Ponori Thewrewk, *A nyelvészet* . . ., p. 10.
[72] *Lectures* I, p. 307.
[73] NyK II, p. 403 (requoted from Hungarian).

of letters."[74] Awareness of the essential interrelations, of the essence hidden "behind the crust" in the depth of superficial manifestations, is an entirely modern conception of law.

Hunfalvy's accurate criticism drew also the attention of the Academy of Sciences to Müller's lectures. The plenary meeting of the Academy on January 22, 1872, set up a committee "to work ... in the interest of having translations made of more eminent products of foreign scientific literature".[75] At the request of the Academy's publishing commission Simonyi in 1873 translated and in 1874 made public Müller's earlier lectures, and the rest appeared, also translated by Simonyi, in 1876.[76] In his capacity as translator, Simonyi made the remark that those lectures "are occasionally one-sided but always witty and interesting dissertations", which "hardly need recommending".[77] In both translations he adduced glosses about the Ugric languages, which is proof that, with very few exceptions, he agreed with Müller's lectures in their entirety.

If, therefore, we examine the theses of Müller's *Lectures* concerning the most comprehensive questions of language (the nature of language, the peculiarities of the laws of language, etc.), then we essentially become acquainted with Simonyi's relevant opinions. Moreover, if we take into consideration that the lectures were translated at the request of the Academy's publishing commission, and that the translated text was published under the auspices of the Academy, we may also presume that the whole Hungarian scientific public was in agreement with the views propounded in two bulky volumes. The translation of the lectures of "good old Max Müller" (Laziczius) is in the first place a document for the history of science, therefore it is worth while to deal with it in detail.

It was not by chance that the Academy's publishing commission turned its attention to Simonyi with a view to having a Hungarian translation made of "more eminent products of foreign scientific literature".

Thanks to his studies and foreign relations, Simonyi proved most apt to explicate in detail the doctrines of the neogrammarian school. During his studies abroad he attended lectures of

[74] Loc. cit., p. 404.
[75] *Fölolvasások* II, first unnumbered page.
[76] Op. cit., third unnumbered page.
[77] *Fölolvasások* I, Preface by the Translator.

Paul, Curtius and Leskien at Leipzig, became a member of Curtius's "Grammatische Gesellschaft", which at the time set itself the aim of studying the new teaching in seminarlike groups.[78] Owing to such scientific education Simonyi became an ardent follower of the new school and took every opportunity to popularize and propagate its doctrines. In his university lectures he was the first to take up comprehensive theoretical questions of linguistics; by involving his zealous students in serious debates during practice lessons he tried to clarify the mode of outlook of the then flourishing neogrammarian school, all essential features of the new principles and methods suggested by the new school. The transmitter and translator of the new, productive thoughts was thus Simonyi, who had started translating Müller's lectures already during his studies at Pest, then Leipzig, Berlin and Paris.

What prompted Simonyi to translate Müller's lectures? The answer is simple and evident. There was and, we may as well say, there is still in contemporary philology no single question of principle which the Oxford professor left unmentioned in his lectures at the Royal Institution; some of them he expounded in detail (often in too much detail), and others only in passing. If we take a cursory glance at the subjects of the lectures, we come to see the wide interest which was characteristic of the London scientific circles and the "educated public at large", and which the lecturer, relying on his extraordinary erudition, tried to satisfy. (The science of language one of the physical sciences; the growth of language in contradistinction to the history of language; principles and methods of linguistic investigation [collection of materials, systematization]; genealogical classification of languages; morphological classification; comparative grammar [theoretical and methodological problems of comparatism]; the origin of language; the theory of language; language and reason, etc.) It follows from the comprehensive character of the subjects that we encounter topics like the importance of the investigation of the living language ("dialectic growth") and, of course, the typical problems of linguistic changes, sound shifts, phonetic laws, which were indeed the most exciting questions of the philology of the time. Hungarian philology in the nineteenth century also was seeking satisfactory answers to these questions, that is why it received with interest the tentative answers from abroad, that is why it turned towards Müller's lectures.

[78] AkNyÉrt XXVI/10, pp. 3, 4.

From the multitude of problems I shall try to pick the principal questions which, in my opinion, are absolutely necessary for a portrait of Müller, and which were in the forefront of interest among contemporary Hungarian philologists (the main peculiarities of language, the characteristics of the laws of language, the proper place of linguistics, the relations between language and thought, the theoretical criteria of a classification of languages, Hunfalvy's related criticism).

Müller believed the task of the science of language was to investigate linguistic phenomena as facts "by means of careful inductive reasoning".[79] This definition of the task follows from his outlook on the nature of language. When seeking to touch upon the nature of language he kept aloof from any definition of language that was deduced not from the evidence of facts.[80] His definition of language, based on inductive reasoning from facts, is as common as possible: "the one palpable distinction between brute and man".[81] This is true on the whole but far too general, because concretely it refers not to the nature of language but to the most essential difference between man and animal. As to its sense, this criterion is identical with Locke's distinction, according to which what distinguishes animals from man is the latter's superior faculty of abstraction.[82] Even so we could accept this general truth—with the reservation, of course, that it refers to *one* of the important aspects of language—if, through the idea of the monogenesis of language, it were not combined entirely with the idea "elevating to the height of divine origin". This specific view regarding the monogenesis of language follows from the intention to reconcile the biblical conception with scientific thinking, and it is an eloquent proof of the slip of the most respectable inductive procedure if it shrinks back from making the final, the most principal inferences. Müller finds himself here in sharp contradiction to the above formulation of the task of linguistics as "fact-respecting and fact-stating" investigation when, with a certainly fine-sounding allegory, he

[79] *Lectures* I, p. 252.
[80] A conventional production, living organism. Op. cit., p. 250.
[81] Op. cit., p. 405.
[82] "I may be positive in . . . that the having of general ideas is that which puts a perfect distinction betwixt man and brutes, and is an excellency which the faculties of brutes do by no means attain to." J. Locke, *An Essay Concerning Human Understanding*, Oxford, 1894, II, ch. IX, pp. 207—8.

writes: "I . . . date the real beginning of the science of language from the first day of Pentecost. After that day of cloven tongues a new light is spreading over the world, and there objects rise into view which had been hidden from the eyes of the nations of antiquity. Old words assume a new meaning, old problems a new interest, old sciences a new purpose."[83]

This slip of Müller's is an instructive example to show also where an inaccurate conclusion formulated with even the most respectable intention can lead. The fact is that in a different place Müller, on behalf of humanity, clearly expresses his indignation against certain American hate-mongering politicians who, in order to devise "scientific" arguments in support of the "unhallowed theory of slavery", urged comparative linguists "to prove the impossibility of a common origin of languages and races".[84] He rightly condemns the kind of "interpretation" of Darwinism on the title-page of an American "scientific" publication made for this purpose, "in which, among the profiles of the different races of man, the profile of the ape was made to look more human than that of the negro".[85] But Darwin cannot be made responsible for this. Against such "aggressive ideas" even the idea of humanity conceived in the most Christian manner is of no use: "The common origin of mankind, the differences of race and language, the susceptibility of all nations to the highest mental culture—these become, in the new world in which we live, problems of scientific, because of more than scientific, interest." [!][86] The above-cited lines, which are unquestionably neatly composed, are very enlightening also to the effect that the natural-scientific (fact-stating) method of linguistic research is not enough in itself if it is not coupled with an unambiguous point of departure (or view), if it does not rest on the firm basis of consistent materialism.

In Müller's view another peculiarity of language is its changing character. Because, as he writes, "whatever the origin of language, its first tendency must have been towards an unbounded variety".[87] How does a linguistic change occur? Through the "natural growth of language",[88] as a result of new usage by

[83] *Lectures* I, p. 141.
[84] Op. cit., p. 13.
[85] Op. cit., pp. 13—14.
[86] Op. cit., p. 141.
[87] Op. cit., p. 62.
[88] Op. cit., p. 63.

certain great men, heroes fit to be imitated, or independently of
the will and consciousness of individual man? Müller holds the
latter view. He sees the essence of linguistic change in the
objectivity of the process of change: ". . . neither of the causes
which produce the growth of language . . . is under control of
man."[89] The continuous changes which take place slowly but
"irresistibly" are "completely beyond the reach or control of
the free will of man",[90] that is why the attempts of some grammarians and purists to improve language are "perfectly bootless".[91]

The form-change of language is caused by "phonetic decay"
(reduction), which in turn "is not the result of mere accident; it is
governed by definite laws".[92] But these laws "were not made by
man; on the contrary, man had to obey them without knowing
of their existence".[93] So many sentences, so many unequivocal
statements about the objective character of language, of linguistic processes, of their productive causes, of the laws governing them! There would be nothing wrong here, since this is
directed against the earlier one-sided subjective linguistic theory.
As one-sided the conception was about the habits of great men,
kings, etc. being the sole language-forming factor, at least so
one-sided and in principle wrong is the "fatalistic" conception of
linguistic law—built upon the total elimination of the subjective
element—which professes the complete helplessness of man and
which regards all philological activity as being entirely hopeless
and "perfectly bootless". (N.B.: Language improvement is here
confined almost exclusively to the possibilities of altering certain
speech sounds, but also here it is wrong to disregard the subjective element.)

According to Müller the laws of form-changes, of "phonetic
decay"—beyond the effects of "dialectic growth"—are in the
first place physiological laws, which can be explained by the
difference of the physical factors surrounding man and influencing his physiological development and condition: ". . . the laws
which regulate these changes [phonetic changes] are entirely
based on physiological grounds, and admit of no other explanation whatsoever."[94]

[89] Op. cit., p. 71.
[90] Op. cit., p. 72.
[91] Op. cit., p. 73.
[92] Op. cit., p. 71.
[93] Ibid., cf. also pp. 40, 41, 43, 44, etc.
[94] Lectures II, p. 192.

The idea is a matter of common knowledge. Since, in addition to making simple statements on the regularities of phonetic changes, the conception of phonetic law has been looking for the productive causes, the Darwinian natural-scientific explanation has occupied first place: the effect wrought by earth, climate, etc. upon the organs of speech, the influence of the latter upon sound changes.[95]

From among the contemporary Hungarian authors even Riedl wrote in his phonetics published in 1859 as follows: "With the changing of earth, climate, mode of living, as the result of thousands of new impacts, there come about new phonetic laws, new word-forms . . ."[96] This phrase is repeated in his grammar published in 1864.[97] The idea of "geographical explanation" occurs in an academic lecture of his in 1873 as well.[98]

The main reason for "phonetic degeneracy" is to be found therefore in physiological factors, including even human sloth, carelessness and love of comfort.[99] This is how "phonetic decay" comes about for lack of muscular energy. Simonyi fully endorsed this idea, as is proved by his addition to Müller's Latin, Anglo-Saxon and French examples of such Hungarian words which have been reduced as compared to the fuller forms preserved by the cognate languages: Vogul *kälm* — Hung. *kém* ('spy'); Ostyak *jenk* — Hung. *jég* ('ice'); Mordvin *šäjär* — Hung. *szőr* ('hair'); Finn. *silmä* — Hung. *szem* ('eye'); Finn. *antaa* — Hung. *ad* ('give'), etc., etc.[100] Simonyi sees an action of the "general law of reduction" even in the transformation of loan-words borrowed from foreign languages. His examples: Turk. *biliži* — Hung. *bölcs* ('wise'); Sl. *opatica* — Hung. *apáca* ('nun'); Latin *tegula* — Hung. *tégla* ('brick'); German *Wanderer* — Hung. *vándor* ('wanderer'); French *gendarme* — Hung. *zsandár* ('gendarme'), etc.[101] The general law of reduction,

[95] A. F. Pott, *Etymologische Forschungen* . . . II, 1836[2], p. 1; H. Osthoff, *Das physiologische und psychologische Moment* . . ., Berlin, 1879, p. 19; F. Kaufmann, *Gesch. der schwäb. Mundart* . . ., Strassburg, 1890, p. XI; J. P. Rousselot, *Les modifications phonétiques du langage* . . ., Paris, 1891, p. 351. Their opponents: B. Delbrück, *Die Lautgesetze* . . ., Leipzig, 1893[3], p. 127; H. Paul, *Prinzipien* . . .[2], p. 56; O. Brenner, *Einleitung zur "Deutschen Phonetik"*, Leipzig, 1893, p. 11; H. Fischer, *Geography* [!] *der schwäb. Mundart*, Tübingen, 1895, p. 79, and many others.
[96] Riedl, *Magyar hangtan*, p. 37.
[97] Riedl, *Magyar nyelvtan* [Hungarian Grammar], Pest, 1864, p. X.
[98] AkNyÉrt III/9, p. 42.
[99] *Lectures* II, p. 193.
[100] *Fölolvasások* II, pp. 197—8.
[101] Op. cit., p. 198.

however, can be neutralized, and even an opposite trend may be promoted, by the aforementioned indolence and leisureliness in the formation of sounds. This is what—beyond the examples taken from various foreign languages—Simonyi had in mind when pointing to loan-words dissolving their initial consonant clusters: Sl. *prostŭ*—Hung. *paraszt* ('peasant'); German *Schnur*—Hung. *zsinór* ('string'); Sl. *dvorŭ*—Hung. *udvar* ('court'); German *Strang*—Hung. *istráng* ('traces').[102]

When, after the mystical theories about the origin of language, linguistic facts are already available, these are subjected to one-sided, physiological examination. We already know today that sound changes are not, and not even in the first place, produced by physical, physiological factors. But we must not lose sight of the fact that the physiological explanation was in essence a groping about for an objective grip, meant to counter the earlier theories of phonetic change on the basis of subjective factors. This explanation claiming to be scientific was advocated by none other than Curtius and his followers. In Hungarian philological literature, besides Simonyi and Riedl, also Z. Gombocz recognized that the cause of change in pronunciation "is to be found in love of comfort, at least in many cases".[103] Gy. Lux wrote in 1927: "Phonetic changes have mainly physiological, psycho-physical causes . . ."[104] What Lux meant by psychophysical causes he clearly explained: ". . . the fundamental cause of linguistic change lies in the imperfection that can be experienced in the perception and imitation of sounds."[105] This explanation is essentially a psychological revival of the theory of "phonetic degeneracy", of the physiologically conceived decay of language. The physiological explanation of sound changes has still been encountered in recent times as well. At the Debrecen philological congress (1966) J. Molnár attributed the unrounding of Hungarian vowels to a fundamental change in the culinary habits of the first Hungarian settlers in the country, more precisely to the resulting change in the arrangement of their teeth.

We have to add in the interest of truth, however, that Müller, when framing his physiological explanation of sound changes, came to several interesting and even enduring conclusions. In his lecture on "Phonetic Change"[106] he dealt separately with the

[102] Op. cit., pp. 199—200.
[103] Nyr XXVII, p. 57.
[104] Gy. Lux, *A nyelv* [Language], Budapest, n. d., p. 44.
[105] Op. cit., p. 45.
[106] *Lectures* II, pp. 176—215.

problems of "imperfect articulation".[107] In this respect he investigated why in the languages of some peoples we do not find certain sounds which play a very important role in the languages of European peoples (sibilants, trills, etc.).[108] By endorsing Kaufmann's view, he explains the absence of sounds like *s*, *sh*, *z* in the Dinka language on the ground that the Dinkas—like other Negro tribes of the White Nile—take out their lower front teeth. He attributes the lisp found in other languages to the fact that certain tribes (for example, the Va-Hereros), for ritual or aesthetic reasons, file off part of their upper front teeth and knock out some of the lower ones.[109]

Müller is also right to say that, in the intermingling of languages, in the borrowing of loan-words or the learning of foreign languages, sound substitution serves to bridge the gap created by the lack of one or another sound of the language of origin in the adopting language. That is how English *steel* became *kila* in Hawaiian: the initial consonant cluster was dissolved, the sounds *t* and *k* could not be distinguished, and a consonant could not remain in final position.[110] The absence of *r* and the elimination of consonant clusters are responsible for Christ to have become *Ki-li-sse-tu*, Europe *Eulopa*, America *Ya-me-li-ka* in Chinese.[111]

According to Müller, a shifting of articulation is the explanation for the alternation of certain existing speech sounds having the same function, a phonetic phenomenon occurring in most languages. Thus, for example, the Latin terminations *-aris, -alis*, as to their function as well as origin, are doubtless identical and alternate depending on the consonant of the word-stem: *saturnalis—secularis, normalis—regularis*, etc.[112] Simonyi adduces Hungarian examples: *fúr — fulánk* ('sting'), *paszúr — paszuly* ('kidney bean'), *csikér — csekély* ('trifling'), *barbier — borbély* ('barber'), etc.[113] Riedl called this "articulation shifting" *dissimilation*.[114]

A thorough examination of the "dialectic growth" also facilitates orientation in the tangle of sound changes because, in

[107] Op. cit., pp. 183—8.
[108] A. Kaufmann, *Das Gebiet des Weißen Flusses und dessen Bewohner*, Brixen, 1861.
[109] *Lectures* II, p. 178.
[110] Op. cit., p. 184.
[111] Op. cit., p. 181.
[112] Op. cit., p. 187.
[113] *Fölolvasások* II, p. 189.
[114] AkNyÉrt III/9, pp. 8—9.

addition to the general physiological explanation of the "phonetic decay", the inquiries into living languages "will amply reward a fresh *battue* of the comparative philologist".[115] Müller thought highly of the investigation of the various dialects. He reverted to the subject time and again,[116] for "the real and natural life of language is in its dialects".[117] He spoke up resolutely against those who maintained that dialects "are everywhere corruptions of the literary language",[118] and he even reversed the question and professed unmistakably that "Dialects exist previous to the formation of literary languages, for every literary language is but one out of many dialects".[119] Even though Müller's explanation for the formation of literary language cannot be fully accepted, the part played there by dialects is not quite negligible.

Also in his subsequent works Müller often stressed the role of dialectic factors besides the physiological explanation of sound changes. He claimed that the lack of muscular energy could explain such cases of the "law of sound shift" (Lautverschiebung) where tenues become mediae: $k > g$, $t > d$, that easier pronunciation would account for the developments of *knight* > *night*, *hláford* > *lord*, *Worcester* > *Woosta*, but that the changes $t > th$, $d > t$ did not serve easier pronunciation, here we have to do with the penetration of dialectic forms into everyday language.[120]

While underlining the objective character of the "minute laws" producing and regulating "the changes of each consonant, each vowel, each accent",[121] Müller recognizes also the role of the subjective factor (the whims of some to change sounds consciously), in so far as such whim becomes a habit. He confines this possibility, however, to the speech of primitive peoples, in which he sees "the childhood of language".[122] Today we know already that modern whims of linguistic usage or eccentric modes of pronunciation may come into fashion, "become objectified". Recognition of subjective factors as having a part in sound

---

[115] *Lectures* II, p. 2.
[116] *Lectures* I, pp. 44, 51—2, 55—6, 64; II, pp. 28—35.
[117] *Lectures* I, p. 52.
[118] Op. cit., p. 55.
[119] Op. cit., p. 56.
[120] M. Müller, *Die Wissenschaft der Sprache*, Leipzig, 1892, p. XIV.
[121] *Lectures* II, p. 45.
[122] Op. cit., p. 43.

changes is only commendable, but it is in direct opposition to the essence of the conception of phonetic law discussed above (total exclusion of the subjective element).

As a matter of fact, this is not the only flaw in Müller's concept of law; its principal defect is its inconsistency, its mistaken starting point, mentioned already in connection with his conception of the genesis of language. Accordingly, the clever order, or regularity, hidden behind the superficial disorders of the material world, behind its apparent and real contradiction, is not a characteristic of matter, but "the reflection of a divine mind" lighting up "the dark chaos of matter".[123] When we penetrate the mysteries of the material world, and disclose its regularities, essentially we come to see "the eye of God beaming out from the midst of all His works".[124] Against this "law" man is really helpless; in the evolution of a law conceived of in this sense the subject really cannot play any role.

As has already been mentioned above, the concept of phonetic law is a cardinal precept of the neogrammarian school, which evolved it on the basis of the natural-scientific discoveries of the time (mechanics, gravitation, regularities of the evolution of the living world, etc.).

The most characteristic trait and principal value of this conception of phonetic law lay in the fact that it tried to discover the regularity and order hidden in the depth of sound change, one of the most interesting and—according to the neogrammarians—most important outward forms of motion of language, to find the causes producing the changes. In the light of this idea and with a critical eye, they re-examined all views which the earlier attempts at linguistic explanations had formed regarding the process and causes of change, and categorically rejected every idea which they believed was no adequate reflection of the phenomena and things. The idea of phonetic law formulated with such theoretical claim was made—as a matter of course— the exclusive explanatory principle and practice of linguistic changes, the touchstone of the rightness or wrongness of etymologies. The concept of phonetic law thus became the guideline of the neogrammarian linguistic theory, the yardstick of almost every idea concerning the development of language, the

[123] *Lectures* I, p. 17.
[124] Ibid.

standard by which any explanation was accepted as adequate or rejected as unscientific. The neogrammarians held their conception of phonetic law to be a fixed point at which even the clearest phonic consonances had to fail if they could not be explained by *regular correspondences* hidden in the depth of sound changes.

To illustrate the fertilizing effect of the concept of (linguistic, phonetic) law of natural-scientific inspiration, we could cite numberless examples from both foreign and Hungarian scholars. The significance of the concept of phonetic law which took shape as an adequate mental reflection of the "motion of things" was clearly formulated by Müller as well: "On the strength of these phonetic laws once established, words which have hardly one single letter in common have been traced back with perfect certainty to one and the same source."[125]

This also is part of Müller's conception of law fraught with flat contradictions. For when relying on his specific education in natural science, Müller builds his formulations on strict examination of the facts of language, and not on a false ideology fading into the fog of mysticism, his answers are to the point.

He considered it highly important to ensure recognition of the concept of phonetic law thus formulated (he reverted to the basic idea in almost every one of his lectures), and looked forward with optimism to the reception of the new idea. "Few people, if any, would doubt any longer that the changes of letters take place according to certain phonetic laws ..."[126] How much he was mistaken! His optimism was unfounded, he did not foresee the almost thirty-year-long desperate struggle which was to come between advocates and opponents of the concept of phonetic law. The fact remains, anyway, that Müller—backing all the progressive elements of the new idea together with its extravagances open to question—was a militant propagandist of the phonetic-law conception of the neogrammarian school.

The concept of a phonetic law "operating blindly" and "admitting of no exceptions" was practically a product of the application of research methods based on truly physical principles. The application of the principles and methods clearly determined also the proper place of linguistics among the physical sciences. The very fact that Müller was lecturing at the Royal Institution of London is eloquent enough proof of his pertinent stand, but

[125] *Lectures* II, p. 27.
[126] Op. cit., p. 192.

he even told so in introducing his second series of lectures when he stated his view about the proper place of linguistics as a theoretical question in the focus of discussion: "One thing I feel more strongly than ever—namely that, without the Science of Language, the circle of the physical sciences, to which this Institution is more specially dedicated, would be incomplete."[127] It is rather indisputable that the basic motive in his classification of linguistics was the dignified claim to scholarliness working with unambiguous notions and methods, and excluding the arbitrary conception of phenomena.

That is how the contemporary scholars viewed the physical sciences, that is why many other neogrammarians also classed linguistic research among them, and that is where other Hungarian scholars besides Simonyi also saw the essence of "classification". About the turn of the century I. Goldziher gave this evaluation of Müller's lectures: "When claiming the science of language for the physical sciences and designating the methods of natural science for observing of the growth of language, Müller took up the cudgel against the one-sidedness of linguistic philosophy [logicism]."[128] In this conception, the "spiritual freedom [!] manifest in history" is not valid for the formation of language; language "is clearly placed under the stringent regularity of natural phenomena as an organic product of nature".[129] Accordingly, the science of language is a natural science in as much as it opposes necessity to human freedom.[130] Speaking of the significance and influence of Müller's view, Goldziher stated that Hungarian philologists received from him a firm argument when they were striving to eliminate individual arbitrariness, when they thus endeavoured to achieve, by explaining the changes of language, "a scholarliness excluding the arbitrary conception of phenomena". "So, therefore, in the eyes of our generation, Max Müller . . . has become an apostle of the natural-scientific outlook on linguistics . . . . And nowadays we can hardly evoke the inspiring effect which this very categorically formulated doctrine exerted not only upon the general linguistic outlook but also, in a practical sense, upon the treatment of living language."[131]

[127] Op. cit., p. 7.
[128] NyK XXX, p. 460.
[129] Loc. cit., p. 461.
[130] Loc. cit., p. 462.
[131] Loc. cit., p. 461.

In possession of such a natural-scientific arsenal, Müller could give only one answer to the much discussed problems of *language and thought*. Acceptance of the objective character of language, the above definition, necessarily led to an identification of language and thought as "one of the best established principles of the science of language", without which it is impossible to imagine "articulate" sounds, sequences of sounds, and thoughts independent of words. In one of his lectures, entitled "Language and Reason", he wrote: "To treat of sound as independent of meaning, of thought as independent of words, seems to defy one of the best established principles of the science of language."[132]

As to the separateness of language from thought, from the process of thought, he would be ready to accept it only if language were considered to have been a result of common agreement, if we conceived of the origin of language so that "certain wise kings, priests, and philosophers had put their heads together and decreed that certain conceptions should be labelled and ticketed with certain sounds".[133]

It was not without irony that Müller connected the quoted hypothesis with the opinion according to which the outward form of language is given by the sound, and its content is formed by the thought. In case the "agreement theory" would be accepted, "we might speak of the sound as the outside, of the ideas as the inside of language".[134] The conventional character of language conceived of in this sense contradicts the most elementary requirements of common sense, because in reality "There never was an independent array of determinate conceptions waiting to be matched with an independent array of articulate sounds. As a matter of fact, we never meet with articulate sounds, except as wedded to determinate ideas . . ."[135] A testimony of linguistic facts in support of the above thesis: λόγος "most rightly and naturally expresses in Greek both speech and reason".[136] The word λόγος comes from λέγειν, its equivalent in Latin is *legere*, which actually means 'to gather', 'to pick', or rather 'to tell', 'to recite': English *tell* and the German *zählen* of the same stem equally have the meaning 'to count' and 'to cast up', too. Therefore λόγος < λέγειν "is nothing more or less than the gathering

---

[132] *Lectures* II, p. 47.
[133] Op. cit., p. 48.
[134] Ibid.
[135] Op. cit., p. 65.
[136] Op. cit., p. 66.

up of the single by means of the general".[137] Simonyi adduces examples from the Hungarian and related languages in support of this view: Hung. *számolni* 'to count' has in some region also the meaning 'to relate', 'to keep telling'; Est. *luge-* also means 'to count', 'to read' and 'to tell'; *lugu* means both 'number' and 'story'; Vogul *lau-* 'to tell', its equivalent in Mordvin: *lovo* 'to read', 'to count'.[138]

The above examples, which demonstrate the particular acts in the process of thinking (to collect, "count up" and "tell" the various conceptual marks) and thereby make an abstraction of concept, really give food for thought. But the result will not be different either when we examine a little more closely the linguistic terms related to the whole process of the acquisition of knowledge. Already Locke firmly held the view that every concept—even the most abstract one—can be traced, directly or indirectly, to concrete sensation.[139] Based on the original and abstract meanings, of the verbs *imagine, apprehend, comprehend, conceive*, etc., Locke comes to an abrupt conclusion: ". . . and I doubt not but, if we could trace them [the above-cited examples and the like] to their sources, we should find, in all languages, the names which stand for things that fall not under our senses to have had their first rise from sensible ideas."[140] According to Müller this formulation based on sensualistic materialism, "though somewhat involved and obscure, is a classical passage", but he finds the facts stated by Locke "to be above all doubt" and says that "those who are opposed to materialistic theories consider it necessary to controvert the facts alleged by Locke..."[141] If, in connection with the data quoted by Locke, we invoke the meanings of the individual elements in support of the essence of Locke's gnoseological idea, we come to the following conclusion. The original meaning of the stems of those verbs clearly points to the lowermost, primary stage of the process of cognition, to

---

[137] Op. cit., p. 67.
[138] *Fölolvasások* II, p. 69.
[139] "It may also lead us a little towards the original of all our notions and knowledge, if we remark how great a dependence our words have on common sensible ideas; and how those which are made use of to stand for actions and notions quite removed from sense, have their rise from thence and from obvious sensible ideas are transferred to more abstruse signif- ications, and made to stand for ideas that come not under the cognizance of our senses." Locke, op. cit., III/1, pp. 4—5.
[140] Op. cit., III/1, p. 5.
[141] *Lectures* II, p. 394.

the moment when the sense organs come into contact with the object to be perceived. Through the sense organs the object perceived sends "part images" to the brain, and the image of the object, the *notion*, appears in the mind. When the notion is abstracted from the multitude of "part images" into symbols mirroring only the most essential features, i.e. when we have *grasped, conceived, apprehended*[142] the essence of the thing, we get to the *concept* of the initially sensed fact, object, etc. If, by examining more closely the meanings of idiomatic expressions, we can trace these undeniably very abstract concepts to sensations arising from concrete processes of apprehension, and if, by physical operations with the "stock concepts" thus devised (through an arbitrary combination of the conceptual marks which exist separately), we get to the concepts *Pegasus, centaur*, (anthropomorphous) *god, heaven*, etc., then we can really understand Locke's joy of "rediscovering" the dictum of Thomas Aquinas: "Nihil est in intellectu, quod non sit prius in sensu."[143]

To support Locke's process of concept-formation (sensation to notion to concept), Müller examines the original meanings of the Latin words *spiritus* (< *spirare*), *anima* (< Sanskrit *an* 'to blow') 'spirit, soul' and finds that both have also the meaning 'breath'.[144] Relying on Budenz's first publication on word comparisons,[145] Simonyi listed the equivalents in cognate languages of the Hung. *lélek* 'soul' in order to demonstrate the quite "earthly" relations of the expression of this concept noted to be of "divine origin". The Hung. *lélek* is originally 'steam, vapour' though Votyak *lul* and Zyrian *lov* mean only 'soul, life', while its equivalents in other cognate languages are: Vogul *lil* 'soul', 'breath', Livonian (dial.) *lävl* 'hot steam', 'soul', Finn. *löyly*, Est. *leil*, Lapp *lievl* mean only 'vapour, evaporation'. The equivalent of the Latin *spiritus* in Hungarian, *szellem*, signified originally 'breath': "zèllèt hol akar ot lehel" = spiritus ubi vult spirat.[146] In the same way Latin *animal* became Hung. *lelkes állat* 'animate brute', shortly *lelkes*, which was equivalent to *élő* 'living'. Here the verb 'live' has the connotation of what one 'lives by': 'food,

---

[142] Cf. the synonymity of English *apprehend, comprehend, conceive* and German *auffassen, begreifen*, too.

[143] *De veritate* II, p. 3.

[144] *Lectures* II, p. 374.

[145] *A magyar és finnugor nyelvekbeli szóegyezések* [Word Correspondences in Hungarian and the Finno-Ugric Languages], Pest, 1868.

[146] Quoted from RMNy III, p. 194, by Simonyi, op. cit., p. 279.

corn, cattle, livestock' (cf. Lapp *ällo* 'flock', Finn. *elo* 'corn', Livonian *jelāmi* 'cattle, stock, property').[147]

The analysis of linguistic facts led Müller to the conclusion that most of the word-stems originally had a general ("material") meaning which made them fit to express precisely even the most abstract concepts. This property of language (of words) points also to its (their) economical nature: ". . . language has been a very good housewife to her husband, the human Mind; she has made very little go a long way."[148] The cited metaphorical (husband vs. wife) relation of language and thought is accordingly unequivocal: the two belong together, they are inseparable; Müller returned to this idea in several places.[149]

I do not wish—nor would I be able—to solve here the problem of the relationship between language and thought, a problem which has been much discussed up to now and is still not settled satisfactorily. The only thing that seems to be certain is that language, word-form, is an inseparable part of the process of thinking, for the final result of the abstracting operation, verbal thinking, is difficult to imagine without the presence of linguistic form.

At the end of the first volume of Simonyi's Hungarian translation of *Lectures*, Hunfalvy again came back, now with full knowledge of the Müllerian conception, to the criticism of Müller's idea, especially of his morphological classification. Just as he emphasizes the significance of Müller's genealogical classification and approves the criteria of the common origin of various languages, so resolutely he argues against his principles of morphological classification and its practical consequences. According to this, the criterion of the classification of languages is "the manner in which roots are put together",[150] the behaviour of the word-elements in the case of different forms, derivations, etc.

On the basis of such a principle of classification Müller distinguishes three stages of the development of languages:

(a) *Radical stage*. Languages belonging to this stage are called

---

[147] Op. cit., pp. 378—9.
[148] *Lectures* II, p. 387.
[149] "Language and thought are inseparable. Words without thought are dead sounds; thoughts without words are nothing. To think is to speak low; to speak is to think aloud. The word is the thought incarnate." *Lectures* I, p. 439.
[150] Op. cit., p. 330.

monosyllabic or *isolating*, e.g. the old Chinese language. Characteristic of the languages belonging to this stage of development is that "roots may be used as words, each root preserving its full independence".[151] This stage "excludes phonetic corruption altogether".[152]

(b) *Terminational stage.* This stage is represented by the languages usually called *agglutinative*, e.g. those belonging to the "Turanian family of speech". In these languages "two roots may be joined together to form words, and in these compounds one root may lose its independence", "the other sinking down to a mere termination".[153] Here, too, the principal root is not liable to phonetic corruption, which is allowed in the secondary, so-called "determinative elements".[154]

(c) *Inflectional stage.* In this are classed the *amalgamating* or *organic* languages, e.g. those belonging to the Aryan and Semitic families. In the languages of this stage "roots coalesce so that neither the one nor the other retains its substantive independence",[155] that is to say, this stage "allows phonetic corruption both in the principal root and in the terminations".[156]

Between languages which are related according to the principle of morphological classification (e.g., the Turanian languages) we cannot discover any kind of family likeness (genealogical affinity) which is so characteristic, for example, of the Semitic and the Aryan languages. The principle of genealogical classification is not even applicable to these languages.[157]

Müller tries to exemplify the difference between the Aryan and the Turanian languages by referring to the difference between good and bad mosaic, and what is more, he considers the above classification to be a qualitative one. Thus he thinks the Turanian peoples were nomadic tribes unfit to establish states, as opposed to the high culture of the Aryans, and he says even that their language was less developed than the "political" pattern of the Aryan languages.[158]

Hunfalvy takes one by one the criteria of this principle of classification. He begins with the linguistic criterion, with what is

---

[151] Ibid.
[152] Op. cit., p. 331.
[153] Ibid.
[154] Op. cit., p. 332.
[155] Op. cit., p. 331.
[156] Op. cit., p. 332.
[157] Op. cit., p. 371.
[158] Op. cit., pp. 335, 340.

called "phonetic decay". He rightly points to the untenableness of Müller's opinion by mentioning the obvious fact — invoked also by Edkins[159] who was referred to even by Müller — that Chinese in former times, as to its phonetic character, also was different from today's Chinese. The same applies to the word-roots of the so-called inflected languages.[160] The linguistic facts of Hung. *hó* 'snow' — *havas* 'snowy'; *van* 'is' — *lesz* 'will be'; and still more *uruzag bele* > *országba* 'into the country', etc. are proof of the rightness of Hunfalvy's critical remarks: "phonetic decay" cannot be a criterion by which to distinguish a special class, for it may occur in languages of either the agglutinative or the inflected class, and so in the "main root" and the terminations alike. For this very reason he proposes instead of "phonetic decay" the term "historical phonetic change" in order to distinguish it from the type of "grammatical phonetic change" which is different in the different languages.[161] If grammatical phonetic change is determinatively different according to (types of) languages, then it can serve as a basis for classification. On this principle of classification he proposes, in place of Müller's threefold system, one of four classes:

(a) There is no grammatical phonetic change (Chinese).

(b) The vowels of the word-root are essential and invariable before suffixes, the word-root affects the suffixes (Finno-Ugric and Turkish languages).

(c) The vowels of the word-root may change before suffixes, thus the root-vowels do not affect the suffixes (Aryan languages).

(d) Root-vowels are unessential, root-consonants are the predominant elements (Semitic languages).[162]

In the wake of Castrén, Hunfalvy comments on this fourfold system in a footnote listing Vogul and Ostyak words in which the root-vowels also change before different suffixes. But, we can add, this applies also to Hungarian. The above-cited example of *hó* — *havas*, just as *hő* 'heat' — *heves* 'heated', *lé* 'juice' — *leves* 'juicy', also argues against acceptance of the principle of classification proposed by Hunfalvy, as today languages are as a rule no longer classified on a morphological basis of this kind.

Hunfalvy rightly criticized Müller's mosaic metaphor; Latin *scio* = *sci-o* is at least as "bad a mosaic" as is Hung. *tudsz* =

---

[159] *A Grammar of the Chinese Colloquial Language*, Shanghai, 1864².
[160] *Fölolvasások* I, p. 397. (Hunfalvy's remarks appended to the Hungarian edition.)
[161] Ibid.
[162] Op. cit., p. 400.

= *tud-sz* ('you know'); moreover, in the *-m* and *-d* of *tudom* ('I know [it]') and *tudod* ('you know [it]'), respectively, "there is concealed an objective suffix together with the personal or subjective ending". If we examine the formation of *tudjuk* ('we know [it]'), we find that it has come from *tud-ja-muk*, so this is "such a perfect mosaic for which there is hardly any match in Sanskrit or Greek".[163]

Hunfalvy in his critical writing again comes back to Müller's letter mentioned before, which is included in Bunsen's book and deals with a description of the Turanian languages. In that letter Müller uses a different angle to qualify the languages divided into three classes on a morphological basis. Accordingly, Chinese is a *household* language, the dialects of the Turanian family are *nomadic* languages, and those of the Aryan and the Semitic families are *state* languages. Hunfalvy rightly points to the weakness of this classification of languages: this procedure in fact leaves out of account that, at the time the languages came into being, none of the tribes or peoples was on such a level of development as to be able to form a state of its own.[164] The main features of the advancement of every people are by and large identical (hunting, stock-breeding, farming). It may happen that we find a state (or its rudiments) among nomadic peoples, while in Hunfalvy's time the Arab people, whose language Müller included in the highest morphological class, undeniably were living the life of nomads, not to mention the Gipsies.[165] Nomadism or statehood cannot therefore be a criterion by which to classify languages.

With regard to the origin of language, Hunfalvy held that Müller's idea of monogenesis might be acceptable but at the same time debatable. On this very basis he challenged Müller's thesis according to which the languages belonging to the so-called Turanian linguistic family are unfit for genealogical classification. In these languages he could find the same degrees of relationship as were discernible in the Aryan-Semitic languages. If this finding is correct—and he adduces eloquent examples to prove it—then the only research method applicable to the languages of the Turanian family is that "which was successful in the investigation of the Aryan languages".[166]

---

[163] Op. cit., p. 401.
[164] Op. cit., p. 402.
[165] Op. cit., pp. 403—4.
[166] Op. cit., p. 408.

This was a very important finding in its time, for if Hunfalvy had agreed with Müller's views, it would have been necessary to invent a different sort of research method for the Turanian languages, although the method of Bopp and Grimm had already proved to be successfully practicable. The investigation of the languages of the Uralo-Altaic linguistic family with the aid of the comparative-historical method, as well as the results of the investigations, vindicated Hunfalvy's views.

That was how for the first time the Hungarian scientific public responded to the lectures of the English propagandist of "European fame" of the new German linguistic theory and method. In the light of the lectures the profile of a very peculiar scholar showed itself to his Hungarian propagators and critics. These were fascinated by his amazing professional knowledge, his commendable thoroughness, his extraordinary intuitions, his capability of recognizing the deeper interconnections, his perfection in general gnoseological questions, his knowledge of the multifacetical "evidence" of language, his astonishing critical sense. At the same time he did not get lost in the greyness of positivism, his inferences drawn from the facts led him to bold generalizations as long as concrete facts of investigation were available. His wild fantasy, however, often carried him to generalizations that incurred sharp opposition from contemporary researchers. His ideological commitment led him utterly astray in the "big questions". In his explanations both of the genesis of language and of the formation of different languages he attempted—without success, of course—the impossible: to reconcile the findings of science with the tenets of the Bible; in the more and more brilliant emanations of the human mind he saw the reflection of a divine spark.

Of Müller's profile composed of great contradictions Simonyi saw only his ingenuity, but Hunfalvy and still more Ponori Thewrewk sharply criticized him for his inconsistency (see above). In any case, it is a fact that his lectures at the time excited great interest in Hungary, where their influence was undeniable. It is a pity that the attention focussed on him was waning with the progress of time and ultimately ceased altogether. It is beyond doubt, however, that it would have been useful to develop some of his doctrines further and to criticize consistently his erroneous ideas. Surely, the point would have been to keep interest alive for the manysided teachings of the neogrammarian school, for the general questions of linguistics. In view of the interest shown the Hungarian environment was fit to accept and develop further the many aspects of the new ideas, to make ever new critical examinations of the particular theses on the basis of new experience, to investigate in detail the "innumerable forces" which make up a language, in the way also Müller, relying upon Hegel, conceived of the process of human cognition as a spiral motion tending upwards and upwards.[167]

The first Hungarian popularizers and active propagators of the neogrammarian doctrines concentrated their activities, understandably, on the search for the inner stimuli of the motion of language, for "the essence hidden behind the crust", the linguistic (phonetic) laws. In the light of the imprints left by the new doctrines in Hungary, this essence was far from being confined to "probing" into the reasons underlying the sound changes, however important it was considered to make the neogrammarian postulate recognized, but the search went on for the "regulating principle" of all kinds of linguistic manifestations, for the internal interrelations behind the apparent superficial chaos. This procedure necessarily followed from the scientific credo which did not want to introduce into language "ideas" from outside, but reviewed, accepted or rejected every linguistic idea on the strength of the objective pattern of motion of language. The authoritarian principle was replaced with principles supported by the evidence of the facts of language, and theoretical findings had continuously to be tested by the severity of linguistic practice, because this was required by scientific exactness, the empiric starting point taken over from the methods of natural science.

And what is in question here is not even any kind of empirics, but a rather definite scientific outlook. An outlook which is based on the principle of the indissoluble ties of science and practice, of practical necessity, an outlook which sees the main stimulus of the development of sciences in the satisfaction of social needs. The role of practice, of empirics thus appears in its full context, in its dialectical unity: since theory serves to satisfy human needs in all forms and manifestations, it is necessary to demonstrate the "practicability" of the theory.

---

[167] "... und der Vorschritt menschlichen Wissens gleicht oft den Schwingungen eines Pendels oder noch besser einer spiralischen Bewegung, in der es immer wieder auf denselben Punkt zurückkehrt und doch stets, so dürfen wir hoffen, bei jeder Drehung zu einem höheren Standpunkt

Conceived in this manner, the unity of theory and practice is well exemplified by the remarkable lines drafted by Riedl more than a hundred years ago: "The basis of our knowledge is experience. Every science, lofty and sublime as its subject should be, eventually took its origin from experience, from the modest daily needs of semibarbarian races. What had induced the most ancient philosophers to engage in so profound investigations was not an ideal of truth, beauty and goodness. It was rather the urgent need of a semisavage and patriarchal society that laid the first foundations which human spirit later developed into so immense edifices. The names of some of the oldest sciences still indicate today their peculiar genesis. Geometry, which seems today independent of any sensual impression and presents its points, lines, surfaces and solids only as ideal forms to be found nowhere in reality; geometry, as appears from its name, began with the measurement of ploughland. Botany, or botanike techne, received its name from the fodder grain . . . The founders of astronomy were not poets and philosophers, but seamen and husbandmen. The names of stars, like the Brooding Hen, the Reaper, etc. indicate that they originate from the practice of agriculturists."[168]

The phenomena observed in practice prompted the scientists of modern times to uncover their internal interrelations. It was by seeing the church lamp move that Galileo came to discover the general laws of pendular movement. Newton was induced to look for the cause of free fall by his observation of the "motion" of an apple that had fallen on his head, and he came to discover the general laws of gravitation. Darwin observed the formation of the breeds of animals in the practice of English stock farmers, and a thorough study of his experience led him to devise his theory "which has already essentially modified the world outlook hitherto accepted and has not failed to affect the science of language either". It was during his translating the Gothic Bible that Grimm became aware of "regular correspondences" between the Latin, Greek and Sanskrit languages, and so Grimm's law was born.[169]

---

gelangt." Müller, *Die Wissenschaft der Sprache* I, Vorw. pp. XVII—XVIII.

[168] A nyelvtudomány alapelvei [The Principles of Linguistics]: Introductory university lecture. *Kalauz*, 1863, p. 11. — "Brooding Hen" is in Hungarian the name for the star cluster called Pleiades in English.

[169] AkNyÉrt III/9, p. 14.

Riedl thought these statements were all the more important as in his time it was generally held that the worth of the sciences lay primarily in their own selves, irrespective of whether they meant anything to practice. "It is sure", he wrote, "that, generally speaking, no branch of science flourished in Europe for a long time if it was unable to promote the interests of society in some respect or other."[170]

I think these findings can stand the test of our present-day knowledge, too. The scientific public of these days recognizes more or less uniformly the social functions of theory, of science. Today it is hardly questioned, if at all, that the various types of the social sciences also serve to satisfy a special need (as promoters of the development of social consciousness), but it is also a matter of common knowledge that the sciences were far differently valued around the middle of the nineteenth century.

For this very reason we have to attach very great importance to Riedl's words — eloquent proof of his scientific faith — where it is not difficult to detect the effect of Schleicherian natural-scientific empirics, nor the fact that already prior to the first translation of Müller the principles and results outlined in Hunfalvy's programmatic speech stimulated the Hungarian scholar, who was highly sensitive and fast reactive to every new doctrine, to engage in a thorough study of the lectures of the Oxford professor.

Riedl's knowledge of Müller's work prompted him to reconsider time and again his own views regarding the most important questions of linguistics. Besides the need of a more intense and meticulous investigation of the neogrammarian theory of language, this reconsideration was further motivated by his intention to try, by means of the new theory and method, to reach the solution of an exciting old problem, that of the conjugation of the Hungarian verbs ending in -ik.[171] Against the background of the opposition of orthology and neology[172] the dispute was, in

170 Loc. cit., p. 12.
171 In the paradigmatic pattern of conjugation in Hungarian some verbs take the suffix -ik in the third person singular of the indicative present.
172 Opposite trends of the Hungarian language-reform movement which began to unfold, as a corollary of emergence to nationhood, in the last decades of the eighteenth and the first decades of the nineteenth century. The neologists (language reformers), striving to create Hungarian terminologies for the various branches of science and to refine Hungarian

Riedl's time, still in full swing with varying ardour, because the issue became (or was made to be?!) a decisive factor in the struggle between the new and the old.

It was thus timely to re-examine the question, and Riedl devoted four lectures to the elucidation of the matter. He read all four lectures at Academy meetings.[173] The series was published in 1873 under the title "Is There an Acceptable Reason for a Special Conjugation of -*ik* Verbs?" [174]

His first lecture started out from Humboldt's idea about the tasks of different sciences, from its application in the field of linguistic research. Accordingly, if linguistics gets only as far as to cognize the phenomena appearing in the different languages, to merely register such phenomena, and if it has no contact with practice either, this sort of work "has no scientific value" and "can be regarded only as sheer sport".[175] Knowledge is thus qualitatively different from all cognition of the phenomena; knowledge begins when we have also "ideas" about the phenomena, that is, when we discover also the internal interrelatedness of their essence. "To know means not only to have cognition of things, but also to possess ideas, that is, from a different point of view, to comprehend the laws of the given phenomena."[176] From this formulation of the task there follows necessarily the principal object of linguistics, "the definition of the laws [of the genesis] of languages".[177]

These objectives induced Riedl to uncover the "natural laws" of the Hungarian language.[178]

His research programme was thus not to construct new rules, nor exceptions, for the multiplication of these would jam the "robust organism of language into a Procrustean bed",[179] but to discover interrelations which had come about independently of the will of individual men, and which are therefore organic

---

literary language, made a copious contribution to the Hungarian vocabulary. This endeavour was not always free from irregular word coinage either. It was against such extravagances that the orthologists stood up and soon they became opposed to deliberate language development: they preferred tradition to reform. Victory in the struggle between the two trends, as a matter of course, was won by the neologists.

[173] April 22, June 3, 27 and 30, 1872.
[174] AkNyÉrt III/9.
[175] Loc. cit., p. 3.
[176] Ibid.
[177] Loc. cit., p. 4.
[178] Ibid.
[179] Ibid.

"formations originated with natural necessity" which admit of no exceptions.[180] Individual (great) men have no influence on the origin and development of such formations. Riedl also mentions the notorious slip of the tongue to which reference is made both in Müller's lectures and in Hunfalvy's commentary. (The mistake came from the lips of the German Emperor Sigismund at the Council of Constance. Yet, despite the imperial will and self-confident attitude, the mistake failed to become a "rule of language".) After underlining again the objective character of language, Riedl came to the following conclusion: "It is my scientific conviction . . . that language must not and cannot even . . . *be made*, but language surely *can* and must be studied in order that, by becoming acquainted with its laws and *obeying* them, we might be masters of it."[181]

How do we cognize the laws of language, and what are indeed those motive forces which prompt man to discover the essential features of some phenomena of the world? Riedl's answer to these important questions of gnoseology is clear: all theoretical knowledge has its source in practice.

This "scientific conviction" formulated with utmost care, on close inspection, says nothing less than that:

(a) One of the fundamental features of the laws of language, their independence, of the will of individual men, is in accordance with the fundamental feature of the laws of nature, their objective character.

(b) Cognition of the laws of language is possible through a profound and "fact-respecting" investigation of the facts of language.

(c) We can cognize them on the basis of practice, by satisfying practical needs.

(d) Once we have cognition of the laws of language which come into being and are operative independently of our will, we are not helpless in face of them, we can "master them".

So many sentences, so many important precepts, whose significance cannot be overemphasized, especially if we oppose them to the idea of "blind operation" suggested by the "extremist" neogrammarian conception of phonetic law, and if we remember how fatalistic even the conception of the law of society looked still in the recent past, and how helpless it considered men to be in face of the operation of social laws (Stalin's views on the most

---

[180] Loc. cit., p. 15.
[181] Loc. cit., p. 13.

characteristic features of the laws of political economy and the nature of their operation).

We have only to add one single remark to this entirely modern idea of law: Riedl's view that the laws of language do not admit of exceptions is not acceptable. It must be said, however, that the "exceptionless" character of the law of Riedl's conception was inspired by the early idea of natural law and was formulated nearly a hundred years ago. On the basis of the natural-scientific results attained since that time we already know that cogency is not the most typical peculiarity of natural laws either. For the sake of truth, however, we have to say also that Riedl uses a more differentiated formulation when he writes of the operation of the laws (assimilation, dissimilation, voicing, etc.) of "word phonetics, . . . perhaps the most important part of scientific grammar".[182] He says that in his time there existed also the word-forms *házval, késvel*, etc. side by side with the actual forms *házzal, késsel* ('with the house, with the knife'), etc. which shows that assimilation was not yet completed in some places,[183] and this in turn points to the limitation in place and time of the operation of the phonetic law.

Different considerations also brought Riedl to turn against the "exceptions". Based on a superficial examination of the phenomena of language, older and contemporary grammars laid down certain rules and described as exceptional or even outright wrong everything that could not be subjected to these—more or less arbitrarily established—rules. In the opinion of such "rule-makers" it was wrong to use the forms *olvasol, nézel, romlasz, bomlasz* ('you read, you look, you degenerate, you go to pieces') in the practice of popular and colloquial language instead of the "regular" forms *olvassz, nézsz (nézesz), romlol, bomlol.*[184]

And now we have come to the main issue of the dispute, the problem of the *-ik* conjugation. Riedl rightly tried to approach the solution from a thorough analysis of the whole system of conjugation and not of sporadically encountered paradigmatic forms, by taking into account both the historical evolution of the system and the place in it of its various parts; or, in our modern terminology—the dialectics of the whole and the part. In forming

---

[182] Loc. cit., p. 6.
[183] Loc. cit., p. 22.
[184] Loc. cit., p. 15.

his opinion, he looked for objective grips instead of the rather subjective-smelling "criterion" to answer the question "Who speak good Hungarian and where ?", even if, as a consequence of the discovery of linguistic facts, of their essential traits and internal correlations, he was compelled to propose, "with the permission of the Academy", an "extensive revision of the whole system of conjugation" laid down in contemporary grammars.[185] This action was in harmony with the recent linguistic trend of his time which "does not want to *make* language" but "*is learning, seeking and probing* without, however, *being imperative* or compulsive".[186]

The representatives of the "camp of -*ik*" leaning on Révai's immense prestige actually referred to the verb-forms occurring in Old Hungarian in order to defend Révai's "system" of -*ik* conjugation, which in Riedl's opinion was the result of misunderstanding. Namely, when examining some of the old conjugational forms, Révai came to the conclusion that the reason for the final -*sz* in *írsz, vársz, kérsz* ('you write, you wait, you ask') is that these verbs have the forms *ír, vár, kér* in the third person singular. By the same logic the forms *aluszol, fekszel, iszol* ('you sleep, you lie [in bed], you drink') end in -*l* because the forms of the third person singular are *aluszik, fekszik, iszik*. But even if it was a peculiar "system compulsion" that made Révai to create a separate -*ik* paradigm, Riedl asked at once what kind of system is that which becomes visible only in two forms of the whole paradigmatic pattern (first and second persons singular of the present indicative) through its own characteristic endings *(-*m** and -*l: feksz-e-*m*, feksz-e-*l*) claiming a separate conjugation. What he does not even enlarge upon, but mentions only in passing, is that we can discover these personal endings in other paradigmatic forms, too: -*m* occurs in the first person singular of the transitive conjugation of the "verbs without -*ik*", while -*m* and -*l* are found respectively in the first and second persons singular of the past tense of verbs with -*ik* and those without -*ik*: *ír-o-*m* a levelet* 'I write the letter' vs. *ír-o-*k* egy levelet* 'I write a letter'; *ír-t-a-*m** 'I wrote'; *ír-t-á-*l** 'you wrote', etc.[187] Accordingly Riedl stated: The endings -*m* and -*l* are personal suffixes which indicate only the difference between persons just as the suffixes -*k* and -*sz* do: *ír-o-*k** 'I write', *ír-*sz** 'you write', etc.[188]

[185] Loc. cit., p. 24.
[186] Loc. cit., p. 16.
[187] Loc. cit., pp. 35—6.
[188] Loc. cit., pp. 36—7.

A re-examination of old Hungarian linguistic records and codices led Riedl to emphasize that, as against the opinion of the "camp of -*ik*", there was in the old language no such clear dividing wall between conjugations with -*ik* and without -*ik*, but even if there had been it does not mean much for today's language: ". . . what is the value, the worth, of linguistic records is not that they regulate the language of today, but really only that they explain today's language . . . The law of nature which says: Die Todten stehen nicht auf !, applies also to language."[189]

Riedl thought that the cause of Révai's "system-creating" mistake was that in his time there did not exist "the alpha of a really scientific grammar, namely phonetics".[190] That is why he could not see that the suffix -*l*, being conceptually equivalent to -*sz* but phonetically more adaptable, is added to the morphemes *alusz-*, *feksz-*, *isz-* as a consequence of the enforcement of dissimilation. The same applies to the opposite case as well: the stem *boml-* takes the suffix -*sz* which is equivalent to -*l*.[191]

Riedl ascribed to the law of "scientific grammar", among them to assimilation and still more to dissimilation (which had been neglected until then), an extremely considerable role in the origin of phonetic changes. He categorically rejected the procedure of previous grammars which, almost without exception, gave euphony as an explanation for the regular alternation of -*nak* and -*nek* in forms like *háznak*, *embernek* ('to the house, to the man'). He questioned with full right the "euphony" of the type of words like *halhatatlanságának* ('to his immortality'), *kegyetlenkedésének* ('to his atrocity'), and mentioned the structure *a pápa csalhatatlanságának tana* ('the dogma of papal infallibility') as a deterrent example. The very same vowels, if they succeed one another many times, are not only unpleasing to the ear, but are outright boresome. He stated the same thing with regard to the assimilation of consonants, too. He asked rightly why *ház-zal* sounded better than *ház-val*, not to mention that this assimilation is not enforced in all cases (*néz-ve*, *lát-va* ['looking, seeing'], etc.). He was right to say that linguistic (phonetic) changes did not as a rule serve to realize the idea of some sort of "absolute euphony" but were fit to help language "to perform as easily as possible its function, which is to become as perfect an expression of thought as possible".[192] The best possible compliance with the commu-

[189] Loc. cit., pp. 19—20.
[190] Loc. cit., p. 33.
[191] Loc. cit., p. 34.
[192] Loc. cit., p. 5.

nicative function of language is an evident explanation also for the productive cause of phonetic changes, which is to be found, according to Riedl, not in the striving after euphony, but "in the laws of the physiological functioning of the speech organs".[193]

To make pronunciation easy and rapid is therefore the basis of both assimilation and dissimilation. The work of the speech organs is fatiguing the muscles, so that after the same muscles have worked for a while, they need some respite, during which the work of other bundles of muscles is required. It is this fatigue factor that causes many mispronunciations occurring with tongue twisters; the fact is that the organs of speech are unable to keep producing for a longer time consonants of the same or similar place of articulation.

Riedl's theory that dissimilation serves to help the communicative function to be fulfilled as easily as possible is acceptable on the basis of the above examples, but it must be added that the primary aim is still precise communication, that is the avoidance of misunderstandings. When the need of easier pronunciation is confronted with the requirement of precise communication, the latter prevails. Just to return to the above examples, the assimilation process *ház-val* > *ház-zal*, *kés-vel* > *kés-sel* has been accomplished in general (there are still exceptions in some dialects: *kés-vel*, *busz-val*, etc.). On the other hand, the word-forms *néz-ve*, *lát-va* have not in general developed into *néz-ze*, *lát-ta*, because the latter forms had been retained for the "communication of information" of a different kind, and a mixing of the two can cause troubles in communication.

This type of exhaustion of the organs of speech is, of course, a regulator or modifier not only in the Hungarian language area but it is generally effective. The aim being to avoid the frequent succession of the same consonants, it is understandable why the suffixes *-lis* and *-ris* in Latin having the same function alternate in words like *spiralis* and *singularis*, and the same cause accounts for the following examples from Romance languages: It. *pellegrino*, Fr. *pélerin* < Lat. *peregrinus;* It. *fratello* < Lat. *frater*, etc.[194] Hungarian examples of the alternation of sounds: *dal* 'song'—*danol* 'sing'; *Antal* < *Anton;* *Selmecz* < *Schemnitz;* *tömlöcz* 'gaol' < *timnuc;* *erkély* 'balcony' < *Erker;* *borbély* 'barber' < *Barbier*. The "regulator" of the suffix clusters *-alék,*

---

[193] Ibid.
[194] Ibid.

-elék and *-adék, -edék* is that dentals are followed by the variant *-l-* and other consonants by the variant *-d-: adalék, töltelék* and *omladék, menedék.* The same regulation takes place with the variants *-kozik, -kezik* and *-kodik, -kedik: hivatkozik, következik; pajtáskodik, részegeskedik,* etc.[195]

The above-cited examples are "live" word-forms taken from the practice of language. The use of *leszesz, teszesz, olvassz,*[196] further *romlol, bomlol,* etc., "created" by the compulsion of the *-ik* paradigm, instead of *leszel, teszel, olvasol,* and *romlasz, bomlasz,* respectively, is contrary to popular and literary usage, but to ordinary linguistic instinct, too. It lives only "in the grammar-trained minds".[197] At the same time the forms *aluszol ~ alszol, eszel, iszol,* etc. perfectly tally with both popular and literary usage, though not because they fit in with the "invented" *-ik* paradigm but because they are regular dissimilatory variants of personal suffixes having the same function.[198]

It was not on the *-ik* verbs in general that Riedl declared war. He formed his opinion with sober moderation when he wrote that, if there are *-ik* verbs in Hungarian—and surely there are lots of them, both basic words and derivatives—then neither he nor anybody else is in a position to wipe them out; or conversely: if such verbs were non-existent, neither he nor any other person or authority could establish them by order. He only challenged that there exists a separate *-ik* paradigm. Those who "believe" in it are victims of a misunderstanding.[199]

Although Riedl did not succeed "in helping us and our descendants to get rid definitively of the *-ik* conjugation",[200] his witty lucubrations add excellent examples to the argumentation based on respect for the facts of language, the practical starting point of theoretical generalization and its reaction upon practice, the shaded picture of the characteristic features of the process of human cognition, in one word—all that we still set down today for cardinal criteria of scientific work.

Riedl's treatise discloses brilliant sagacity and excellent debating capacity, and it draws attention to the following important

[195] Loc. cit., pp. 8—9.
[196] This latter Rield calls a "phonetic monster". Loc. cit., p. 10.
[197] Loc. cit., p. 11.
[198] Ibid.
[199] Loc. cit., p. 28.
[200] Loc. cit., p. 61.

circumstance: in the light of Riedl's scientific conception and mainly of the practical application of his theory, we came to a decisive stage in the development of the concept of linguistic law in Hungary.

The point is not that the term law in Hungarian linguistic literature is first encountered in Riedl's works. It can be found in earlier studies, too. As far back as 1843 J. Fogarasi distinguished "universal and superior laws" from "special proper laws".[201] The former ones—as "supreme laws in any possible human language, the universal laws"—include "preciseness, pleasing sound and shortness".[202] As to their nature, however, these *a priori* laws based on transcendentality[203] are not even laws but rules, or rather viewpoints to be respected "in the establishment of linguistic rules and in the cultivation of language".[204] It is true, on the other hand, that also Riedl had already surmised the significance of the phonological peculiarities of sounds when, for example, he called attention to the importance of distinguishing in pronunciation between e and ë (his symbol was *é),* since "this *é* not only makes speech pleasingly variegated [pleasing sound] but also plays a prominent role in inflections".[205]

[201] J. Fogarasi, *Művelt magyar nyelvtan elemi része* [Elementary Part of a Cultured Hungarian Grammar], Pest, 1843, p. 4.

[202] Op. cit., p. 5.

[203] Op. cit., p. 4.

[204] Op. cit., p. 11.

[205] Op. cit., p. 39. When mentioning the opposition of e and ë, he adduced no example for "the prominent role played in inflections"; what he had in mind was something like *mentek* ('those exempted'), *mentëk* ('I rescue'), *mëntek* ('they went'), *mëntëk* ('you go'). In his grammar he consistently distinguished in notation between the two different e sounds, although this was neglected in "common writing". He even made the remark that it would not be needless to use two letters also in writing for the two sounds, but he nevertheless did not propose this course of action because "our writing is already overflooded with accent marks" (op. cit., p. 39). In other places he stressed the importance of distinguishing between long and short vowels with reference to such examples as: *vagy* 'or'— *vágy* 'desire'; *vad* 'wild'— *vád* 'accusation' (op. cit., p. 35).
It was out of the same consideration that he drew attention to the distinction, through pronunciation "with utmost care and precision", between "rough and gentle letters" [unvoiced and voiced consonants] as well, because they "are never confounded in the Hungarian language, except in case of necessity". Here, as appears from his later examples, he had in mind some cases of the assimilation of consonants. His examples (where the critical consonants "are to be learned well"): *pap* 'priest'— *bab* 'bean'; *fagy* 'frost'— *vagy* 'or'; *tudás* 'knowledge'— *dudás* 'piper', etc. (op. cit., p. 35).

It struck him in the eye also that the possible associations of speech sounds, the phonetic combinations, take place according to some rule, too. The arrangement of the sounds in speech ensures the rhythm of "utterance" (pronunciation or, in a wider sense, speaking): ". . . vowels as softeners are everywhere in the most beautiful proportion to consonants of a harder nature".[206] The evidence of the "objective nature of language" made him perceive also the phonetic peculiarity that "in clear, precise utterance" the Hungarian language "tolerates neither many vowels . . . nor many consonants directly side by side". And if such cases nevertheless occurred, "it helps with intercalations, elisions, contractions, etc. . . This is how it also naturalizes foreign words".[207] Consequently, this is how—through dissolution of consonant clusters—Lat. *schola* changed to *iskola* and *claustrum* to *kolostor* in Hungarian, etc.[208]

Under "The Main Laws of Word Formation"[209] the author presented the regularities to be observed "in utterance".

The transcendentalism of the universals, "the metaphysics of language",[210] mixes in this conception of law with an intuition of the phonological regularities of sounds, and the demand for euphony or pleasing sound with an inkling of certain elements of the regularities of sound combinations.

Riedl's opinion of the significance of the comprehensive character of linguistic laws sounds far more categorical: "*Determination of the laws of languages* is therefore the principal task, if not the only one, of today's linguistics . . . Starting out of this position I have studied and still study the Hungarian language, not in order to squeeze its robust organism into a Procrustean bed by piling up all kinds of *rules* and *exceptions*, but in order to pick out those natural laws upon which is built the existence of this so very interesting organism."[211]

The "natural laws" of language, "this so very interesting organism", appear in Riedl's conception as "phonetic laws" or "laws of sound change" and are the following:

[206] Op. cit., p. 40.
[207] Ibid.
[208] Ibid.
[209] Section title, op. cit., p. 282.
[210] *A' magyar nyelv metaphysicája vagy a' betűknek eredeti jelentése. A magyar nyelvre alkalmaztatva* [Metaphysics of the Hungarian Language or the Original Meaning of Letters: Applied to Hungarian], Pest, 1834. A work by Fogarasi. As explained in his preface, "*metaphysics*" here should mean 'science of knowledge'.
[211] AkNyÉrt III/9, p. 4.

(a) autonomous metaphony (sound alternation),
(b) conditioning,
(c) metathesis,
(d) elision,
(e) sound extension,
(f) palatalization,
(g) zetacism,
(h) assimilation,
(i) dissimilation.[212]

In his study in question criticizing the -*ik* conjugation he presented the essence and function of dissimilation. On the basis of the position explained in his paper, the "natural law of sound change" can be interpreted in one way only: it is nothing else but the physiological explanation of the regularities of sound changes and the stressing of their objective character. For it was in this very character that he saw the most typical feature of contemporary linguistics already in his phonetics published in 1859, because it "proceeds from the objective nature of language and relies on its indisputable state".[213] He attributed great significance to the phonetic laws based on the objective nature of language, the laws of phonetic change, because he held that orientation amidst related languages, determination of the degree of linguistic kinship, is made possible by the "laws of sound change".[214]

He described "*vocal harmony*" as "the most remarkable fundamental law" of the Altaic languages which "is based on the difference between back and front vowels".[215]

Riedl regarded the law of progressive assimilation based on vocal harmony *(ember-nek)* as "a very special phonetic law

[212] Loc. cit., pp. 5—6.
[213] Loc. cit., p. 56.
[214] Loc. cit., p. 61.
[215] Rield, *Magyar hangtan*, p. 75. It should be noted here that even Schleicher, who knew many languages and wrote in Hungarian with good grammar, considered vocal harmony one of the most characteristic phonetic laws distinguishing Hungarian from the languages of the Indo-European family. Cf. AkNyÉrt III/7, p. 13. In his own words: "Übrigens setzt gerade das Gesetz der Vokalharmonie einen nicht flektirenden [!] Sprachorganismus voraus: es basirt [!] sich auf der Unveränderlichkeit des Wurzelvokals, und soll die Wurzel vor dem Verdunkeln durch zahlreiche und schwere Suffixe bewaren [!]. Hier wirkt die Wurzel auf die Vokale der Suffixe ein, in den flektirenden [!] Sprachen dagegen die Suffixe freilich in anderer Weise auf die Vokale der Wurzel." Quoted by Riedl, *Magyarische Grammatik*, Wien, 1858, pp. 14—15.

peculiarly typical of all Altaic languages",[216] and he wrote even about *"phonological laws"* in his book.[217]

Riedl's categorical conception of law had a great influence on the formation of the linguistic law ideas of his contemporaries and successors as well.

In J. Szvorényi's Hungarian grammar we can find a detailed description of almost all those phonetic, morphological regularities which were discussed also by Riedl, only with a different terminology. To him vocal harmony is *order of sounds*, according to which Hungarian words may be *velar, palatal, mixed* or *sharp* (containing the vowels *é* and *i: irigység* 'envy', *bilincs* 'handcuffs', *szépít* 'beautify', etc.).[218] What is lurking behind the "clear sharp pronunciation" of consonants is the realization of the phonological opposition of these sounds: *bor* 'wine'—*por* 'dust'; *czipő* 'shoe'—*csípő* 'hip'; *dér* 'hoarfrost'—*tér* 'space', etc.[219] In the section entitled "Nominal Suffixes" under the chapter on "Word Morphology"[220] the author deals in detail with the regularities of the association of stems and suffixes.

"Probing" into the regularity hidden behind the objective facts of language was the primary motive of the activity of S. Brassai, too, who stated unmistakably so in his paper entitled "Word Order and Accent". In the "accentuation" of the word preceding the verb he viewed such a characteristic trait of Hungarian which "must be based on some natural [objective] law or laws, and this law governs both accent and word order, these being unaffected by each other. It has thus been our scientific duty . . . to probe into this law".[221]

In his above-mentioned evaluation of Gyarmathi, too, Hunfalvy characterized the "law of the change of letters" as a possi-

---

[216] *Magyar hangtan*, p. 98; cf. also *Magyar nyelvtan*, pp. 5—6.

[217] *Magyar hangtan*, p. 130. Obviously the question here is not of phonology or phonological laws taken in the modern sense. As is commonly known, after the former terminological uncertainty (psycho-phonetics: Baudouin de Courtenay and his pupils) it was the Prague conference of December 18 to 21, 1930, that uniformly determined the scope of phonology. If this is so—and it certainly is—we cannot deny the profound impression of the Schleicherian conception of phonetic law upon Riedl, the scientific systematizer of the speech sounds of Hungarian.

[218] J. Szvorényi, *Magyar nyelvtan, tanodai s magánhasználatra* [Hungarian Grammar for School and Private Use], Budapest, 1876⁴, pp. 18—20.

[219] Op. cit., p. 22.

[220] Op. cit., pp. 63—92.

[221] AkNyÉrt XIV/9, p. 11.

bility to discover the essence concealed behind the "crust", behind the apparent chaos of linguistic phenomena.

According to Balassa, too, the "strict laws" of sound changes are "the guarantee of the progress of linguistics".[222] In other places Balassa warned against viewing the "order of phenomena" through subjective, "coloured glasses", because this method "makes it difficult . . . to see clearly . . . the motion of the things we are to get to know".[223] If new bits of knowledge challenge the effect of laws held unquestionable so far make them unacceptable, the linguist who is aware of the new facts ". . . has to abandon his former faith and conviction, to sacrifice even his most beautiful dream in the interest of truth . . ."[224] It is an honouring task for any science, for any scientist to uncover the truth, the law, and the discovery of the truth should be based upon the fact "that the order of notions corresponds to the order of phenomena, i.e. the motion of thought follows the motion of things".[225]

The aforecited opinions clearly exemplify the profound impression which the concept of natural law elevated to the rank of a central category of natural science made upon Hungarian philology, especially upon the reception in Hungary of the concept of linguistic law. The conception of linguistic (phonetic) law presenting also the limits of the natural-scientific knowledge of the time reflected almost all those essential features which in our days, too, we regard as the cardinal criteria of laws.

Even on the evidence of its contemporary reception in Hungary, the acceptance of phonetic law was the objective grip recognized as the touchstone of the rightness or wrongness of linguistic—primarily etymological—ideas, for this is the basis which "puts a stop to wild etymologies".[226]

[222] Nyr XIII, p. 289.
[223] Nyr XXV, p. 59.
[224] Ibid.
[225] Ibid.
[226] "Das Lautverschiebungsgesetz hilft also wilde Etymologie bündigen und ist sie zum Prüfstein geworden." J. Grimm, *Deutsche Grammatik²* I, p. 588.

3. THE CONCEPT OF SYSTEM CHARACTER

The thought, or at least its germ, of the system that evolved equally under the influence of natural science came up in the Hungarian literature of linguistics relatively early, well before the appearance of the neogrammarian school. Already in 1834, under the pressure of a certain system compulsion, Fogarasi used the *ö* sound in suffixes in which *e* was used as a rule. In defence of the *ö* of *fejtöget* 'explicate', *követközött* '[it] followed', *nyelvhöz* 'to language', and even to popularize it, he resorted to the following arguments: If we take for a basis by analogy the velar suffixes *(-ogat, -kozik, -hoz, -kodik)* of the word-forms *irogat* 'keep writing', *hadakozik* 'make war', *házhoz* 'to a house', *gondolkodik* 'think', etc., then, in his view, the suffixed forms like *fejtöget*, etc., and not the arbitrarily used variants like *fejteget*, etc. are the more regular.[1] What is essential in this explication is not that the thought of labial–illabial conformation gets lost, but that suffixes based on the palatal–velar opposition of vowels are recommended. The fact is that Fogarasi investigated very carefully the principal traits of the regular arrangement of Hungarian speech sounds, and in his grammar published in 1843 he even worked out the "order" built on the correspondence of vowels according to length and shortness:

short	*a*	with the corresponding long			*á*
„	*ȧ*	„	„	„	„	*ȧ́*
„	*e*	„	„	„	„	*ê*
„	*ė (ë)*	„	„	„	„	*é*

short	*i*	with the corresponding long			*í*
„	*o*	„	„	„	„	*ó*
„	*u*	„	„	„	„	*ú*
„	*ö*	„	„	„	„	*ő*
„	*ü*	„	„	„	„	*ű*.[2]

That the systemlike behaviour of the linguistic elements was recognized at the time appears also from the book *A magyar nyelv rendszere* [The System of the Hungarian Language] published in 1848 under the auspices of the Hungarian Learned Society. The

---

[1] Fogarasi, *A' magyar nyelv metaphysicája . . .*, Preface p. 3.
[2] Fogarasi, *Művelt magyar nyelvtan . . .*, p. 29.

very title already refers to the need of investigating a *system*, but over and above this, in the chapter on morphology, some of the regularities operating independently of the individual speaker are pointed out also in the linking of word-roots and suffixes. Thus: "The pure nominative case [absolute word-root] takes any suffix." The limitations existing in the further suffixation of "inflected nominative cases" [suffixed word-roots] are also observed, with the point made that "the nominative plural and the nominative with a possessive ending take on any simple suffix . . . but mutually exclude each other". Possible "suffix associations" are thus: *kert-ek-ben* 'in gardens', *kert-em-ben* 'in my garden'; impossible associations: *kert-em-ek, kert-ek-em*.[3] A similar examination is made of the regularities seen in "verb inflection" (derivation) with the presentation of possible associations of the possibilitative verbal suffix.[4]

In his grammar published in 1864 Riedl already purposefully investigated the order of associations of verbal suffixes on the basis of his recognition of the objective interrelations of language. There he devoted a separate chapter to the *"Laws of the Succession of Suffixes"*.[5]

We read in that chapter, among other things: ". . . not every suffix may be added to any root, just as less can the suffixes with one and the same stem morphemes succeed one another in any order . . . their succession is subject to certain laws."[6] Thereafter follows a table of the possible occurrences in the "succession of suffixes". It is worth a closer inspection.

I. Stem morpheme + possibilitative suffix: *zár-hat,*

II. Stem morpheme + frequentative suffix: *hajóz-gat,*

III. Stem morpheme + factitive suffix: *zár-at,*

IV. Stem morpheme + frequentative + possibilitative: *zár-ogat-hat,*

V. Stem morpheme + frequentative + possibilitative [obviously a misprint for "factitive"]: *zár-ogat-tat,*

---

[3] Op. cit., pp. 153—4.
[4] Op. cit., p. 192.
[5] Op. cit., p. 164.
[6] Ibid.

VI. Stem morpheme + factitive + frequentative:
zár-at-gat,
VII. Stem morpheme + factitive + possibilitative:
zár-at-hat,
VIII. Stem morpheme + frequentative + factitive + possibilitative: zár-ogat-tat-hat,

IX. Stem morpheme + factitive + frequentative + possibilitative: zár-at-gat-hat.[7]

If we leave out of consideration whether the striving for completeness was crowned with success or not, and we watch only
the need and character of systematization (objective order and
not voluntaristic disarray), then we can see the significance of
Riedl's experiment. Let us compare it to some lines of a study
which appeared exactly a hundred years later: "The structural
model of the process of communication at the level of morphemes
is no different from the exact system of morphology: in fact we
find here what morphemes succeed one another in the course
of communication, what is a one-dimensional mosaic like which
can be regularly composed of the members of the morphemic
system."[8]
    Another remarkable fact is that in the same book Riedl, with
his vowel classification according to the "opposition of back and
front vowels", preceded the phonological school's conception of
an oppositive phonetic system. In explaining the Hungarian
speech sounds he also expressly referred to "the systemlike
nature of sounds".[9]
    It is indeed the idea of systematism that is borne out by the
theoretical starting point used in the -ik polemic, when Riedl
tries to approach the solution of the problem, not from the
sporadical occurrence of one or another conjugational form, but
from the evidence of the whole conjugational system, by taking
into consideration the historical emergence and evolution of the
system as well as its synchronic peculiarities: in today's terminology—the dialectics of the whole and the part.

[7] Op. cit., pp. 165—6.
[8] F. Papp, Nyelvi rendszer, közlési folyamat és ezek néhány matematikai modellje [System of Language, Process of Communication, and
Some of Their Mathematical Models], ÁNyT II, pp. 75—88; loc. cit., p. 81.
[9] Chapters and sections of his grammar bear titles like *The Vowel
System* (p. 72), *The System of Hungarian Consonants* (p. 79), *The Influence
of Accent on the Hungarian Vowel System* (p. 102).

The thought of a system, of systematism coming up also in earlier linguistic works was thus put in a new light in the scientific activity of Riedl: this was already more than a "brilliant intuition" of one of the basic peculiarities of language, of systematism, this was the formulation of regularity, of the law that can be unraveled on the concrete evidence of systematism, and all this nearly half a century before the publication of Saussure's posthumous work!

The authors quoted provide the opportunity of a rather unequivocal answer to the question raised at the beginning of this chapter. All great comprehensive problems of the century that made linguistics a science elicited at once a lively response from the best Hungarian scholars. So many authors, so many substantial statements, so many resolute positions taken up in favour of the modern principles and methods. Prominent representatives of Hungarian linguistics eagerly adopted the new ideas. They even had sufficient energy to develop further critically one or another of the new doctrines (Hunfalvy, Riedl); what is more, the linguistic theory inspired by natural science affected also general philosophical thinking in Hungary, and in the most important question of philosophy, the relationship between matter and the elements of consciousness, it enforced a clearly materialistic position (Ponori Thewrewk). The individual active propagators of the new ideas were joined by the Academy with its authority as the offical forum of the popularization of the new doctrines. The Academy did so not only by hastening the Hungarian translation of a popular compendium of the neogrammarian doctrines, but also by electing the foreign celebrities of the school of linguistic history its "associate members" (J. Grimm, Schleicher).

The brisk intellectual life of the second half of the nineteenth century—an organic part of which was the upswing of linguistic thinking in Hungary, too—was not a chance episode of the development of Hungarian public mentality but an inevitable concomitant of the peculiar process of evolution of Hungarian society. Though with a great phase lag as compared to the rate of progress of other European societies, the development of bourgeois mentality started in Hungary as well. In the initial, progressive stage of development the bourgeoisie inevitably came into conflict with the retrograde institutions and ideas, and regarded the representatives of progressive thought as its ideological "reinforcement" as long as the progressive ideas helped it to win and consolidate its positions. And the big natural-scientific discoveries were just a vital element of the establishment and furtherance of industrialization, and the materialistic thoughts arising practically as its "by-products" also supported it, at the very beginning, in fighting the "conservative ideologies". The effervescence of theories and the promotion of progressive ideas in Hungary were thus an ideological impact of a passing cross-fire between the spheres of interest. But as soon as the interests of the advancing bourgeoisie were adapted to the power positions, the theoretical brotherhood in arms came to an end, and even the ideological weapons were soon pointed at one another: a stop was put to the respectability of materialistic and progressive ideas in general.

This is what produced the short-lived confluence with the mainstream of European progressive ideas; this can account for the sudden advance of Hungarian philology in the second half of the nineteenth century but also for its sudden change of course about the turn of the century. It was thus no accident that the lively interest shown as a promising start gradually faded away and ultimately shrank to a simple and "respectable" sort of psychologism of linguistic history.

As though nothing had happened in the reception in Hungary of the manifold new ideas, of the great theoretical problems of linguistics, as though Hungarian scholars had said not a word about the general criteria of language, the linguistic laws, the interrelations of language and thought, the most important questions of the genesis of language. As though total darkness had shrouded those brilliant and bold thoughts which came out from the pens of Hungarian authors under the stimulating in-fluence of the neogrammarian doctrines. As though there had vanished into thin air all those ingenious partial findings which, coming ahead of the main currents of modern linguistics, were published in Hungarian as a result of the investigations into the pattern of the synchronic motion of languages (phonological peculiarities of speech sounds, germs of the idea of systematism). As though total darkness had obscured also those brilliant and bold ideas which had arisen from the polemic about the lin-guistic theory motivated by natural science. The essence of the polemic (efforts to devise a materialistic theory of language) got lost, its by-product (organism theory) was brushed aside, and so was the conclusion of this theory concerning the linguistic (phonetic) laws, their exceptionless operation resulting from the exaggeration of the objective character. "Schleicher the genius" was described only as a simplifier who had slipped over the direct adaptation of natural-scientific principles and methods of research, as one whose theoretical precepts—because of his wrong starting point—are not worthy of attention, for the linguistic laws were said to have no similarity to the natural laws. As though the subject of a litigation lasting three decades in the second half of the nineteenth century had not been this very neogrammarian conception of law designed to find out whether linguistic processes take place independently of the consciousness of the individual speakers, whether the stimuli of these processes are objective, and to what extent the linguistic laws are characterized by objectivity.

The activities of Hunfalvy, Riedl, Ponori Thewrewk and, last but not least, Simonyi hallmark the rapid rising cycle in the advance of Hungarian linguistics. The "European character" of their conceptions of linguistic theory was ensured by their purposeful joining the mainstream of the progressive ideological trends. The vital element and stimulating force of Simonyi's rich and manyfold work lay just in the fact that he consistently abided by the progressive elements of the new ideas also when they had begun "to fall out of fashion"; this also can account for the tragic end of his life. They were all very colourful and critical representatives of Hungarian linguistics, who took over and developed further the new ideas, but they were not obsessed with the neogrammarian dogmas, they were not fanatics stymied between the bounds of the fatalist conception of blindly operating phonetic laws and of the subsequent trend of linguistic psychologism.

4. THE "AFTER-LIFE" IN HUNGARY OF THE NEOGRAMMARIAN DOCTRINES

The rediscoverer and "perhaps a little belated" propagator of the "most important theses" of the neogrammarian school,[1] Z. Gombocz, in 1898 saw the essence of the entire teaching in the linguistic dissemination of Paul's individual psychologism: "To explain every linguistic phenomenon from the position of individual man, to trace the general use of every sound, word-form, meaning or structure back to the individual—this is the basic thought that runs through Paul's book with consistency, almost

---

[1] Gombocz: Nyr XXVII, p. 6.

with obstinacy, and this guiding idea is more or less clearly expressed also by the rest of the neogrammarians."[2] The problem of the "general use of sound, word-form, meaning or structure" is typically a question within the province of the investigation of synchronical phenomena, but even apart from the fact that Paul was still not the originator of the synchronic methods of investigation, this is an extremely narrow viewpoint and method compared to those which came to light, in synchronic linguistic research, from under the pens of Fogarasi, Riedl and Szvorényi some decades before the publication of Gombocz's writing.

But this is not the point. The point is that for quite a length of time Gombocz recognized, in his general theory of language, only the justification of the diachronic investigation of language, taking the psychological interpretation of linguistic evolution to be the main task of linguistics. Still in 1922 he stated in his work establishing his theoretical and methodological principles that "linguistics has no ahistorical disciplines".[3] This conception clearly challenges the justification of other methods of linguistic research and even precludes the feasibility of any different kind of solution. Accordingly the "ahistorical" interpretation is in fact "likely to lead only to inadequate and worthless or directly wrong results".[4] The categorical formulation indisputably indicates that early in the twenties Gombocz classed linguistics "in the group of the historical sciences", because he held that only the historicity of language might make it possible to understand its essence, to sketch out its characteristic features.

How can the researcher get to know the essence of language and sketch its characteristic features on the basis of what he knows about its historical development; what are the reasons that motivate the historical development of language; what are the identical and the different traits of linguistic evolution and human thinking, and of the development of society; in short, are there normative rules—or, if you like, laws—that serve as a basis for a description of the historical development of language, for an explanation of its essence? These are the most important questions of principle to which contemporary Hungarian linguistics also has to provide a clear-cut answer if it claims to be a science.

---

[2] Loc. cit., p. 8.
[3] Z. Gombocz, *Nyelvtörténeti módszertan* [Methodology of Linguistic History], Budapest, 1922, p. 3.
[4] Ibid.

If the Hungarian linguists of the early twentieth century classed linguistics "in the group of the historical sciences", it would have been expectable that the explanatory principle of the course of evolution of linguistic phenomena should be a historical one, i.e. in investigating the regularities of linguistic change and development recourse should be had to the regularities discovered by the science of history. Since, however, the contemporary Hungarian science of history tried to sketch the factors motivating the development of human society by resorting to rather variegated and often contradictory theories which failed to meet the historical requirements of the period, scholars were seeking different, more exact (or exact-looking) explanations to detect the productive causes of the evolution of language. In this way, as is commonly known, they came to the application of the results of psychology in the field of linguistic researches. As early as 1898 Gombocz saw Steinthal's principal merit in the fact that "he applied the results of Herbartian psychology from the point of view of linguistics",[5] and what is more, he thought that the conduct of (historical) linguistic researches on a psychological basis was the fundamental principle of the neogrammarian school: "We have thereby come to the basic principle of the neogrammarian school . . . linguistics must stand not on logical but on psychological foundations."[6] The application of Herbart's psychological methods and really appreciable results he took for the principal gain of linguistics because he regarded psychological factors to be one of the main causes of linguistic evolution: "The causes which shape historical development are first of all psychical ones."[7] Uncovering of the psychical causes of the development of language is the only way that can lead to the discovery of the regularities of the development of language—this is the essence of Gombocz's theoretical and methodological standpoint, which is rooted in Paul's psychologism. Gombocz wrote in 1902: "Paul opposes psychology as a law-making science to linguistics as a historical science."[8]

This sketch of the conception of linguistic theory and the methodological standpoint clearly show the task of linguistics, which Gombocz—in the wake of Herbart, Steinthal, Wundt and

---

[5] Gombocz: Nyr XXVII, p. 6.
[6] Loc. cit., p. 8.
[7] Gombocz, Változás és törvény a nyelvtudományban [Change and Law in Linguistics]. *Társadalomtudomány* I, pp. 194—201; loc. cit., p. 195.
[8] Gombocz: Nyr XXXI, p. 358.

Paul—described in these terms: ". . . the psychological interpretation of the development of language, more strictly the investigation of the individual and collective psychological conditions of the development of language."[9]

Gombocz's great prestige determined the "profile" of linguistic research in Hungary for long years ahead. Historical psychologism, i.e. the privileged and even exclusive place of historical research in linguistics, psychological methods and explanatory principles—this is the summary of the principles and practice of Hungarian linguistics in the first quarter of the twentieth century. In one of his later writings (1927) Gombocz expressed his view of this situation as follows: "It is beyond doubt that in the past few decades our linguists focussed their attention almost exclusively on the history of the Hungarian language and the problems of Finno-Ugric comparative linguistics."[10]

Being desirous to throw off the shackles of its former one-sided logicism, Hungarian linguistics got caught by historicism, psychologism. Again it waived the right to a relative autonomy and willingly reduced the scope of its investigations to the historical development of language, thereby ruling out in advance the possibility of proper and complete linguistic explanations. As far as I know, A. Horger alone criticized, rather flexibly but at the same time categorically in my view, the exclusiveness of historicism and psychologism professed by Gombocz. By acknowledging the psychical character of linguistic processes, Horger found it natural that in the explanation of those processes— either those of today or those of old—"we always have to make allowance for their psychological foundation, too; so psychological interpretation is an integral part, a concomitant of historical linguistic research and is not a separate method independent of it. Abstracted psychological speculation which disregards the facts of linguistic history leads at best to erroneous results".[11] In the same work, in defence of the justification of the synchronic methods of linguistic research, he disapproved of Gombocz's one-sided and rigid historicism.[12]

[9] Gombocz, op. cit., p. 8.
[10] Gombocz, MNy XXIII, p. 1.
[11] A. Horger, A nyelvtudomány alapelvei [Principles of Linguistics], Budapest, 1926, p. 11.
[12] Op. cit., p. 3. In the early thirties the one-sidedness of linguistic psychologism was sharply criticized also by Ries, a scholar of great reputation: "Eine reine psychologische Satzdefinition ist noch keine sprachwissenschaftliche." Was ist ein Satz? 1931, p. 30.

It is also part of the historical truth that Gombocz's linguistic theory did not bog down in diachronic one-sidedness, but developed further. Having made the acquaintance of Saussure (a fact revealed by a very sketchy book review[13]), he changed his opinion: he recognized the justification of the synchronic investigation of language. "I need not underline separately", he wrote five years after the publication of the aforecited declaration he had made against synchrony, and therefore it is not needless to emphasize, "that both the synchronic and the diachronic linguistic view can be justified, and consequently it would be wrong to oppose descriptive grammar, as an unscientific grammar, to historical grammar."[14] Under the influence of the phonological lectures given at the 1928 Hague conference on philology, and being impressed by "Laziczius's grandiose phonological study",[15] Gombocz viewed as indisputable "the decisive influence of Saussure's posthumous work upon the development of postwar linguistics",[16] and at the Philological Society meeting on January 22, 1934, he devoted his lecture to the exposition of the "functional linguistic outlook".[17]

Despite all this it can be stated that the hegemony of historicism based on psychological explanatory principles visibly delayed the spread in Hungary of the newer trends unfolding with Saussure's activity and popularized by the Prague Circle initiated by B. de Courtenay. Although the new trend has some remarkable representatives in Hungary as well (J. Györke, I. Papp and Gy. Laziczius), official linguistics was somewhat late in taking notice of the entirety of the teaching of the new school. This delay was characterized by the fact that the Hungarian translation of Saussure's posthumous work was published as late as 1967, when the new methods, built on the principle of systematism, on the structural principle, had become fairly far removed from the originator of the idea.

The retrograde cultural policy of the years following the turn of the century did not favour the propagation of progressive theories; in the interwar years it even combated them most aggressively and with administrative measures. It is not by

[13] Gombocz: MNy XX, pp. 141—3.
[14] MNy XXIII, p. 4.
[15] MNy XXX, pp. 2—3.
[16] Loc. cit., p. 1.
[17] Loc. cit., pp. 1—7.

chance therefore that the linguistics of the first half of the twentieth century was also unable to escape these negative influences, and it took a very long time to find its way back into the current of European and extra-European new theories and methods.

5. REOPENING OF THE BIG LITIGATION

I wrote at the end of Section 1 of this chapter that the first big litigation had been essentially closed by history upon the brilliant results of comparative historical linguistics. This statement does not mean that the neogrammarian conception of phonetic law has won through in every detail once and for all. Its drawbacks and vulnerable points prevented this. At any case the fact is that with its system of criteria claiming exactness it gave an enormous impetus to the development of linguistics. This is clearly demonstrated by the very quick and definite response of pre-eminent representatives of Hungarian linguistics and by the results achieved with the effective aid of the new outlook and new methods.

As if the Müller–Simonyi prophecy had come true, according to which the imposing spell and practical utility of the rational kernel of the neogrammarian doctrines allow no one to doubt that sound changes take place according to certain phonetic laws.[1] The cross-fire of debates was unable to break down the cardinal thesis that linguistic and phonetic changes are not due to arbitrariness, they are not mere accidents, but they follow a regularity immanent in the phenomena. Every explanation of scientific pretension had behind it this fundamental idea, which Delbrück himself had recognized, too.[2]

The struggle around the phonetic laws was essentially waged for a scientific phonetics; those who entered the arena to make the phonetic law accepted did not advocate the dogma of an abandoned altar, but fought for the progress of scientific research in phonology and for a decisive turn in the character of investigation. The recognition of the regularity of sound changes was regarded also by Szinnyei as a "firm basis" without which "no step can be taken in linguistics".[3] The authors of TMNy also date "the recent methodological progress of our science" from the propagation of the "stricter conception" of phonetic laws —

---

[1] Müller, *Lectures* **II**, p. 192.
[2] Delbrück, *Einleitung in das Sprachstudium*, Leipzig, 1880, pp. 114—5.
[3] Szinnyei: NyK XV, p. 253.

the seventies of the nineteenth century.[4] They speak out clearly what they took over from the neogrammarian conception of phonetic law: "What we call phonetic law does not mean that some change has to take place under any circumstances, but . . . it means that the sounds in the same situation in a language at a certain time undergo the same change. Therefore, sound changes are not exceptionless but regular, and every exception to or departure from the rule has its special cause."[5]

This is an extremely important statement not only because at the time (1895) it eliminated in careful and flexible terms the stumbling-block of the neogrammarian postulate of phonetic law, the blind and exceptionless working of the law, but also because it hit upon the dynamic unity of rule and exception: what is considered an exception from one angle is accounted a strict regularity from another aspect. This conception of the law was fit to explain convincingly such developments as could not be explained by the rigid neogrammarian postulate. The "regularity" of both the divergent and the convergent phonetic evolution could be demonstrated on this basis of principle: departures from the expected phonetic development may be explained either by some time lag or by dialectic divergence or by other circumstances (phonetic situations).

The heated debates over the phonetic law thus seemed to have calmed down, the fire of arguments for and against had consolidated the elastic conception of phonetic law, which then eliminated the terms 'phonetic rule' and 'sound alternation'; it seemed that Wechssler, who described the polemic in detail would be right in his final conclusion: "So there is nothing to prevent the term 'phonetic law' from being used now as before. On the contrary, it denotes the actual relationships much better than the expressions 'phonetic rule' or 'sound alternation' which have again come into use lately."[6]

What made Wechssler so optimistic about the future of the term phonetic law? It was that, in his opinion, the results of the

---

[4] TMNy I, p. IX.
[5] Op. cit., p. 54.
[6] "So steht nichts mehr im Wege, den Terminus 'Lautgesetz' nach wie vor zu brauchen. Im Gegenteil, er bezeichnet die thatsächlichen Verhältnisse weit besser als die neuerdings wieder üblich gewordenen Ausdrücke 'Lautregel' oder 'Lautwechsel'." Wechssler, *Gibt es Lautgesetze?* 1900, p. 528.

latest researches made it possible and even necessary to reject the parallelism "forced" by Schleicher with the laws of nature and the natural sciences in general, and that phonetic law had to be regarded as a psychological law built on the principle of causality.[7] In place of the conception of law burdened with the natural-scientific parallelism "forced" by Schleicher he recommended the "newer scientific" concept of law hallmarked by R. Chr. Eucken, who expounded it in the chapter entitled "Über die philosophischen Grundbegriffe der Gegenwart" of his "mind-stirring" work.[8] Accordingly it is mistaken to conceive of law as if it were the severe redeemer of processes and events, as if the connection of the general and the particular were lying in the things themselves. Wechssler quoted from Eucken: "As recent science understands law, the general is substituted for by particular cases *only in our view, but not in the real nature of things.*"[9] And he adds this to the above quotation from Eucken: "In reality, in the case of phonetic laws just as in that of the natural law of the conservation of energy, the expression 'law' states the existence of three criteria" [the connection of the general and the particular is only a product of consciousness].[10]

Wechssler's above-cited conception of law finished once and for all the consolidation of the concept of linguistic law. This conception had not a bit of those progressive elements which — together with all their extravagances — were definitely formulated in the neogrammarian postulate of phonetic law (behind the change of things and processes are to be found only the motives inherent in their essence — objective character — and from this point of view the principal peculiarities of natural laws and linguistic laws are identical). This conception of law formulated on a subjective-idealist platform was good only to disavow all those efforts which the most progressive linguists in the last part of the nineteenth century made in order to develop linguistics into a real science.

---

[7] Op. cit., pp. 527—8.
[8] R. Chr. Eucken, *Die Grundbegriffe der Gegenwart historisch und kritisch entwickelt,* Leipzig, 1893², p. 178.
[9] "Wie die neuere Wissenschaft das Gesetz versteht, erfolgt jene Ablösung des Allgemeinen von den einzelnen Fällen *nur in unserer Betrachtung, nicht in einer realen Natur der Dinge.*" Wechssler, op. cit., p. 528.
[10] "In Wirklichkeit wird bei den Lautgesetzen, so gut wie bei dem Naturgesetz von der Erhaltung der Energie, durch den Ausdruck 'Gesetz' nur das Vorhandensein drei Merkmale ausgesprochen." Ibid.

The bulky volume which was prepared with the intention and the promise of closing the debate around the concept of phonetic law and drawing the lessons from it gave rise to fresh disputes, and only widened the gulf between linguists divided into two camps by the criterion of phonetic law. If the anti-Schleicher camp of the time could rightfully criticize the extravagances of the concept of law based upon the tenets of natural science, this applied still more to Wechssler's theory of phonetic law conceived on a subjective-idealist basis.

The Wechssler–Vossler–Finck linguistic theory built on the subjective-idealist concept of law which had come to light in Eucken's revised formulation left only very faint traces in the Hungarian linguistic works following the turn of the century. As far as I know, it was only in a programmatic article published by *Nyelvtudomány*, a short-lived journal founded to counteract linguistic positivism, that G. Petz spoke up in favour of this trend, underscoring its most important elements: ". . . let us not transpose the subjectivity of the human soul into reality, the linguist should not seek in the phenomena for causes, goals and laws, because the causal principle exists not in phenomena but in human reason."[11] To this axiom Petz added only one nostalgic-ringing remark: linguistics in Hungary is not of such a "theoretical standard" as to solve its task in the way required by Vossler and Finck, it can undertake this kind of work "only in a distant future".[12] Until the theoretical standard of Hungarian linguists has reached the desired level, we have to rest satisfied with the "positivist" procedure.[13]

As Petz suggested, the term phonetic law based on the conception of law evolved by the revaluation of the causal principle must not be rejected, only it must be well interpreted. What he meant by proper interpretation is not difficult to find out: application of the subjective-idealist principle of causality to the explanation of phonetic changes. "There is indeed no reason", he wrote, "to reject wholly the expression 'phonetic law', but we have to interpret it properly, and we are doing so when by the exceptionless regularity of phonetic changes we mean again only the application of the causal principle in the field of phonetics."[14]

---

[11] G. Petz, Nyelvtudományi irányok és feladatok [Linguistic Trends and Tasks]. *Nyelvtudomány* I, pp. 1—11; loc. cit., p. 10.

[12] Loc. cit., p. 11.

[13] Ibid.

[14] Loc. cit., p. 4.

If causality, regularity, is not an immanent peculiarity of things and processes, but a product of the controlling mind, then in fact the exceptionless operation of phonetic laws does not—and cannot—cause any harm, and the entire dispute around this question is a meaningless waste of time and energy, the problem seems to be a pseudo-problem. Phonetic changes are rather tangled, intercrossing and puzzling processes in which order is introduced by the systematizing human mind, and in this sense they have nothing in common with the mechanically occurring natural processes.

Similar considerations moved M. Rubinyi to stand up against the parallelism principle of natural law; true enough, he did not popularize Vossler, nor did he criticize his subjective idealism,[15] and what is more, in one of his works explaining the exceptions, he seemed to be haunted by Vossler's conception of law: "...there are some forms which contradict the established laws."[16] Linguistic laws must not and cannot be established, they either exist or do not exist, and if they do we can at most get to know and discover them.

The position of "inexorable phonetic laws",[17] of the "strict laws" which are "the guarantee of the progress of linguistics"[18] was shaken, their main strength, their objective character appearing in the armour of natural science, began losing its original ringing in face of the metamorphosis of the concept of linguistic law. Not—or not necessarily—under the influence of the Vosslerian trend, there came ever more to the forefront those views which tended to place stress on the difference between natural and social laws and even on their irreconcilable antagonism: no kind of identical feature was recognized between them. Instrumental in this was certainly also the exaggeration in the opposite direction of the contemporary postulate of linguistic law (absolutization of the objective character, the blindly working process, etc.). It is equally true, on the other hand, that by the time of the turn of the century the advocates of phonetic law had given up most of these extravagances. There was thus no reason to reopen the litigation in order to combat the initial excesses and on this basis to criticize and reject the phonetic-law conception as a whole.

---

[15] Loc. cit., pp. 158—9.
[16] M. Rubinyi, Általános nyelvtudomány [General Linguistics], p. 57.
[17] J. Szinnyei: NyK XV, p. 258.
[18] Nyr XIII, p. 289.

I think M. Müller was right when he summed up the lessons of the first big litigation by stating that the determining motive of the difference of opinion between the two camps was to be found in a fundamental philosophical difference of opinion. Those who saw in the genesis of man, of language "the supreme blossom of nature" *(die höchste Blüte der Natur)*, while recognizing the difference *(Grenzlinie)* between the human race and the animal kingdom, inevitably became adherents of the natural-scientific linguistic outlook. Those who, on the other hand, were unwilling to recognize any kind of genetic connection between the human race and the animal kingdom inevitably drifted into the opposite camp and not only condemned the extravagances of the natural-scientific theory of language but attacked the whole theory relentlessly.[19] Even though Müller—as we have seen before—dated the cleaving of the human tongue "from the first day of Pentecost", he was always a courageous fighter for the linguistic view hallmarked by a demand for exactness.

The dispute was thus renewed and it has been lasting—with varying intensity—up to these days.

The polemic centred, besides the old controversial issues (linguistic processes, the character of changes, the causes of changes, linguistic laws and natural laws, the role of objective and subjective factors), on topics like the course of changes (gradual or abrupt), law and tendency, based upon the recent results of research.

Those who, when digging up the hatchet, attacked the cardinal point of the postulate of phonetic law, questioned one of the fundamental traits of the concept of law in its modern sense—its objective character. This appeared also from Gombocz's writing of 1898, where he rightly criticized the view which put the phonetic laws "on an equal footing with natural laws", but what he inferred by proceeding from this position already has a bearing on the essence of the concept of law: "Phonetic law is a correspondence observable between accomplished facts [a rule ascertainable on the basis of superficial behavioural pattern] and has no affinity with the natural laws, at least in such a sense as it is applied in physics or chemistry."[20] If we recall only for a moment the rational kernel of the "old" concept of phonetic

---

[19] M. Müller, *Die Wissenschaft der Sprache* I, Vorwort, pp. V—VI.
[20] Gombocz: Nyr XXVII, p. 17.

law, its real value (linguistic changes result from immanent peculiarities of language, they are due not to arbitrariness but to objective necessity, individual man cannot halt this process), and we "confront" it with this concept of law, our eye is caught at once by the latter's simplified empiricism, its nature of being "a rule" limited to a statement of facts. That this conception does not want to look below the surface, behind the "crust", and that it does not pretend to discover the interrelations existing there, is clearly stated by Gombocz a few lines later: "Phonetic law is nothing else than the ascertainment of the change in the phonic state [!], limited in place and time, occurring with greater or lesser uniformity."[21] This rather pessimistic-ringing conception of law refers not only to linguistic laws but also to the so-called empirical laws of natural history, which also only ascertain the changes and their uniformity, but are incapable of finding out their causes and grasping the essence of the changes. If there is anything in which phonetic laws resemble the laws of natural history, it can be — according to Gombocz — their empirical character. As he wrote in another paper: "As regards the method of our investigations, it might be undeniable that especially the phonetic laws remind us, to a certain extent, of the empirical laws of natural history; the laws of linguistic development are also empirical laws, which merely ascertain *the complex uniformity of the occurrence,* of the change, which can either by no means or only in part be broken down to its primary conditions."[22] In his view linguistic law is identical with "the expression of a psychological regularity that is still unknown to us".[23] It was from this position that he criticized Müller's and mainly Schleicher's conception of (blindly operating and exceptionless) phonetic law,[24] although in other places, speaking of the so-called independent or regular sound changes (*temlec* >*tömlöc* 'gaol', *ser* > *sör* 'beer', *gyengy* >*gyöngy* 'pearl'), he also said that these are "not infrequently exceptionless in the strict sense of the word".[25]

On the basis of the foregoing it is rather difficult to find out what Gombocz understands by law, and this becomes still more

[21] Ibid.
[22] Z. Gombocz, Változás és törvény a nyelvtudományban [Change and Law in Linguistics], ÖM I, p. 73. It is repeated word for word in another work by the same author: *Nyelvtörténeti módszertan* [Methodology of Linguistic History], 2nd ed., p. 11.
[23] Ibid.
[24] Ibid.
[25] ÖM I, p. 69.

complicated in another place, where he wrote about the relation-ship between law and regularity as follows: "On the basis of all this it is evident that, in connection with phonetic laws, we can-not talk of *exceptionless operation*, but we can speak only of *exceptionless regularity* [?]."[26] It is not at all evident on what strength we can speak of the "regularity of phonetic laws"! What should we mean by the "regularity of law"? Does he oppose law to regularity? Or is "regularity" a characteristic feature of law? The uncertainty is also not dispelled if we read Gombocz's interpretation resorting to the causal principle: ". . . all sorts of change in the sound-form are subjected to strict causality, which is given expression partly in generally operative laws, partly in some stray ones [obviously laws] which counteract the effect of the former."[27] The confusion only grows in conse-quence of the fact that in another place of the same book the author denies the causal character of linguistic laws: "The laws of linguistics are not laws of causality: they present the changes not as effects of unknown or partly known causes, but as the function of temporal and local conditions."[28] Causality is always a law of general validity, it never has a stray variant. It points to what does, or more precisely can, occur under the given cir-cumstances. In case of complicated effects and interactions one of them can possibly produce some change and the other cannot. Any sound change is thus always produced by some (physiologi-cal or other) cause, that is either by one or by another. *Cause* and *law* are not identical concepts. The discovery of law is always aimed at grasping the general and does not direct attention to stray phenomena. The general character of law is one thing, and the issue of the general operation of the law is another thing. If two laws — hence not a general one and a stray one — counteract each other's effect, one of them may neutralize the other's, and that is how stray phonetic changes differing from the general trend of development, but not stray laws, come about. That a phonetic change differing from the general trend of development has a reason of its own, this fact — being a trivial one — is not worth discussing, but this does not mean at all that we can speak of general and stray laws.

I think we can best approach the gist of Gombocz's idea if we take his concept of law as he himself formulated it in some place:

[26] Gombocz, *Nyelvtörténeti* . . ., p. 22.
[27] Ibid.
[28] Op. cit., p. 12.

when applying the term 'law' he had in mind not the natural-scientific category taken in the philosophical sense, but he used it only metaphorically: "We think of this regularity of linguistic changes when we speak of the development of language—with a metaphor taken from organic life—and mention the *regularity* of linguistic development."[29]

The "exceptionless regularity" of Gombocz's conception of phonetic law comes up almost word for word in a work by J. Schmidt, too: "Phonetic law means therefore no exceptionless validity, but *exceptionless regularity*—it means that every case of phonetic change is strictly dominated by causality."[30]

The cause of exceptions to the "regular" phonetic changes of general validity was much better described by Gy. Lux, who stated: "In so far as there are departures from regularity, they are again due to the effect of other regularities [laws]."[31]

A more exacting—though not faultless (see below)—conception of law appears also from the opinion of A. Horger who strongly opposed, as Gombocz did, phonetic laws to natural laws, but when writing of the task of linguistics, he was seeking to discover such laws "which sum up and *explain* the particular changes that can be observed in the history of languages".[32]

Laziczius's conception of law is already entirely differentiated and covers also the sound changes, the phenomena of both the state and the process of development. To explain the varying pronunciation *(o* vs. *a)* of the root-vowel in Russian *воɗ-а,* he refers to its stressed or unstressed position: "Such alternation is of absolute validity; if the phonetic cause is in action, the change sets in without exception."[33] At the same time he recognizes the justification for existence of the exceptions to regular sound

---

[29] Op. cit., p. 11.
[30] J. Schmidt, *A nyelv és a nyelvek* [Language and the Languages], Budapest, 1923, p. 67.
[31] Gy. Lux, *A nyelv* [Language], Budapest, n. d., p. 45.
[32] A. Horger, *A nyelvtudomány alapelvei* [Principles of Linguistics], Budapest, 1926, p. 6. It is true that this conception limits the law to the explanation of the changes observable in diachronic processes, yet this limitation is weakened to some extent by the remark to be read on the same page, where, defending the justification of synchronic linguistic description and explanation, Horger criticizes Gombocz's known thesis according to which "linguistics has no ahistorical disciplines".
[33] NyK XLVIII, p. 5.

changes without questioning, however, the regularity of the process of change. Relying on Szinnyei, he tries to explain the behaviour of the Hungarian equivalents of the Finno-Ugric *k, especially the essence of the couple of exceptions where the original sound has remained k also before a velar vowel in Hungarian words of Finno-Ugric origin (kap 'get', kum dial. vers. of huny 'shut one's eyes'). He supposes a Finno-Ugric medio-palatal *k which, in the ancient Hungarian language territory, started in general to become velar before a velar vowel, the end-result being *k > x > h. According to this hypothesis, however, there ought to have existed an ancient Hungarian dialect where the medio-palatal *k failed to become velar, the original *k having remained k. The struggle of these two tendencies in general resulted in the change *k > h, which in turn modified the ancient Hungarian consonant system: the appearance of the new phoneme in Hungarian brought with it a shift in functional stress, while in a few cases (exceptions) the old /k/ triumphed in the clash of the tendencies.[34] From the point of view of a regular, necessary process *k > x > h, the change *k > k is accidental, but this does not refute the regular character of the process.

Whether we accept the hypothesis built upon Szinnyei's idea or not, Laziczius's explanation indicates an entirely modern conception of law.

6. LAW AND RULE

Law used in a metaphorical sense is, in Gombocz's conception, identical with rule which is observed, established and formulated by the linguist. In his methodology the most important task of phonological research is still "to observe the regularity of phonetic changes, to establish the phonetic laws".[1] In his paper on phonology, however, we read only about the "formulation of those changes having taken place more or less regularly" which resulted in the "emergence of today's Hungarian phonetic structure".[2]

J. Schmidt expresses himself more clearly, taking phonetic laws to be synonymous with phonetic rules: "The phonetic laws

---

[34] Loc. cit., p. 361.
[1] Gombocz, Nyelvtörténeti ..., p. 19.
[2] ÖM II, p. 63.

are then only phonetic rules . . . to the effect that we state that somewhat took place somewhere sometime."[3] These phonetic rules are but "empirical formulae".[4]

M. Zsirai also speaks of the "regularity of sound correspondences", although he admits that "phonetic rules have a catalytic nature".[5]

Law therefore was soon to be superseded by rule, not to speak in detail about the rule complex of modern descriptivist trends.

If, however, we take a closer look at the essence of Gombocz's original dilemma (the cogency of phonetic laws), we can draw from it interesting lessons. As we have seen, Gombocz criticized the neogrammarian postulate of phonetic law just because it accepted as a cardinal criterion of the law its blind operation admitting of no exceptions. If we examine the essence of the "establishment of phonetic laws"—a rather unfortunate expression already quoted from Gombocz's methodology—it becomes clear that he, in accord with an earlier formulation by Melich, understands by phonetic law just what the neogrammarians did. He writes: ". . . we can formulate as a *phonetic law:* the short *u* of the final open syllable, which existed in the Arpadian age, has disappeared."[6] In a more general way: ". . . the short vowels pronounced with the tongue raised high in final open syllables disappeared during the thirteenth century."[7] Melich held this view: "In the Hungarian language the short vowels in final open syllables have all disappeared without exception."[8] Phonetic law is thus, also according to them, a process of phonetic change where there are no exceptions. True, Gombocz fails to mention in this place the widely accepted physiological explanation (reduction) as the cause of the disappearance of the short vowels of final open syllables; if we add this explanation, which was generally accepted in Gombocz's time, we come directly to the neogrammarian concept of phonetic law: the only cause of exceptionless phonetic change is a physiological one.

[3] Schmidt, op. cit., p. 61.
[4] Ibid.
[5] *A modern nyelvtudomány magyar úttörői* [Hungarian Pioneers of Modern Linguistics], Budapest, 1952, p. 44.
[6] Op. cit., p. 20.
[7] Ibid.
[8] MNy VI, p. 158.

Those who had formerly adopted the neogrammarian postulate of phonetic law also understood by phonetic law only the sound changes which could be explained by physiological causes and which admitted of no exceptions.

It was from this position that as long ago as 1895 Balassa criticized M. Grammont's view on the laws of dissimilation as universals, expounded in the chapter entitled "Les lois de la dissimilation" of Grammont's book *La dissimilation consonanti-que dans les langues indo-européennes et dans les langues romanes* (Dijon-Paris, 1895). "We cannot approve", argued Balassa, "that the cases of dissimilation are called laws by Gram-mont, as though the sounds in such position ought in any case to act upon one another in this way."[9] As regards the Hungarian language, he also admitted that the second *r* was replaced by *ly* in the words *borbély* (< *Barbier*) 'barber', *erkély* (< *Erker*) 'balcony', but he found it wanting in the case of *mártír* 'martyr'. Hence dissimilation cannot be a linguistic law, because a single exception degrades its status of law. True, the editor (Szinnyei) —again from the position of cogency—defended Grammont's thesis when he added to Balassa's critique: "In the old literature, however, we find forms of dissimilation as well (e.g. *martel'*, *martely, martyll*)."[10] That Balassa also professed the conception of phonetic law being explainable by physiological causes is proved by his comment on the explanation of Grammont's physiological laws of dissimilation ("la loi du plus fort"—struggle of sounds for life!): "Moreover, in most cases, we have to seek no phonetic (physiological) cause for dissimilation but . . . we have to explain the sound changes on the basis of popular etymology, puns, analogy, and similar reasons."[11]

What can only be inferred from Balassa's position is expressly spoken out by H. Schmidt for the explanation of exceptionless-ness. According to him, in fact, the reason why it is possible to give a definite and positive answer to the exceptionless working of phonetic laws is that it applies to "qualitative sound change", and this is "an organic physiological process in every phenom-enon".[12]

[9] NyK XXVII, p. 105.
[10] Ibid.
[11] Loc. cit., p. 111.
[12] NyK XXXVI, p. 72.

The exceptionless nature of the changes dependent on phonetic position was advocated also by I. Kniezsa in his different etymologies, but this appears also from his explanation of the process of voicing. "We should regard it as very strange that the process of voicing", he writes, "would have applied only to the *s* coming from an original *ž*—and this without exception in every phonetic position—while carefully avoiding the *s* sounds deriving from the etymological *š*."[13] If then voicing is exceptionless in certain phonetic positions, it is "not strange".

L. Tamás, who uses as synonyms the terms 'phonetic law' and 'phonetic rule', nevertheless explains exceptionlessness also on a physiological basis, by the automatism of speech motions: "The question of the exceptionless operation of phonetic laws, phonetic rules can readily be fitted in the framework of what has been said of the automatism of speech motions."[14] The exceptions to changes of this nature he attributes to analogical automatism: "By analogical automatism we on our part mean the socially given tongue-moving, language-enriching faculty which over and again interferes with the process of sound changes which is automatic and is thus tending towards exceptionlessness."[15]

Most recently F. Papp has stood up for the regularity, "admitting of hardly any exceptions", of the modification of linguistic elements: "It was a tremendous discovery by the science of language of the last century that the particular elements of a language change not indiscriminately—which would also be conceivable in principle—but according to strictly applicable laws which admit of hardly any exceptions."[16] It was again this author, and in the same paper, who categorically stated his position—by formulating the common feature, the objective character, of natural and social laws alike—in favour of this important criterion of the concept of law: "As in all other domains of nature and society, here also the situation is that the system is not introduced by us into our material of investigation, but we only get to know better and better, and formulate more and more precisely, the objective regularities found there."[17]

---

[13] MNy XXIX, p. 96; cf. also loc. cit., p. 148.
[14] MyN XLIII, p. 165.
[15] Loc. cit., p. 166.
[16] ÁNyT II, p. 75.
[17] Loc. cit., p. 76.

And finally it is not indifferent either with regard to the dispute over the nature of phonetic changes that, after all, sound changes took place in the course of speech, and that is how they developed into linguistic changes, or they died off at the moment of their birth as non-socialized individual variants, peculiarities. If, in the last analysis, sound changes are speech-sound phenomena, products of natural processes, it is undeniable that natural, physiological factors are, to some extent, responsible for their occurrence. If we recognize that phonology, the science dealing with the speech-sound phenomena and their properties, is a discipline of the physical sciences,[18] which is indissolubly linked to linguistic phonetics, we will at once see in a new light the neogrammarians' physical explanation of phonetic law!

I. Papp holds this view on the automatically prevailing phonetic regularity of sound combinations: "... sounds take part in building up words and larger speech units not only according to their functions, but sound combination has also regularities which operate, regardless of the function and the intention of speaking, with automatic certainty."[19] Again he expresses his opinion on the phonetic laws in such terms: "The various phonetic laws ensure the smooth occurrence of the linguistic sound phenomenon: they are rooted in the mechanism of the phonic material. On the other part, however, the phonetic laws are good also to express faithfully, with a plain-going, smooth and sufficiently articulated sequence of sounds, the unity and arrangement of the thought content of language. Thus the phonetic laws, in spite of the fact that as a phonetic compulsion they often counteract and jeopardize the sense-distinguishing role of sounds, still eventually serve the interests of the communication of thought."[20] It is obvious that in the quoted passages Papp speaks of regularities of the mechanism, not of phonetic change, but of sound combination; however, his convincing arguments can be used as analogy to illustrate the heuristic joy which must have filled the neogrammarians over the discovery of the physiological

[18] "The speech-sound phenomena are natural processes, and phonetics can thus be classed as a natural science, just like anatomy, physiology and acoustics ... Linguistic phonetics sets itself the aim of explaining the linguistic sound-phenomena and the phonetic changes in linguistic history." I. Papp, *Leíró magyar hangtan* [Descriptive Hungarian Phonetics], Budapest, 1966, pp. 9—11.
[19] Op. cit., p. 121.
[20] Ibid.

regularities of sounds, and really there is not much to wonder that the discovered objective regularity enthralled them, and that they elevated it to the rank of an exclusive sound-changing factor.

It is instructive to look into Horger's case which can be seen from his bulky study analyzing the behaviour of vowels in two open syllables. His starting point is that phonetic laws are exceptionless: "The phonetic laws, however—provided, of course, that they are established and laid down in a rule [!] with perfect accuracy—admit of no exceptions."[21] He tries to demonstrate this thesis by examining an immense mass of material; if a pair of identical vowels occur in two open syllables, the one contained in the second open syllable would always drop out; the fact is that the elided vowel is always of a more palatal formation: "... if both open syllables contained the same vowel, it was always the second one of them that was elided ... if two open syllables contained vowels of different quality, then the one to be elided was that which, compared to the other, was formed more in front in the oral cavity."[22]

When, however, he is confronted with the words berkenye 'sorb' and Terbegóc, he describes them as "unruly facts" and timidly calls them exceptions to the regular "elisions" (which are of a more palatal formation without exception).[23] "If therefore berkenye and Terbegóc did not exist, we could again say that the sound of a more palatal formation dropped out."[24]

Regular sound changes tolerating no exceptions, more precisely also those which show exceptions, have to occur with absolute regularity (regularity of the exceptions), and if some "unruly facts" cannot be placed under one or another rule and cannot be explained on the basis of the strictest causality, then "we have to avow sincerely" that we are unable to do anything with them. This recoiling is all the more conspicuous because Horger in the same paper laid his finger (by accident?) on one of the possible explanations of the origin of such "unruly facts". True, this is to him a negative argument. According to him, it cannot be a rule for the behaviour of vowels in two open syllables when, for example, somebody finds, in a note from Fejér County, kukrica

[21] Horger: NyF, pp. 65, 34.
[22] Loc. cit., p. 22.
[23] Loc. cit., p. 19.
[24] Loc. cit., p. 20.

instead of *kukorica* 'maize', because it may be due to the fact that a peasant of the region, "perhaps in fast or jabbering talk", so pronounced the "word which is pronounced *kukorica* all over the country".[25]

How many data of this kind might have been noted down from the recorded history of our language! How many "unruly facts" noted down as a result of "mishearing" we have to do with, especially from the time when scribes were not, or were hardly at all, familiar with the Hungarian language!

From the point of view of the "operation" of phonetic law surrounded with strict causality, how many such accidental cases we have to reckon with, and this fact does not influence the "regular" character of the general process. It is possible to agree perfectly with Horger that the cases like *kukorica — kukrica* "are really of such trifling significance that they can safely be ignored".[26] But thus they really have to be safely ignored even if such a case "sticks out a mile" from the generally unambiguous-looking process and cannot be fitted in it. It is also true, on the other hand, that recognition of this principle would impair the postulate of phonetic law which, also according to Horger, no one could ever demonstrate.

The most interesting and — we might as well say — most contradictory aspect of the dispute about exceptionlessness is that the Hungarian linguists of the twentieth century have attacked the postulate, and rightly so, in principle, but they accepted it as a guidepost in practical work, and yet they saw the great progress of Hungarian linguistics in the "inexorable application" of the postulate of phonetic law.[27] The same contradictoriness appears still more clearly from Horger's following lines: "For it is true that in linguistic practice we unconditionally have to proceed *from the principle* that *phonetic laws admit of no exceptions*, but no one has ever before been able to prove this beyond doubt. This is a postulate *without which we cannot work efficiently*, but which nevertheless is still only a postulate."[28] I have already presented Gombocz's conception of law. In one of his variants, as we have seen, he refused the concept of linguistic law even the minimum of causality. Despite all this he also recognized the

[25] Loc. cit., p. 22.
[26] Ibid.
[27] Lux, op. cit., p. 65.
[28] Horger, loc. cit., p. 42.

significance of the application of the law in practical work: "Such a formulation of the linguistic law ... of course detracts nothing from its practical value."[29] G. Bárczi makes the status of linguistics as a science dependent upon whether practical work keeps track of the perfect phonetic correspondences. He writes: "The importance of phonological tendencies is indisputable ... Correspondences of words, morphemes can be regarded as perfect only *if the phonetic correspondences are perfect* or if we can explain the causes of occasional departures. Without phonological tendencies linguistics would cease to be a science."[30]

A side-issue of the dispute about exceptionlessness clad in the armour of physical science was the limitation in place and time of the operation of the phonetic laws, more precisely the reformulation of this view. The reason why I take it as a side-issue is that this dispute was closed already in its first stage: even the neogrammarians recognized in this sense the limitations involved. The fact in itself that the formerly closed controversial issue was reformulated would not have mattered at all, but the way we see this in itself right conclusion applied in practical etymological works is not entirely reassuring.

B. Kálmán, for example, applies the principle of time-limitation elastically in his explanation of the origin of a new phoneme, *zs*. He thinks it is imaginable, in fact, that the new phoneme is not necessarily a result of foreign language influence, of the contact with Slavic peoples, but the result of internal linguistic evolution. After the disappearance of unaccented and functionless vowels in final position a shift occurred in the consonantal combinations of structures like **vosu belül:* it could become **vos beleül, "the physiological law of assimilation according to voicing came into force"*, and a *zs* is heard at the end of the word *vos*.[31] Already Simonyi remarked in his examples supporting the cases of "genuine assimilation" that the difference in pronunciation of the assimilation of a physiological nature might produce also phonological value—even if he failed to emphasize this difference. For the change *n > m*, besides *tehén + ből*, pr. *tehémből* ('out of a cow'), etc., he mentioned *uru + mk*, pr. *urunk* ('our lord'); besides *bomlik* 'decompose' (v.i.) he noted also *bont* 'de-

[29] Gombocz, Nyelvtörténeti ..., p. 12.
[30] G. Bárczi, *Bevezetés a nyelvtudományba* [Introduction to Linguistics], Budapest, 1953, p. 65.
[31] MyN LXI, p. 399.

compose' (v.t.), and for the change $d > t$ he mentioned a derivative of *szid* 'reprove': *szitkozódik* 'vituperate'.[32]

Whether Kálmán's explanation for the origin of the phoneme *zs* is acceptable or debatable, it is a very valuable hypothesis indicating how it is possible—and even necessary—to draw on the merits the practical conclusions from the proper correction of a formerly formulated postulate of phonetic law: linguistic facts anyway support it.

But the way M. Horváth applies the restrictive criterion of the limitation in place, but especially in time, is strongly debatable. In one of his etymologies (*ostrom* 'siege'), professing the categorical nature of the temporal limits of the unrounding of vowels, he considers "negligible" every attempt that, in the etymological explanation of *Sturm* > *ostrom*, permits a form with *u* originating from a time when "the change $u > o$ was no longer to be expected".[33] What should we say to the existence of today's vernacular "unrounding" phenomena of the kind of $u > o$, such as *kommunista* ∼ *komonista* 'communist', *csuda* ∼ *csoda* 'miracle', *unoka* ∼ *onoka* 'grandchild', *uzsonna* ∼ *ozsonna* 'snack', not to mention the vernacular occurrences of the opposite tendency[34] (*kum* instead of *huny* 'shut one's eyes', *hun* instead of *hol* 'where', *házok* instead of *házak* 'houses', etc.). Inflexibility cannot fight inflexibility, and dogma cannot be defeated by dogma!

7. THE ROLE OF SUBJECTIVE FACTORS IN PHONETIC CHANGES

The undeniably most important lesson of the new dispute over the nature of linguistic (phonetic) changes is provided by the view on the role of subjective factors.

It is not by chance that this problem has become a central topic of recent disputes. The neogrammarians, as we have seen, when combating subjectivism and voluntarism, fought to have

---

[32] NyK XIV, pp. 71—2; cf. also: *romlik* 'spoil' (v.i.)—*ront* 'spoil' (v.t.); *hámlik* 'peel' (v.i.)—*hánt* 'peel' (v.t.); *ömlik* 'pour' (v.i.)—*önt* 'pour' (v.t.), etc.

[33] MNy LXI, pp. 31—2.

[34] "... regression: preserved antiquity". Hajdú, *Bevezetés az uráli nyelvtudományba* [Introduction to Uralic Linguistics], Budapest, 1966, p. 30.

the objective character of linguistic changes recognized. That was what they took as the cardinal criterion of the science of language, that was why they explained linguistic changes on a physical-physiological basis, and why they classed linguistics among the physical sciences. The stressing of the objective character of linguistic changes was indubitably a progressive element of this struggle, but the confounding of subjectivism and voluntarism with the idea of recognizing the role of the subject, the conscious element, was not. Those who identified linguistic laws with natural laws recognized no role whatsoever of the subject, as they could not even recognize it from this standpoint.

The reopening of the litigation was aimed at grasping the identical and different features of natural and social processes, and, as is usual in disputes, it necessarily led to polarization and boiled down to the known alternative: either there is total identity between the two processes, or there is no resemblance whatever between them. Both positions unavoidably determined also the views on linguistic laws, but left their marks upon the evaluation of the role of the conscious element, the subject. On the philosophical plane this appeared in the metaphysical opposition of blindly working necessity to human freedom, determinism to indeterminism, but it was just this metaphysical opposition that pushed polarization further.

All the more striking and extremely remarkable was the dynamical intuition of this alternative at the time, which can be seen from a pertinent statement by Riedl. As a conscious and militant Schleicherian, Riedl classed linguistics among the "physical" sciences and determinedly combated the view which conceived of linguistic development as a function of the will of certain great men. (The lack of response to the notorious lapse of the tongue of the Emperors Tiberius and Sigismund.) At the same time, however, he recognized that the development of language is not a necessary consequence of an automatism working in itself and for itself, but that the individual also has a definite role to play in it. Also according to him, the development of language starts out from individuals, but such individual efforts can succeed only if they "correspond to the common disposition" of the collectivity.[1] The "common disposition" of the

---

[1] Sz. Riedl, A nyelvtudomány alapelvei [The Principles of Linguistics]: Introductory university lecture. *Kalauz*, 1863, p. 36.

collectivity is essentially based on the laws which do not depend on the individual, and which the individual can recognize; and if he does, he can influence their operation. The point at issue here — and Riedl does speak it out — is no less than the dialectical unity of opposite factors observable in the process of linguistic changes: "The course followed by the development of language comprises the two opposite circumstances — compulsiveness [determinism, necessity] and freedom."[2] In Riedl's brilliant idea we can find the rudiments of the dialectic of the individual and the community, of the individual and the social.

In matters relating to the problems of the opposition of the objective regularity governing the development of language and of the conscious ability and intention of the individual to develop the language, also the Academy had to take a stand because of the spread of the neologistic movement and in order to form a correct judgment on the many uncommon and even faulty word-formations existing in the sea of neologisms. That is why in 1872 it announced a Competition basically intended to fight against wrong word-formations. The Competition read notably: "It being proved by daily experience that, since the justification of the language reform has not been brought into question, and our literature and especially the periodical and daily press have grown continually richer, our language has unnecessarily been flooded with numberless . . . new idioms formed after phrases of other languages . . . Let therefore those principles be expounded which must be kept in mind when new idiomatic expressions are coined."[3]

The Competition was answered by two essays. One of them was that mentioned above, the other was written by S. Imre.[4]

Both competitors started out of an adaptation to the laws "moving, governing" the development of language. They judged the new forms by "the spirit of language", vernacular speech,[5]

---

[2] Cf. "In der Beschränkung zeigt sich erst der Meister, und das Gesetz nur kann uns Freiheit geben" (Goethe); "Freedom is a recognized necessity" (Marx).

[3] Quoted by E. Ponori Thewrewk, A helyes magyarság elvei [Principles of Correct Hungarian], Budapest, 1873, p. 1.

[4] S. Imre, A magyar nyelvújítás óta divatba jött idegen és hibás szólások bírálata, tekintettel az újítás helyes módjaira [Critique of the Foreign and Bad Phrases that Came into Fashion since the Hungarian Language Reform, with Regard to the Proper Methods of Reform], Budapest, 1873.

[5] ". . . by the sum-total of all phenomena of the aboriginal Hungarian people." Ponori Thewrewk, op. cit., p. 93.

and established the rightness or wrongness of conscious word-formation on the basis of comparison. The "intentional developers of language"[6] were thus not corrupters of language according to the official position of the Academy either, they besieged the law-making and even law-preserving bastions of *veneranda antiquitas* with the knowledge and "consent" of the Academy. In this revolutionary stage of the struggle between old and new, the victory of the new was promoted through conscious intervention by the active camp — not devoid of extravagances either — whose members are called neologists in the history of science.

The peculiar alloy, or rather mixture, of the objective viewpoint ("the spirit of the aboriginal Hungarian people") and the subjective opinion have never been thrown into such relief as in the judgment of new creations. Everyone tried to distinguish by the (objective) standard of "linguistic instinct". To illustrate the extent to which this distinction contained subjective elements and the kind of value shift it has undergone to this day, it is enough to adduce a few new expressions which were judged to be wrong by contemporary linguistic consciousness according to Imre's essay. (I deliberately placed in Group I words which mean to today's linguistic instinct practically nothing, being "empty sequences of sounds" and consequently untranslatable; on the other hand, the words classed in Group II are of the kind which few of the "average speakers" know to be neologistic formations, and without which social intercourse in our days would be, so to speak, unimaginable.)

I	II	
áholog	*ábra*	illustration
bánlal	*állvány*	scaffold
csarna	*beruház*	to invest
emle	*bőrönd*	suitcase
falárd	*csarnok*	hall
gyű	*csend*	silence
hibcsiny	*életképes*	viable
iroma	*elvhű*	true to principles
jégne	*felmond*	to give notice
kemne	*felsorol*	to enumerate
lábtyú	*felülvizsgál*	to supervise
mezőcz	*gép*	machine
	gondnok	guardian

[6] Op. cit., p. 1.

hátralék	arrears
inger	stimulus
járda	sidewalk
képvisel	to represent
kézbesít	to deliver
láttamoz	to countersign
merev	rigid
munkaképes	capable of work
nővér	sister
nyugta	receipt
okmány	document
ön	you
rendelkezik	to dispose
sorakozik	to form up
szabvány	standard
tanár	professor
újonc	recruit
ünnepély	festivity
vágy	desire
zöm	bulk.[7]

The above examples are also good to illustrate that the objective consciousness of language as the community's controller of correct speech comes about through the co-operation of a great variety of conscious elements — mainly cultural influences — and undergoes great development in a relatively short time. It is also difficult enough to find out why the objective standard of "the aboriginal Hungarian people", when sifting words of identical formation, rejects one (*éleny*)[8] and endorses another (*higany* 'mercury'), why a word like *csalárd* 'fraudulent' remains in usage to survive and why another like *falárd* perishes, etc. It is doubtless that accident also plays a role in the "objectification" of the productions of the conscious development of language, and thus accident also has to be reckoned with as a factor in this development.

The elasticity of Riedl's theory of linguistic change, the relative flexibility of the Academy's position regarding the language reform, however, stopped progressing. In this an undeniable part was played also by the overwhelming vigour of the neo-

[7] Imre, op. cit., pp. 206—10.
[8] A neologism proposed for '*oxygen*'.

grammarian conception of law. Not only the propagators but also the opponents of this conception recognized one of the determining features of linguistic processes, and they saw it in the objectivity. The role of the intention, of the conscious element, in the origin and influencing of these processes was more and more dwindling, and it was even reduced to nil in the view of some. Szarvas wrote, for example: *"Change takes effect by itself, without the assistance of consciousness, there being no trace even of intentionality."*[9] Balassa thought the language-reform movement was a forcible intervention in the process of the objective development of language, he held that its emergence was not necessary but exceptional: *". . . every change* in the life of language *takes place unconsciously*; conscious and at the same time forcible changes like our language reform constitute exceptions in the life of the languages."[10] In a review written on the occasion of the publication of the third edition of Paul's book *(Prinzipien)*, G. Petz specially underlined the significance of Paul's idea that "the unconscious, unintentional nature of the linguistic processes makes possible their exact scientific cognition".[11] Gombocz in his earlier writings specially stressed the unconscious character of changes, and his later works also took as non-existent the speaker with his conscious intention to cultivate the language. He wrote in 1898: "We have to emphasize first of all that a change of usage does not take place consciously."[12] He formulated the idea just as definitely also in one of his books: "The fancies, intentional changes, invented by the individual usually disappear without a trace . . . In the changes of language only a very inferior role is played by direct volitive influences and deliberateness."[13]

The view of the subjective idealist Vossler, who represented the opposite extreme, and according to whom "Every expression of language . . . as free and individual creation must be explained from the individual intuitions of the speakers",[14] found almost no response in the relevant opinions of Hungarian linguists.

[9] Nyr X, p. 165.
[10] TMNy I, p. 43; the idea comes up on the next page again.
[11] Petz: NyK XXIX, p. 110.
[12] Gombocz: Nyr XXVII, p. 11.
[13] *Nyelvtörténeti módszertan* [Methodology of Linguistic History], Budapest, 1922, pp. 10—11.
[14] "Aller sprachlicher Ausdruck . . . soll als freie und individuelle Schöpfung aus den individuellen Intuitionen der sprechenden Individuen erklärt sein." K. Vossler, *Positivismus und Idealismus in der Sprach-*

Overwhelming objectivity, denial of the intention and possibility of consciously shaping and developing the language, non-acceptance of this kind of function of subjective factors—this would be, in general outlines, the linguistic attitude reflecting the essential features of the changes of language in the early decades of the twentieth century.

This one-sided explanation is all the more striking as a writing dated from the end of the eighteenth century also hinted that language is changing through speech, and in the act of speech one has nilly-willy to take into account the speaker with his subjective intentions, his taste, his habits of speech, his manners, etc. The actualized spoken variants, changes of language can also be observed. It can be seen, as was also noted by F. Kempelen, that individual variants and peculiarities of pronunciation differing from the usual can come into fashion, can become objectified. Kempelen noticed the pronunciation of the French r, because when in Paris he was puzzled by the fact that about a quarter of the Parisians spoke with a strong uvular r, and not because a changed articulation basis prevented them from producing the dental r, but simply because the uvular r became fashionable, and this fashion was accepted and took deep roots, passing from father to son.[15] The significance of Kempelen's observation is only enhanced by the fact that his conception of language was progressing with the improvement of his talking machine, and this conception was greatly influenced by mechanical factors. Evidence of this is also the title of his work *(Mechanismus . . .)*. And besides, being an observer with attentive ears and eyes, he did not fail to notice the non-mechanical processes — or the facts producing them—which influence the changes of language (a fashion started by individuals and originated in theatrical usage).

It is also a fact worth considering that one of the militant propagators of the objective character of the neogrammarian

---

wissenschaft: Eine sprachphilosophische Untersuchung, Heidelberg, 1904, p. 88.

[15] "In Paris schien es mir, als wenn wenigstens der vierte Theil der Einwohner schnarrte, nicht weil sie das rechte R nicht aussprechen können, sondern weil man eine Annehmlichkeit darein gesetzt hat, und es einmal zur Mode geworden ist, und diese Mode kann nicht wie andere Moden aufhören, denn ganze Familien haben das Zungen-R verlernt, und das Schnarren wird sich bey ihnen auf Kindeskinde fortpflanzen." Op. cit., p. 331.

conception of law, M. Müller, equally reckoned with the possibility of individual initiative in the origin of the processes of phonetic change, and even took into account the distortion of words under the impact of taboo names: some primitive tribes not only avoided to utter the banned word but deliberately altered other words phonemically similar to it. But this deliberate change or distortion of pronunciation is observed not only in the case of taboo names, some tribes departed from the usual pronunciation also for the fun of it or out of mere freak, as was noted by H. W. Bates in his work on the customs of the tribes living on the river Amazon:[16] "When Indians, men or women, are conversing amongst themselves, they seem to take pleasure in inventing new modes of pronunciation, or in distorting words . . . I think it, therefore, very probable that the disposition to invent new words and new modes of pronunciation, added to the small population and habits of isolation of hordes and tribes, are the causes of the wonderful diversity of languages in South America."[17] If linguistic facts of some kind get into contradiction with principles established by theory, the facts cannot be suppressed; this realization runs right through Müller's lectures, as attested clearly by the following passage: ". . . we learn at least this one lesson, that there often is more in real language than is dreamt of in our philosophy."[18]

Saussure's pertinent statement, worth noticing, also escaped general attention. What has become commonly known is that he strictly separated the individual *(parole)* and social *(langue)* aspects of language *(langage)*, although he clearly stated that neither of them is conceivable without the other.[19] When, for the sake of a more thorough investigation, he separated the two aspects of language, all he essentially did was to oppose the individual products of speech activity variegated by accidental factors, and consequently relying on them as well, to the regularity inferable from the colourful facts of *parole*, to the essential, the crystallized social will, the objectified linguistic sign.[20]

---

[16] H. W. Bates, *The Naturalist on the Amazons* I, pp. 329—30.
[17] Quoted by Müller, *Lectures* II, p. 44.
[18] Op. cit., pp. 43—4.
[19] "Le langage a un côté individuel et un côté social, et l'on ne peut concevoir l'un sans l'autre." Saussure, *Cours* . . ., p. 24.
[20] "En séparant la langue de la parole, on sépare du même coup: 1° ce qui est social de ce qui est individuel; 2° ce qui est essentiel de ce qui est accessoire et plus ou moins accidentel." Op. cit., p. 30.

His grasping the objective character of the linguistic sign was also more elastic than in the attitude of his contemporaries and his successors. According to him, the sign as a fact of *langue* is not a category wholly independent of the will of society and its individual members, but a linguistic element which society and the individual alike must accept as it is, it being to a certain extent always independent of the individual or social will.[21] It is no unnecessary philological meticulousness to recall and even stress this idea, and this for two reasons. First, the objectivity of the linguistic sign examined from the synchronic point of view is put in a different light from that generally attributed to Saussure. Second, if Saussure formulated so elastically that synchronical facts are independent of the human will, recognition of the role of the subjective factor—beside that of social objectivity—evidently applies still more in the origin of diachronic processes. Also according to Saussure, speech is the vehicle of all changes; changes can be observed first with individuals, as a result of either conscious or spontaneous activity; and depending on several factors they either fade out on the speaker's lips or "come into fashion", become socialized, objectified. The diachronical facts generate and "regulate" the synchronic system, the course of the diachronic process can be influenced by the human will.[22]

The propagators of Saussure's theory overlooked these factors because, for fear of the charge of subjectivism, they viewed the only basic criterion of erudition in the stressing of the objective character of language, of linguistic changes.

Against the one-sidedness of the adaptation and criticism of the neogrammarian doctrines, G. Bárczi recognized the language-forming function of the conscious element when explaining the circumstances of the origin of slangy elements as follows: "This actual slang is only to a certain extent the result of spontaneous, subconscious linguistic development, word creation, to a great extent it is conventional distortion of language or at least arbitrary, conscious or half-conscious word-formation."[23]

---

[21] "Car le signe échappe toujours en une certaine mesure à la volonté individuelle ou sociale." Op. cit., p. 34.
[22] ". . . la volonté préside à un changement de ce genre." Op. cit., p. 127; see also p. 138.
[23] G. Bárczi, *A "pesti nyelv"* [The Lingo of Budapest], Budapest, 1932, p. 3.

Although Bárczi's statements apply to the genesis of the "wildings" of the Hungarian language, their principled positiveness was of very great significance at the time when the language-shaping nature of consciousness was generally forgotten. (Not including, of course, Vossler and his followers, who only muddled up everything with their linguistic explanations based on subjective idealism.) Bárczi's sharp eyes noticed the subjective factor hidden among the language-shaping forces, and he formulated this discovery in a positive manner.

What can be stated of slang applies, *mutatis mutandis*, to the facts and factors characteristic of the general evolution of language. Namely, assisting in the production of slangy elements is, on the one hand, the intention to make them special tools of communication intelligible only to the initiated and, on the other, the daredeviltry fomented by exhibitionism "to startle the old fogeys". Whoever has once enjoyed the success of a stunt shocking the "passers-by" can hardly forget the experience of success, not to mention the stooge character and "occult field-values" of that singular morphology and syntax. No matter how long-established a truth it is that expressions screening the intended message with deformed morphological garb, syntagmatic chains reflecting the wildest associations are cut to fit in with the basic categories of "ordinary" morphology and syntax, the essential thing is the conscious formation (deformation) of language, the production of emotional effects planned beforehand, the deliberate scandalization of the "simple souls". In given conditions and social situations this "dialect"—the hooligan language—may grow to social dimensions, or at least conquer whole age-groups, and as such may fulfil a special function.

Such a special function is exercised by the idiom of the so-called "beat movement" which has attained great popularity especially among the young people. J. D. Salinger's book *The Catcher in the Rye* was a smashing success amidst teen-agers in Hungary, but also adults enjoyed it although they would have needed a kind of "hooligan glossary" to read the book, since they did not know all elements of the *"lousy vocabulary"* of the hero. Salinger's hero is a teen-ager, a son of the beat generation, who devises his own weapons, his vocabulary and singular phraseology, to express his disagreement with the adults. He uses his weapon to describe his bleak childhood, as if presenting the adults with a mirror: look at the poor figure you cut!

This peculiar idiom has thus been established in literature;

what is more, how eminent a place it holds in Hungarian literary translations is eloquently shown by the Hungarian edition of J. Kerouac's book *On the Road*, which was reviewed by the critic under the title "Translation from English into Hooligan".[24] The critic, É. Zentai, demonstrates the "language-generating power" of the translator (Gy. Déry) by the following lines: *"Dilis krapekok battyognak San Francisco lepra utcáin, megskubizzák a csajokat, zsernyákok hipiseznek minden sarkon, a piti bejzlik tele wurlitzerező, begerjedt félcédulásokkal, akik meg akarják kúrni a mólés babákat, és kénytelenek cigarettát újítani, mert soha nincs egy alzó grandjuk se."*[25] (Dotty bums are pegging along the crummy streets of San Francisco, scrutating the janes; dicks are snooping around at every corner; the stale joints are full of juke-boxing, hepped-up nuts, who want to make the grogged babes and have to lift cigarettes, because they have never got a red cent.)

It should take no philistine prudery for one to sneer at this meaty, milieu-creating "stylistic art", at this eager overbidding, since our literary magazines and chiefly our translators have inured us to the "odour" of slang. But why Déry saw fit to render "cold-water pad" as *lepra odú* 'dirty hole' and *nyomortanya* 'slum'; or why "bar" was turned into *bejzli* or *csehó* 'joint'; "to peek at" into *megskubizni* 'to scrutate'; "cop" (which is now so common a word that its only acceptable Hungarian equivalent can be *rendőr* 'policeman') into *zsernyák* and *hekus* or *dekás* 'dick', 'flat-foot'; "drunk" into *tintás* or *mólés* 'grogged'; "kid" into *krapek* 'bum'; "girl" into *csaj* 'jane' or *baba* 'babe' used disparagingly, is known—in addition to the manager of Magvető (Seedsower) Publishers—only to the editor who revised the translation, A. Varannai.

Shocked as the reader with a refined taste is at the act of the publishers (who sowed no good seed by publishing this "translation"), the fact unhappily remains a fact: the "gems" picked at random from the distorted text are all known terms "commonly used" by certain strata. No matter how short their past history may be, the role of subjective "taste" and individual initiative in their genesis and vigorous spread is undeniable.

The conception of the spontaneity of linguistic changes, precluding any conscious influence, of necessity led to the opinion that the process of change can only be slow and gradual, for

[24] *Nagyvilág* XII, p. 610.
[25] Ibid.

sudden, abrupt changes would jeopardize even mutual understanding, and so language does not suffer sudden changes. As Szarvas put it: *"Change is gradual, progressing at some length or faster . . . and it makes no leaps."*[26] According to Balassa the transition from one linguistic form to another is slow, "fading by degrees".[27] Gombocz also accepted the hypothesis according to which "the final cause of a regular phonetic change lies in the slow transformation of man's psychic organism".[28]

The neogrammarian "dogma" of the slow, gradual and blind working of phonetic changes was first "consciously" contested in Hungary by Laziczius. Instead of the phonetic viewpoint applied until then to describe and explain the process of phonetic changes, he used phonological criteria to approach the essence and productive causes of such changes. While phonetics is concerned with every kind of phonetic change, historical phonology treats only of changes which have a bearing upon the entire sign system, and looks into the motion of changing language behind the changing sounds.

Sievers's school of phonetics based the idea of the gradualness of phonetic changes on the fact that the particular sound types in the immense multitude of speech sounds display a rather great degree of similarity as to the place and mode of their production, so that they are not as remote from one another as we might think. Indeed, with the countless number of glides (transitional sounds, *Übergangslaute*) added, the explanation presented itself: owing to the shades of difference between sounds or sound types, the transition from one sound to another can take place without a hitch; thus the process of phonetic change can only be a slow, gradual one without leaps, made possible by a slight change or shift in the place and mode of production of sounds.[29] The rare occurrences where this smooth gradualness could not be used as an explanatory principle *(k > t)* were not even called sound change but sound alternation. But since the neogrammarian school failed to disclose the nuanced variants and to give an acceptable explanation of the sound change, Laziczius described the neogrammarian teachings concerning the gradualness of phonetic changes as "dogmatic" tenets based on phonetic conclusions.[30]

[26] Nyr X, p. 165.
[27] TMNy I, p. 40.
[28] Gombocz: Nyr XXXI, p. 538.
[29] E. Sievers, *Grundzüge der Phonetik*, Leipzig, 1901³, pp. 225 ff.
[30] Laziczius: NyK XLVIII, p. 357.

335

Against the phonetic (physiological, physical) explanation Laziczius proposed a phonological theory (which takes account also of the psychical background). He wrote in this connection: "If the phonetic changes were only physical, this explanation [the theory of gradual change precluding leaps] would even be right, but since the question here is of linguistic processes, we must not forget about the psychical background against which these physical processes take place."[31] In Laziczius's conception, consideration of the psychical background is bound to direct attention to the correlation of the so-called sound intention *(Lautabsicht, Lautintention)* and of the realized speech sound.[32] According to him, it is characteristic of every language that the speaker's sound intention is expressed within a determined scope of realization, where the (physical, physiological) qualities of the realized sounds may vary. Until the variation has crossed the determined limits, the same sound intention is realized, so that there can be no question of phonetic change. As soon as the actual (realized) sound crosses the limits of the determined scope of realization, there obviously can be no longer any question of the realization of the same sound intention, for at that moment a phonetic change occurs.

"Language knows neither transitional sound intentions nor transitional phonemes." This is the summary of the train of thought of Laziczius, who necessarily arrives at the only kind of conclusion: "Consequently *phonetic changes in language are always and without exception abrupt."*[33] To the already mentioned idea of Shcherba, a member of Wundt's school, he adds a quotation from Sommerfelt, according to which "abrupt change is a psychological necessity".[34]

The "psychophonetic" explanation of phonetic change was a natural reaction to the conception of the neogrammarian school,

---

[31] Ibid.
[32] The idea of the relation between intention and realization comes up already in the work of Shcherba [Щерба] entitled *Русские гласные в качественном и количественном отношении* [The Russian Vowels in Terms of Quantity and Quality], St. Petersburg, 1912.
[33] Laziczius, loc. cit., p. 358.
[34] "Le changement par saut c'est une nécessité psychologique." *Journal de Psychologie* XXV, p. 689. Cf. Laziczius, loc. cit. The importance of the difference between the phonetic and the phonological explanation of sound changes was pointed out by Laziczius in one of his earlier writings, where he called attention to the wrongness of the established conception which "disposed of *all* phonetic changes by a physiological and mechanical explanation". MNy XXVI, p. 266.

whose theory of the phonetic change taking place with "blind necessity" (to the total exclusion of the conscious element) came into conflict with the contribution of the conscious element, the sound intention. The views which emphasized the "equality of rights" of speech sounds, the slightness of the differences between sounds or sound types, and the existence of transitional sounds (the phonetic classification of sounds), were replaced by a conception pointing to the significance of the linguistically important sounds, of the phonemes relevant for the realization of the sound intention.

After Shcherba, Laziczius gives the following example to illustrate the difference between the phonetic and phonological classification of sound changes. For a phonetic explanation the formation of the sounds *n* and *m*, respectively, in Hung. *ront* (< arch. *romt*) 'spoil' (v.t.) and *színpad* (pr. *szímpad*) 'stage' is of the same value: both are products of assimilation. The fact that in the first case we have a change *m* > *n* and in the other *n* > *m* is phonetically irrelevant and does not affect the essence of assimilation. Both are due to regressive assimilation. In the first example the preceding bilabial sound (*m*) was affected by the following dental (*t*) and was pushed towards a dental position to become *n*. In the second example the preceding dental (*n*) is affected by the following bilabial (*p*) to become a "pure" bilabial *m*.

We arrive at an entirely different result, Laziczius continues his train of thought, if we examine the phonological value of the change. We have two "regular" sound changes in the case of the element *n* in *romt* > *ront* as well as in the etymon *(szín)* of *színész* 'actor', *színház* 'theatre', etc. if it appears in the compound *színpad*, while phonologically we have to make a definite distinction between the phonetic changes *m* > *n* and *n* > *m*, and this on the basis of the sound intention inducing the change. "It is clear", writes Laziczius, "that in the case of *romt* > *ront* the way of assimilation led from a sound intention *m* to a sound intention *n*; that is, an evident change occurred psychically as well, but no such thing happened to the word *színpad*, because the sound intention here is *n* even when we pronounce *m*: we utter a phoneme *n* but it turns out to be *m*."[35]

When could we speak, in cases like *színpad* pr. *szímpad*, about a phonetic (phonemic) change *n* > *m* that would be also phono-

---

[35] Laziczius: NyK XLVIII, p. 350.

logically "regular" according to Laziczius? "Surely", he writes, "if once the word *szinpad* as a compound would become obscure, if the first constituent . . . would lose its connection with our words *szín*, *színész*, *színház*, etc., then it would be possible for us not only to say *szimpad* but also to want to say so. Then it would be possible to speak about change phonologically, too, but now it is not."[36]

The "genuine" phonetic changes therefore—according to this conception—take place solely owing to the existence and contribution of psychological momenta, of forms of motion. When the realization value of actual speech sounds clashes with the psychical value, with the sound intention, the latter prevails in the phonological evaluation of the realized speech sound.

The explanation of phonetic change attempted on the basis of Wundt's and Shcherba's psycholinguistics is itself psychologistic and grossly exaggerates the function of the subjective load of the sound intention, taking it as the only sound-changing factor. Accordingly, the presence or absence of phonetic change wholly depends on what we want to pronounce or to hear. Hence, if somebody, for example, "with an intention *u* pronounces a sound which is physically exactly intermediate between *u* and *o*" and the hearer perceives the sound heard with an intention *u*, there is no phonetic change, but if he does so with an intention *o*, "a change *u* > *o* occurs without transition".[37]

It would be difficult to deny the role of psychical factors, the role of the subject, in the start and process of phonetic changes, but it is at least as difficult to accept them as the only sound-changing factors. Let us consider for a moment the very last quotation and examine it from a practical point of view. Let us suppose that a speaker with an intention *u* utters a sound which is physically realized between *u* and *o*, say, for the sound *u* of the word *unoka* ('grandchild'). The word is pronounced in the presence of two hearers: one is accustomed to the standard form *unoka*, the other hails from a place in whose dialect the word is pronounced *onoka*. According to Laziczius the first hearer "identifies the sound heard with his own intention *u*",[38] the other with his own intention *o*. In the "judgment" of the first hearer no phonetic change took place, but according to the second "a

---

[36] Ibid. Changed spelling is obviously also a function of the change of sound intention; though Laziczius does not say so, it logically follows from his train of thought described above.

[37] Ibid.

[38] Ibid.

change $u > o$ occurred without transition". Because if somebody uttered a sound u of impure timbre with the intention u, and if all hearers perceived it with the intention u, then there would be no particular trouble: the subjective intention of the speaker and the hearers could be taken as an objective standard or criterion, and there would not be a shade of doubt that no change occurred in the "objective sound intention". But the question arises at once: What is the objective criterion of phonetic change in case the speaker's sound intention does not coincide with the hearer's sound intention? Why is only the hearer's sound intention decisive in such cases?

The sound intention is due to conscious subjective activity. To declare the subjective sound intention, which is considerably influenced by all sorts of psychical, cultural, etc. factors, to be the basic criterion of a theory is to build on a rather shaky ground. If I asked a number of people to state their opinion on their sound intention n or m in the word *ront* ($<$ *romt*), for example, I would have to expect pretty different answers. These would depend on what the persons asked knew about language, linguistics and linguistic history, especially if the construction of their sound intention would be coloured by the undeniable kinship of the etymons of the word *romlik — ront*. What is the difference in sound intention between *szid — szitkozódik* and *romlik — ront*? If in the case of *ront* the sound intention n is indisputable, is it likewise possible (or necessary) to disregard *szid*, the still extant etymon of the derivative *szitkozódik*, or rather the sound intention formed in connection with its element d? Is it spelling that should decide upon the sound intention in the case of words like *szid — szitkozódik* as against words like *pad* 'bench' — *padka* (pr. *patka*) 'small bench'? The derived nature of the word *szitkozódik* has become obscure, and the word has lost connection with our words *szidni, szidom, szidás* 'to reprove, I reprove, reproof', etc. Is this the reason why it has become possible for us "not only to say *szitkozódik* but also to want to say so", and "to speak about change phonologically, too", in the case of *szid — szitkozódik*?

The questions are difficult to answer on the basis of Wundt's, Shcherba's and Laziczius's theory of sound intention!

The matter in question is not that the unusual conscious "extravagances" of pronunciation do not or cannot have any linguistic function, nor that such extravagances might not come into fashion and even cover whole language areas to become thus sound-changing factors. Let us recall Kempelen's observation of the uvular *r* in the speech of about a quarter of the Parisians influenced by theatrical speech. A fashionable way of pronunciation initiated by individuals has gained ground and produced a "regular" phonetic change. This way of pronunciation is today almost general. It is also true that an unusual conscious change always has some positive or negative linguistic value, whether or not it gains ground in a given language area, because either it is an expression of intellectual or affective or conative elements, or it has a situation-creating value. The "regular" French *oui* is often replaced by the word *ouais* (ä) with a highly pejorative connotation, as was noticed already by B. Zolnai.[39] It would be equally difficult to disprove the strong pejorative load in the case of Hung. *(ronda >) randa* 'ugly' or the slighter shift of emotion in the German changes *e > ö, i > ü*, for which Laziczius, in Jespersen's wake, adduced examples: *schreckliche > schröckliche, tiefe > tüfe, Finsterniss > Fünsterniss*,[40] or the humorous shade of difference in the changes *ö > e, a > e* in Hungarian, as in the words *öcsém > ecsém* 'young man', *barátom > barétom* 'my friend'.[41] The change *a > e*, the pronunciation of the root

---

[39] B. Zolnai, *Szóhangulat és kifejező hangváltozás* [Emotional Elements in Words and Expressive Sound Change], Szeged, 1939, p. 150.
[40] Laziczius: NyK XLIII, p. 20. It is a different matter that Laziczius regards the linguistic elements expressive of emotion as "phonemic variants" outside the sphere of phonological changes, as "occasional or stylistic variants" *(variantes stylistiques)*, because these means are not used in language for significative distinctions or for grammatical purposes. Loc. cit., p. 18. Though if we do not confine the function of language to significative distinction, but if we consider it a perfect tool of human intercourse, a connecting link of the conscious life of individuals, the phonological character of such changes cannot be denied. The recent results of physiological and psychical research also draw attention to the fact that "conscious life cannot be characterized by only the processes of thought; emotions play an important role, they sanction and confirm the success of action". *Magyar Filozófiai Szemle* X, p. 139. "Consciousness is formed by the unity of the spheres of thought, will and memory." Loc. cit., p. 143. — "... every linguistic phenomenon and every linguistic change has, from the point of view of the function or justification of language, its own — positive or negative — value", writes G. Bárczi. "Namely, we have to consider every linguistic phenomenon from the point of view of how it helps man in expressing his thoughts, his emotions and his will as clearly, as explicitly, and even as economically as possible." G. Bárczi, A nyelvi változások értékelése [The Evaluation of Linguistic Changes], MNy LXII, pp. 129—34; loc. cit., p. 132.
[41] Zolnai, op. cit., p. 151.

vowel at a higher pitch generally betrays a greater affective load in the case of the words *hallatlan* > *hällatlan* 'preposterous' and *gazember* > *gäzember* 'scoundrel'. "The more offensive the speaker's voice", Zolnai writes, "the more the pronunciation of *a* is shifting towards *e*. (This pronunciation is not only a physiological need, but also an intentional distortion, a display of emotion through a change of sound.)"[42]

The conscious, individual introduction of other changes and modes of pronunciation is fairly incontestable. Speaking with a uvular *r*, which was once in vogue in Hungary, but which became outmoded and even turned inside out as to its effect, like the affected pronunciation of the illabial *å (kåszino, åbszolute,* etc.), was a product of conscious imitation and held to be an aristocratic mode of pronunciation; to illustrate this mannerism, Zolnai quoted from the memoirs of actress Mari Jászai, who wrote the following about the manner of speech of her predecessor, Mrs. Laura Mátray-Szép: "Not for all the world would she have said *a*, for she held it rustic; instead of *atyám* [Father] she said *etyém*, and instead of *páva* [peacock] *péve*."[43] The pronunciation *a* > *é* considered aristocratic at a time grew to such dimensions that K. Kardeván wrote an article in defence of the Hungarian *á* sound.[44] Zolnai stated: "Thus, for aesthetic-psychical reasons, the various social strata contribute towards phonetic development."[45] This is probably so, indeed; there may be also types like this among the factors producing phonetic changes, as there were in the past (the replacement of the dental *r* by the uvular *r* in French; the short life of the uvular *r* and the affected *á* sound in Hungarian), but his general conclusions drawn from the phenomena mentioned above are hardly acceptable.

Zolnai exaggerates the role of the conscious intention or activity in starting processes of phonetic change. As to the phenomenon whereby the initial consonant cluster *sc* in Latin is resolved *(sc > esc)* in some Romance languages, he puts forth the following idea: "That much is certain, anyway, that the same phonetic change (e.g. *sc > esc*) may come about on a physiological basis at any time and any place, but for it to become a regu-

---

[42] Ibid.
[43] Op. cit., p. 152.
[44] A magyar *á* hang védelme [In Defence of the Hungarian *á* sound], *Magyarosan*, 1936, pp. 34—5.
[45] Zolnai, op. cit., p. 154.

lar phonetic change it needs the contribution of social and conscious factors."[46] To support this categorical statement he refers to the conditions in which the so-called "overcorrected" forms are created. For the sake of aristocratic style, as is well known, the authors of the overcorrected forms would "reconstruct" a certain form held regular also where such form has never existed.[47] This seems convincing in the given examples. But it is impossible to accept them as leading to conclusions like these: "The snobbish-pedantic 'linguistic instinct' obstructs the spread of phonetic changes"; or: "Phonetic changes, it seems, most often start out from the upper social strata", and finally: "The mechanistic conception of phonetic laws can be replaced by a human [conscious, voluntaristic] explanation."[48]

The affected force of individual conscious changes is entirely disarmed if it comes up against social resistance, and it may even become utterly ridiculous in a given social situation: it may be good only to recall anachronistic figures of bygone periods and situations swept away by the tide of social evolution (the uvular *r* and the illabial *å* in Hungarian). A fairly known fact of the development of the Hungarian language is also that immense numbers of initiatives developed by some neologists on the basis of forced analogies were killed in the fire of social criticism directed against the single overcorrected word *páholy*, etc., etc.

When therefore Zolnai, under Vossler's influence, is looking for a "human" explanation to replace the mechanistic conception of phonetic laws, he falls into the same error which was committed also by the subjective idealist Schuchardt, who could attribute the phonetic changes only to conscious individual initiative of great personalities, princes, famous speakers and actors, and considered it unquestionable that the origin of phonetic changes is arbitrary.[49]

It did not take long for linguists to criticize the explanation based on the exaggeration of the role of subjective intention hidden among the sound-changing factors. L. Tamás in his polemic treatise *Are Phonetic Changes Conscious?* responded

[46] Ibid.
[47] It. *storia* for *istoria* < *historia*; Hung. *páholy* 'box' (in theatre) < *pahó;* op. cit., pp. 154—5.
[48] Op. cit., p. 155.
[49] "... so läßt sich auch die Möglichkeit nicht bestreiten, daß der Ursprung eines Lautwandels ein willkürlicher sei." H. Schuchardt, *Ueber die Lautgesetze: Gegen die Junggrammatiker*, Berlin, 1885, p. 15.

to the views absolutizing the sound-changing function of the conscious element.[50]

Tamás sees clearly that the views declaring phonetic changes to be the results of *merely* conscious individual intention are an exaggerated reaction to the neogrammarian conception of phonetic change. The theory of the exceptionless phonetic change taking place with blind necessity is really inconsistent with the conception admitting even a minimum contribution of the conscious element. As we have seen above, the proponents of the neogrammarian theory of phonetic change built their conception on a very specific theoretical and ideological basis and — understandably — kept to it. In the start and process of phonetic changes they thought they discovered the contribution of the same blindly working forces of nature on whose basis the other natural processes take place (naive, mechanistic materialism). They saw in this conception of the processes of phonetic change the fundamental criterion of a really scientific phonetics, and they combated mercilessly every kind of idealistic — or supposedly idealistic — explanation of phonetic change.

The sound-change theory which sprang from the soil of firm militancy and later ended up in a sort of rigidity met the same militancy on the part of the opposite camp, and it is no wonder that the subjective-idealist theoretician Schuchardt expressed his anti-neogrammarian views also in the title of his study of phonetic laws *(Ueber die Lautgesetze: Gegen die Junggrammatiker)*. He raised the war-cry not against the known neogrammarian rigidity — which was not the first kind of theoretical rigidity in the history of science — but against the whole neogrammarian conception, together with all its progressive features, especially its materialistic elements. What provoked the implacable struggle against the neogrammarian conception of phonetic law was not the suppression of the "conscious or at least half-conscious" activity but the inspirer of the idea of a blindly operating mechanism — natural-scientific materialism. The theory of "sound intention" reformulated by Laziczius is — as to its basic tone and arguments — only a moderate voice in the steady crescendo in which the neogrammarian theory of phonetic change was attacked. And the first militant participant of this offensive was Schuchardt.

If we look for the cause of Schuchardt's style and rigid subjectivism in his ideological stand, we will at once not find "in-

[50] Tamás: MNy XLIII (1947), pp. 92—102, 161—72.

343

credible"[51] the bunch of arguments and categorical statements underlying Schuchardt's theory of phonetic change. The smoke of incense of the absolutization of conscious or half-conscious efforts was meant to exorcize the devil of phonetic change taking place with natural-scientific necessity, in order to clear the hall of linguistics "stained" with materialistic ideas. The "blind wirkender Factor" was replaced by the language-shaping disposition of "great men endowed with linguistic talent", by their conscious activity and its conscious imitation, as the single explanatory principle (Puscarin, Jespersen, Menzerath and their followers). The essence of the turn was not new: the "dogmatic" extravagances of the neogrammarians were replaced by rigid dogmas grown out of the soil of subjectivism.

On the other hand, it followed necessarily from the nature of the disputes that the dogmas of the subjectivist linguistic theory initiated by Schuchardt could not be destroyed by a rigid formulation in a different direction, according to which "every explanation concerning a linguistic phenomenon which *assumes a conscious activity on the part of the speaker must be rejected in advance and considered invalid*".[52]

Tamás essentially accepts the position of Henry who defends the neogrammarian conception of phonetic change. Polemizing, and rightfully so, with the extremist subjectivists, he uses as a weapon the automatism of the speech act by further developing the mechanism theory of the neogrammarians, but he criticizes from this position of principle also all those views which admit the role of the conscious element, of the subjective intention, in the shaping of language, in the starting of phonetic changes. He disapproves the "sound intention" conception of the school of psychophonetics, criticizes Laziczius's pertinent views, and appealing to "sound-formation having the character of collective automatism" he states: "Automatism and intention being opposite, mutually exclusive factors, this conception obviously cannot be substantiated."[53] On the same basis he argues with the conception of G. Sebestyén, who in Menzerath's wake "speaks of a single articulation intention in connection with the word as a whole . . ., although it seems better to speak of a whole of automatic motion with a single start".[54] He criticizes also the neo-

[51] Loc. cit., p. 97.
[52] Quoted in Hungarian, with reference to V. Henry's book in question, by Tamás, loc. cit., p. 98.
[53] Loc. cit., p. 97.
[54] Ibid.

grammarian views regarding analogy and its function (a conscious psychic activity impeding the exceptionless operation of the phonetic laws), and accepts the opinion of those (P. G. Goidanich, Gy. Zolnai) who referred to the "automatic", "unexpected", "unconscious" nature of analogy.[55] He resolves the much debated pair of opposites "unconscious" — "conscious" in the "psychic automatism", "analogical automatism" by having recourse to Ch. Bally's and H. Frey's term *instinct analogique*.[56] He recognizes the "unmistakable traces of consciousness" only in the case of euphemisms and various bizarre fashions.[57]

Tamás explains the functioning of linguistic automatism by the general tendencies of automatism when he accepts A. Sommerfelt's pertinent opinion according to which "the general tendencies of automatism explain the facts which can be found in the phonetic changes of every language".[58] According to him, such a general mechanical "tendency" is the already cited Grammont law *(la loi du plus fort)* "in virtue of which it is always the sound which is stronger for mechanical, psychological or linguistic reasons that assimilates or dissimilates the weaker one".[59]

To the question of the disputed origin of sound changes he replies in these words: ". . . an 'individual' innovation awakens social response only if it accepts in advance the conditions rooted in the nature of collective automatism, if therefore it is not individual in this sense",[60] or more precisely, if it expressly denies the possibility of individual innovation, as evidenced by the following passage: "Since collective cultivation is by definition a social function, we have to say that a phonetic change can take place only if and when it is realized simultaneously by quite a few in the same linguistic community."[61]

By generalizing his position negating the possibility of the sound-changing function of consciousness, of the subjective element, he writes this: "It can be stated, however, that recently linguists almost unanimously adhere to the principle of unconsciousness, even though they do not always give more precise reasons for these views considered to be obviously natural."[62]

[55] Loc. cit., p. 98.
[56] Loc. cit., p. 99.
[57] Loc. cit., p. 96.
[58] *Journal de Psychologie* XXV, p. 660; quoted by Tamás, loc. cit., p. 96.
[59] Tamás, ibid.
[60] Loc. cit., p. 164.
[61] Ibid.
[62] Loc. cit., p. 98.

345

In his treatise under discussion Tamás displays principled determination in arguing with representatives of the subjectivist theory of phonetic change when he refreshes the essence of the pertinent neogrammarian view, developing it even further by making use of the results of recent psychological research. His treatise has the indisputable merit that it assails the subjectivist extravagances and again emphasizes an extremely important feature of linguistic changes—their objective character. But he also is caught in the tide of the polemical defence of the recognized partial truth and is prompted to make flat formulations. He also fails thereby to resolve the rigid antinomy of objective–subjective, unconsci–ousconscious and to close the debate dragging out for several decades. To his view formulated twenty years ago, that "linguists almost unanimously adhere to the principle of unconsciousness", let me add the following convincing lines from Bárczi's article referred to above: ". . . even if linguists[63] . . . refuse to take notice of it, the speaker himself certainly keeps evaluating, tries to make his speech clearer, more specific, more appealing, he makes his choice of linguistic tools, and this fact is one of the most important language-shaping forces which continually influences also the production of phonetic changes . . . every Hungarian is in his own speech and writing, in however modest a measure, a language-shaping factor".[64] R. Jakobson also calls attention to the role played by the purposive language-shaping tendencies of individuals in producing phonetic changes.[65] In recent Hungarian literature S. Károly often points to the importance of recognizing the subject, the conscious element, as a language-changing factor.[66]

The answer to the question ("Are phonetic changes conscious?") can thus be neither a categorical *yes* nor a categorical *no*. This is anyway borne out by the lessons of the periodically recurring battle between the alternatives polarized owing to the attractive or repelling power of the two extremist positions.

When recognizing the role of the appearance of diachronic phonology, its epochal importance for phonological research, we

[63] Here Bárczi has in mind, first of all, the neogrammarians and their followers.
[64] Bárczi: MNy LXII, pp. 132—3.
[65] *Selected Writings* I: Phonological Studies, s'Gravenhage, 1962, p. 17; ÁNyT III, pp. 241—2.
[66] S. Károly, *Általános és magyar jelentéstan* [General and Hungarian Semantics], Budapest, 1970, pp. 7, 177, 179, etc.

have to recognize at the same time that the physical-physiological explanatory principle has been superseded by the linguistic principle. On the other hand, the starting point of linguistic changes is the speech act of individuals, which means also recognition of a selective exploitation of the potentialities within definite limits, and even the disposition to conscious change, but also the possibility of such change. When the exact registration of the facts of linguistic (phonetic) changes is replaced by the demand for a planned investigation into the productive causes of changes, when therefore the spread of the causal principle characterizes the questions posed by historical phonology, it is impossible to neglect the role of subjective factors in the examination of the causes producing the changes. Let me add immediately that this stand does not mean that historical phonology can look for *only* subjective factors among the causes of phonetic changes (this would amount to the same mistake of which I have tried to give a critical illustration), but it means that the subjective factors cannot be neglected either beside the objectively determined factors.

In fact, the reason why the polemic in question came to a deadlock was that always extremes of "either-or" characterized the various stages of the dispute, that the debating parties firing at one another from the two poles forgot the truth that the social and at the same time individual processes of language are determined by the simultaneous contribution of objective and subjective factors.

The question arises why, in spite of the recognition of these evident-looking truths, the said irreconcilable polarization came about; or more clearly, why even Marxist linguistic literature had for a relatively long time neglected the investigation of the role of the subject; why the significance of the factors objectively determining the linguistic "behaviour" of *only* the subject was stressed, even in addition to the extent to which it was absolutely necessary to emphasize it against the subjective-idealist conceptions; why emphasis was placed *only* on the fact that man, the subject, is born into a linguistic situation determined by objective factors (which is beyond argument, indeed) and consequently can and even must *only* accommodate himself to the situation; and it was forgotten that the objectively determined linguistic situations had been created by men, who can for this very reason change it consciously, in accordance with the given requirements.

In my judgment the delay of the answer to the question can be explained if we view the problem as part of the general history of theories and take account of its particular features.

Until recently Marxist philosophy has failed to deal sufficiently with the role of the individuality. Apart from statements confined to generalities (recognition of the role of the individuality, including eminent personalities, in the development of society), the problem of the human individuum, of the personality, has not been examined in detail. Here again the old truth has prevailed: since Marxist theoreticians did not satisfactorily deal with the theoretical questions concerning the personality, some philosophical schools alien to Marxism have monopolized, as it were, the formulation of answers to these special questions *(Persönlichkeitstheorie)*, eliciting only a one-sided refusal from Marxists. Because people could not receive answers from elsewhere, they had to draw upon the said theories. It is a different question whether these theories were able to provide satisfying answers, but since there was no other answer, very many came under the influence of the diverse idealistic tendencies. It was no accident, for example, that the existentialist philosophy which became fashionable all over Europe, especially in intellectual circles, had such a great influence on the various literary currents and their reading public.

It would only be proper to ask why things went this way, why Marxist theoreticians joined in studying these problems with a considerable time lag. The answer was formulated by Schaff, who wrote in these terms:

"First of all, because the union of Marxism with the revolutionary labour movement made it imperative to concentrate upon the problem of the regularity of social evolution, the regularity of the transition to the socialist form of society and its construction; briefly, upon the problems related to movements and struggles of the masses.

"These practical, political interests of Marxism pushed the questions concerning the human individuum and his specific problems into the background."[67]

---

[67] "Vor allem, weil die Verbundenheit des Marxismus mit der revolutionären Arbeiterbewegung gebot, sich auf das Problem der Gesetzmäßigkeit der gesellschaftlichen Entwicklung zu konzentrieren, auf die Gesetzmäßigkeit des Überganges zur sozialistischen Gesellschaftsformation und auf deren Aufbau, kurz: auf die mit Bewegungen und Kämpfen der Massen verbundenen Probleme.

A realistic assessment of the role of the personality must be based on the relation, the interaction, of object and subject, which is possible only by solving the following contradictions: Can man as a social creature act at the same time creatively upon social life? Does not historical necessity set limits to the human individuum's displaying his activities freely? In other words (interpreted according to man's role played in linguistic changes): Is man a slave at the mercy of a socially determined linguistic situation, or can he produce a determining effect on the development of language; that is, how can the objective character of language, of linguistic changes, be reconciled with the idea of man's language-forming faculty?

In attempting to answer the above questions, we must not for a moment forget that language occupies a very important place among the factors causing the social determinedness of man, and this only enhances the significance of the relation of man to language. The only means of accumulating information about reality is language, which is at the same time a means of communicating socially gathered information. Consequently, language has a tremendous effect on the formation of the human psyche, from the "learning" of the meaning of the first word of childhood to the very high-level abstract operations, so much so that the system of language influences the system of thought, the way in which man sees the world (the function of language in the psychical reflection of the external world) and classes the particular phenomena of reality.[68]

"Die praktischen, politischen Interessen des Marxismus drängten die mit dem menschlichen Individuum und seinen spezifischen Problemen verbundenen Fragen in den Hintergrund." A. Schaff, *Marx oder Sartre?* *Versuch einer Philosophie des Menschen*, Vienna, 1964, p. 15.

[68] "Die Sprache ist so alt wie das Bewußtsein — die Sprache *ist* das praktische, auch für andre Menschen existierende, also auch für mich selbst existierende wirkliche Bewußtsein." K. Marx, F. Engels, *Die deutsche Ideologie: Kritik der neuesten deutschen Philosophie in ihren Repräsentanten, Feuerbach, B. Bauer und Stirner, und des deutschen Sozialismus in seinen verschiedenen Propheten*, Berlin, 1953², p. 27. — "The cognition of the objective world surrounding men is realized in a new form of psychical reflection, in language, in speech." Zs. S. Huck, A marxista tudatfelfogás néhány problémája [Some Problems of the Marxian Conception of Consciousness], *Magyar Filozófiai Szemle* X, 1966, pp. 128—49; loc. cit., p. 142. — "Сознание есть отражение действительности, как бы преломленное через призму общественно выработанных *языковых* значений, понятий." [Consciousness is a reflection of reality as refracted through a prism of socially processed *linguistic* meanings and notions.] А. Н. Леонтьев. *Проблемы развития психики* [Problems of the Development of Psychics], Moscow, 1965, p. 281.

From the point of view of social determinedness, however, man is not only a creature but also a creator *(homo agens)*; the human psyche not only reflects the phenomena of the external world, not only is it determined, but it also determines, being *"in charge of active pursuits"*.[69] Man not only adapts himself to objectively given situations (including the linguistic situation), but also makes use of them, and even transforms his environment, "rising above it", to the conscious satisfaction of his needs.[70]

Man's socially determined state does not mean that it precisely fixes, so to say from outside, every act of the individuum. Marxist determinism conceives of historical necessity not as a "blind force" which acts outside of men and independently of them: on the contrary, it considers it as a realization of human activity. As Schaff puts it: "History is made by men, but the actions and decisions of men are influenced by the conditions surrounding them and by the needs occasioned by these conditions. Nothing happens here outside of men, nor independently of them."[71]

Whoever fails to recognize this dialectical interaction in the relation between social determinedness and conscious human activity, to grasp its essence, can be a believer of either the most pessimistic sort of fatalism or the most subjective sort of idealism.

The conception of "objective" and "subjective" in this sense makes it possible to uncover the causes producing the processes of phonetic change, to grasp the essence of these processes, if we conceive of the linguistically determined nature of the subject as we have discussed its social determinedness.

The thought of "recognized necessity" as a guiding principle can protect against both subjectivist voluntarism and dogmatic fatalism. The dialectics of determinism and of the freedom of human activity may bring closer the end of the dispute over the concept of phonetic law and thereby an understanding of the essential features of linguistic laws.

---

[69] *Magyar Filozófiai Szemle* X, p. 139.
[70] Loc. cit., p. 137.
[71] "Die Geschichte wird von Menschen gemacht, aber die Handlungen und Entscheidungen der Menschen werden von den sie umgebenden Bedingungen und den durch diese Bedingungen hervorgerufenen Bedürfnissen beeinflußt. Nichts geschieht hier außerhalb der Menschen, noch unabhängig von ihnen." Schaff, op. cit., p. 86.

The principal lesson learned from the dispute going on with varying intensity for nearly a hundred years, and being revived (or rehashed) from time to time, is that the efforts exerted to uncover the essential traits of linguistic processes either sprang from the analogical compulsion of existing and supposed similarities and even identities (language is a living organism, the regularities of its processes—types of motion—entirely correspond to those of "other" natural processes) or recognized no similarity at all between regularities of linguistic and natural processes. In a more general way: the rigidity of "either-or" concealed a view which, on the one hand, thought that natural and social processes were identical in every detail and, on the other, cut a gap between the two kinds of process. Both modes of outlook, the one rooted in the theoretical views of positivism, social Darwinism, and the other built on the theoretical basis of neo-Kantianism, are contrary to the facts, to our up-to-date knowledge of the essential features of natural and social processes. In reality, namely, the correlation of nature and society displays the relation of identity and difference, owing to the simple fact that society, considering both its genesis and its existence, is an inseparable part of nature. The unity of nature and society, as conceived in the final analysis of natural and social processes, follows from the material unity of the world; this is ultimately reflected also by the main laws of materialist dialectics which, by dint of their general character, reflect the principal correlations of the natural and social and thought processes alike. This unity, however, does not mean perfect identity—society is not only *some* part of nature, but a *specific* part of it, "the highest form of motion".[72] This is just where there is an important philosophical innovation of Marxism, namely that it conceived of social motion as a specific process of natural history. From this conception it follows of necessity that one of the most characteristic features of the laws revealing the motives, the internal interrelatedness of this specific process of natural history, the social laws, is that they are operative owing to the action of men possessing consciousness and will, hence they are inseparably linked with the conscious human activity: "The life of society is inconceivable without thinking and acting men."[73]

Of course this conception does not mean that every kind of

[72] *Történelmi materializmus* [Historical Materialism], Budapest, 1964/1965, p. 52.
[73] Op. cit., p. 58.

individual action is "making law", nor that individual actions can rigorously be opposed to law. In fact, the law is ultimately realized in individual actions. But the law is law just because it not only manifests itself in the given individual actions, but is present and effective *"also in the social conditions and inter-relations, in the historical continuity"* of human actions.[74]

Just as it would be a mistake to construe an irreconcilable contradiction between the world processes of social history and nature, so also it would be incorrect not to take into consideration the relative difference existing within the fundamental unity.

If language is a product of society, being at the same time a specific formation of "natural history" creating society, then in discovering the regularities reflecting its internal interrelations and its motion we have to reckon with the above peculiarities of social laws because what in general applies to the totality of the forms of motion of society cannot be otherwise in the case of the forms of motion of language either. If we conceive of language not as a sovereign network of metaphysically isolated elements, but as a system based on the interdependence of phonemes, signs and symbolic associations, that is if we attribute sovereign existence to none of the language-forming factors, then and only then do we have the right—for the sake of a more thorough investigation—to draw from the results of our inquiry conclusions regarding general regularities of the forms of motion of language. In this and only in this sense can we—to avoid mistakes—speak of essential features of phonetic laws, of the laws reflecting adequately the movement of the phonemes, and accordingly make valid conclusions concerning the essential features of the linguistic laws.

I seek therefore to proceed by keeping permanently in view the correlation of the part and the whole, the drop and the sea, when I shall discuss only phonetic laws, "torn out of their interconnections", just in order that, in the light of and relying upon the conception of law taking shape as a result of the most recent researches, we might come closer to the conception of linguistic law destined to satisfy also the modern requirements.

The clarification of the concept of law is extremely important not only for the purpose of closing the unending dispute in a

[74] *Társadalmi Szemle* 1965/1, pp. 77—8.

reassuring manner, but also because the undecided question is still in our days a source of many misunderstandings. The "use of the term phonetic law"[75] not only gave rise to many misunderstandings and disputes in the periods of heated debates about the phonetic law, but as a result of misunderstandings and misinterpretations it was even proposed that we should not speak of phonetic laws, but only of tendencies of phonetic development, phonetic changes. Natural laws and social laws, the role of the object and the subject in the operation of social (linguistic) laws, the opposition of the terms law and tendency constitute the complex of questions which, I think, should be elucidated in order to get closer to a realistic picture of the determining features of linguistic laws.

8. THE CONCEPT OF LAW IN OUR DAYS

As opposed to the conception of all manner of idealist gnoseology traceable to the hypostasis of concepts in the Platonian ideology, a cardinal thesis of the Marxist theory of knowledge is that concepts are reflections of the reality existing outside and independently of consciousness, that mental reflection is only a more or less precise, an approximately true image of actual interrelations and processes. Since reflected reality is infinite, to speak about a total, adequate reflection of reality is a gnoseological absurdity, but this is not some sort of gnoseological pessimism, for the Marxist theory of knowledge, professing the knowability of the world, suggests just that the mental reflection of reality comes ever closer to the structures of actual interrelations and processes.

The concepts formed of reality, of its various segments, are always based on the body of knowledge of the given period. Just as knowledge about the particular momenta, processes and changes of reality is enlarged, so the content of the concepts is transformed and new concepts arise. Change in the content of concepts and the emergence of new concepts necessarily go with an uninterrupted growth of human knowledge. The most mobile and revolutionary elements of the concept embodied in the word are just the conceptual marks, which are always true mirrors of the collective body of knowledge, of the emotive-

[75] NyK XXIII, p. 452.

evaluative momenta, etc., and find room for a long time in the sound-form obtained with the birth of the new concept. This "elasticity" of the correlations of linguistic form and content marks is the starting point for explaining a very characteristic type of semantic change. The type of semantic change in question is the one in which the "social value" of the word undergoes a very considerable change, so that it can be turned inside out in the given social situation. Let us take the steep descent of the Hungarian words *úr* 'lord' and *asszony* 'lady': *Úristen* 'the Lord God', *király úr* 'Royal Majesty', *Miasszonyunk* 'Our Lady' $> < ez$ *olyan "úri" dolog* 'this is something the upper classes do' (with an extremely pejorative connotation), *jóasszony* 'silly woman',[1] and the ascending semantic development of *paraszt* 'peasant': *büdös paraszt* 'stinking boor' $>$ *munkás-paraszt hatalom* 'worker-peasant power'.

This feature of the content marks of concepts is characteristic not only of "common concepts", the same applies also to the so-called scientific terms and the semantic change of the established concepts (e.g., *atom* 'indivisible particle of matter' $>$ *atom* 'composite part of matter made up of divisible elementary particles').

An excellent example of the change in the content of concepts is the motion of the conceptual marks of *törvény* 'law', *törvény-szerűség* 'legality, regularity'. The concept 'law, legality' traceable to the primarily and fundamentally practical terms 'rule, regularity' of the science of the Orient of antiquity, as we have already seen above, sprang from the soil of mechanical materialism, found shape in the fundamental traits of natural law, and became a central category of the natural science of modern times, but enriched also all science of the times. The concept of natural law consummated in the teachings of Newton was used for centuries by classical physics, and the same concept figured also in the philosophy of the period (Locke, Hobbes, Spinoza, etc.). For all that, the idea of natural law that was understandably limited by the scientific knowledge of the period, and confined to the recognition of the mechanical forms of motion of nature, comprised the fundamental criteria which still today we take as the fundamental criteria of law.

[1] For more detail, cf. F. Kovács, *A magyar jogi terminológia kialakulása* [The Development of Hungarian Legal Terminology], Budapest, 1964, pp. 14—27.

The so-called "physical revolution" that began around the turn of the twentieth century shook the supposedly "fixed points" of classical physics based on the regularities of the mechanical forms of motion. At the same time the evolutionism of Darwinian biology added new colours to the determining marks of the concept of natural law. Accordingly the concept of natural law based on the theses of classical mechanics was transformed.

The new concept thus formed was in many respects different from the Newtonian type. Again it was a known consequence of the metamorphosis of the concept of natural law, including chiefly also the material doctrine ("matter has disappeared") of the so-called scientific revolution, that the currents of idealistic philosophy gathered a new impetus in their struggle against the philosophical doctrines of materialistic inspiration, launching a concentrated attack against the philosophical concept law reflecting the most general interrelations of reality, the objective-causal interdependence of its internal processes.

It is no accidental phenomenon of the history of science, but an unavoidable concomitant of the transformation of the concept law, that also the struggle against the neogrammarian concept of law intensified in this "scientific environment". It is not difficult to see the common theoretical basis, on the one hand, of Schuchardt's implacable, and sometimes ironical, hostility towards the phonetic law and, on the other, of the idealistic philosophical interpretations distorting the essence of the new scientific discoveries of the physical revolution. That is where the theoretical roots of what is called Vosslerism are to be found.

All this does not mean, of course, that the mechanistic conception of law of modern times was fundamentally erroneous, that the scientific laws of the period wrongly reflected the regular interrelations of reality. In the course of scientific cognition, understandably, it is the "most conspicuous" dominant interrelations of material reality, its regular momenta, that become known and are reflected in the "collective consciousness" and are formulated in the laws of science.[2] The law crystallized on the

---

[2] Literature distinguishes the concepts of *law* and *regularity*. By regularity is meant the objective interrelatedness of nature and society, while by law is meant "the scientific theorem, the theory, which expresses and reflects it and is mostly mathematically formulated". Gy. Nádor, *A természettörvény fogalmának kialakulása* [Evolution of the Concept of Natural Law], Budapest, 1957, p. 19. — Likewise Erdey-Grúz makes a dis-

basis of the Newtonian world outlook reflected these most conspicuous traits of the forms of motion of matter, the mechanical form of motion, and considered them to be the most characteristic features of matter.

With the enlargement of knowledge the less conspicuous interrelations of matter were also cleared up, the essential traits

---

tinction between the two concepts and says that their use as synonyms is a confusion of ideas due to slipshodness. T. Erdey-Grúz, *A világ anyagi szerkezete* [The Material Structure of the World], Budapest, 1965, p. 169. This author speaks in this sense also about "the establishment of a law". Op. cit., p. 174. — Considering that the scientific public does not regard the difference between the two concepts as positive and final, I for my part use only the term *law*, applied to the objective interrelatedness of both natural and social processes, as well as to the scientific notions reflecting them, by distinguishing them through special qualifiers (*natural law, law of natural science*, etc.). Of course I do not wish thereby to close the terminological dispute. The writer of the relevant entry in ÉrtSz (obviously a philosopher) defines the two concepts just the other way round, differently from the above definitions. Accordingly, *törvény* ('law') is "A permanent and absolute connection, relation between phenomena of the objective world independent of human consciousness; a regularity prevailing in the process of the phenomena" (item 7 under *törvény*). If we compare this to what we find under *törvényszerűség* ('regularity'), the confusion will only grow further, because there we can read about "*unfixed law*": "A consistent normality uniformly prevailing in observed similar phenomena under similar conditions, a law which is usually not settled, not fixed yet with absolute certainty." The permanent and absolute connection that exists independently of human consciousness between phenomena of the objective world, the conformity *(law)* prevailing in the process of the phenomena, must not and cannot be settled, it is objectively given; if we settle it, if we uncover it, we are already faced not with laws of objective reality but with laws of science. Besides, the expression 'establishment of a law' has a rather voluntaristic look and is heavy with diverse ideological loads. In spite of all this — mainly in works on natural science and mathematics—we often encounter expressions like "*establishment of a law*", "*application of different laws*", etc. (See, for example, Kiefer's conception of law discussed above.) If, therefore, I use hereinafter the "unitary" term *law* to denote the objective interrelatedness of nature and society as well as "specific scientific notions", it is always to be understood that the latter are approximately precise reflections of the former. The subjective here should be construed as the mental reflection of objective reality. Cf. "*objective law*", "*reflected law*"; the first is "*a law of nature* as a real part of the objective regular interrelation of natural phenomena", and the second is "*a law of science, a law of natural science* as the reflection of natural laws in human consciousness in form of specific concepts". B. M. Kedrov, *A természettudományok tárgya és kölcsönös kapcsolata* [The Subject of the Natural Sciences and Their Interrelation], Budapest, 1965, p. 60; cf. also *Magyar Filozófiai Szemle* X, 1966, p. 504.

of the so-called basic forms of motion were also discovered; and since they could no longer be described by the "classical" laws of natural science, it became necessary to "modernize" them, to "adjust" them to the regularities uncovered by the recent scientific results. This does not involve, for example, the overthrow of the "classical" law of the change of physical state which says that water boils at 100° C under the pressure of one atmosphere, that it passes from one state into another; that under different conditions the phenomenon takes place differently, but in a way clearly determined by the new conditions (for example, the boiling point rises with the increase of pressure). This physical law even today reflects rightly *one* of the forms of motion of matter, the objective pattern of the change of physical state taking place at the ordinary temperature and pressure, but this is an infinitesimal part of the very complex forms of motion of matter. Only let us stick to the aforementioned example. Besides the three classical physical states, natural science today already knows about several different kinds, the so-called "degenerated states" existing under extreme circumstances: the state developing at high temperature, the quantum gas state and the superfluid state observed at low temperature, the degenerated solid state obtaining at extremely high pressures.[3] All we come to see therefore—but this is not negligible—is that the scientific law about the "degenerated state" reflects more truly the objective interrelations, the objective laws of nature which existed even before they had been discovered by the searching mind. In general, the more that human knowledge penetrates the "tangle" of the complex forms of motion of reality, and the more fully it is able to uncover their internal interrelatedness, the more it will be necessary to change the internal content of old concepts and laws, to replace them, under the given conditions, with new ones.

Does all this mean that—on the basis of the recent scientific results—we have to give up the fundamental categories of the natural-scientific concept of law based on materialism, the world outlook that professes natural determinism, the objective causality, the objective necessity of nature, or at least we have to

[3] P. Rádi, Kísérlet a mozgásformák rendszerének korszerű leírására [Attempt at an Up-to-date Description of the System of Forms of Motion]. *Magyar Filozófiai Szemle* XI/3, pp. 369—406; loc. cit., p. 382; cf. also Erdey-Grúz, op. cit., pp. 31—40.

speak about the "degeneration" of these categories? Of course, this is not the point. The new natural-scientific achievements do not challenge the existence of the fundamental categories, but they contest their inflexibility based on previous defective knowledge. The dispute about the modern concept of law has delved into many categories, only in order to make them clearer, stricter — or, if you like, more elastic. In other words, the debate was characterized by a striving to refine the categories in order that the "modernized" scientific categories might approximate more, and reflect, the forms of motion of the real processes.

Let us think of one of the cardinal theses of the classical concept of natural law, the interpretation of causality: if the objective conditions are given, the expected phenomenon must occur "with blind necessity, without exceptions". As we have seen, this teaching inspired also the neogrammarian postulate of phonetic law.

The modern natural-scientific discoveries do not hammer the bulwarks of causality, but they contest the principle of absolute and exceptionless laws. The natural scientist often faces *also* phenomena which do not fit in with the absolute character of the classical change of physical state which, in general, do not meet the requirements that might be expected according to classical (Laplacian) determinism. (The improvement of methods, the formulation of the laws of nature with the exactness of mathematical formulae make possible a clear-cut prediction of the course of events and processes.) In studying the processes of the microcosm one often comes across phenomena which "show that classical determinism not only does not correspond to the laws of nature, but it does not make it possible either to define them precisely enough".[4] The extent of differences between specific mechanical motion and "specific nuclear motion" is described by Erdey-Grúz as follows: "Within the atomic nucleus the laws of motion of matter differ from the laws applicable to macroscopic bodies to such an extent that the latter do not even present us with an approximately true picture of reality."[5]

---

[4] V. A. Fok, A kvantummechanika interpretációjáról [Interpreting Quantum Mechanics]. Published in the volume *A modern természettudományok filozófiai problémái* [Philosophical Problems of the Modern Natural Sciences], Budapest, 1962, pp. 265—93; loc. cit., p. 285.

[5] Erdey-Grúz, op. cit., p. 189.

A characteristic trait of these phenomena is that—as is expressed in the language of mathematics—"in the presence of a certain complex C of conditions *the phenomenon may or may not take place*".[6] The mathematicians call such phenomena stochastic (στοχαστικος), which otherwise may be called "accidental".[7]

Natural science examines the accidental character of mass phenomena, not of individual ones. The disintegration of the atoms of radioactive elements, for instance, is an accidental mass phenomenon: whether or not *one* atom disintegrates under the given circumstances in a specified time cannot be predicted, it is accidental. It can, however, be calculated in advance what proportion approximately of a specified quantity of a radioactive element will disintegrate. The fact is, namely, that—as to the number of disintegrated atoms—minor differences can be observed from the law describing the speed of disintegration.[8]

Thus the rigid formulae of classical determinism are increasingly superseded by formulations where exceptionlessness is replaced by the probability character of description, according to which a distinction is made between what is potentially possible and what is actually realized. This means at the same time making precise the concept of causality, in as much as—in the stated conception—it applies directly to probability, "consequently to potentially possible events, but not to events which actually took place".[9]

To avoid misunderstandings (for such things still exist!), it is necessary to note that such a formulation of causality does not mean that the so-called stochastic phenomena have no direct productive causes. Nothing of the kind. The stochastic phenomena and events are also causally determined. The phenomena classed in the "accidental" category also have their causes, but these are outside the "complex C" of the conditions considered, either because—owing to their unimportant role—they are negligible in the mesh of the multiplicity and complexity of causes, or because we still do not know these existing and effective causes. Implied in this formulation of the necessary and the accidental is also the fact that what is realized and what

[6] I. Ruzsa, *Matematika* [Mathematics], Budapest, 1966, II, p. 321.
[7] Ibid.
[8] Op. cit., p. 324.
[9] Fok, loc. cit., p. 285.

is not, out of the potentially possible events, under the given circumstances, is independent of our consciousness (objective character).

"At a more searching examination most causal phenomena of the natural sciences appear stochastic", writes Ruzsa. Then he proceeds: "This is understandable, for in nature really everything is related to everything: consideration of all causes is therefore impossible."[10] And as Erdey-Grúz puts it: *"The necessary . . . usually becomes visible through accidents.* Accidental events, however, are not exceptions to the law[11] but are caused by incidental interactions disregarded (deliberately or, because of defective knowledge, under compulsion for the time being) in the law. In this sense the law includes also the accidental events."[12]

Realization and recognition of the dialectical correlation of the necessary and the accidental is of primary importance from a theoretical point of view but no less so from the point of view of the construction of the modern concept of law. This is the very conception that separates us from the causal conception of metaphysical materialism and of idealism: the first takes all causes to be equally important, it does not distinguish between essential and unessential; the second negates the causal dependence of the accidental. The theoretical significance of the accidental is clearly exemplified by the fact that the investigation of the objective regularities of accidental mass phenomena belongs in the province of a separate branch of mathematics, the calculus of probability.

The significance of the most recent natural-scientific discoveries related to the different forms of motion of the complicated structure of the microcosm was recapitulated by S. T. Melyukhin, from the point of view of causal correlations, as follows: "In a general way, the deeper we penetrate into the structure of matter, the more we happen to meet with an endless multitude of processes, and the more striking is their unspecified, probability character. Accordingly the variety of the behavioural possibilities of the micro-objects is growing uninterruptedly, while in the act of interplay always only an insignificant part of the mass of possibilities turns into reality."[13]

---

[10] Ruzsa, op. cit., p. 323.
[11] Thus, according to Erdey-Grúz: the laws of science.
[12] Erdey-Grúz, op. cit., pp. 178—9.
[13] S. T. Melyukhin, *A szervetlen természet fejlődési dialektikája* [Dialectics of the Development of Inorganic Nature], Budapest, 1963, p. 222.

The findings of quantum mechanics and in general the most recent results of natural science concerning the content elements of older scientific notions made it imperative to perform philosophical generalizations which can and must be deduced from the results.

This task urged, first and foremost, the re-examination of a central category of science, the concept law, because—as we have seen—the laws formulated on the basis of the results of classical physics can no longer explain the newly uncovered facts, and "do not even present us with an approximately true picture of reality".

More and more coming to the fore in the philosophical literature of recent years is the realization that the general character of the scientific law is "mostly inconsistent with all variants of a given phenomenon which present a structure that is not plain but complex".[14] In order to solve the arising contradiction it has become necessary "to proceed from the abstract general towards the concrete general, to explicate from the abstract regularity the whole circle of the subordinated regularities which clarify the complex phenomena, the entire variational province of phenomena".[15] Relying on the categories of the old concept of law alone, it is impossible to iron out the contradiction of the complex structure of general and individual phenomena, and this very reason has made it inevitable to reformulate the concept of law, to evolve, to "establish", a conception of law of the kind which is a more approximative reflection of the recently discovered regularities of the forms of motion of objective phenomena and processes.

In the philosophical literature of our days we can read about two kinds of law, more precisely two aspects of the law, called dynamic and statistical laws. The dynamic laws are those which "are precisely describable by means of classical physics".[16] On the other hand, the statistical laws are those "in which the function of probability is essential, which consequently are made up not (or not only) of precise relationships, and thus, a role is

---

[14] J. Szigeti, Ismeretelméleti-módszertani megjegyzések [Comments on Gnoseological Methodology]. *Magyar Filozófiai Szemle* VIII, pp. 819—40; loc. cit., p. 830.
[15] Ibid.
[16] J. Fodor, Dinamikus és statisztikai törvények [Dynamic and Statistical Laws]. *Magyar Filozófiai Szemle* X, pp. 488—506; loc. cit., p. 488.

played in them also by accident (which, in accordance with the classical view, is usually excluded from the definition of dynamic law)".[17]

Keeping in view the absolute ("regular") predictability of the process, some attach to the dynamic laws a predeterministic character; what is more, Sh. Amsterdamski describes the relations called dynamic laws as deterministic laws.[18] So-called classical physics knew only such laws.

For the purpose of clarifying the relationship of the two kinds of law, attempts were made to reduce the statistical laws to the dynamic ones, and the former were even considered secondary as compared to the latter. In our days, on the other hand, it is an increasingly accepted opinion that what is characteristic of the laws of nature is rather that they are statistical in character; consequently modern science operates primarily with statistical laws, because these are "more widely applicable instruments of the description of nature than are the dynamic laws".[19]

In the objective processes, however, the dynamic and statistical regularities appear always together; to stress or separate one or another of them is possible only because also in the processes now one and now another of them comes to the forefront or falls into the background: "The separation of the dominant and inferior aspects, the absolutization of either the dynamic or the statistical character, however, is carried out by man, and therefore ontologically—in terms of objective determinedness—it is wrong to speak of (purely) dynamic and (purely) statistical laws."[20]

When we speak of statistical and dynamic laws, therefore, the attributes basically refer to the laws of science which, in the process of human cognition, always reflect the laws of reality, the actual interrelations, only with approximative accuracy, since they are subjective copies of various segments of the complicated reality reflected in the human mind. The statistical and dynamic laws—as laws of science—are two aspects of the objective interrelatedness of material reality and display the opposition of general character and concreteness: the generality of the law is statistical in character with regard to the individual,

[17] Loc. cit., pp. 488—9.
[18] *Magyar Filozófiai Szemle* IX, p. 672.
[19] Fodor, loc. cit., p. 489.
[20] Loc. cit., p. 505.

it refers to the accidentality of the individual phenomena. At the same time the law has to reflect also the indissoluble connection with the individual phenomena, because the general exists in the individual phenomena, and only in them (dynamic character). In this sense (contradictoriness being dissolved in a dialectical unity) we can speak of the dynamic and statistical character of the laws of science.

In the phenomena described by statistical laws the result of an effect exerted on the object is no unambiguous change but what is called dispersion: it shows only the probability of change, a whole gamut of possible changes, and this throws a different light also upon the causality theory based on classical determinism. According to this, the dispersion of the expected or expectable succession of events is objectively determined (regularity). Determinedness of the several elements of the expected succession of events is out of the question: "... a statistical regularity", writes Melyukhin, "expresses a form of causality where the initial state of the system determines the subsequent states not in an unambiguous way but with a certain measure of probability, and here the probability itself is an objective yardstick of the possible realization of the given future state."[21]

M. E. Omelyanovsky describes the statistical laws as follows: the statistical law is realized "only as a dominant tendency, as a necessity forcing its way through a multitude of accidents and manifesting itself in these accidents, as the mean value of a great number of accidents".[22] When emphasizing the tendency character of the concept of statistical law reflecting the complicated interactions of reality with approximate precision, Fodor states: "That the tendency character of the law is dominant in microdomains can cause problems only to the logic based on (classical) physical thought, for the domains of reality are characterized rather by such complicated interactions; only in a few specialized domains are there groups of phenomena in which the interactions can clearly be separated into essential internal and negligibly unessential external factors."[23]

[21] Melyukhin, op. cit., p. 221.
[22] M. E. Omelyanovsky, V. I. Lenin és a modern fizika filozófiai problémái [V. I. Lenin and Philosophical Problems of Modern Physics]. A modern természettudományok filozófiai problémái, pp. 47—119; loc. cit. p. 87.
[23] Fodor, loc. cit., p. 503.

9. SOCIAL LAWS, LINGUISTIC LAWS

If we put the question as to what conclusions can and must be made, on the basis of the modern concept of natural law built on the most recent results of natural science, about the peculiarities of the concept of social law, inclusive mainly of linguistic law, we have to proceed from the fundamental ontological thesis that society and in it man himself are part of nature taken in the broader sense, because the different domains of reality picture different forms of motion of matter. That is exactly why the qualitatively different domains of an infinitely manifold world ultimately display congruent features, identical or similar structures. "This is", writes Klaus, "what enables us to find the models of one domain in another domain as well."[1] From the models of natural science we can thus draw conclusions applicable also to the domain of the social sciences. Only we have to bear in mind that in the social processes, in the scientific laws which reflect them, "the particular, the individual, . . . as against the general, is of much greater importance than in the realm of nature".[2] Klaus states as a general law: "The higher the stage of development of matter (the higher the form of motion) in question, the greater is the weight of the particular, the individual, against the general."[3] This statement follows of necessity from the almost commonplace thesis that society itself is also a product of material reality, but what is usually not taken into due consideration is that society is not only an organic part of nature but it rises from it and reacts upon it by conscious action, as it "creates" an artificial image of nature, producing a cultural scenery, a cultural sphere. "As this relative rising of society from nature takes place", writes Rádi, "so the active and purposive reaction of man upon nature, upon the geographical blanket, becomes visible. This interaction of society and nature brings about the artificial nature."[4] In respect to its genesis, therefore, society rises from biological forms of motion but, as regards its existence, is qualitatively different. The evolution of living creatures leads by a tremendous leap to the evolution of man,

---

[1] G. Klaus, *Bevezetés a formális logikába* [Introduction to Formal Logic], Budapest, 1963, p. 348.
[2] Ibid.
[3] Ibid.
[4] P. Rádi, *Kísérlet a mozgásformák rendszerének korszerű leírására* [Attempt at an Up-to-date Description of the System of Forms of Motion]. *Magyar Filozófiai Szemle* XI/3, pp. 369−406; loc. cit., p. 385.

just as the development of biocoenosis leads to the formation of society.

When therefore we compare the laws of nature with the laws of society and establish the extent of isomorphism between them, we have always to bear in mind the qualitative differences between them.

In grasping the characteristic features of social laws we have to start from Engels's idea—which is formulated in his work *Dialektik der Natur* and whose principles have been lucidly proved by scientific results—that the material world is an involved system of qualitatively different forms of motion and of structures "underlying them". The closed system of the material world shows the dialectics of identity and difference. Engels divided the many forms of motion of the material world into five kinds of so-called basic forms of motion (physical, chemical, biological, conscious, social).

On the basis of the scientific results of the nearly eighty years that have passed since that time, newer tentative classifications distinguish six to eight kinds, and most recently there has been talk about classes of forms of motion instead of basic forms of motion.
Mention is made of the possibility of distinguishing three classes of forms of motion:
(a) the class of chemicophysical forms of motion (non-living or inorganic nature);
(b) the class of biological forms of motion;
(c) the class of social forms of motion.[5]
According to this division the different classes of forms of motion include different kinds of motion, they are "constructed" of them (mechanical, chemical, metabolic, sensation, language, thought, etc.). One kind of motion may belong to more than one form of motion; the kinds of motion characterizing the lower forms of motion are as a rule included among the higher ones.[6]

---

[5] Rádi, loc. cit., p. 370; В. М. Букановский, *Принципы черты классификации современного естествознания* [Principles of the Line of Classification of Modern Natural Science], 1960, ch. IV; J. Horváth, A világ anyagi egységének helyes felfogásához [On the Right Conception of the Material Unity of the World]. *Magyar Filozófiai Szemle* VI/1, pp. 21—33; loc. cit., p. 27.
[6] Rádi, loc. cit., p. 388.

The threefold classification of the forms of motion (their sequence is designed to demonstrate also their hierarchical succession) seems to show the qualitative differences between the different forms of motion (non-living, living, social) more plastically than did the former classifications.

Non-living nature is characterized by a "particular complex" of chemical and physical forms of motion.

In living organisms there appear, besides the kinds of (chemical, physical, etc.) motion of non-living nature, also qualitatively new specific kinds of motion characteristic of life (metabolism, reproduction, sensation, activities observed with animals of higher order, etc.), which are subject to new regularities. With a view to maintaining and continually regenerating its own internal equilibrium, the living organism reacts to the changes of its environment by making expedient changes in its own position or state (motions of a teleological character which do not exist in non-living nature). These expedient motions are called also functions. Biological expediency is not a sort of category that is introduced from outside into the living organism (idealist teleology), but self-determinedness, or adaptability, formed in the course of evolution and conditioned by the environment and structure of the organism, i.e. an objective category.[7]

In the class of the social forms of motion—in addition to those mentioned—again there are qualitatively new forms of motion (labour, production, thought, language, motion of the elements of the basis and the superstructure, etc.). The expediency typical of the specifically biological forms of motion here is promoted to purposiveness, which is precisely a distinct peculiarity of the social forms of motion.[8]

Consequently, every form of motion is a complex phenomenon, a complex of different kinds of motion. "The form of motion is always the motion of some structure and at the same time the structure of different motions."[9]

If we want to determine the role of society, of man, in the tangle of the different forms and kinds of motion of material reality, we have to define it as part of nature taken in the broader sense, and to underline the priority of external nature, but this makes sense only if we regard man as being distinct from nature.[10]

[7] Loc. cit., p. 392.
[8] Ibid.
[9] Loc. cit., p. 395.
[10] "Allerdings bleibt dabei die Priorität der äußeren Natur bestehen,

"The human organism is . . . the most highly organized member of the evolutionary series of individual structures, and society is that of a series of collective structures."[11]

The definition of consciousness in the light of the system of the forms of motion sketched above is: *"Consciousness is a peculiar aspect of the mode of existence of human organization (society), such a complex kind of motion, such a functional structure of peculiar motions linked to the brain, which is capable of presenting an immensely deepening reflection of the phenomena and essential interconnections of reality, and of guiding man's purposive action corresponding to the reflected objective relationships and manifesting itself also in their expedient transformation."*[12]

The dialectics of social determinism and conscious human action, of necessity and freedom, in the projection of the peculiarities of the social forms of motion is defined as follows: "The complexity and the high order of the class of the social forms of motion lie precisely in the qualitative diversity, in the complicated and supreme character and interaction of the specific kinds of motion characteristic of that class. These properties make possible, with the evolution of man and society, *the emergence of a form of determinism in which freedom, the capability for active self-determination and for the active and conscious reflection of the world can reach a new level never before approached in any other domain of nature."*[13]

On the basis of what has been said it becomes possible to remove all that rigidity which characterized the earlier conception of law. It is possible to get a reassuring answer to those questions of detail posed by the protracted dispute which appeared in the interpretation of the objective character of law, if we accept the construction according to which the objective character of laws "most generally means that the laws are, in their primary, real nature, substantial determinednesses of material reality",[14] and if, besides, we take into account the quali-

---

und allerdings hat dies alles keine Anwendung auf die ursprünglichen, durch generatio aequivoca [Urzeugung; Entstehung organischer Wesen aus anorganischen Stoffen] erzeugten Menschen; aber diese Unterscheidung hat nur insofern Sinn, als man den Menschen als von der Natur unterschieden betrachtet." Marx–Engels, *Die deutsche Ideologie*, p. 42.

[11] Rádi, loc. cit., p. 402.

[12] Ibid.

[13] Ibid.

[14] *Társadalmi Szemle* 1964/12, p. 91.

tative difference existing between laws of nature and society as to their objective character. Well, as is commonly known, the gnoseological roots of the objectivist distortion of the social laws are to be found in the fact that the distortionists conceived the objective character as "a natural determinedness independent of human relations", in which the greatest mistake was "the disruption of the material, practical activity of the social laws and men, the opposition of the regular determinednesses of social processes to the historical role of human activity".[15] According to this conception "the masses . . . not only carry out and serve the laws which are independent of them, but . . . they degrade the 'crystal-clear' requirement of law to a tendency. In this conception it is not the scientific law that is 'narrow, incomplete, approximative', but the phenomenal world which only approaches the law as a 'true' reality".[16]

On the other hand, as we have seen, both in nature and in society the laws usually become operative as tendencies, that is in an approximate manner, in the form of statistical averages. Because material reality is of the most diverse kind, its forms of motion influence one another, the several laws are not isolated from one another, they are in interaction, they strengthen or weaken—in certain circumstances even can wholly neutralize—one another's functioning and operation. In addition to all this, the operation of the laws of society is influenced by many other circumstances, including the fact that they are an involved network of conscious human aspirations, come about as a result of the collision of different intentions, and can be construed as their resultant. Nevertheless, "the tendencylike operation of the laws cannot be regarded as a sort of exclusive social peculiarity".[17]

The tendency is the outward form of the law, the realization of its effect. Marx uses them as synonyms when he speaks metaphorically of "the natural laws of capitalist production", that is, of the "tendencies working with iron necessity towards inevitable results".[18]

[15] Loc. cit., pp. 91, 92.
[16] Loc. cit., p. 101.
[17] Történelmi materializmus [Historical Materialism], p. 59.
[18] K. Marx, Capital, New York, n. d., Vol. I, p. 13.

10. PHONETIC LAW OR SOUND-CHANGING TENDENCY?

This formulation of the question, together with the answer given to it, is the alternative at the last stage of the dispute about the phonetic law.

We can decide the justification of this alternative, in my opinion, by probing into the peculiar marks of the general concept of law based on the essential features of the modern law of nature. More precisely, if we accept Rádi's classification of the forms of motion (language is one of the kinds of motion classed among the social forms of motion),[1] we have to start from the peculiarities of the laws of society.

The terms law and tendency are used in different ways in the technical literature both abroad and in Hungary. For instance, E. Gamilscheg[2] treats the two terms as synonyms when the development is different, but he gives the name "Entwicklungstendenzen" to the motives producing cases of identical types. The same applies to V. Brøndal.[3]

In one of his works L. Deme also refers to the lack of uniform usage: ". . . in general usage the word tendency at times denotes laws of development and at other times general laws hidden behind similar processes of development."[4] He himself uses the two terms as synonyms: ". . . tendencies . . . are those general characteristics of a dialect which are hidden behind the various phenomena as common regularities."[5] He speaks in this sense about "concentration into tendencies", by which he means the grasping of the essential interrelations.[6] So far this is clear and unambiguous. The technical term tendency completely covers the conceptual marks of law taken in the present sense. The trouble begins when "the particular regular sound correspondences" are called by him "parts" or "members", "quasi out-

---

[1] P. Rádi, Kísérlet a mozgásformák rendszerének korszerű leírására [Attempt at an Up-to-date Description of the System of Forms of Motion]. *Magyar Filozófiai Szemle* XI/3, pp. 369—406; loc. cit., p. 393.

[2] E. Gamilscheg, *Die Sprachgeographie*, Leipzig, 1928, pp. 15—16.

[3] V. Brøndal, *Substrat et emprunt en roman et en germanique*, Copenhague–Bucureşti, 1948, pp. 73—4.

[4] L. Deme, A magyar nyelvjárások néhány kérdése [Some Questions of the Hungarian Dialects], NytudÉrt I, 1953, p. 102.

[5] Ibid.

[6] Loc. cit., p. 103.

ward forms" of the tendency.[7] As a matter of fact, the tendency—as we still shall come to speak about it later—is the outward form of the law, its realization. The confusion is only increased by the fact that further on in his study, at variance with the above-cited phrases, the word tendency is approximating to its everyday usage. To dissociate himself from Bárczi's conception (see below), Deme writes the following: "The tendency therefore, in our opinion, is not a process of change that takes place once, nor is it a cause of it; but it is *in its function the endeavour* of the dialect to choose consistently one of the manifold possibilities of development."[8] It does not at all help to clear the picture that later on he again identifies the tendencies of diachronic processes with the law: "The tendency as an internal law of development of the dialect."[9]

The contradictory character of Deme's conception of tendency, the rigid formulation of some of his assertions, was pointed up also by L. Benkő in his introductory lecture at the debate organized by the Main Committee on Linguistics of the Hungarian Academy of Sciences.[10] Besides, L. Benkő puts the word tendency between quotation marks.[11] His following lines do not betray that he would fully agree: "In our recent literature on phonology it is much in fashion to class phonetic changes of major extent among the so-called tendencies."[12]

J. Berrár criticizes the neogrammarian fetish of phonetic law with wise moderation, by adducing telling examples from the Hungarian and foreign languages.[13] In a sketchy summary of recent research in historical phonetics, she succinctly refers to the intertwining character of the productive causes of sound changes (phonetic position, stress conditions, assimilation, dissimilation, less frequently semantic factors; she makes no mention of the role of subjective factors), and sets elastic limits in time and place to the phonetic changes. She opposes the rigid

[7] Loc. cit., p. 102.
[8] Loc. cit., p. 133.
[9] Title of chapter. Loc. cit., p. 137.
[10] L. Benkő, Megjegyzések Deme Lászlónak A magyar nyelvjárások néhány kérdése című tanulmányához [Remarks on László Deme's Treatise Entitled "Some Questions of the Hungarian Dialects"], IOK VII, pp. 500—523.
[11] Pais-Eml, p. 81.
[12] Loc. cit., p. 86.
[13] Zs. Telegdi, *Bevezetés a nyelvtudományba* [Introduction to Linguistics], Budapest, 1963, II, pp. 73—82.

neogrammarian schema by the dynamic conception of the process of such changes. Namely, according to the neogrammarians, a specific sound of a given language in identical phonetic position changes in an identical way and at the same speed; the sound being in an appropriate phonetic position changes simultaneously in every word in the speech of the inhabitants of the given language area: the change starts and ends everywhere at the same time. On the other hand, the facts of language indicate—even if we examine only the unrounding of the vowels of Old Hungarian—that a certain sound change begins in the usage of some speakers, and the changed sound will for a while coexist with its "unchanged ancestor". Well discernible morphological doublets come about this way: *fuk ∼ fok* 'degree', *bukur ∼ bokor* 'bush', *Bolatin ∼ Balatin*, etc. In the competition of doublets usually the newer, the unrounded type of vowel survives,[14] unless it is prevented by some opposite agency (intermingling of dialects, influence of the surrounding sounds, occasionally the preservative force of meaning and often even the force of analogy).

This is a clear, unambiguous and convincing explanation. Its convincing nature is enhanced just by the generalization resulting from the manifold, "dynamic" examination of the linguistic facts. This conception of the start and process of phonetic changes is really apt to explain the bounds and limits of the operation of the general laws of phonetic development, the exceptions to the general line of development, and even the possibility of a course of development in the opposite direction (*onoka ∼ unoka* 'grandchild', *ozsonna ∼ uzsonna* 'afternoon snack', etc.). But it is hard to accept that from all this one may—and even must—draw the conclusion that "instead of phonetic laws we can today speak rather only of sound-changing tendencies".[15]

It is difficult to understand what is the difference of principle between historical phonetics and synchronic phonological investigation, of which Telegdi himself states that although it "is not based on the historical view, . . . yet it is indisputably a science".[16] And if we look at what provides the scientific stamp for the discipline which "is not based on the historical view", we can see that it nevertheless is a science, because it uncovers "the

---

[14] Already Simonyi drew attention to this "duel", and even pointed out that some dialects preserved the older form with the close vowel: *kokas ∼ kakas* 'cock', *magos ∼ magas* 'high', etc. Nyr VIII, p. 486.

[15] Telegdi, op. cit., p. 78.

[16] ÁNyT I, p. 7.

order hidden behind the phenomena, the laws of phenomena".[17] Is there no order hidden behind phonetic changes? Or if there is some kind of order, is it only a tendency because it does not work with absolute effect, because there are exceptions to it, and can even an opposite "tendency" work? Berrár does not spell this out, but it seems obvious that something like this trend of thought made her also degrade the phonetic laws to "mere" sound-changing tendencies.

To contest the existence of phonetic laws, G. Bárczi and P. Hajdú resort to arguments of the same kind and, for this very reason, use instead of phonetic law the term *tendencies of phonetic development* or *regular phonetic changes*. "These tendencies", writes Bárczi, "sometimes produced complete, one-hundred-per-cent results, that is they took place in all cases . . . At other times . . . they were accomplished only in the overwhelming part of cases. Owing to this high degree of regularity they were previously called *phonetic laws*, and this technical term is still often encountered in today's literature."[18] He has entirely good reasons to contest the validity of the views according to which the phonetic laws, just like the laws of nature, are operating without exception. He writes: "They were considered exceptionless, effective in all cases."[19] From a comparison with the laws of nature (at a pressure of one atmosphere water always and everywhere boils at 100° C) he draws a conclusion against the phonetic law: this same exceptionlessness is not valid for the accomplishment of phonetic changes, that is why we cannot speak of phonetic laws. "Precisely in the Hungarian language the phonetic changes having a hundred-per-cent validity are relatively scarce; so it is more appropriate, and more in conformity with the facts, to speak only of tendencies of phonetic development."[20] The issue and the related argument are repeated word for word in the textbook edition of Bárczi's notes published under the same title a year later.

It is also true, on the other hand, that elsewhere in his notes (and his textbook) we again find regularity mentioned instead of tendency of phonetic development or regular phonetic change: "The alternations of suffixes were produced in the first place

[17] Ibid.
[18] *A magyar nyelv története* [History of the Hungarian Language] I. Lecture notes. Budapest, 1966, p. 114.
[19] Ibid.
[20] Op. cit., p. 115.

by phonetic regularities."[21] Hence, it does not appear clearly what the authors in question understand by regularity.

According to Hajdú, the idea of phonetic law is to be rejected also because it cannot bear comparison with the concept of law in general: "The regularity manifesting itself in phonetic changes, however, cannot be compared to the severe order of natural laws . . . The exceptionlessness going with the concept of law, however, is not characteristic of a regular phonetic change, whose operation can be obstructed, in addition to factors of geography and time, by different tendencies of phonetic development, stray phonetic changes and other causes."[22] The concept of linguistic law, equally measured by the standard of "natural-scientific exactness", is again the loser in a writing of Antal: "The regularities of language reflect developing tendencies, and in this manner we cannot expect the regularities observed [the essence of the recognized objective processes? !] to betray natural-scientific exactness."[23]

As appears from the foregoing, the dispute over the neogrammarians' rigid natural-scientific adaptation is going on on the basis of the natural-scientific arguments of the time of Brugman and Osthoff.

To what extent the content of the modern concept of natural law concerning the objective course of natural processes — just as a consequence of the recent natural-scientific results — has changed until our days, I have already outlined above. How much, on this basis, the general (philosophical) concept of law has been "adjusted" to the new scientific results, I have also mentioned in a few words. Also I have discussed what qualitative differences, besides essential identities, can be established between natural and social laws. I have also pointed out that this necessarily allows conclusions to be drawn with a view to formulating the concept of linguistic (phonetic) law in a way satisfying the modern requirements.

What becomes evident by all means is that both Bárczi and Hajdú are entirely right in combating the rigidity of the old

---

[21] Op. cit., pp. 280 and 229.
[22] P. Hajdú, *Bevezetés az uráli nyelvtudományba* [Introduction to Uralic Linguistics], Budapest, 1966, p. 29.
[23] Antal: MNy LVI, p. 57.

postulate of phonetic law, and they do so with success on the basis of linguistic facts. Their writings of a polemic tone clearly display a desire to help the science of language to make uninterrupted progress, but also a sense of responsibility, when they wish to throw doors and windows open for life-breathing fresh winds to blow away the stifling air of entrenched dogmas.

Bárczi, for example, in an article on linguistic changes,[24] stood up with passionate fervour and convincingly against the views grown out of the soil of rigid doctrines heedless of the evidence of linguistic facts, and emphatically stressed the role of "speaking man", of the subject, the role which "constantly influences also the development of phonetic changes", claiming that "every ...man... in however modest a degree... is a language-forming factor". The "love of words" and respect for linguistic facts prompted the conscientious scholar to engage in battle in order that literature should accept the fact, which can be observed in human practice hundreds and thousands of times, that every speaker is seeking to make his speech not only more plain, but also more pleasing and even more impressive (a shaded formulation of the might of word) and for this very reason consciously chooses from among the linguistic tools.

Hajdú's writings also need no introduction to the expert public. It is especially needless to waste time introducing the results of his above-mentioned monograph which convincingly applies new principles and methods (modern procedures of typology, statistical interpretation of "regular phonetic changes", the use of synchronic data in linguistic history, an elastic sketch of the essential features of the reconstructed original language, etc.). Of all this, however, we have to point to his opinion regarding the fundamental motive of linguistic changes: "The most important mover of linguistic development ... is the tension which is permanently present between the need for an adequate communication of thoughts and sensations [emotions?] and the available linguistic tools."[25]

So many indications, so many fruitful ideas; so many details, so many new realizations; all of them deserve the attention of the linguists searching for the essence of linguistic processes — but the attention of non-linguists as well!

[24] G. Bárczi, A nyelvi változások értékelése [An Evaluation of Linguistic Changes], MNy LXII, pp. 129—34.
[25] Hajdú, op. cit., p. 22.

The proper realization of the many part truths therefore has not grown into a modern concept of linguistic law in the final conclusion of the authors quoted, and even both of them negate a part of it, the phonetic law. This is not a negation of the negation in the philosophical sense, it does not negate the old conception of phonetic law in the sense that it criticizes its rigidity while retaining its progressive elements in the new concept and even further developing them, but it rejects the whole conception of phonetic law together with its deficiencies. In my judgment the question here is not, or at least not only, about a terminological dispute, but about an interpretation of the term law as a fundamental scientific category. Both authors have the same conception of law: a law can be only that which is effective to one hundred per cent and operates without exceptions.

On the basis of a Klausian evaluation[26] interpreted not in the spirit of Klaus, for example, Hajdú abandons the principle of causality, more precisely he opposes it by the principle of teleology taken in the modern sense,[27] and draws from this the already known conclusion that linguistics has the task of "exploring rather the *how* than the *why* of the changes".[28] I think I did not misunderstand the quotation: it refers not to sequence in time but to the order of importance, which is supported also by the author's following opinion: "we have to take note also that we do not always succeed in obtaining an insight behind the immediate causes of change".[29] I do not intend, nor would I be able, to argue against the latter view. But it is hard to imagine that this should lead to the conclusion that linguistics could renounce uncovering the causes and the mutual dependence of linguistic processes. The point is not that the researcher of language ought to look for single isolated changes and for the singular causes

[26] Fodor: NyK LXV, p. 299.
[27] In his book quoted Hajdú still formulates in a differentiated manner and writes that "the principle of causality can be developed, extended towards purposiveness". (Op. cit., p. 22.) We can agree with this opinion—by accepting the critique of the causality theory based on the former rigid conception of determinism—but the way he summarizes his pertinent views in his Theses published a year later is very contestable: "I am looking for the motive of [linguistic] changes, in conformity with the recent theories, not in causality but in purposiveness." *Bevezetés az uráli nyelvtudományba* [Introduction to Uralic Linguistics]. Theses of a doctoral dissertation. Budapest, 1967, p. 5.
[28] Op. cit., p. 23.
[29] Op. cit., p. 22.

producing them (Hajdú is right to polemize against this view), but it must be investigated "what kind of shifts and rearrangements in the system are induced by one or another linguistic change".[30] But let me add: it must also be investigated what further changes can be produced by the shifts and rearrangements, brought about by those changes, in the system and in the functional load, and so forth.

No science can give up discovering the internal interrelatedness of structures and their changes, the complicated cause-effect relationships producing the changes. This opinion does not wish to return to the rigidity of the previous causal principle, but it claims the application of the principle of the cause-effect relation conceived in the modern sense.

Fodor failed to grasp the essence of the matter just when he interpreted the Klausian criticism of the rigid conception of causality as meaning that Klaus had renounced the principle of causality. Klaus does not operate with such rigid "if not — then" schemata; more appropriate to his train of thought is the conception of negation in the sense formulated by him, when he regards the relation between colloquial language *(Umgangssprache)* and technical language as a relation of dialectical negation, and of this latter he declares: "The new negates the original concept, raises it to a higher level, but preserves it at the same time as a special case."[31] This is what corresponds to the Marxist conception of the negation of negation, to the dialectics of the replacement of old concepts by new ones, and also to the train of ideas by which Klaus explains and stresses the necessity of replacing the old principle of causality by a new one.

The examples and linguistic facts presented by Hajdú are unambiguous and convincing; they give satisfactory answers to more than one "why" and, let me add, they witness *for* the concept of phonetic law purified of the neogrammarian distortions. The proto-Uralic sound *s* has the equivalent *t* in Vogul. In spite of this the word *säje* 'pus' of the Uralic original language behaves in Vogul not in the expected manner, it is not *täj* but *saj*. Why did not the expected "regular" phonetic change take place? According to Hajdú, it was "because the initial consonant

---

[30] Ibid.
[31] "Der neue negiert den ursprünglichen Begriff, hebt ihn auf eine höhere Stufe, bewahrt ihn aber zugleich als Speziallfall auf." G. Klaus, *Semiotik und Erkenntnistheorie*, Berlin, 1963, p. 132.

of this word, under the influence of the medial palatal consonant, became palatalized ($> *\acute{s}$) still before the phonetic change $*s > t$ took place, and this circumstance prevented it from changing to t".[32] He thinks it was due to such a secondary palatalization that the Hung. *fészek* ($<$ proto-Uralic $*p\check{i}s\ddot{a}$) 'nest' retained its original sound $*s$, in contradistinction to the initial sounds $*s$ which were lost in Hungarian. It was in order to avoid syncretism that the vowel of the first syllable of the Zyrian *purni* 'to bite' remained at the "original $*u$ stage", in spite of the fact that we might expect y on the strength of "regular phonetic change"; in this case, however, it would have coincided with the verb *pyrny* 'to enter'. Some of the Hungarian final vowels "regularly" became short: *látá* $>$ *láta* 'he saw', but *látá* also survived because it had a function of indicating a difference of meaning.[33]

Analogy can also interfere in the process of "regular phonetic changes". The proto-Finno-Ugric $*s\ddot{a}pte$ or $*s\ddot{a}p\ddot{a}t(e)$ would be expected to have the equivalent *ét* or *éz* in Hungarian. Since, however, *hat* 'six' is a member of the same sequence of numbers and the two even stand next to each other, a form *hét* 'seven' appears in place of the expected form.[34] Other "impeding factors": the Vogul *soj* 'sound, noise' ($\sim$ Finnish *soi-* 'sound, ring') would have the "regular" equivalent *szaj* in Hungarian, yet the Hung. *zaj* 'noise' is obviously "explainable by the onomatopoetic character of the word".[35] Hajdú's examples illustrating the limitations in time and place of the accomplishment of phonetic changes also form an array of unambiguous arguments.[36]

This train of thought is very clear and convincing. Linguistic changes are really governed by a sort of regulator or prime mover, which makes it, if you like, a *law* for the tensions arising out of the performance of the communicative function to be removed, the misunderstandings to be reduced to the minimum. Hajdú stated essentially the same in his aforecited opinion,

[32] Hajdú, op. cit., p. 30.
[33] Ibid. Already Delbrück called attention to the fact that sounds with a functional load resist phonetic changes. *Einleitung in das Sprachstudium*, Leipzig, 1880, pp. 105—6. — T. Mikola also adduces telling linguistic facts to support this theorem on the basis of the transformation of Finno-Ugric *mp* and its Hungarian equivalent *(mb >) b*. If the preservation of the original sound combination is "functionally justified", it resists change: *tompor* 'buttock', *domb* 'hill' $> <$ *dob* 'drum'. MNy LXI, p. 36.
[34] Hajdú, op. cit., p. 30.
[35] Op. cit., p. 31.
[36] Op. cit., pp. 31—2.

with which it is possible to agree completely. By this opinion, however, Hajdú perfectly explained the essence of phonetic exceptions resisting the so-called "regular phonetic changes". In spite of all this Hajdú's final conclusion is as follows: "Hence it is justifiable by all means that, instead of the still often usual term 'phonetic law' we should apply the expression 'phonetic change' or 'tendency of phonetic development'."[37]

If tendency is the realization, the outward form of the law — and in this sense the two may be conceived of as synonyms — then the term 'tendency of phonetic development' is unacceptable because it is opposed to the mechanical concept of law (barring the influence of conscious human activity and admitting of no exceptions) grown out of the soil of "classical" determinism. Law and tendency are not mutually exclusive but complementary categories, their opposition is resolved in the dialectics of the general and the particular. The general and the particular (single, individual) are different sides of an integral whole, neither can exist without the other; the general exists only owing to the individual, through the individual; the individual is also a part of the general, it is inconceivable without connection with the general.

The arguments against the term 'regular phonetic change' in turn are the following:

(a) The *rule* is first of all a term for a lower, empirical stage of cognition: it comprises the superficial "behavioural" norms of phenomena, hence it is unfit to reflect the internal, essential interrelations, particularities of phenomena and processes. It is no accident that it became a favourite term in the antitheoretical period of modern descriptive methods, because these examined only the formal behaviour of linguistic utterances ("manifestations"), its "regularity", and gave up uncovering the internal interrelations.

(b) *Regular* is a debatable qualifier of phonetic changes also because these are not "absolutely" regular, they are liable to *exceptions*. If, on the other hand, we conceive of exceptions in the sense that "they prove the rule", then — as regards the essence of the thing — there might be agreement between us, with only a terminological difference of opinion, but — as we have seen — this is beside the point.

[37] Op. cit., p. **31.**

On the basis of the foregoing, therefore, we do not have to abandon the term *phonetic law*: what is more, only by accepting the concept embodied in that term can we be "on firm ground". Not quite so as the "champions of law" imagined in the light of the teachings of Humboldt, Bopp, Schleicher, Brugman and Osthoff and in the militant polemical climate of neogrammarian adaptations, but by retaining the rational kernel of that conception of law and making at the same time allowance for the new realizations which have become public property of mankind, thanks to the scientific efforts of the past century.

If we regard *phonetics* (not only physiological, acoustic, etc. phonetics, but—and in the first place—phonology in both its synchronic and diachronic projection) as a discipline of the science of language, we cannot renounce the concept of *phonetic law as a linguistic category which reflects with approximate precision the internal interrelatedness of the sound system (structure), the causes of changes, the consequences of the shift in the "conditions of equilibrium" due to the changes, the objective correlations of the motion of word and content.*

The above italicized passage is not destined to be the definition of a new phonetic law. I emphasized only those criteria which I consider the most important ones and without which it is hardly possible to speak about phonetic law in the light of the modern concept of scientific law.

I have no intention of giving a new definition of *linguistic law* either. However, what I have told about the fundamental criteria of phonetic law applies, *mutatis mutandis*, to the most characteristic traits of the linguistic laws. The relation between phonetic and linguistic laws is namely to be conceived as the relation of the part and the whole, in the sense of the above explication.

That is to say, if we hold that language as a structure is not only a network or aggregation of formal relationships (this would unjustifiably narrow down the concept), but if we "adjust" it to the modern concept of structure formulated in the philosophical sense,[38] then *the categories reflecting the immanent peculiarities of*

[38] "The structure is nothing but a system of elements and their interactions" (Rádi, loc. cit., p. 372), which according to Svidersky is in close connection with the quality, essentially being the internal content of the quality: ". . . any phenomenon, as regards its essence, . . . appears as the unity of the elements and the structure . . . Any quality is the above unity of the elements and the structure." *Magyar Filozófiai Szemle* VI/1, p. 52.

*this complicated structure with approximate precision can be said
to be linguistic laws, which are related to social laws as the part is
related to the whole, the kinds of motion of language being a peculiar
part of the classes of the forms of motion of society.*

What we have already said about the characteristics of the
classes of the forms of motion of society, and about the social
laws reflecting them, is valid, considering the specific traits
(whole and part), also for the kinds of motion of language and
the linguistic laws reflecting them. Namely the concrete individual structures can be included in classes of the forms of motion
on the basis of their common essential marks.

There is, however, one thing that must always be borne in
mind. Like sociological research in general, linguistics also "has
to penetrate behind a multitude of accidents in order to uncover
the more profound, more latent interrelations".[39] To this we have
to add that the science of language also cannot rely on such
"experiments" as are made by natural science, which very often
makes use of the potentialities brought about artificially, by
creating "ideal" conditions for experimenting, and which in
this way can observe, and even repeat, the phenomena in a form
practically "purified" of disturbing influence. Hence, the "re-
striction" which Marx established for sociological research is
valid also for the research methods applied in linguistics: the
experiments here must be replaced by the "force of abstraction".[40]

---

[39] *Történelmi materializmus* [Historical Materialism], p. 60.
[40] "In the analysis of economic forms, moreover, neither microscopes
nor chemical reagents are of use. The force of abstraction must replace
both." K. Marx, *Capital*, New York, n. d., Vol. I, p. 12.

CONCLUDING THOUGHTS

It is difficult to close the investigation of the development of "linguistic thought". Countless questions of detail of the period I have discussed might still be, and ought to be, probed into. Even the details that I have deliberately neglected would provide a great deal of general lessons. What brought me to make a very definite selection was not merely the limits set by the size of this volume and by the possibilities but also my endeavours outlined in the Introduction, which stimulated me to keep track of the development of the theories concerning the most general questions of language.

In the polemical parts of the various chapters, occasionally also at the end of chapters, I expounded my own views. I have no intention of repeating them here in a "summary".

I am fully aware that I was not able — nor did I perhaps want — to solve all of the problems I was investigating: I wished only to draw attention to the fundamental aspects of some of the key problems.

Even if my study is not a guide to "a new passage to India", it may possibly contain a few ideas utilizable in the further "practice of navigation".

At least that was my purpose.

BIBLIOGRAPHY

ALBRECHT, E: Die erkenntnistheoretische Problematik des sprachlichen Zeichens: Zur Auseinandersetzung mit der idealistischen Zeichentheorie in der modernen Sprachwissenschaft, DZfPh 1961/3, pp. 358—67.

A magyar nyelv története és rendszere [History and System of the Hungarian Language]: Lectures at the International Philological Congress at Debrecen, Budapest, 1967.

AMMER, K., *Einführung in die Sprachwissenschaft*, Halle, 1958.

AMMER, K., MEYER, G. F., Bedeutung und Struktur. *Zeichen und System der Sprache* III, Berlin, 1966, pp. 5—27.

ANTAL, L., *A magyar esetrendszer* [The Hungarian Case-System], Budapest, 1961.

ANTAL, L., *Questions of Meaning*, The Hague, 1963.

ANTAL, L., *A formális nyelvi elemzés* [Formal Linguistic Analysis], Budapest, 1964.

ANTAL, L., *Content, Meaning and Understanding*, The Hague, 1964.

ARISTOTLE, *Organon*. Ed.: S. Szalai. Budapest, 1961.

BALDINGER, K., *Die Semasiologie: Versuch eines Überblicks*. Vorträge und Schriften, Deutsche Akademie der Wissenschaften zu Berlin, 1957.

BÁRCZI, G., A nyelvi változások értékelése [An Evaluation of Linguistic Changes], MNy LXII, pp. 129—34.

BÁRCZI, G., *A "pesti nyelv"* [The Lingo of Budapest], Budapest, 1932.

BÁRCZI, G., *Bevezetés a nyelvtudományba* [Introduction to Linguistics], Budapest, 1953.

BÁRCZI, G., BENKŐ, L., BERRÁR, J., *A magyar nyelv története* [History of the Hungarian Language], Budapest, 1967.

BELGERI, L., *Les affriquées en italien et dans les autres principales langues européennes*, Grenoble, 1929.

BENFEY, TH., *Geschichte der Sprachwissenschaft und orientalischen Philologie in Deutschland seit dem Anfange des 19. Jahrhunderts mit einem Rückblick auf die früheren Zeiten*, München, 1869.

BENFEY, TH., Die Spaltung einer Sprache in mehrere lautverschiedene Sprachen. *Gött. Nachr. 1877*, pp. 533—58.

BENVENISTE, E., *Problèmes de linguistique générale*, Paris, 1966.

BERRÁR, J., A mondat formai ismertetőjegyei [The Formal Distinctive Marks of the Sentence], ÁNyT I, pp. 53—76.

BEZZENBERGER, A., Besprechung von Osthoff und Brugman: Morphologische Untersuchungen I. *Gött. Gel. Anz. 1879*, pp. 641—69.

BLOOMFIELD, L., *Language*, New York, 1933.

BLOOMFIELD, M., On the Probability of the Existence of Phonetic Law. *The Amer. Journ. of Phil.* V, pp. 178—85.

BOPP, F., *Über das Conjugationssystem der Sanskrita-Sprache in Vergleichung mit jenem der griechischen, lateinischen, persischen und germanischen Sprache*, Frankfurt a. M., 1816.

BOPP, F., *Ausführliches Lehrgebeude der Sanskrita-Sprache*, Berlin, 1827.

BRENNER, O., *Einleitung zur "Deutschen Phonetik"*, Leipzig, 1893.
BRIDGMAN, P. W., *The Logic of Modern Physics*, New York, 1927.
BROCKELMANN, C., *Arabische Grammatik*, Leipzig, 1953¹³.
BRÜCKE, E., *Grundzüge der Physiologie und Systematik der Sprachlaute für Linguisten und Taubstummenlehrer*, Wien, 1876².
BRUGMAN, K., *Zum heutigen Stand der Sprachwissenschaft*, Strassburg, 1885.
CARNAP, R., *Foundations of Logic and Mathematics. International Encyclopedia of Unified Science* I/3, Chicago, 1955, pp. 139—213.
CASSIRER, E., *Philosophie der symbolischen Formen. Die Sprache*, Berlin, 1923.
COLLITZ, H., *Besprechung von Osthoff—Brugman: Morphologische Untersuchungen* I. *Anz. f. deut. Altertum* V, pp. 318—23.
CURTIUS, G., *Einleitung zu: Grundzüge der griechischen Etymologie*, Leipzig, 1858.
CURTIUS, G., *Bemerkungen über die Tragweite der Lautgesetze, besonders im Lateinischen und Griechischen. Ber. der kgl. sächs. Gesellsch. der Wissenschaften. Phil.-hist. Kl.* 1870, pp. 1—39.
DELBRÜCK, B., *Einleitung in das Sprachstudium*, Leipzig, 1880.
DEME, L., *A magyar nyelvjárások néhány kérdése* [Some Questions of the Hungarian Dialects], NytudÉrt I, Budapest, 1953.
Descartes's Letter to Mersenne, 1629. *Corresp.* Ed.: P. Tannery. Paris, 1959.
DEZSŐ, L., *A szemantika és a lexikológia néhány kérdése* [Some Questions of Semantics and Lexicology], ÁNyT IV, pp. 31—67.
DITTRICH, O., *Die Probleme der Sprachpsychologie*, Leipzig, 1913.
DUNS SCOTUS, *Grammatica spec. nova ed.* Ed. M. F. Garcia. Quaracchi, 1902.
EASTON, M. W., *Analogy and Uniformity. The Amer. Journ. of Phil.* V/6, pp. 164—77.
ERDEY-GRÚZ, T., *A világ anyagi szerkezete* [The Material Structure of the World], Budapest, 1965.
EUCKEN, R. CHR., *Die Grundbegriffe der Gegenwart historisch und kritisch entwickelt*, Leipzig, 1893².
FIRTH, J., *The Technique of Semantics. Papers in Linguistics 1934—1951*, London, 1957.
FODOR, J., *Dinamikus és statisztikai törvények* [Dynamic and Statistical Laws]. *Magyar Filozófiai Szemle* X, pp. 488—506.
FODOR, J. A., KATZ, J. J., *The Structure of a Semantic Theory. Language* XXXIX, pp. 170—211.
FOGARASI, J., *A' magyar nyelv metaphysicája vagy a' betüknek eredeti jelentése: A magyar nyelvre alkalmaztatva* [Metaphysics of the Hungarian Language or the Original Meaning of Letters: Applied to the Hungarian Language], Pest, 1834.
FOGARASI, J., *Művelt magyar nyelvtan elemi része* [Elementary Part of a Cultured Hungarian Grammar], Pest, 1843.
FOK, V. A., *A kvantummechanika interpretációjáról* [Interpreting Quantum Mechanics]. *A modern természettudományok filozófiai problémái* [Philosophical Problems of the Modern Natural Sciences], Budapest, 1962, pp. 265—93.
FRIES, C. C., *Trends in European and American Linguistics 1930—1960*, Utrecht–Antwerp, 1961.
GARDINER, A., *The Theory of Speech and Language*, Oxford, 1951.
GOMBOCZ, Z., *A jelenkori nyelvészet alapelvei* [The Principles of Con-

386

temporary Linguistics], Nyr XXVII, pp. 6—13, 53—63, 97—103, 193—201, 433—8, 481—6.
GOMBOCZ, Z., *Nyelvtörténeti módszertan* [Methodology of Linguistic History], Budapest, 1922.
GOMBOCZ, Z., *Jelentéstan* [Semantics], Pécs, 1926.
GOMBOCZ, Z., Változás és törvény a nyelvtudományban [Change and Law in Linguistics]. *Társadalomtudomány* I, pp. 194—201.
GRAUR, A., *Studii de lingvistică generală: Varianță nouă* [Studies in General Linguistics: New Variant]. Bucharest, 1960.
GREENBERG, J. H., Some Universals of Grammar with Particular Reference to the Order of Meaningful Elements. *Universals of language*, Cambridge, Mass., 1963.
GREIMAS, A. J., *Sémantique structurale: Recherche de méthode*, Paris, 1966.
HAJDÚ, P., *Bevezetés az uráli nyelvtudományba* [Introduction to Uralic Linguistics], Budapest, 1966.
HALL, R. A., *Introductory Linguistics*, Philadelphia, 1964.
HARRIS, Z. S., *Methods in Structural Linguistics*, Chicago, 1951.
HECHT, M., Sprachwissenschaft und Philosophie zum Bedeutungsproblem. *Blätter für deutsche Philosophie*, Berlin, 1930/31.
HENRY, V., *Antinomies linguistiques*, Paris, 1896.
HERMAN, J., Az alak és a jelentés kapcsolatának kérdéséhez [On the Question of the Relation of Form and Meaning], ÁNyT I, pp. 125—42.
HERMAN, J., Antal László, Questions of Meaning, ÁNyT III, pp. 242—58.
HJELMSLEV, L., *Prolegomena to a Theory of Language*, Baltimore, 1953.
HORGER, A., *A nyelvtudomány alapelvei* [Principles of Linguistics], Budapest, 1926.
HORVÁTH, J., A világ anyagi egységének helyes felfogásához [On the Right Conception of the Material Unity of the World]. *Magyar Filozófiai Szemle* VI/1, pp. 21—33.
HUCK, Zs., A marxista tudatfelfogás néhány problémája [Some Problems of the Marxian Conception of Consciousness]. *Magyar Filozófiai Szemle* X, pp. 128—49.
HUMBOLDT, W., *Gesammelte Schriften*, Berlin, 1905.
HUNFALVY, P., A nyelvtudományról [On Linguistics], NyK II, pp. 69—95.
HUNFALVY, P., Észrevételek Müller Miksa nyelvtudományi felolvasásaira, különösen a nyolczadikra [Remarks on Max Müller's Lectures on the Science of Language, with Special Regard to the Eighth Lecture]. In Steiner (Simonyi), Zs., *Müller Miksa fölolvasásai a nyelvtudományról* [Max Müller's Lectures on the Science of Language], Budapest, 1874, pp. 395—413.
IMRE, S., *A magyar nyelvújítás óta divatba jött idegen és hibás szólások bírálata, tekintettel az újítás helyes módjaira* [Critique of the Foreign and Bad Phrases that Came into Vogue since the Hungarian Language Reform, with Regard to the Proper Methods of Reform], Budapest, 1873.
IPSEN, G., *Sprachphilosophie der Gegenwart*, Berlin, 1930.
JUNKER, H., *Sprachphilosophisches Lesebuch*, Heidelberg, 1948.
KALMÁR, L., Matematikai és nyelvi struktúrák [Mathematical and Linguistic Structures], ÁNyT II, pp. 11—74, 166—72, 295—304.
KÁROLY, S., *Általános és magyar jelentéstan* [General and Hungarian Semantics], Budapest, 1970.
KATZ, J. J., Mentalism in Linguistics. *Language* XL, pp. 124—37.

KATZ, J. J., *The Semantic Component of a Linguistic Description*, M.I.T., 1964.

KAUFMANN, F., *Das Gebiet des Weißen Flusses und dessen Bewohner*, Brixen, 1861.

KEDROV, B. M., *A természettudományok tárgya és kölcsönös kapcsolata* [The Subject and Interrelation of the Natural Sciences], Budapest, 1965.

KEMPELEN, W., *Mechanismus der menschlichen Sprache nebst der Beschreibung seiner sprechenden Maschine*, Wien, 1791.

KIEFER, F., *A jelentéselmélet formalizálásáról* [On the Formalization of Semantic Theory], ÁNyT IV, pp. 105—55.

KLAUS, G., *Bevezetés a formális logikába* [Introduction to Formal Logic], Budapest, 1963.

KLAUS, G., *Semiotik und Erkenntnistheorie*, Berlin, 1963.

KLAUS, G., *Die Macht des Wortes*, Berlin, 1964.

KLAUS, G., SEGETH, W., Semiotik und materialistische Abbildtheorie, DZfPh 1962, pp. 1245—60.

KRONASSER, H., *Handbuch der Semasiologie*, Heidelberg, 1952.

KRUSZEWSKY, N., *Die Laute und ihre Gesetze. Prinzipien der Sprachentwicklung: Techners Zeitschr. f. intern. Sprachwissenschaft* I, pp. 301—4; II, pp. 260—8; pp. 145—70. (The article is an abridged version of a book published in Kazan.)

KUKENHEIM, L., *Esquisse historique de la linguistique française*, Leiden, 1962.

LAZICZIUS, Gy., *Bevezetés a fonológiába* [Introduction to Phonology], Budapest, 1932.

LAZICZIUS, Gy., *Általános nyelvészet* [General Linguistics], Budapest, 1942.

LAZICZIUS, Gy., *Fonetika* [Phonetics], Budapest, 1963.

LEIBNIZ, G. W., Lingua Adamica, *Filoz. Irat.* VII, p. 148. Ed.: C. J. Gerhardt. Berlin, 1875.

LEIBNIZ, *Opuscules et fragments inédits*. Ed.: L. Couturat. Paris, 1903.

LENIN, V. I., *Materialism and Empiriocriticism*, Moscow, 1947.

LEONTYEV, A. N., *A pszichikum fejlődése* [Development of Psychics], Budapest, 1964.

LESKIEN, A., *Die Declination im Slavisch-Litauischen und Germanischen*, Leipzig, 1876.

LOCKE, J., *An Essay Concerning Human Understanding*, Oxford, 1894.

LUX, GY., *A nyelv* [Language], Budapest, n. d.

MARTI, E., *Psychologische Untersuchungen zur Bedeutungslehre*, Leipzig, 1901.

MARTINET, A., La double articulation linguistique. *Travaux du cercle linguistique de Copenhague* V, pp. 30—7.

MARTINKÓ, A., Hozzászólás Balázs J.: "A stílus kérdései" c. ref.-hoz [A Contribution to J. Balázs's lecture on "Questions of Style"]. *Általános nyelvészet, stilisztika, nyelvjárástörténet* [General Linguistics, Stylistics, History of Dialects]: Lectures at the Third National Congress of Hungarian Linguists, Budapest, 1956, pp. 197—219.

MARX, K., *Capital*, Vol. I, New York, n. d.

MARX, K., ENGELS, F., *The German Ideology*, London, 1942.

MARX, K., ENGELS, F., *Die deutsche Ideologie; Kritik der neuesten deutschen Philosophie in ihren Repräsentanten, Feuerbach, B. Bauer und Stirner, und des deutschen Sozializmus in seinen verschiedenen Propheten*. Berlin, 1953².

MASTERNAN, L. M., Fictitious Sentences in Language. *Essays on and in Machine Translation by the Cambridge Language Research Unit*, Cambridge, Engl., 1959.

MELYUKHIN, S. T., *A szervetlen természet fejlődési dialektikája* [Dialectics of the Development of Inorganic Nature], Budapest, 1963.

MORRIS, C. W., Foundations of the Theory of Signs. *International Encyclopedia of Unified Science* I/2, Chicago, 1955, pp. 77—137.

MORRIS, C. W., *Signs, Language and Behavior*, New York, 1955.

MÜLLER, F. M., *Lectures on the Science of Language*, Vols. I—II, London, 1871[6].

MÜLLER, M., *Die Wissenschaft der Sprache*, Leipzig, 1892.

NÁDOR, GY., *A természettörvény fogalmának kialakulása* [Genesis and Evolution of the Concept of Natural Law], Budapest, 1957.

NEEDHAM, R. N., PARKER-RHODES, The Questions of Lattice Theory. *Essays on and in Machine Translation by the Cambridge Language Research Unit*, Cambridge, Engl., 1959.

OMELYANOVSKY, M. E., V. I. Lenin és a modern fizika filozófiai problémái [V. I. Lenin and Philosophical Problems of Modern Physics]. *A modern természettudományok filozófiai problémái* [Philosophical Problems of the Modern Natural Sciences], Budapest, 1962, pp. 47—119.

OSGOOD, CH. E., *Universals of Language:* Report of a Conference held at Dobbs Ferry, New York, Apr. 13—15, 1961 (The M.I.T. Press, Cambridge, Mass., 1963), pp. 234—254.

OSGOOD, CH. E., SEBEOK, T., *Psycholinguistics*, Baltimore, 1954.

OSTHOFF, H., BRUGMAN, K., *Morphologische Untersuchungen auf dem Gebiete der indogermanischen Sprache* I, Leipzig, 1878.

PAPP, F., Nyelvi rendszer, közlési folyamat és ezek néhány matematikai modellje [System of Language, Process of Communication, and Some of Their Mathematical Models], ÁNyT II, pp. 75—88.

PAPP, I., *Leíró magyar hangtan* [Descriptive Hungarian Phonetics], Budapest, 1966.

PAUL, H., *Prinzipien der Sprachgeschichte*, Halle, 1898.

PETZ, G., Nyelvtudományi irányok és feladatok [Linguistic Trends and Tasks]. *Nyelvtudomány* I, pp. 1—11.

QUINE, W., *The Problem of Meaning in Linguistics*, Cambridge, 1953.

RÁDI, P., Kísérlet a mozgásformák rendszerének korszerű leírására [Attempt at an Up-to-date Description of the System of Forms of Motion]. *Magyar Filozófiai Szemle* XI/3, pp. 369—406.

REGNAUD, P., *Éléments de grammaire comparée du grec et du latin*, Vol. I: Phonétique, Paris, 1895.

REICHENBACH, H., *Elements of Symbolic Logic*, New York, 1947.

RIEDL, Sz., *A magyar nyelvrendszer alapvonalai: Magyar hangtan* [The Basic Features of the Hungarian Language System: Hungarian Phonetics], Prague—Leipzig, 1859.

RIEDL, Sz., A nyelvtudomány alapelvei [The Principles of Linguistics]: Introductory university lecture. *Kalauz*, 1863.

RIEDL, Sz., *Magyar nyelvtan* [Hungarian Grammar], Pest, 1864.

RIES, J., *Was ist ein Satz?* Beiträge zur Grundlegung der Syntax. Heft III, Prague, 1931.

RUBINYI, M., *Általános nyelvtudomány* [General Linguistics], Budapest, 1907.

RUSSEL, B., *Logic and Knowledge*, London, 1956.

RUZSA, I., *Matematika* [Mathematics], Budapest, 1966.

SAUSSURE, F., *Cours de linguistique générale*, Paris, 1955[3].

SCHAFF, A., Die Bedeutung der 'Bedeutung', DZfPh 1961, pp. 610—22, 708—24.

SCHAFF, A., *Marx oder Sartre? Versuch einer Philosophie des Menschen*, Wien, 1964.

SCHAFF, A., *Einführung in die Semantik*, Berlin, 1966.

SCHLEICHER, A., Zur vergleichenden Sprachgeschichte (Zetazismus). *Sprachvergleichende Untersuchungen* I, Bonn, 1848.

SCHLEICHER, A., *Die Darwinsche Theorie und die Sprachwissenschaft:* Offenes Sendschreiben an Herrn Dr. Ernst Häckel, a. o. Professor der Zoologie und Direktor des zoologischen Museums an der Universität Jena, Weimar, 1863.

SCHLEICHER, A., *Über die Bedeutung der Sprache für die Naturgeschichte des Menschen*, Weimar, 1865.

SCHLICK, M., *Gesammelte Aufsätze 1926—1936*, Wien, 1938.

SCHMIDT, J., *A nyelv és a nyelvek* [Language and the Languages], Budapest, 1923.

SCHUCHARDT, H., *Ueber die Lautgesetze: Gegen die Junggrammatiker*, Berlin, 1885.

SEBAG, L., *Marxisme et structuralisme*, Paris, 1964.

SIEVERS, E., *Grundzüge der Phonetik*, Leipzig, 1901³.

SIMONYI, ZS., *Müller Miksa újabb fölolvasásai a nyelvtudományról* [Max Müller's Recent Lectures on the Science of Language], Budapest, 1876.

SMIRNITSKY, A. I., A szó jelentése [Meaning of the Word], NyIK VI, pp. 276—90.

STEINER (SIMONYI), ZS., *Müller Miksa fölolvasásai a nyelvtudományról* [Max Müller's Lectures on the Science of Language], Budapest, 1874.

STEINTHAL, H., *Die sprachphilosophischen Werke Wilhelms von Humboldt*, Berlin, 1884.

STEINTHAL, H., *Geschichte der Sprachwissenschaft bei den Griechen und Römern mit besonderer Rücksicht auf die Logik*, Berlin, 1890—1891².

STERN, G., *Meaning and Change of Meaning*, Bloomington, 1931.

SZIGETI, J., Ismeretelméleti-módszertani megjegyzések [Comments on Gnoseological Methodology]. *Magyar Filozófiai Szemle* VIII, pp. 819—840.

SZVORÉNYI, J., *Magyar nyelvtan, tanodai s magánhasználatra* [Hungarian Grammar for School and Private Use], Budapest, 1876⁴.

SZVORÉNYI, J., *Fejlődési tünemények a nyelvben, fő vonatkozással a nyelvújításra* [Phenomena of Evolution in Language, with Special Reference to the Language Reform], Eger, 1877.

TAMÁS, L., Tudatosak-e a hangváltozások? [Are Phonetic Changes Conscious?], MNy XLIII, pp. 92—161—72.

TAMÁS, L., A "signe linguistique" vitájához [Contribution to the Polemic About the "signe linguistique"], Pais-Eml, pp. 35—9.

TELEGDI, ZS. (ed.), *Általános nyelvészeti tanulmányok* [Studies in General Linguistics], Budapest, 1963—.

TELEGDI, ZS., A nyelvtudomány meghasonlásáról [On the Dichotomy of Linguistics], ÁNyT I, pp. 295—305.

TELEGDI, ZS., *Bevezetés a nyelvtudományba* I [Introduction to Linguistics], Budapest, 1963.

TEMESI, M., A nyelvi jel hagyományos fogalmának kialakulásáról [On the Development of the Conventional Notion of Linguistic Sign], ÁNyT IV, pp. 199—212.

THEWREWK (PONORI), E., *A nyelvészet mint természettudomány* [Linguistics as Natural Science], Pest, 1869.

THEWREWK (PONORI), E., *A nyelv optikája* [The Optics of Language], Pest, 1870.
THEWREWK (PONORI), E., *A helyes magyarság elvei* [Principles of Correct Hungarian], Budapest, 1873.
THOMAS AQUINAS, *Opuscula 15: De natura verbi intellectus.* Ed.: Grabmann, Toulouse, 1906.
THRACIS DIONYSII, *Ars grammatica.* Ed.: G. Uhlig, Lipsiae, 1884.
TRÓCSÁNYI, D., *Humboldt Vilmos nyelvbölcseleie* [Wilhelm Humboldt's Linguistic Philosophy], Budapest, 1914.
TRUBETZKOJ, N. S., *Grundzüge der Phonologie*, Göttingen, 1962³.
ULLMANN, S., *Précis de sémantique française*, Berne, 1952.
ULLMANN, S., *The Principles of Semantics*, New York, 1952.
VOSSLER, K., *Positivismus und Idealismus in der Sprachwissenschaft: Eine sprachphilosophische Untersuchung*, Heidelberg, 1904.
VYGOTSKY, L. S., Denken und Sprechen, Berlin, 1964.
WECHSSLER, E., *Gibt es Lautgesetze?* Festgabe Suchier, Halle a. S., 1900.
WEINREICH, U., On the Semantic Structure of Language. *Universals of Language*, Cambridge, Mass., 1963.
WEISGERBER, L., Die Bedeutungslehre — ein Irrweg der Sprachwissenschaft? *Germ. Rom. Monatschrift* XV, pp. 161—83.
WEISGERBER, L., *Muttersprache und Geistesbildung*, Göttingen, 1929.
WEISGERBER, L., Sprachwissenschaft und Philosophie zum Bedeutungsproblem. *Blätter für deutsche Philosophie*, Berlin, 1930—1931.
WHITNEY, W. D., Further Words as to Surds and Sonants, and the Law of Economy as a Phonetic Force, *Proc. of the Amer. Phil. Assoc.* July 1889, pp. XII—XVIII.
WILLAMOWITZ, U., *Platon*, Berlin, 1959.
WITTGENSTEIN, L., *Tractatus logico-philosophicus*, London, 1955.
WUNDT, W., Der Begriff des Gesetzes in den Geisteswissenschaften. *Logik*, Stuttgart, 1906.
WUNDT, W., *Die Sprache und das Denken*, Leipzig, 1885.
ZHOLKOVSKY, A. K., A szemantikai analízis szabályairól [On the Rules of Semantic Analysis]. A Hungarian translation by P. Szántó, still in manuscript, of the article "О правилах семантического анализа" published on August 17, 1964, in МППЛ pp. 17—32.
ZOLNAI, B., *Szóhangulat és kifejező hangváltozás* [Emotional Elements in Words and Expressive Sound Change], Szeged, 1939.
ZVEGINCEV, V. A., A jelentéstan helye a nyelvészeti diszciplinák sorában [The Place of Semantics among the Linguistic Disciplines], NyIK VI, pp. 267—75.
ZSIRAI, M., *A modern nyelvtudomány magyar úttörői* [Hungarian Pioneers of Modern Linguistics], Budapest, 1952.
Апресян, Ю. Д., Современные методы изучения значений и некоторые проблемы структурной лингвистики [Modern Methods to Investigate Meanings and Some Problems of Structural Linguistics]. *Проблемы структурной лингвистики* [Problems of Structural Linguistics], Moscow, 1963, pp. 102—50.
Апресян, Ю. Д., К вопросу о структурной лексикологии [On the Question of Structural Lexicology], ВЯ XI/3, pp. 38—46.
Виноградов, В. В., Основные типы лексических значений слова [The Main Types of Lexical Word Meaning], ВЯ 1953/5, pp. 3—29.
Виноградова, О. С., Эйслер, Н. А., Выявление систем словесных связей при регистрации сосудистых реакций [Demonstration of Systems of Word Connections as Registered by Vascular Reactions], ВПсих № 2.

Виноградова, О. С., Лурия, А. Р., *Тезисы конференции по машинному переводу* [Theses of the Conference on Machine Translation], Moscow, 1958.

Звегинцев, В. А., *Семасиология* [Semasiology], Moscow, 1957.

Мельчук, И. А., К вопросу о грамматическом в языке-посреднике [On the Question of the Grammatical in the Intermediary Language], МППЛ 1960/4.

Щерба, Л. В., *Русские гласные в качественном и количественном отношении* [The Russian Vowels in Terms of Quality and Quantity], St. Petersburg, 1912.

INDEX

Abélard, P. *42*
Ábrahám, S. 162
Akhmanova, O. S. *205*
Albrecht, E. *41*, 45, 46, 47, *49*, 52, 385
Ammer, K. *52*, *127*, 385
Amsterdamski, Sh. 362
Antal, L. 53, 54, 55, 59, 60, 61, 62, 63, 64, 66, 67, 68, 70, 71, 72, 73, 75, 77, 78, 79, *82*, 86, 87, 89, 90, *92*, 93, 95, 97, 99, 100, 101, 102, 104, 105, 106, 107, 200, 201, 213, 214, 215, 373, 385
Apresian, Y. A. 71, 72, *127*, *131*, 132, 133, *134*, *138*, 139, 140, 141, *158*, 391
Aristotle 33, 34, *36*, 203
Augustin, A. 44

Balassa, J. 296, 318, 335, 384
Balázs, J. *129*
Baldinger, K. 67, *129*, 385
Bally, Ch. 345
Bárczi, G. 323, 332, 333, *340*, 346, 370, 372, 374, 385
Bates, H. W. 331
Bauer, I. *48*
Becker, K. F. 16
Belgeri, L. 385
Benfey, Th. 233, 235, 246, 385
Benkő, L. 104, 370
Benveniste, E. *20*, *133*, 385
Berrár, J. 370, 385
Bezzenberger, A. 235, 385
Bierwisch, M. 48, 57
Bloch, B. *205*
Bloomfield, L. 23, 52, 53, 59, 60, 61, 63, 64, 108, 109, 110, 175, 205, 285
Bloomfield, M. 235, 237, 385
Bopp, F. 223, 224, 225, 239, 240, 246, 247, 249, 257, 379, 385
Bréal, M. 259
Brenner, O. 235, 267, 386
Bridgman, P. W. 88, 386
Brockelmann, C. *212*, *213*, 386
Brøndal, E. 369
Brugman, K. 221, 232, 233, 235, 238, 239, 254, 373, 379, 386
Brunot, F. *221*
Brücke, E. 208, *209*, 386
Brückner, A. 239
Bucanovskij, V. M. *365*
Budenz, J. 276
Bunsen, Ch. J. 260

Buysenns, E. 48
Bühler, K. *19*, 128

Carnap, R. 87, 139, 140, 386
Cassirer, E. 36, 39, 386
Castrén, M. A. 279
Chomsky, N. 56, 172, 174, 191, 192
Collitz, H. 235
Courtenay, B. 103, 306
Couturat, L. 36
Curtius, G. 220, 226, 235, 237, 238, 263, 268, 386

Darwin, Ch. R. 227, 228, 230, 251, 265, 283
Delbrück, B. *224, 225, 231, 233,* 234, 238, 239, *267,* 307, 377, 386
Deme, L. 369, 370, 386
Déry, Gy. 334
Descartes, R. 35, *293,* 386
Dezső, L. 135, 136, 137, 138, 178, 179, 180, 182, 386
Diefenbach, L. 228
Dionysius, T. 34, 203, 391
Dittrich, O. 120, 386
Dixon, R. M. W. 9, *60*
Duns, S. *203,* 386

Easton, M. W. 235, 386
Edelspacher, A. 252, 253
Eisler, N. A. 134, *134,* 138
Elekfi, L. 193
Engels, F. 96, *349,* 365, *367*
Erdey-Grúz, T. *355,* 356, 358, 360, 386
Eucken, R. Chr. 309, 386

Fernandez, M. *36*
Firth, I. *131, 133,* 386
Fischer, H. 267
Fodor, I. *375,* 376
Fodor, J. 361, *362, 363,* 386
Fodor, J. A. 95, 162, 386
Fogarasi, B. *151, 152*
Fogarasi, J. 292, *293,* 297, 303, 386
Fok, V. A. 358, 386
Frege 139, 140
Frey, H. 345
Fries, C. C. *59,* 386

Gabelentz, H. G. *9,* 246
Galileo, V. 283
Gamilscheg, E. 369
Gardiner, A. 108, 386
Gerhardt, C. J. *36*
Goethe, J. W. *326*
Goidanich, P. G. 345
Goldziher, I. *256,* 273

394

Gombocz, Z. 44, 45, 268, 302, 303, 304, 305, 306, 312, 313, 314, 315, 316, 317, *323*, 335, 383, 386, 387
Grammont, A. 318
Grammont, M. 345
Graur, A. *236*, 387
Greenberg, J. H. 56, *57*, 387
Greimas, A. J. 92, *140*, 144, 387
Grimm, J. 16, 222, 245, 246, 283, 296, 300
Gyarmathi, S. *9*, 245, 246, 249, 261, 295
Györke, J. 306

Hajdú, P. *324*, 372, 373, 374, 375, 376, 377, 378, 387
Hall, R. A. 110, 387
Harris, Z. S. 23, 53, 56, 171, *192*, 205, 206, 210, 211, 212, 213, 218, 387
Häckel, E. 226, 227, 228
Hecht, M. 112, 387
Hegel, G. W. F. 96, 226, 230, 231, 254, 260, 282
Helmholtz, H. 46, 47
Henry, V. 237, *238*, 344, 387
Heraclitus 32, 33, 203
Herbart, J. F. 16, 304
Herman, J. 66, 67, 68, 69, 87, 106, 209, 387
Hjelmslev, L. 23, *71*, 387
Hobbes, T. 354
Horger, A. 305, 315, 321, 322, 387
Horváth, J. *365*, 387
Horváth, M. 324
Huck, Zs. 349, 387
Humboldt, W. *9*, *36*, 224, 225, 245, 246, 247, 249, 285, 379, 387
Hunfalvy, P. 247, 249, 256, 257, 258, 259, 260, 261, 262, 264, 277, 278, 279, 280, 281, 284, 286, 295, 300, 302, 387
Hutterer, M. 55
Huxley, Th. H. 251

Imre, S. 326, 328, 387
Ipsen, G. *36*, 387

Jakobson, R. *27*, 346
Jászai, M. 341
Jespersen, O. 340, 344
Junker, H. *36*, 387

Kálmán, B. 323, 324
Kalmár, L. 26, 198, 200, 201, 387
Kardeván, K. 341
Kardos, L. *150*
Károly, S. 98, *99*, 102, 346, 387
Katz, J. J. 110, 162, 387, 388
Kaufmann, A. 269
Kaufmann, F. 267, 388
Kedrov, B. M. *356*, 388
Kempelen, F. 208, 330, 340, 388
Kerouac, J. 334

Kiefer, F. 135, 137, 138, 162, 163, 164, 165, 166, 167, 168, 169, 170, 171, 172, 173, 174, 175, 176, 177, 178, 182, 183, 184, 185, 186, 188, 189, 190, 191, 192, 193, 194, 195, 197, 198, 207, 356, 388
Klaus, G. 28, *39*, 119, *127*, *139*, *140*, 149, *150*, *152*, 160, 161, 364, 375, 376, 388
Kniezsa, I. 319
Kovács, F. 354
Kronasser, H. 58, 59, 109, *129*, 388
Kruszevsky, N. 235, 388
Kukenheim, L. *221*, *223*, 224, *233*, 288
Kuriłowitz, J. 48

Laziczius, Gy. 14, 16, 19, *20*, *22*, *36*, 103, 121, *205*, 262, 306, *315*, 316, 335, 336, 337, 338, 339, *340*, 343, 344, 388
Leibniz, G. W. 35, 160, 161, *203*, 221, 388
Lenin, V. I. 46, 47, 96, *97*, *150*, *154*, 242, 388
Leontyev, A. N. *205*, *349*, 388
Leontyeva, N. N. *133*
Leskien, A. *232*, 263, 388
Linnaeus, K. *19*
Locke, J. 264, 275, 276, 354, 388
Lotz, J. 102, 147, *148*
Luria, A. R. 134, 138, *205*
Lux, Gy. 268, 315, 322, 388

Maróth, M. *212*
Martemianov, Y. S. *133*
Marti, E. 120, 388
Martinet, A. 48, *205*, 388
Martinkó, A. 129, 130, 388
Marx, K. 95, 96, *124*, *326*, *349*, *367*, 368, 380, 388
Masternan, L. M. *139*, 388
Mátray-Szép, L. 341, 344
Meier, G. F. 49, 50, *727*
Melchuk, I. A. 140, 392
Melyukhin, S. T. 360, 363, 389
Mikola, T. *377*
Molnár, J. 268
Morris, C. W. 53, 62, 79, 80, 81, 82, 83, 84, 85, 86, 87, 89, 139, *171*, 175, 176, 389
Müller, M. 233, *234*, 256, 257, 258, 259, 260, 261, 262, 263, 264, 265, 266, 268, 269, 270, 271, 272, 273, 274, 275, 276, 277, 278, 279, 280, 281, 282, 283, 284, 307, 312, 313, 331, 389

Nádor, Gy. *222*, 2, *355*, 389
Needham, R. N. *139*, 389

Ogden, C. K. 128, 129
Omelyanovsky, M. E. 363, 389
Osgood, Ch. E. 102, *140*, 389
Osthoff, H. 232, 233, *234*, 235, 239, 267, 373, 379, 389

Pais, D. 383
Papp, F. 196, 200, 201, *299*, 319, 389

397